# Significant Contributions to the History of Psychology 1750-1920

## 1750-1920

Edited and with Prefaces by

DANIEL N. ROBINSON

Georgetown University

# Series B
# PSYCHOMETRICS AND EDUCATIONAL PSYCHOLOGY

## Volume II
## J. H. Pestalozzi

# Significant Contributions
# To the History of Psychology
# 1750—1920

## HOW GERTRUDE TEACHES HER CHILDREN
Johann Heinrich Pestalozzi

## PESTALOZZI'S EDUCATIONAL WRITINGS
Johann Heinrich Pestalozzi

Edited and with Prefaces by
### DANIEL N. ROBINSON
Georgetown University

UNIVERSITY PUBLICATIONS OF AMERICA

Copyright © 1977 by University Publications of America, Inc.,
Washington, D.C.


International Standard Book Number: 0-89093-163-1


Library of Congress Catalog Card Number: 77-072191

Manufactured in the United States of America

# CONTENTS

═══════════════════

*How Gertrude Teaches Her Children*
by Johann Heinrich Pestalozzi

*Pestalozzi's Educational Writings*
by Johann Heinrich Pestalozzi

# Sources

---

*How Gertrude Teaches Her Children* has been reprinted from the translation of Lucy E. Holland and Frances C. Turner which was published in Syracuse in 1898 by C. W. Bardeen.

*Pestalozzi's Educational Writings* has been reprinted from the translation of J. A. Green which was published in New York in 1912 by Longmans, Green & Co. as part of its Educational Classics series. (The present publisher acknowledges the cooperation of the Cleveland Public Library in supplying a copy of the original edition.)

# Significant Contributions to the History of Psychology 1750-1920

## GENERAL INTRODUCTION

In the last pages of the 1892 edition of his *Psychology*, William James is found examining the state of the discipline and assessing the claims made in its behalf by new and loyal adherents. Accepting that, indeed, psychology is a natural science, he then notes that this fact does not confer stability or even validity:

> It means just the reverse; it means a psychology particularly fragile, and into which the waters of metaphysical criticism leak at every joint . . . A string of raw facts; a little gossip and wrangle about opinions; a little classification and generalization on the mere descriptive level; a strong prejudice that we *have* states of mind, and that our brain conditions them: but not a single law in the sense in which physics shows us laws, not a single proposition from which any consequence can causally be deduced. . . . This is no science, it is only the hope of a science. . . . The Galileo and the Lavoisier of psychology will be famous men indeed when they come, as come they some day surely will . . . When they do come, however, the necessities of the case will make them "metaphysical." (pp. 467-468)

And in 1976, the presidential address to the annual convention of the American Psychological Association sounded a note not very different from James's; eighty-four years later, psychology is still in pursuit of a single law, still found lengthening a string of raw facts, still awaiting its Galileo and Lavoisier.

It is not my purpose here to dispute such appraisals. Rather, I would offer a construction of them that differs from the one provided by James and, more recently, by Professor McKeachie. I would submit that the *apparent* sluggishness of psychology's growth is, to a very considerable degree, the result of the extraordinary perspicuity of its eighteenth- and nineteenth-century founders who, themselves, extended their vision by standing on the high ground established by earlier generations of philosophers and metaphysicians. It was in these two centuries that those *isms* with which any developed psychology would have to reckon were advanced in nearly modern form: empiricism, nativism, materialism, utilitarianism, positivism. These were the centuries of Condillac, Cabanis, La Mettrie, Rousseau, Berkeley, Hume, J. S. Mill, Kant, Hegel, and Fichte. And to these names we could easily and aptly add dozens more. These were, as well, the centuries of such astonishing fecundity in the biological and physical sciences. Thus, as our own century emerged, its psychologists found themselves competing with many of the most tutored and capacious minds in all of intellectual history; minds seldom neglectful of even the subtlest nuance or most elusive epistemological possibility. It would not require a pessimistic temperament to sustain the conviction that only "a string of raw facts; a little gossip and wrangle about opinions" were left over to us by this legion of savants.

We do not account for periods of uncommon achievement by merely noting that figures of great genius were responsible. Aside from their specific contributions, the men and women of the *Enlightenment* and of the *Victorian* period are indistinguishably woven into the same fabric of humanity that covers all of human history. They are not instances of a strange species and, in many cases, they were not even well born or well bred. But if I were pressed to set them, *en bloc*, apart from the larger community of any age, I would be tempted to do so on the basis of their familiarity with what was known and written by those who came before them. It is in this only relevant sense of the term that we can call all of them *educated*. The long list of eminent men who never earned academic degrees includes Hume, J. S. Mill, and T. H. Huxley, but it contains none who was ignorant of what Matthew Arnold so fondly called "the best things said and done in the world." And with no intention to be reproachful, I would say that this characteristic sets them off most vividly from our own generation whose commendable energy and eagerness become listless when stalled by historical reflection. Yet, in the absence of this reflection, strings of facts can only be lengthened meaninglessly and discussion of fundamental issues can only be reduced to a wrangle about opinion.

The scholars of the eighteenth and nineteenth centuries were, on the whole, confident and optimistic. Indeed, we find so much of their writing innocent because of these characteristics. We also wonder how people of such broad and deep intelligence could sustain so cheery and self-contented a disposition. At the risk of simplifying matters, I would again point to their command of the history of ideas. Since they knew how far others had advanced in the search for truth, they were able to measure the range of their own progress. They did not have to worry about repeating the obvious. When they discovered coal, they did *not* bring it to Newcastle! Their assessments of earlier thought were often harsh and biased, not to say wrong, but they knew what had been thought. With us, the situation is different. Our historical studies are generally the briefest of all our formal exercises and are usually confined to summaries. In psychology, especially, there is a tendency to divide the season of inquiry into a bright experimental one and that gray and sullen eon that kept truth hidden until laboratories brought the light. We put off the day when the findings made possible by these laboratories meet those "necessities of the case" which make them "metaphysical." It might not even be too harsh to say that we avoid, consciously or otherwise, the very forms of inquiry that are likely to unearth these necessities.

Whatever the brooding and unreachable motives may be, I leave to those better suited to such matters. The *fact* we have to deal with is the growing distance between contemporary psychology and its moorings; the growing distance dividing today's psychologist from the achievements of those who created his discipline. It is a fact that presents a problem, and it is to this problem that the present volumes are addressed. The modern psychologist labors under the burden of specialization, a burden that does not permit his eyes to wander too far beyond the prosperous if tiny kingdom of his interest. And we may add to this burden the effects that fashion and commerce have had on the general availability of many of the most significant contributions to psychological thought. That all this has become more widely perceived can be seen in the appearance of the multitude of secondary sources and burgeoning anthologies meant to facilitate periodic excursions back to psychology's original ports of embarkation. Yet, it is a paradoxical measure of the success of these ventures that, increasingly, secondary sources and anthologies are held in marginal and only grudging esteem. They have driven readers to the primary works, and the readers, thus enlightened, have come to question the aptness of interpretation and the aptness of selection displayed by historians and anthologists.

It would not be correct to say that the mounting distrust of texts and collections has diminished their authority. Rather, the distrust has weakened the real contributions such editions can make while not significantly protecting readers from the damage they can do. Secondary sources are *exegetical* by nature and can be, therefore, nothing but handbooks if they are not animated by a personal perspective. Accordingly, a text on the history of psychology *succeeds* when its reader finds himself disagreeing with this or that interpretation. Only when one recognizes that any worthwhile secondary source is an original work in itself is one likely to redeem the assets and avoid the liabilities of the genre. But to be repaid by the originality of such editions, the reader must be fully conversant with the primary sources under consideration. Ideas and issues of moment are not easily assimilated. The burden can be lightened by sharing. This, then, is the aim of exegetical writing; not to introduce the reader to ideas and issues but to provide yet another perspective against which he can test his own. And this is precisely the reason that secondary sources are such poor devices for introducing readers to the literal, unadorned, and faithfully rendered thoughts of others. The reader who is utterly ignorant of the original expositions necessarily cannot have any perspective on them and, as a result, can only take on faith the validity and the fidelity of the secondary treatments.

That this has not gone unnoticed can be discerned by anyone who has watched the steady procession of anthologies marching forth from every major publisher in the Western world! It would be arduous, indeed, to locate a major figure in the history of thought whose books or essays have not been excerpted in the past twenty years. Nor is this a fact to be despised since anthologies of the sort in mind serve the useful function of allowing the reader to test the waters before taking a headlong leap. Nonetheless, this overall approach must be counted as even less desirable than introductions given by exegetical writing. Anthologies may conceal—but they do not eliminate—the mixed blessing of *interpretation* since the anthologist still stands as both bridge and barrier to the original works. Moreover, the principle guiding the preparation of such collections is that of economy of effort, a principle which often serves the reader at the expense of the authors whose great and careful works have been boiled down to a few conclusions—with all the analysis boiled off.

A moment's reflection is enough to convince the wary mind of the problems courted by those who rely upon such collections. The history of ideas, even in its fullness, does not offer a broader range of opinion on most matters than the range embracing the commoner spheres of conviction. As a result, little more than vanity is served or abused when we learn only of the conclusions reached by the better minds of history. The value of study is not to be found in statistical tabulations or the voting patterns emerging from three millenia of reflection. If the labors of the scholar are to be repaid, he must pursue the lines of argument and analysis followed by others and compare these with his own. What matters more than the conclusions reached are the methods and the reasons invoked in their defense. The mere fact, if it is a fact, that Socrates believed in the existence of innate ideas or that Leibnitz was a "psychophysical dualist" or that Thomas Reid's philosophy conformed to the canons of his Presbyterian faith can have little standing in the courts of inquiry. Facts of such a sort are, at most, *biographical* and only loosely historical. They bear the same relationship to a knowledge of the thoughts of another as a street address bears to a knowledge of the life lived by the resident.

Where choice must be confined to excerpted works or secondary elaborations, the latter may well be more safely advised. It is doubtful that a serious author would prefer to be judged on the basis of several pages copied from his *magnum opus* than to be ignored entirely. And it is just as doubtful that the prepared mind would spend itself on the authorship of three hundred pages of text if the point at issue could be settled in three. Human history, as Collingwood teaches, is the history of thought. Human history is a history of actions and these, if they are to be more meaningful than simple reflexes, proceed from *reasons*. But in noting this, we offer no veiled endorsement of what has come to be called "psychohistory." When we seek, for example, Giordano Bruno's reasons for subscribing to the Hermes legends, we are concerned as historians not with Bruno but with ourselves, with human invention at large. To the extent that Bruno's convictions can be explained by the unique details of his life, his convictions cannot be of any general and historically informing value. We assume, that is, that Bruno's defense of his beliefs would proceed along rational and not autobiographical

lines; that he would urge upon us an argument and not a "revelation"; that he would set forth an analysis and not merely a
diary. To inquire into the factors that may have led Bruno to the
path he subsequently followed is to study Bruno. To review his
defense of this as the right path is to study history. Those who
accept this distinction will need no further warnings in the matter of excerpts and will readily agree that the value of an abridg-
ed work decreases in proportion to the degree of abridgement.

In assembling materials for *Significant Contributions to the
History of Psychology* I have not by any means overcome all the
objections stated or implied above. Each volume reflects, after
all, what *I* judged to be a significant contribution and there are,
no doubt, many missing volumes which could have given readers
access to works others would judge to be superior to those I have
chosen. By way of explanation and apology, therefore, I should
summarize the criteria governing my selections. And I should
quickly add that I have not even been undeviatingly loyal to
these. To avoid being overly actuarial, I will say only that each
selection satisfied at least two of the criteria and three quarters
of the selections satisfied all of them.

The criteria, themselves, can be stated briefly but only defended at length. The first of these is, of course, the *significance*
of the work in question. Of the several criteria, this is the only
one that is dependent exclusively on judgment. I consider a work
significant to the history of psychology when it is addressed to
an issue or method which neither contemporary psychology nor
any plausibly imaginable system of psychology can ignore.
Broadly set forth, these issues and methods include—but are
not limited to—cognition and affect, experience and action, and
the ontogenetic and phylogentic manifestations of these. Surrounding and often penetrating each of these, we will find recommended methods of investigation and proof and these, too,
become celebrated issues in their own right.

An issue may be significant but still treated in an unworthy
manner. A subject such as hypnosis or "animal magnetism," for
example, enjoyed such popularity in the nineteenth century that
one could easily fill thirty volumes with articles and books devoted to it. It is not ungenerous, however, to observe how many
of these articles and books failed to shed light on the causes,
uses, or importance of the phenomenon. Many expositors limited their assessments to the analgesic powers of hypnotism; others fixed their enthusiasms to its putative spiritual significance;
still others sought to find God through its application. We do not

find modern psychology's indebtedness to the nineteenth century by examining works of this kind. Here, again, we face the burden of judgment: Given this or that issue to be an important one, has it been ably served or has it been obscured by this or that treatment of it?

In addition to the significance of the issue and the aptness of the treatment, I have been guided by the criterion of *accessibility*. This criterion can be applied with more objectivity than the first two, but judgment is not entirely suspended. I may illustrate this with a question: How accessible is the recently reprinted essay of 200 pages which is priced at $40.00? Fortunately, in only a few instances has it become necessary to include in these volumes works which, in being made *physically* accessible, have been rendered *economically* out of reach. But there have been more than a few—though still not many—instances where inclusion has been warranted because of the poor quality of recent republications or because the republications have been so destitute of editorial comment as to render the work unintelligible to all but experts. Both of these latter considerations are rough measures of the actual accessibility of a work. The relevance of the quality of production is too obvious to need discussing, and only a few words are in order in regard to editorial contributions.

Active minds are often changeable, and the views expressed in one major work may be qualified or even abandoned later. It is also the case that an author relies on the attitudes and the ordinary acceptations of words and phrases prevailing among his readership. In a different and later century, such attitudes may have few adherents and what was once an ordinary acceptation may have become extraordinary or even unknown. It is the editor's task to anticipate problems of this sort which the modern reader may confront; to alert the reader and to translate for him the older attitudes and locutions into a familiar language. And here I do not use the term "translate" metaphorically but literally. The editor's PREFACE has, among its varied duties, that of providing a conceptual Lexicon, one that establishes the intellectual and broad social boundaries within which the older works were fashioned. In the absence of such a Lexicon, "old" and "dated" become synonymous. To conclude, then, I note that in some instances I have chosen material which, though available in a recent reprinting, is *conceptually* inaccessible to all but those who have mastered the period.

Of course, the most confidently applied measure of accessibility was that emerging from a careful study of the National Union Catalogue, which yields a sufficiently precise assessment of how readily obtainable a given edition is. Without going into details, I will only say that the works offered in these volumes would, with the noted exceptions, be extremely difficult to obtain at all but the major national and university libraries. Indeed, many are not to be found even in the majority of these.

Those who examine all the volumes will note also that a number of original translations have been included. These were subjected to the same criteria that guided the balance of the selections. In addition to these original translations, I have, of course, included many non-English works translated at or near the time of their authorship. But in mentioning these facts I would not want to create the impression that an "international" flavor was either sought or achieved. For reasons that can only be set forth in far more space than the present occasion provides, the significant contributions, in modern times, to the history of psychology have come almost entirely from those quarters in which the scholar's language has been English, French, or German. One hopes and trusts that this will no longer be a fact decades hence when the native genius of men and women the world over is nurtured by those peculiar conditions on which the inquiring mind depends.

The last and most arbitrary criteria are those of *period* and *organization*. In regard to the first, I shall state but not defend the decision to confine selections to works authored between 1750 and 1920. There is nothing historically compelling about the choice of the earliest date except that, before 1750, works of a psychological nature are actually and purely philosophical. I needn't defend the significant contributions made to modern psychology by Aristotle, Descartes, et al., but in the case of such extraordinary figures, the happy availability of their writings removed them from consideration. Clearly, the period of greatest fertility *vis à vis* modern psychology is the nineteenth century and especially the second half. This is a fact honored by the space devoted in these volumes to that period.

A project involving 28 volumes and nearly 200,000 pages presents an editor with grave organizational problems. In no case is a work completed in a second volume, this to serve the reader's convenience and to save his expense. Add to this the desire to keep all volumes roughly equivalent in size and it soon becomes clear that some juxtapositions will be less than apt.

Mechanical solutions to this problem were all unfitting. Neither an alphabetical nor a chronological organization satisfies the aim of the project or the constraints imposed by the realities of production. Thus, to every possible extent, I have tried to give each volume a *thematic* integrity and I have bolstered this attempt by dividing the entire collection into *series*. The reader who is willing to overlook my failures here and to focus attention on the selections themselves will, I am sure, find direction and even inspiration in the writings of bygone but ever eminent psychologists. Nor is it too much to hope that the student of the past will find in these pages but another proof of the timelessness of the human imagination and the arbitrariness of merely temporal divisions.

DANIEL N. ROBINSON

===============

> *We are born weak, we need strength; help-*
> *less we need aid; foolish, we need reason. All*
> *that we lack at birth, all that we need when*
> *we come to man's estate, is the gift of educa-*
> *tion.*
>
> Rousseau, *Emile*

No leading philosopher has ever been entirely silent on the
subject of education, and no developed society has been too
modest to deny how superior its system of education is when
compared with what came before. But once we set aside all that
is merely self-congratulatory and illusory, and once we choose
to ignore those historical nuances that are purely technical or
administrative, we discover that the *ideal* of education, throughout Western history, has been animated by two conflicting
views of man; by two alternative visions of society; by two
counterpoised *metaphysics*. One of these is the idea of *Harmony*; the other, *Progress*. The first of these is the world in-
vented by the Greeks of antiquity; the second, the modern
world of the *Renaissance* and the *Enlightenment*.

The "Greek view," as the Western world received it from
the philosophers and dramatists of antiquity, was one con-
ditioned by the principles of hierarchy, order, place, season.
That which was sudden and inexplicable was interpreted as
evidence of man's limited comprehension of the cosmos; of his
intellectual weakness and his proneness to deception. Long
before Socrates and Plato, a latent philosophy had been adopted
by the *Hellenes*. This was the "philosophy" contained in the
epic works of Hesiod and Homer. There is very little, indeed,
in the literary and intellectual achievements of the Hellenic
Age which is not thoroughly beholden to this older and per-
vasive influence. Its traces are easily discerned in the four-
element physics of the pre-Socratic natural philosophers of

Ionia, and in the catechism of the Pythagoreans. But it is seen,
as well, in the systematic writings of Plato and Aristotle, though
in a manner that is somewhat different from the pre-Socratic
and Pythagorean expressions.

The ethical and political writings of Plato and Aristotle
display anthropocentric concerns only touched upon by the earlier philosophers of Ionia. And they are far more down-to-earth
than anything found in Pythagoreanism—at least to the extent
that our little knowledge of the latter is valid. Nevertheless,
the Socratic and Aristotelian analyses retain the traditional
commitment to *Harmony* as the goal of life, and, in significant
respects, this commitment is antithetical to the idea of progress.
On the ancient account, harmony is a condition of being, a
fixed point on the continuum of being. To move *past* this point
—i.e., to "progress"—is to return to vice and ignorance.

It is only by keeping this Homeric theme before us that we
are able to reconcile the "earthiness" of the Platonic and Aristotelian systems with their abiding suspicion of and contempt
for "the facts of sense." There is no *fact* that can conduce to
a condition of being, as there is no "experience" that can reveal the eternal and immutable. One does not "see" Harmony,
one *deduces* it. Accordingly, all true philosophy is the gift of
reason, not experience. But the flowering of reason does not
occur unconditionally. If one is to attain the state of ration-
ality, through which the affairs of life are governed by the harmonic relationship among intellect, will, and passion, one must
be nurtured from infancy. One's character must be shaped by
rewards and punishments. One must be offered musical examples of harmony, and must learn, through martial training,
those habits which mirror harmony. Thus educated, the young
man is now ready for that formal, philosophical analysis which
proves *certainly* and *axiomatically* those principles which were,
heretofore, merely illustrated.

The education prescribed for the youth of Athens emphasized discipline and restraint. It took for granted that what
was "natural," by way of adolescent inclinations, was wicked
and degrading. The aim of education was to tame the natural
appetites so that the mind might be appealed to, when the time
was right. Education, then, was not designed to facilitate some
assumed "natural progression," but to ensure that "natural
stagnation" would be overcome. For the Greeks, each period in
life—infancy, early childhood, childhood, adolescence, manhood, senescence—carried with it fixed capacities and pro-
clivities. Aristotle, in his *Rhetoric*, carefully delineates these

stages, and notes the assets and liabilities of each. The stages, themselves, are *natural* but not necessarily temporary. There is no age at which, without the benefit of tuition, we are fully rational beings. Rather, at each stage, we meet new and sterner challenges, all threatening to destroy what small degree of harmony we might have cultivated to that point. Left at the mercy of nature, we become no more than brutes—called "natural slaves" by Aristotle—able to follow rational arguments, but unable to articulate them for our own benefit.

During the thousand years of Christian hegemony in the West, the Ancient Greek idea of education was adopted wholecloth, with reinforcement coming from the Stoic and Epicurean schools of Rome. For the Christian, too, the world has been set up as a test and an arena; an arena that is lawful, harmonious, invisibly but rationally governed. At the same time, man is free to choose his course of action, but so saddled by the burden of his original state (of sin) as often to choose poorly. Through discipline, governance, example, and exhortation, the child may be brought to that state of being in which he surrenders his entire life to "Reason and the Will of God." There are, then, only *two* conditions of being: the condition of sin, and that of salvation. The former leads to eternal suffering; the latter, to eternal peace (harmony). In the most important respect, individual and collective "progress" is a concept without meaning. This is not to say that good habits will not result from practice, or that a man might not be a better Christian tomorrow than he was today. It is to say, rather, that progress, *per se*, is not the goal; that progress is not even the means. Progress is that merely and trivially accidental correlate of Faith guiding Reason and perfecting it.

As Christianity passed from its Patristic to its Scholastic period, and as Aristotelian rationalism began to replace the more transcendental features of neo-Platonism, there began the tradition of "religious science." This tradition, from the thirteenth to the sixteenth centuries, would yield both the "natural magic" and the "spiritual magic" of the *Renaissance*; and, both the witchcraft and the natural science of the seventeenth century. But in both of these manifestations, "religious science" introduced the Western community to the idea of progress—first as the hope of influencing and manipulating nature, and then as the goal of controlling and opposing nature. Ironically, then, in the very century in which we find the Church re-establishing itself on Aristotelian foundations, we find a movement away from the orthodox Hellenic restraint, the age-less Homeric diffidence in the face of the Cosmos. This is not to say that the Scholastics misinterpreted Aristotle or that they abandoned Plato. Rather, in an era of greater security and economic expansion, the Western community found antique principles and passages that were more consonant with emerging confidence and hopefulness. And, with the *Reformation*, what had once been the relatively isolated shift in the perspective of intellectuals, now became a more general, cultural phenomenon. In the storms of anti-authoritarianism, Sweet Harmony was brushed aside and the Idea of Progress was installed as the new religion of Humanism.

These tendencies culminated—or, shall I say, reached their first plateau—in the *Enlightenment*. The later revolutions of 1848 were of a radically different sort, and even these are to be understood more as prolongations of *Enlightenment* energies than as renewed battles of principle and philosophy. The salient figure in 1848 is the Plain Man; in 1789, the *philosophes* and their first-born. Between these upheavals we find both the revival of classical values and the impatient urge to accelerate the march toward the goals of the *Enlightenment*. In the field of education, the tensions as the nineteenth century begins are between nationalism and brotherhood, freedom and moral purpose, scientific materialism and the human spirit, commercialism and naturalism. Each of these pairs is, of course, a version of every other, and all are bound up in what was soon to be called the Spirit of the Age.

The life of Johann Pestalozzi spanned many of these developments and was uniquely affected by them. He was sixteen when Rousseau published *Emile* (1762). He issued his first *Gertrude* piece in 1781. Pestalozzi was forty when Frederick the Great died; Karl Marx was nine when Pestalozzi died (1827). One of his admiring critics was Herbart, and one of his students was Froebel. He fought bravely for Prussia in her wars and suffered neglect during the intervals of peace. Yet, as the world became ever more uncertain, and as his own fortunes shifted precariously and without warning, his resolve quickened and stiffened. For a half-century, he labored in behalf of the education of the young, seeking to fit them to the world as it is, while preserving the gifts which nature had bestowed on them. It is less than surprising that even he, especially he, recognized that his "ideal" could never be attained. It was, after all, the Greek ideal:

> Every philosophical investigator of human
> nature is ultimately compelled to admit that
> the sole aim of education is the harmonious
> development of the faculties and dispositions
> which, under God's grace, make up person-
> ality. (*Views and Experiences*, p. 159)

In some respects, the modern reader is likely to feel more
at home with the philosophy of education advanced by Pestalozzi than would be expected, given that this philosophy is
nearly two centuries old. Western man, and particularly the
Western intellectual, lives in the patrimony of Rousseau, and
continues to defend his habits and yearnings in terms first
articulated by the *philosophes* and later defended by the able
essayists in the Liberal tradition of the nineteenth century.
Certainly most students in the contemporary American university will agree with Pestalozzi's tirelessly repeated claim that
"Life is Education." And only one given to spasms of sedition
would, today, argue against the Pestalozzian resolution to educate, "the whole man," who becomes "whole" only when education appeals to "head, heart, and hand." Moreover, there
is a general and an increasing enthusiasm for practical, earth-
bound education, and a general, though stable, suspicion aimed
at high-bound, "irrelevant," classical education. Would not
more than one sophomore applaud the following claim?:

> This disproportion, ruinous for the human
> mind, between the advantages of the upper
> and the misery of the lower classes, or rather
> the beginning point from which this striking
> disproportion . . . dates, is the invention of
> the art of printing . . . I might almost say it
> was forced to make this universal instrument
> of knowledge a mere letter-eye, and us mere
> letter-men. (*Gertrude* Letter-X, pp. 222-223)

Pestalozzi's complaint with books, like the modern teacher's fears of television, is that passivity becomes the rule, self-
activity the exception. As the world becomes more manageable
by economic and technical means, the already great chasm
separating the lot of the classes is widened, and the literate
society comes to master the illiterate. Worse, the masters rule
by words, not deeds.

We can find the same notions in *Emile* or, for that matter,
in Marx. But ideology aside, these notions, in the hands of

Pestalozzi, spring from a systematic philosophy of education, one that is by no means either dated or endangered. On the authority of Rousseau and of his own deliberations, Pestalozzi insists that *Nature* is our school, and *Life* is our principal tutor. The formal school, therefore, succeeds to the extent that it anticipates the demands which Life and Nature impose upon us; it fails to the extent that it sacrifices the *real* to the *abstract*, the *practical* to the purely *speculative*. And life, finally, is *experience* and *action*.

On the fundamental question of epistemology, Pestalozzi is unhesitating: All that we know, we know through the mechanisms of sensation. The knowable world enters our being through the organs of sense, and, until this has happened, we know nothing. However, the senses alone can convey only showers of disconnected and chaotic experiences. The prepared mind is one which forges *thought* from these sense-impressions, and here the role of language is essential. Language is the means by which mere sense-impressions are converted into thought and organized into coherent concepts and memories.

> My method of instruction is particularly distinguished in this:—it makes greater use of language as a means of raising the child from vague sense-impressions to clear ideas, than has ever been done before. Also, it is distinguished by the principle of excluding from the first elementary instruction all collections of words presupposing actual knowledge of language or grammar. (Gertrude Letter-VII, p. 178)

There are two emphases in this passage: one relating to the primacy of language in the formation of thought, and one which restricts language-teaching to the concrete realm of the sensible. The real bondage of the lower classes is that they cannot comprehend the barrister, the clergyman, the businessman. They are the butt of humor and the objects of exploitation because their schooling has steeped them in verbal swamps containing no recognized sign-posts; containing nothing common to their daily experiences. Therefore,

> . . . as *definitions before sense-impression* lead men to presumptuous chatter, so word-teachings about virtue and faith, preceding

the realities of living sense-impressions, lead
men astray to similar confusion about them.
(*Gertrude Letter-XIII*, p. 281)

Every clear idea is an idea about *something*, and this requires that the senses have commerce with the *thing* before the
mind can form ideas about it. It is no less so in the realm of
morals than in the realm of facts or of science or of craft. Instruction which is purely verbal—that is, destitute of concrete,
perceptible examples—is literally *nonsense*, and can do no
more than confuse the young mind. As Rousseau argued, the
child must learn, "not from books but from things." (I might
note, however, that in advancing this argument in *Emile*, Rousseau draws his inspiration from *Robinson Crusoe*—a book!)

Were Pestalozzi to stop here in his analysis, he would provide no more than a fashionable *empiricism*, no different from
that advanced by, say, Helvetius or La Mettrie. But Pestalozzi
is an empiricist without being a radical environmentalist, and
a naturalist without being a radical materialist. Note, then,
that in his own philosophical development, he finds it necessary to cool the smug assurances of the *Enlightenment* in the
shadows of traditional wisdom. Thus, his *empirical* psychology
is the first step toward a *cognitive* psychology, and this, the
first step toward a practical (moral) *social* psychology. To stop
at the stage of empirical psychology—and from this point to
seek to unfurl all varieties of metaphysical and ethical slogans
—is to revive the errors of the *Enlightenment*:

This led to the disappearance of all *humanity*
from political systems; this again to the dissolution of a few political systems which had
ceased to be human. But unfortunately this
did not work to the advantage of humanity
. . . the deficiencies of European instruction
. . . has brought this part of the world *where
it is now;* . . . there is no remedy for our present and future overturn in society, morality,
and religion except to turn back from the
superficiality, incompleteness, and giddy-
headedness of our popular instruction, and
to recognize that *sense-impression is absolutely the foundation of all knowledge* . . .
(*Gertrude Letter-X*, p. 227)

But, while it is the *foundation* of all knowledge, it is not the limit of what we know. Rather, it is the first step in the formation of *clear ideas* which, themselves, are the beginning of our sense of duty. We move, then, from the fact, to the principle, to the action, educated in such a way as to render all our actions conformable to the facts of the situation, and to the principles which blanket these facts. We find the clearest illustration of this point in "The Art of Measuring" (*Gertrude* Letter-VIII), where education in geometric forms and proportions elevates the (mere) power of observation to an awareness of *rules* (p. 193). And the same applies in *moral* instruction, where the teacher's love and justice—displayed in *particular* instances—are offered with such reliability and generality that the child becomes aware of the moral *principle* that forms the foundation (justification) of the actions.

With the perspicuity of a Freud, Pestalozzi constantly insisted that all education begins within the home, and that its most important features were those first and most completely in the hands of the family—and especially the mother. The early schools he established for orphans gave him direct exposure to the ravaging effects of the parentless childhood, and his hardly concealed lack of confidence in governments persuaded him that children are best educated by those most personally and emotionally committed to them. In his *ABC of Anschauung,* mothers are reminded of the disproportionate influence of the early years on later life. As Professor Green noted in his *Introduction* to the edition of 1912, Pestalozzi anticipated Wordsworth in recognizing that "the child is father to the man." What the child must learn from his mother is that which mere sense-impressions will not convey. I speak here of *moral principles* and of *the awareness of God.* These principles and this awareness are, finally, of a transcendental nature—or at least are the gift of a transcendent Being—but they must originate in and be founded upon experience. That is, they must make their first appeal to the mind of the child through the senses, if there is to be a clear idea of them. In this, the mother is the indispensible model, the irreplaceable teacher. The love that flows between mother and child becomes the *exemplar* of God's love for man. The justice and concern of the mother are, too, instances of a more general feature of the world. These lessons cannot be learned at the knee of Nature any longer:

> Not God's first creation but *this* world decoys
> the child to the giddy dance of the whirlpool
> of the abyss whose depths are the home of
> lovelessness and moral death. Not God's cre-
> ation, but the brute force and art of bringing
> about its own ruin, is what *this* world puts
> before the child's eyes. (*Gertrude* Letter-XIV,
> p. 291)

Rousseau's *noble savage*, if he ever lived, will no longer find uncorrupted nature standing by as *alma mater*. The real world is one of war, self-deception, pretense, oppression, moral bankruptcy. The child who will evade the traps of this world, and who will survive in it as a whole person, a moral person, must be prepared for it by human intervention and by human example. And in this, we discover what the many pages of arithmetic instruction, drawing, physical exercise, language-training, and manual labor were all about. We see that the aim of Pestalozzi's program is not to produce only the competent craftsman or the disciplined professional. The aim, in Pestalozzi's own words, is this:

> . . . to prevent the selfishness of the reason
> by preserving the purity of the heart from
> error and one-sidedness; and, above all, to
> *subordinate* my sense-impressions to my con-
> victions, my eagerness to my benevolence,
> and my benevolence to my righteous will.
> (*Gertrude* Letter-XIV, p. 293)

I suggested earlier that Pestalozzi's idea of education is likely to meet with approval when reviewed by the modern world. But this is not to say that the grounds upon which the approval rests are the same as those set forth by Pestalozzi. Nor is it to suggest that a modern reader will applaud everything which Pestalozzi believes follows from his system.

The defense of experience and the celebration of "life" as our most effective teacher are, in Pestalozzi's theories, inextricably bound to his class-oriented perception of society. He can discern no justification for forcing the sons of farmers to master Latin phrases or the speculations of metaphysicians. He openly laments that system of universal education which ignores differences in background, prospect, native ability, and personal inclinations. For Pestalozzi, the head, heart, and hand must be nurtured coextensively largely because the child will, more than likely, find himself working with his hands most of his life.

But even more than this, Pestalozzi believes that psychological development was a matter of sensory-motor integration, and that early manipulative training was essential to ultimate cognitive skill. Note, then, that the defense of "doing" is as much Piagetian as it is Rousseauean. That is, it is based upon a theory of cognitive development and not merely on the putative virtue of manual labor!

Note, too, that the education which life provides is offered by Pestalozzi to those who have already become mentally and morally disciplined. His concern, as an educator, is to ensure that, of the mixed opportunities made available by daily life, the child entering the real world will not become corrupted and "giddy-headed" by the procession of sense-impressions. Accordingly, from his earliest years, the child is shaped by the moral examples set by the members of his family, and further refined in his thinking by a program of instruction which can only be called *regimental*. To seek a defense of modern "experiential" education in the writings of Pestalozzi is, therefore, hazardous. Few recent writers of so-called liberal persuasion have proposed curricular reform on grounds which Pestalozzi would claim as his own—or, for that matter, on grounds which Pestalozzi would be likely to comprehend. He would consider it psychologically suicidal to take the product of the typical modern family and hurl him into the waters of life's experiences. Man, as he tells us, "must gather experience amongst the ruins of his primitive instincts, which shall convince him of the errors and worthlessness of his animal nature, and lead him to the recognition of moral worth" (*Early Writings*, p. 72). Relevant and constructive experience, then, can occur only "among the ruins" of that psychological equipment which the completely untutored brings into the world.

In this same connection, Pestalozzi was disinclined to place much importance on the socio-economic "status" of children as a factor calling for special methods or warranting special concerns. Although he constantly kept before him a picture of the sort of life the child would come to live, and the unique occupational demands which seemed to go hand-in-glove with the child's family background, he held steadfastly to the conviction that the psychological faculties are common to all people, and that their nurturance was the principal responsibility of the teacher. He puts his conclusions clearly in the *Address to My House, 1818:*

> Amidst the ups and downs of my experience,
> I soon found that the problem of education is
> in its essentials the same whatever the social
> position of the children, and that it does not
> consist in communicating special knowledge
> or special dexterities, but in developing the
> fundamental human powers (*which are, of
> course, the same for rich and poor*). (p. 198)

To develop these faculties, the teacher must pace the child through the intricacies of language, number, and form. He must see to it that the mechanisms by which the sense-impressions are formed and registered become subservient to cognitive rules which, in turn, impose requirements on actions. These steps are as essential to the farmer as they are to the craftsman or the General. Thus, no matter what the background, the individual must develop his powers *as a condition* of being educated in the several theaters of life.

As language, number, and form are not the only *formal* elements of the child's education—only the most basic—so the family is not the only setting in which the moral dimensions of life are cultivated. In Letters V, VI, and VII of "Views and Experiences," Pestalozzi provides us with conjectures which are at once Freudian, Piagetian, and Wordsworthian. He notes the egocentric perspective of the infant; a perspective which is necessitated by the biological requirements and by the perceptual and motor limitations of the newborn. Soon, however, the child comes to recognize himself as one among several; then as one among many. His social circle widens, and pure dependency and selfishness become transformed into interdependence and a sense of society. Nature, too, serves as a great teacher. The child learns of waste and death; of the fruits of labor and the wages of laziness; of the essential *harmony* among God's creations. We appreciate, then, that the Pestalozzi "system"—which Herbart thought was all exercise and discipline—is but the application of *naturalism* to education. It is the pedagogical version of that sentiment which, in letters, will guide the Lake Poets; in art, the masters of the landscape and seascape; in music, the Romantics. The sentiment, of course, is impelled and amplified by the idea of harmony, and it is a return to the Greek vision, a turning away from *progressivism*. This is but one more of our modern ironies, for, what we ordinarily mean today by "progressive" education—education based on "learning by doing," on "experience," on "real life"—is, in fact, a reactionary idea, and one with impeccable "conservative" credentials.

One is, perhaps, most impressed, in reading these essays by Pestalozzi, with the self-consciously *psychological* orientation of the author. He does not set out to provide a philosophy of education, but an educational psychology. His program, at every stage, seeks support from the known or presumed principles of learning, memory, cognition, motivation. And as a psychologist, Pestalozzi compiles a mixed but interesting record. On the issue of the acquisition of language, he is clearly in the associationistic-mimetic tradition, and, for this reason, his exposition is dated and dry. He seems unwilling to subject language to the same kind of analysis which he brings to bear upon the relationship between sense-impressions and "clear ideas." With respect to the latter, he adopts the notion of fixed mental faculties or powers which permit the organization of sensations. The disciplined and prepared mind now processes the impressions according to rules or principles, such that what might have been no more than a din of experiences is now an ensemble of coherent ideas. With respect to language, however, he is content to let imitation and rewarded practice work their magic and, somehow, convert a din of words into grammatical speech. It is clear, then, that, although Pestalozzi anticipated the seminal theories of Professor Piaget, he did not anticipate those of Professor Chomsky.

In his recognition of the social and socializing character of education, Pestalozzi was clearly ahead of his time, even in light of the impetus provided by Rousseau. His discussions here are filled with allusions to peer-pressure, "modelling," role-playing, and the like. And, although he never uses the term or its specific equivalent, he is clearly aware of the phenomenon of "critical periods of development." Everywhere, he emphasizes "readiness" on the learner's part as the crucial factor in determining the success of tuition.

In the more restricted compartment of educational psychology, Pestalozzi is both prophet and leader. He urges the establishment of rural colleges devoted to agricultural science; vocational schools designed to produce good craftsmen; technical institutes for the training of teachers. He insists that a major problem in education can be solved by making available to parents and teachers a set of manuals—"how-to" books—in which the psychological techniques and principles developed in his own schools are discussed clearly and with a practical

bent. He argues, further, that he has only scratched the surface of what will finally be educational *science,* and that future
workers will have to undertake serious experimental investigations of learning, memory, child-development, etc. In this connection, he proposes the creation of experimental schools (*Probe
Schule*) devoted to exploring the issues and hypotheses which
he has already brought to light.

It is of interest, also, that a man so eager to preserve and
to elevate what Pestalozzi calls "the national culture"—a man
anxious and hopeful that the well-educated child will be of
value to the State—should be sorely troubled by the governmental control of the schools. Part of his reservation is, to be
sure, understandable in terms of the tragic political events in
his own lifetime. He tells us in several places that, all things
considered, individuals are better at doing most things than
are governments. But at a deeper and essentially non-historical
level, Pestalozzi seems to fear that no government is ever restful in the face of a morally enlightened citizenry; that governments, by and large, will not impose a system of education
likely to produce such a citizenry. And he fears, also, the tendency toward moral mediocrity displayed by corporations and
communities of men, as opposed to the generally high tone of
conduct witnessed in the transactions between individuals
(*Gertrude* Letter-XIII, pp. 273-275). He mistrusts the masses
and prefers that they not all be instructed by a common tutor
—especially the State.

We learn from Professor Green's *Introduction* to the edition of 1912 that, "hardly a country in Europe was not affected
by [Pestalozzi]" (p. 13). Although his efforts were focused on
the earliest years of education, his influence necessarily spread
to higher education as well. What modern college or university
does not proclaim its responsibility to the "whole man"? What
modern college or university degrades the part played by calis-
thenics and athletics in the education of this "whole man"?
And while they would hardly associate themselves with *all* that
Pestalozzi has to say about the education of women, most university officials certainly would agree that,

> It is a mere prejudice to suppose that the
> acquirement of knowledge and the cultiva-
> tion of the intellect must either not be solid
> and comprehensive, or that they are apt to
> take away from the female character its sim-
> plicity and all that renders it truly amiable.
> (*Greaves* Letter-XXVII, p. 245)

But again we are advised not to impute too much modernity to our author. Contemporary education has, indeed, incorporated many of the suggestions developed and promoted by Pestalozzi. Our schools are bloated with personnel who care for the bodies, the psyches, and the "inter-personal relations" of the students. "Self-activity" is proclaimed, and every truly "progressive" school now is lined with "open classrooms" in which the most relevant aspects of every-day life are explored. All this, however, is only *half* of Pestalozzi's program. The other half—the *first* half—is *language, number, and form;* that trinity of mental powers whose harmonic integration is the necessary forerunner of those cadences which we call a rational life.

In a sense, modern education has outdistanced Pestalozzi. It has rushed directly into the ends of life and has tended to abandon the means to these ends. Pestalozzi, much in the fashion of the Medieval philosopher, conceived of the developed person as one whose knowledge of the world was gained through experience; as one whose judgments were formed by the disciplined correlation of knowledge and action; as one whose moral character was established by the integration of knowledge, action, and will. For Pestalozzi, as for the Medieval scholar, none of this was imaginable in the absence of some higher principle, according to which man—as an active and a moral being—has been fitted to the world in which he lives. This, then, is the *naturalistic* element; this, the sense in which the true teacher is like the gardener,

> . . . under whose care a thousand trees blossom and grow. He contributes nothing to their actual growth; the principle of growth lies in the trees themselves . . . He gives neither life nor breath. He only watches lest any external force should injure or disturb . . . But he must recognize fully the peculiar constitution of man's mind, adapted as it is to unite man's various powers in the interest of his final mission. (*Address to My House, 1818,* p. 195)

## BIOGRAPHICAL AND BIBLIOGRAPHICAL NOTES

*Johann Heinrich Pestalozzi* [1746-1827]

Pestalozzi was born in Zurich, where his father was a member of the clergy. The cantons of Switzerland had figured importantly in the rise of the European nation-states and had been small centers of protest and activism for centuries. Again in the eighteenth century, reform filled the Swiss atmosphere with leaders such as Lavater proclaiming the virtues of national culture. For a time, the young Pestalozzi was a follower of Lavater's, known more today for his odd theories of physiognomy than for his political and religious influence. Lavater, himself, had studied the ideas of the British "sentimentalists" and laid great stress on the "natural" inclinations of man as a moral being. How much of this rubbed off on Pestalozzi is, of course, a matter for conjecture.

Pestalozzi was already in his forties when the French Revolution erupted, but his early enthusiasm for liberal causes cooled quickly as he came to measure the full impact of radical liberalism. Indeed, in his *Evening Hours of a Hermit* (1780) we catch glimpses of that conservative tone which will come to dominate his later works.

Over the years, Pestalozzi established many schools, but none of them achieved the lasting success which Pestalozzi's own reputation would suggest. His first was at Neuhof, and it went bankrupt. In the year of the Revolution, he set up a school for orphans at Stans, but this soon became one more casualty in the battles between France and Switzerland. But successively, his schools at Burgdorf, Münchenbuchsee, and Yverdon increased his fame as an educator of young children.

As with political liberalism, Rousseau's "nature philosophy" was more attractive to the youthful Pestalozzi than to the more seasoned educator. Anticipating the "biogenetic" principles of Haeckel, he came to view each person as containing within him the total progress of the race, such that every man must wrestle with the inner tension between instinct and ethics. Even in the most optimistic of the *Gertrude* letters, there is the strain of worry and doubt; doubt in regard to the aims of governments, the will of the people, the future of the race.

Of the writings included in this volume, the *Letters to Greaves* are of qualified authenticity. His complete works have appeared in several German editions, the most recent under the editorship of Paul Baumgartner (Zurich, 1944-1949). An excellent recent biography has been provided by Käte Silber, under the title, *Pestalozzi: The Man and His Works* (London, 1960).

All of the notes appearing in the present volume were provided by the translators and editors of the editions of 1898 and 1912.

# HOW GERTRUDE
# TEACHES HER CHILDREN

An Attempt to Help Mothers to Teach their own Children

AND

## AN ACCOUNT OF THE METHOD

*A Report to the Society of the Friends of Education, Burgdorf*

BY

## JOHANN HEINRICH PESTALOZZI

TRANSLATED BY

## LUCY E. HOLLAND AND FRANCES C. TURNER

AND EDITED, WITH INTRODUCTION AND NOTES,

BY

## EBENEZER COOKE

*Second Edition, from Wholly New Plates*

SYRACUSE, N. Y.
## C. W. BARDEEN, PUBLISHER
1898

# CONTENTS

Page

# EDITOR'S PREFACE

*The Method* in time and thought precedes *How Gertrude Teaches*. It may be read after Letter I., for in this letter Pestalozzi gives the history and circumstances which led him to those principles he first definitely stated in *The Method*. The *First Letter from Stanz* also belongs to this period. It will be found in De Guimps's Life (Syracuse edition, pages 88-95) and in Quick's *Essays on Educational Reformers* (Syracuse edition, pages 221, 222). These works form a complete group, and are his most important educational works. They are undoubtedly his own ; of later works this cannot be said until we come to the *Swan's Song* and *My Experiences*.

The portions of *How Gertrude Teaches* in Biber's *Life of Pestalozzi* are all that have been translated. Its peculiar terms, such as *Anschauung* (see pp. 7–14) may partly account for this neglect. These terms are difficult, for apparently we do not grasp Pestalozzi's thought. We neither read nor follow him. If we walk in his ways, we may see what he saw ; if we repeat his experiments, we may in some measure share his thought. Doing leads to knowing. He has been blamed for not defining his terms. He gives instead the history of his conception, the circumstances which led to it, its development, and his schemes founded on it. "There are two ways of instructing," he says; "either we go from words to things, or from things to words. Mine is the second method." His meaning may become clearer if the reader will substitute *Anschauung* for "sense-impression" and for all other equivalents throughout the work. It has, and can have, no equivalent in English. We may partly learn its meaning, as we have learned that of some other words, from its use. If definitions are desired, the most helpful will be found at the beginning of Kant's *Critique of Pure Reason*. Kant's method is to begin with definitions.

We have tried to translate this work literally, without pharaphrase and without omissions : no difficult passage has been left out. Much might be improved. The more we learn from him the more evident this is. Any help which will make his thought still clearer will be gladly and thankfully received.

Pestalozzi foresaw, on its first morning, when he began *How Gertrude Teaches*, the nature of the coming century : "The whole earth the beauty wore of promise." We have entered into it. From Wordsworth's *Prelude*, "dedicate to Nature's self and things that teach as Nature teaches," written at exactly the same time, and in the same spirit, as *How Gertrude Teaches*, to our latest schemes of technical education, we have been thinking

and working in the same ways, with but little of his
direct influence.    Education generally ; the doctrine of
development ; the culture and knowledge of the body,
practically by exercise, theoretically by physiology ;
science and art, both included in his elementary means
—form, both founded on *Anschauung;* the training of
teachers, based on psychology ; our social schemes for
the welfare of the people—are all and more to be found
in this work.

In other minds similar ideas germinated independently.    Portions of the truth Pestalozzi perceived were
seen by many.    Soon after the middle of the century
much of it was re-embodied by the Rev. F. D. Maurice
in the Working Men's College.    His faith in both
"learning and working" are in the name.    In his
deep religious feeling and human sympathy, his perception of principles in the common facts of every-day
life, the unity of all studies, their relation to work, in
his desire to educate, exercise, and develop the whole
being, and in many other ways he resembled Pestalozzi.
At a time when the "mutual instruction" of Stanz
had been twisted here to support the monitorial system, the reality itself reappeared in the conversational
teaching—allied to Socratizing—which was generally
adopted at the College.    Men taught men in a non-
professional way, for the social and human elements
were considered as important as learning.    In this

direct action of mind on mind was to be found something of the "mutual self-vivification" of Stanz.—The unselfish devotion of Mr. Maurice's fellow-workers to a common purpose is a significant contrast to the divisions at Yverdun.

Among his associates, Mr. Ruskin, who may have been influenced by Rousseau, maintained the supremacy of Nature, and insisted as strongly as Pestalozzi himself on learning "to see" and on "seeing" as the beginning of art and thought. He claimed for form sense-impression and doing, a place in education. " Every youth should learn to do something thoroughly with his hands to know what touch means," he said. In many other ways he continued Pestalozzi's thought. Another associate, Rossetti, restored to form its old power of expressing thought, and unconsciously illustrated—as did all the Pre-Raphaelities—the Pestalozzian principle ;—the development of the individual follows that of the race. The College was perhaps at its best nearly twenty years before Payne's lecture on Pestalozzi.

The privilege and duty of continuing Mr. Ruskin's teaching in one class fell to me, and after several years this attempt to teach from nature naturally led me to Mr. C. H. Lake. He watched with much sympathy my attempts to teach drawing and natural science. Of these things he professed to know nothing, but his

profound knowledge of psychology, educational principles, and of Pestalozzi's spirit—he had been friend
and fellow-worker with Payne for many years—made
him the best guide and critic possible, perhaps the only
one. He entered into the work with great interest, for
he delighted in experiments, and to bring actual school
work to the test of principles. He was a master of
Socratizing, believed in inductive teaching, and, with
Pestalozzi and Maurice, in that "mutual instruction"
which brings minds into direct contact by conversation.
To him I am much indebted. I was compelled to fall
back on the unforgotten lessons of my boyhood, and I
expected to find the methods and principles of Pestalozzi established, well known, even extended, and his
own work easily accessible; but only Biber's fragments were available. Blind to its difficulties, I long
failed to induce friends to translate *How Gertrude
Teaches*, until, trying for myself, help was for the first
time offered ; Miss L. E. Holland translated not only
this work, but several others which threw light on it.
There were difficulties, and the late F. C. Turner
revised the whole work, and reduced the number. He
sought in both French and German literature to verify
passages and for help generally, even during his long
and painful illness. The amount and kind of help of
these friends could only have been given by those who
fully sympathised in the work.

Some doubtful passages remained ; for these several friends were consulted, and the various readings compared. In this way we had help from Mme. Michaelis, Miss F. Franks, Fraulein H. Seidel, Mr. A. Sonnenschein, and others. We have added the index.

*April,* 1894.

# NOTE ON TWO DIFFICULT WORDS

*Anschauung* is here usually translated "sense-impression". When another equivalent is used it is indicated by (*Ansch.*). "Sense-impression" is frequently used by Mr. Sully. "Sense-impressions are the alphabet by which we spell out the objects presented to us." (*Teacher's Handbook of Psychology*, 1886, ch. viii.) It was one of the most suitable words, but we are indebted to Mr. J. Russell for fixing it. The first draft of the translation of this work was made before his translation of R. DeGuimps' *Life of Pestalozzi* was published, but he suggested this term, and said he had used it. "Intuition" was impossible; instead of conveying it hides Pestalozzi's meaning, and it has caused much mischief. Mr. F. C. Turner shows that "intuition" has not the same meaning for us that *Anschauung* had for Pestalozzi.

The language of Pestalozzi presents considerable difficulties to the translator. He tells us (p. 140) that he is "incapable of philosophic thought." His words do not always express his full meaning, but that is partly because his thought is still growing and imperfect. A year earlier he did not really know the foundation of his method, and his expressions, like his thought, are in some ways still immature, changing and confused. His sentences are often over-burdened with qualifications and saving clauses, characteristic of him.

Sometimes he uses words with local meanings differing from their usual signification.

The greatest difficulty, however, is in dealing with that word which is the keystone of his whole theory, *Anschauung*. Its meaning has grown under his hands, and it connotes for him much more than it ever did before. It has, and can have, no satisfactory English equivalent. The early writers and translators used the word "*intuition*", and quite recently Mr. Quick has sanctioned its use. It has the advantage of being etymologically an equivalent of *Anschauung*, but so have *contemplation* and *inspection*, by which no one would propose to translate it. It has, moreover, the fatal objection of connoting a philosophical idea and theory which is far removed from Pestalozzi's *Anschauung*. To show this, we give the most authoritative account we can find of the two words.

### ANSCHAUUNG

*Contemplatio, intuitio, experientia*

"*Anschauung ist eine sich unmittelbar auf den Gegen-stand als einzelnen sich beziehende Erkenntniss.*" *Anschauung* is a knowledge which is directly obtained from a special object.

"*Anschauung ist eine Vorstellung so wie sie unmittelbar von der Gegenwart des Gegenstandes abhängen würde.*" *Anschauung* is a mental image, such as would be produced directly by the presence of the object. (Kant, *Kritik der reinen Vernunft*.)

"*Ein unmittelbares Bewusstsein heisst Anschauung.*" A direct consciousness is called *Anschauung*.

"*Sie sollen es fassen nicht im Denken sondern in leben-*

*diger Anschauung.''* You must grasp it not in thought, but in vivid *Anschauung.* (Fichte.)
—Grimm's *Deutsches Wörterbuch.*

## INTUITION

1. Mental perception of anything; immediate knowledge.

" The truth of these propositions we know by a bare, simple intuition of the ideas, and such propositions are called self-evident.''

2. Knowledge not obtained by deduction of reason, but instantly accompanying the ideas which are its object.

" All knowledge of causes is deductive, for we know nothing by simple intuition, but through the mediation of the effects, for the causality itself is insensible.'' (Glanville.)

" Discourse then was almost as quick as intuition.'' (South, *Sermons.*)

" He these single virtues did survey
By intuition in his own large breast.'' (Dryden.)
—Latham's *Johnson's Dictionary.*

It is evident that the two words have not the same connotation, and that the English word " intuition " does not imply the presence of the object before the senses with the same strictness that *Anschauung* does in the mouths of Kant and Pestalozzi.

Pestalozzi uses the word *Aunschauung* :

1. For the *knowledge* obtained by the direct contemplation of the object before the senses—*sense-impression.*

2. (*a*) For the *mental act* by which the above knowledge is obtained—*observation.*

(*b*) And for the *mental faculties*, by which it is obtained—*the senses*.

(*c*) And again, for *objects of the world*, about which such knowledge is gained—*seen objects*.

Allied to this is the meaning in the following passages:

" Culture brings before me the sea of confused *phenomena* (*Ansch.*) flowing one into the other." (*The Method*, page 318.) So also *Anschauungbücher*, picture books, page 67.

(*d*) Objects seen possess form, number, color, light, and shade, etc. Pestalozzi considers that *form* is common to all, and so he frequently uses *Anschauung* as a synonym for FORM, not for form alone, but for form plus something else. The nearest equivalent for *A B C der Anschauung* is alphabet of form, though the expression is often used in other and wider senses. As Pestalozzi found drawing impossible without measurement, the *A B C of Anschauung* was used for measurement also. Therefore *A B C of Anschauung* meant form, and a means of measuring form (MEASURE-FORM).

3. For knowledge obtained by contemplation of ideas already in the mind, which have not necessarily been derived from the observation of external objects. This meaning seems at first to contradict the foregoing ; but it is obvious, on reading the passages in which this meaning occurs, that Pestalozzi regarded the ideas in question as possible objects of an internal or subjective observation: *e.g.*, " Knowledge gained

by *sense-impression* teaches me the properties of things that have not been brought before my *senses* by their likeness to other objects that I have observed. This mode of *observation*," etc. (page 184). For this meaning the word *intuition* can appropriately be used.

4. *Es* (*der Kind*) *lebt in seiner Anschauung* (*d. h. Gottes*). " The child lives in *contemplation* of God " (page 336).

The word *intuition* is used by Pestalozzi, but not as an equivalent of *Anschauung*, unless it be for meaning 3. " I live entirely upon convictions that were the result of countless, though for the most part forgotten intuitions " (page 56). " Speech was a means. . . . of representing the actual process of making ideas (*Intuitionen*) clear " (page 236). In both these passages it means something different from *Anschauung;* it means *Anschauungen* with the mental process which combines them into unity of idea superadded." (F. C. T.) " Intuitive ideas given by nature and art " (p. 71), is nearer *Anschauung*.

Pestalozzi summarizes his views of *Anschauung* on pp. 183–185.

(1) *Impressions* made by all that comes *accidentally* into contact with the five senses. The objects are *in no order*, but in natural confusion. The action on the mind is limited and slow. There is but little if any active living interest in the mind. No attention.

(2) *Attention.* Teachers call *attention* to what they consider important, and so arouse *consciousness*, and deepen the impression. There is order in the presenta-

tion, and the thought is connected. The *Art of teaching guides* the selection, and exercises the thought.

(3) *Spontaneous efforts.* But what the teacher presents does not always absorb the whole attention, sometimes not at all. The child has its own interests. Some knowledge it strongly desires, and therefore will seek this of its own free will, and throw its whole soul into the search. The will, stimulated by *self-activity of all the faculties*, prompts to *spontaneous* efforts. This is a step towards moral self-activity and independence.

(4) *Necessary work.* Man must satisfy his wants and wishes, he must work, he must know and think that he may *be able to do*. This is especially considered in Letter XIII. To know, *Anschauung* is necessary, and *knowing and doing* are so intimately connected that if one ceases, the other ceases also. *Anschauung* and *Fertigkeit* observation and experiment, seeing and doing, impression and expression united, lead to clear ideas, generalizations, and education.

(5) *Analogy* and *Subjective observation.* The unseen is understood by its likeness to the seen. We classify and know by analogy. What we can remember we compare, reason about, judge and generalize. " The *results of sense-impression are changed into the work of my mind and all my powers.*" This wider meaning includes the whole psychological sequence.

Pestalozzi's *Anschauung* covers as much or more than Wordsworth's " imagination ":

> " Which in truth
> Is but another name for abstract powers
> And clearest insight, amplitude of mind
> And Reason in her most exalted mood."—*Prelude.*

Prof. Ruskin has always insisted on the value of seeing. " The sight is more important than the drawing." (*Elements of Drawing.*) Compare one of his many passages. " How many manner of eyes are there ? Your physical-science students should be able to tell us painters that. We only know in a vague way the external aspect and expression of eyes. We see, as we try to draw the endlessly grotesque creatures about us, what infinite variety of instruments they have; but you know far better than we do how those instruments are constructed and directed. You know how some play in their sockets with independent revolution,— project into near-sightedness on pyramids of bone,—are brandished at the points of horns, studded over backs and shoulders,—thrust at the ends of antennæ to pioneer for the head, or pinched up into tubercles at the corners of the lips. But how do the creatures see out of all these eyes ?

" No business of ours you may think ? Pardon me. This is no Siren's question—this is altogether business of ours, lest perchance any of us should see partly in the same manner. Comparative sight is a far more important question than comparative anatomy. It is no matter, though we sometimes walk—and it may often be desirable to climb—like apes; but suppose we should only *see* like apes or like lower creatures ? I can tell you the science of optics is an essential one to us, for exactly according to these infinitely grotesque directions and multiplications of instrument you have correspondent not only intellectual but moral faculty in the soul of the creatures. Literally, if the eye be pure, the body is pure; but, if the light of the body be but darkness, how great is that darkness." (*The Eagle's Nest*, 1887, pp. 127–8.)

---

After *Anschauung*, the most difficult word to translate is *Fertigkeit*, which literally means (1) *promptitude* or *readiness;* (2) *readiness and skill in performing some action.* It is not easy to find a satisfactory English equivalent in this sense. The following quotations given in Grimm, in addition to one from *Wie Gertrud*, will make the meaning quite clear. (The English equivalent in each case is in italics.) " *Da nemlich, es kurz zu sagen, diese Reinigung in nichts anders beruhet als in der Verwandlung der Leidenschaften in tudendhafte Fertigkeiten.*" " As, to put it shortly, this purification consists of nothing less than the transformation of the passions into *habits of* virtuous *action.*" (Lessing.)

" *Ihr alle reimt mit gleicher Fertigkeit.*" " You all rhyme with equal *facility.*" (Gellert.)

" *Die Eigenschaften, die Fertigkeiten des Lichts rege zu machen.*" " To bring the properties, the *capabilities* of light into play." (Goethe.)

" *Er besitzt eine ausserordentliche Fertigkeit in Geigen.*" " He possesses extraordinary *skill* in fiddling." (F. C. T.)

" *Fertigkeiten* " we have generally translated " activities ", but several other equivalents are used, *e. g.* (1) acts, actions; (2) powers of doing, skill, practical skill, technical skill; (3) practical ability, abilities, faculties, capacities; —*e. g.* (1) " We are far behind the greatest barbarians in the *A B C of acts or actions (gymnastics)* and their skill in striking and throwing," etc. " These contain the foundations of all possible *actions* on which human callings depend." (2) "The people do not enjoy in regard to culture in skill (technical education) one scrap of that public and universal help from government that each man needs. In no way do they enjoy the culture of those *practical abilities*." (3) "The abilities (capacities, talents, etc.) on the possession of which depend all the powers of knowing and doing (*Können*) that are required of an educated mind and noble heart, come as little of themselves as intelligence and knowledge." "*Powers of knowing and doing*." "Can" and "ken" are derived from the same root as the German *könden* and *kennen;* the present tense "can" is the preterite of the obsolete verb meaning *know*, so that its real meaning is *I have known* or *learnt*, and therefore *am able to do*. I *ken*, therefore *I can;* knowledge and skill are inseparable. See Murray's Dictionary.

This whole series of meanings, as with *Anschauung*, are connected. "Knowing and doing are so closely connected that if one ceases the other ceases with it." Doing has a double function; by doing thought is expressed, and by doing thought is also gained and made clear. It is *Anschauung*, by experience, through the sense of touch or active movement; impression and expression combined. The whole psychological sequence of Pestalozzi is impression, clear idea or knowledge, and expression. Observe, think, do, and know. One kind of *Anschauung*, he says, Letter VII, is obtained "by working at one's calling". He connects observation and experience.

For Pestalozzi's use of Form see Note 44, page 363; for his use of Oval see Note 65, page 372.

# AUTHORITIES

It has not been possible to give authorities for notes except where they are quoted entire. We have consulted and are indebted to the following editions of Pestalozzi's: *Wie Gertrude ihre Kinder lehrt*, Ed. 1, Gessner, Zürich, 1801.—*Pädagogische Bibliothek*, Albert Richter, Leipzig, 1880. This is the text we have generally followed. Seyffarth, *Pestalozzi's sämmtliche Werke*, vol. XI. Brandenburg, 1872.—*Pädagogische Klassiker* III, Karl Riedel, Wien, 1877.—*Ausgewählte Schriften berühmter Pädagogen*, IV, Dr. K. Aug. Beck, 1887.—*Universal Bibliothek*, Leipzig, 991, 992, 40 pf., a small popular edition without notes.

Dr. Darin, *Comment Gertrude instruit ses infants*, Ed. 2, Paris, 1886. Also the following biographies, etc., Biber, E., *Henry Pestalozzi and his Plan of Education, being an account of his life and writings*, London, 1831.—R. DeGuimps. *Pestalozzi, his Life and Work. Translated from the edition of 1874 by Margaret Cuthbertson Crombie*, Syracuse, 1889.—Morf, *Zur Biographie Heinrich Pestalozzi's*, Winterthur, 1868–1885.—Guillaume, J., *Pestalozzi, Etude Biographique*, Paris, 1890. *Pestalozzi Blätter*, Zürich, 1878–1892—Herbart, *Päd. Schriften*, 1880.—J. P. Rossel, *Allgemeine Monatschrift für Erziehung und Unterricht*, Aachen, 1828, etc., etc.

# How Gertrude Teaches Her Children

## PREFACE *

If these letters may be considered in some respects
as already answered and partly refuted by time, and
thus appear to belong to the past rather than to the
present, yet if my idea of elementary education has
any value in itself and is fitted to survive in the future
then these letters, so far as they throw light on the
way in which the germ of the idea was developed in
me, may have a living value for every man who considers the psychological development of educational
methods worthy of his attention.

Besides this general view of the matter, it is certainly remarkable that this idea, in the midst of the
simplicity and artlessness of my nature and life, came
forth from the darkness within me as from the night.
In its first germ it burnt within me like a fire that
showed a power of seizing on the human mind; but

* This preface was added to the second edition, Collected Works, vol. v., Cotta, Stuttgart, and Tübingen,
1820. The first edition (1801) has no preface. This
therefore gives us Pestalozzi's views twenty years after
he published the book.

afterwards, when men looked upon it and spoke of it as a matter of reason in its deeper meaning, it did not maintain its first vitality, and even seemed for a time to be quenched.

Even in this early stage Ith, Johannsen, Niederer,[1] and others gave a significance to my own expression of my views, which went far beyond that which I gave them myself, but which therefore stimulated public attention in a way that could not be sustained. Gruner, von Türk, and Chavannes[2] about the same time took up the actual results of our experiments in just as marked a way, and brought them before the public in a manner which went far beyond my original view of the subject and the power that lay at the basis of my efforts.

It is true there lay deep in my soul's consciousness a prevision of the highest that might and should be aimed at, through a deeper insight into the very nature of education; and it is indisputable that the idea of elementary education was implied in the view I took in its full significance, and shimmered forth in every word that I spoke. But the impulse within me to seek and find for the people simple methods of instruction, intelligible to every one, did not originate in the prevision that lay in me of the highest that could come from the results of these methods when found; but on the contrary this prevision resulted from the reality of the impulse that led me to seek these methods.

This soon led me naturally and simply to see that intelligible methods of instruction must, as a general principle, start from simple beginning points; and that if they are carried on in a continuous graduated series the results must be psychologically certain. But this view of mind was far from being philosophically and clearly defined and scientifically connected. As I was unable by abstract deductions to arrive at a satisfactory result, I wanted to prove my views practically; and tried originally by experiments to make clear to myself what I really wished to do and was capable of doing, in order by this path to find the means of accomplishing my purpose. All that I strove for then and strive for now is closely connected in my mind with that which twenty years before I had tried on my estate.

But the higher significance that was given to my views, so loudly, so variously, and I must say, so carelessly and hastily, gave a direction to the form and method of carrying them out in my Institute that was not really the outcome of my own soul nor that of the people round me, nor that of my helpers; and I was in this way led away from myself into a region strange to me, which I never trod before. Certainly this visionary world, into which we fell as from the clouds, was not only quite new ground to me, but with my eccentricity, with my want of scientific culture, in the singularity of my whole being, as well as my age at that time,—in these things there were reasons why I could scarcely expect even a half-lucky star to shine upon this course.

Insurmountable difficulties seemed to obstruct the hope of being able to advance in this region to happy results. These lay in the peculiarities of my assistants, who though they were in part quite helpless themselves should have stretched out helping hands to me in my efforts on this new ground. Meanwhile a lively impulse to tread this region was roused in our midst. But the cry " We can do it " before we could, " We are doing it " before we did it, was too loud, too distinct, too often repeated, partly by men whose testimony had a real value in itself and deserved attention. But it had too much charm for us; we made more of it than it really said or meant.

Briefly, the time as it was dazzled us; yet we still worked actively, in order practically to approach our end. We succeeded in many respects in the way of bringing a few beginning subjects of instruction into better order and to a better psychological foundation; and our efforts on this side might have had really important results; but the practical activity, which alone could secure the success of our purpose, was gradually lost in our midst in a lamentable manner. Matters strange and far removed from our duty soon absorbed our time and powers, and gave a mortal blow to the simplicity, the progress, the concentration, and even the humanity of our original efforts. Great ideas for improving the world, which rose out of elevated views of our subject, and which soon became exaggerated, filled our heads, confused our hearts, and made our hands careless of the needs of the Institute that lay before our eyes.

In this state of things the loss of the lofty spirit of our first union was inevitable; our old love could be the same no more. We saw more or less all the evils under which we suffered, but no one sought for them enough and saw them where he ought,—in himself. Every one blamed the other more or less; every one required of the other what he himself neither did nor could do; and our greatest misfortune in this condition was that our very efforts, special and one-sided, led us to seek help against the evils of our house in deep philosophical researches.

We were, in general, unfit to find in this way what we sought. Niederer alone felt his own strength in this region in which we now ventured; and since in this power he had for many years stood alone in our midst, he gained such an overwhelming influence not only over those around me but also over me, that I actually lost myself in myself; and against my nature, and against all possibility of success, I tried to make myself and my house that which we ought to have been, in order to make any progress in this region.

This preponderance that Niederer gained in our midst and the views he laid down on this subject so caught hold of me and led me on to such a resigned subjection and complete sacrifice and forgetfulness of myself, that I, as I know myself, can and must now say clearly, it is quite certain if he had been with us when I wrote these letters, I should have considered their whole contents and consequently the idea of elementary education as it then lay before me like a vision glimmering in the clouds, as coming from him and carried from his soul into mine.

In order to believe this statement and look upon it as naturally and innocently as it comes from me you must really know me more; you must distinctly know how I am, on the one side, animated by the conviction of how much I was and still am wanting in clear, philosophical, definite ideas on this subject; and on the other side, the degree of my trust in the lofty views of my friend, and the weight which he would necessarily have upon those ideas lying dim within me, vague and limited.

That Herr Niederer was not with us when I wrote these letters, is the only circumstance that makes it possible for me to see clearly what was Herr Niederer's service in our efforts in elementary instruction, and what I may consider as coming from myself. I know how little this is, and how much and what it still requires if it is not to be a mere nothing, or at least if something is to come out of it. In the last respect my reward is greater than my merit. In any case it is quite clear to me that the deductive view of our efforts, advancing in front of the practical perform- ance, far surpassing it, and leaving it behind, was Herr Niederer's view; and that my view of the subject came out of a personal striving after methods, the ex- ecution of which forced me actively and experimentally to seek, to gain, and to work out what was not there and what as yet I really knew not.

These two efforts opened the ways on which each of us must go to reach the common end, and for which each of us felt in himself a special power. But we did not do this, and hindered one another because we forced ourselves long, too long, to go with him hand in hand, I might say in the same shoes and at the same pace with him. Our end was the same; but the road which we should take to get to it was marked out for each of us differently by Nature, and we ought to have recognized sooner that each of us would reach his end with more ease and certainty if he would step and go along it in perfect freedom and independence.

We were too different. The crumb lying on the road arrested me if I thought it would afford the least bit of nourishment to my effort and further it. I must pick it up, I must stop at it and examine it; and before I know it enough in this way I cannot possibly consider it critically and look upon it as instructive for me, in universal connection and combination with all the relations, which as a single thing, it bears to our efforts. My whole manner of life has given me no power and no inclination to strive hastily after bright and clear ideas on any subject, before, supported by facts, it has a background in me that has awakened some self-confidence.

Therefore to my grave I shall remain in a kind of fog about most of my views. But I must say if this fog has a background of various and sufficiently vivid sense-impressions it is a holy fog for me. It is the only light in which I live, or can live. And in this peculiar twilight of mine I go on towards my goal in peace and content so long as I go in peace and freedom; and at the point I have reached in striving after my ideal I stand firm to my conviction that while I have done very little in my life to reach ideas that can be defined with philosophical certainty by words, yet in my own way I have found a few means to my end, which I should not have found by such philosophical inquiries after clear ideas of my subject, *as I was capable of making.*

Therefore I do not entirely regret my backwardness. I ought not.  I ought to pursue my way of *experiments,* which is the way of my life, willingly and gladly, without desiring the fruit of a tree of knowledge that for me and for the idiosyncrasy of my nature is forbidden fruit.  If I pursue the road of my experiments, however limited, honestly, faithfully, and energetically, I think by doing so I am what I am and know what I know; and my life and action, though imperfect, is not merely a blind groping after experiments not really understood.

I hope it is more.  I hope in my way to make some few points of my subject philosophically clear that could not so easily be made equally clear in any other way.  The idiosyncrasies of individuals are, in my opinion, the greatest blessing of human nature, and the one basis of its highest and most essential blessings; therefore they should be respected in the highest degree.  They cannot be where we do not see them, and we do not see them when everything stands in the way of their showing themselves, and every selfishness strives to make its own peculiarity rule and to make the peculiarities of others subservient to its own.  If we would respect them it is necessary that we should not sunder that which God hath joined together, and also that we should not join together that which God hath put asunder. Every artificial and forced joining together of heterogeneous things has according to its nature the result of checking individual powers and qualities; and such unsuitably joined, and therefore checked and confused individual powers and qualities express themselves then in every case as unnatural, forcibly brought forward; and work upon the whole mass, in whose interest they were thus brought together, in a destructive, confusing and distorting manner.

I know what I am not, and therefore may honestly say I would not be more than I am. But in order to use the powers that may fall into my hands as I am, I must use my powers freely and independently, however little they may be, that the words " To him that hath, shall be given," may be true for me, and the others, " He that hath not, from him shall be taken away even that which he hath," may not be too depressingly fulfilled in me.

As I now look in this way upon the value that this book may have for me and the world, I must let it appear exactly in the shape in which it had the courage to step forward twenty years ago. Meantime I have given the necessary account of our pedagogic progress in educational practice and methods since then in some of my new works. I will go on doing this, and especially in the fifth * part of Leonard and Gertrude I will throw more light on this point than I have yet been able to do.

But whatever historical and personal concerns I touch upon in these letters, I shall now enter on no more. I cannot well do so. I smile over much and look on it with quite different eyes than I did when I wrote it. But over much I would rather weep than smile. But I do not this either. Now I can speak neither weeping nor smiling. My conscience tells me the hour of my silence is not yet passed; the wheel of my fate also is not yet turned. Smiling and weeping would alike be premature; if not with locked doors, harmful.

Many of the subjects and views touched upon in this book may perhaps soon be changed. Perhaps I shall soon smile over much whereat now I should weep; and perhaps I shall shortly think very earnestly about things which I now pass with a smile. In this state I have left the book almost unaltered. Time will explain the contrast between what is said there and my present

---

* The fifth part of Leonard and Gertrude never appeared, for the manuscript was lost with other works left behind by Pestalozzi, when it was sent to Paris to Josef Schmid, in the beginning of 1840, to be published.

opinions about the things said, and will also explain those which appear incomprehensible and inexplicable, if it is necessary. I hardly think it will be. But if it is necessary beyond my grave, may it be in mild, not glaring colors.

PESTALOZZI

YVERDUN, *June 1st, 1820*

I *

MY DEAR GESSNER,

You say it is time that I published my ideas on the instruction of the people.

Now I will do it; and as Lavater[3] gave his views on eternity to Zimmermann in a series of letters, so will I give you my views, or rather make them as clear to you as I possibly can.

I saw popular instruction like a bottomless swamp before my eyes; and waded round and round with difficulty in its mire until at last I learned to know the sources of its waters, the causes of its obstructions,

---

* The letters are not numbered by Pestalozzi, but they are distinctly divided. See Mr. Quick's copy of Ed. 1, 1801, Teacher's Guild Library, London. There are fourteen letters, but Seyffarth divides Letter seven, and so makes fifteen. This has caused some little confusion; but there is really no difference in the text. They are addressed to Heinrich Gessner, publisher, Zürich, son of Solomon Gessner, the poet. He was a member of the " Patriotic Party ", a society of young men founded in 1762, whose object was to improve the condition of the people.

and the places from which there might be a possibility of diverting its foul waters.

I will now lead you about for a while in this maze of error, out of which I extricated myself after a long time more by accident than by sense and skill.

Ah! long enough! ever since my youth, has my heart moved on like a mighty stream, alone and lonely, towards my one sole end—to stop the sources of the misery in which I saw the people around me sunk.

It is more than thirty years since I put my hand to this work which I am now doing. " Iselin's Ephemerides "[4] bear witness that my dreams and wishes which I was then trying to work out are not less comprehensive now than they were then.

But I was young; I knew neither the needs of my scheme, nor the attention that its preparation required, nor the skill that its realization called for and presupposed. My ideal scheme included work in the fields, the factory, and the workshop. I had a deep but vague feeling of the value of all three departments; I looked upon them as safe clear paths towards the realization of my plan; and verily, I have come back after all the experiences of my life to nearly my early views on the essential foundations of my plan. Yet my confidence in their essential truth, founded upon the apparent certainty of my instinct, was my ruin.

The truths of my opinions were truths in the air;

and my confidence in my instinct, in the foundations
of my work, was the confidence of a sleeper in the
reality of his dream. I was in all three departments
in which my experiments should have been made an
inexperienced child. I wanted facility in details that
careful, persevering, and accustomed handling from
which the blessed result, towards which I strove, alone
could come. The consequence of this positive unfitness for my task was soon felt. The pecuniary means
to my end went quickly off in smoke, all the sooner
because I neglected to furnish myself in the beginning
with a satisfactory staff of assistants in my task.
When I began to feel keenly the need of such persons
as could properly supply that in which I was wanting,
I had already lost the money and credit which would
have made the organization of this staff possible to me.
Such a confusion in my circumstances soon arose that
the wreck of my scheme was inevitable.

My ruin was complete; and the fight against fate
was the fight of underlying weakness against an enemy
of ever increasing strength. Struggles against disaster
led to nothing. Meanwhile I had learnt in the immeasurable struggle immeasurable truth, and had
gained immeasurable experience; and my conviction
of the truth of the principles of my views and efforts
was never greater than at the moment when they were,
to the outward eye, entirely destroyed. My heart still

moved on unshaken towards the same object, and I
now found myself in misery, in a condition in which
I perceived on the one hand the essential needs of my
work, and on the other the ways and means by which
the surrounding world of all sorts and conditions,
really thinks and acts about the object of my endeavors.
So that I perceived and comprehended the truth of
these opinions, as I never should have done in an apparently happy issue from my premature attempts.

I say it now, with inward exaltation and gratitude
towards an over-ruling Providence, that even in my
misery I learned to know the misery of the people and
its causes deeper and deeper, and as no happier man
knows them.[5]   I suffered as the people suffered; and
the people showed themselves to me as they were, and
as they showed themselves to no one else.   I sat long
years among them, like an owl among birds.   But in
the midst of the scornful laughter, in the midst of the
loudest taunts of the men who rejected me—" You
poor wretch, you are less able than the meanest day
laborer to help yourself, and do you fancy you can help
the people ?"—in the midst of these jeering taunts,
which I read on all lips, the mighty stream of my
heart ceased not, alone and lonely, to struggle towards
the purpose of my life—to stop the springs of the
misery in which I saw the people around me sunk.   In
one way my strength became ever greater.   My mis-

fortunes taught me always more and more truth for my purpose. That which deluded no one else deluded me; but that which deluded every one else deluded me no more.

I knew the people as no one about me knew them. Their pleasure in the prospect of profit from the newly-introduced cotton manufacture ; their increasing wealth, their brightened houses, their abundant harvest, even the " Socratizing " of some of their teachers, and the reading circles among the under-bailiffs' sons and the barbers, deceived me not. I saw their misery; but I lost myself in the vast prospect of its scattered and isolated sources; and while my insight into their real condition became ever more wide, I did not move a step forward in the practical power of remedying the evil. Even the book that my sense of this condition forced from me, even " Leonard and Gertrude ",[6] was a proof of this my inner helplessness. I stood there among my contemporaries like a stone that tells of life and is dead. Many men glanced at it, but understood as little of me and my aims as I understood the details of skilled labor and knowledge that were necessary to accomplish them.

I was careless of myself, and lost myself in the whirl of powerful impulses towards outward operations of which I had not worked out the foundations deeply enough.

Had I done this, to what an inner height should I have been able to raise myself for my purpose, and how soon should I have reached my end! This I never found because I was unworthy; for I only sought it from without, and allowed my love of truth and justice to become a passion which tossed me about like an uprooted reed upon the waves of life. I myself, day by day, hindered my torn-up roots from fastening again into firm ground and finding that nourishment which they so essentially needed for my end. Vain was the hope that another might rescue this uprooted reed from the waves, and set it in the earth in which I had delayed to plant it.

Dear friend! Whoever has a drop of my blood in him now knows how low I had to sink; and you, my Gessner, before you read further, dedicate a tear to my fall.

Deep dissatisfaction devoured me now; things eternally true and right seemed to me in my condition mere castles in the air. I clung with obstinacy to words and phrases which had lost within me their basis of eternal truth. So I sank day by day more towards the worship of common-places, and the trumpet blare of quacks with which this modern age pretends to help the human race.

Yet it was not that I did not feel this sinking and struggle against it. For three years I wrote, with incredible fatigue, my " Inquiries into the Course of Nature in the Development of Mankind ",* particularly with the view of agreeing with myself as to the progress of my pet ideas, and of bringing my innate feelings into harmony with my conceptions of civil rights and of morality. But this work, too, is to me only an evidence of my inner helplessness, a mere play of my power of questioning, one-sided, without proportionate skill against myself, and void of sufficient effort towards that practical power which was so necessary for my purpose. The disproportion between my practice and my theories only increased: and that deficiency in myself which I was bound to supply for the accomplishment of my purpose became greater, and I less able to supply it.

Besides I did not reap more than I sowed. The effect of my book was like the effect of all my doings on those around me; nobody understood it. I did not find two men who did not half give me to understand that they looked upon the whole book as a " galli-

---

* *Inquiries into the Course of Nature in the Development of the Human Race.* This study of the evolution of man was written at Neuhof at Fichte's suggestion. Published, 1797. Niederer, writing to him early in 1801, says, " I look upon it as containing a most valuable discovery; I may call it indeed the germ of your whole method ".

maufry ".* And only lately, a man of importance, who rather likes me, said with " Swiss " familiarity: " But really, Pestalozzi, do you not feel yourself, that when you wrote that book, you did not exactly know what you wanted?"

Yes, that was my fate, to be misunderstood and to suffer injustice. I ought to have been used to it, but I was not. I met my misfortune with inward scorn and contempt of mankind, and thereby injured my cause at those inmost foundations which it should have had in me. I did it more harm than all those by whom I was misunderstood and despised could have done it. Yet I swerved not from my purpose; but it was now sensibly atrophied, and lived on in an unsettled imagination and a disordered heart. I became more and more confirmed in the wish to nourish the sacred plant of human happiness on unconsecrated ground.

Gessner! In my " Inquiries " I lately defined the claims of all civil rights as mere claims of my animal nature; and, in so far as they are a real hindrance to the only thing that has any worth for human nature, looked upon them as hindrances to moral purity. But I now lowered myself under the provocation of external force and internal passion to expect a good issue from

---

* Nonsense, hodge-podge. *Winter's Tale*, Act iv., sc. 3.

the tinkling cymbals of civil truth; to expect ideas of right from the men of my time, who with few exceptions live only to make themselves comfortable and hanker after well-spread tables.

I was grey-haired, yet still a child but a child deeply disturbed within myself. Still in all this stormy time I moved on towards the purpose of my life; but my way was more one-sided and erring than ever. I now sought a way to my end generally in the discovery of all the old sources of public ills; in passionate statements of civil rights and their foundations; in the employment of the spirit of violence that had risen up in revolt against the individual suffering of the people. But the purer doctrine of my early days was only noise and words to the men around me:—how much more must my present view of things be foolishness to them! As usual, they steeped this kind of truth also in the mire, remained as they were, and behaved towards me as I ought to have expected, but did not expect because I hovered in the air in the dream of my wishes and no selfishness opened my eyes to the men about me. I was deceived not only in every knave but in every fool. I trusted every one who came and spoke fair words.

Yet I knew the people, perhaps as no one else knew them, and their bewilderment and degradation. But I cared for nothing but damming up these springs and stopping their mischief; and Helvetia's new men (*novi homines*), who did not want so little and who knew not the people, of course found that I was not made for them. These men, who in their new place like shipwrecked women took every straw for a mast by which the republic might be carried to a safe shore, despised me as a straw at which no cat would clutch. They knew it not and intended it not, but they did me good, more good than ever men had done me. They restored me to myself and left me (silently wondering at the sudden transformation of their ship's repair into shipwreck) nothing but the word which I spoke in the first days of that overthrow, " *I will turn schoolmaster.*" For this I found confidence. I became one; and ever since I have been engaged in a mighty struggle (forced upon me in spite of myself) to fill up those internal deficiencies by which my ultimate purposes were formerly hindered.

Friend! I will openly reveal to you the whole of my being and doing since that moment. I had during the first Directory won confidence through Legrand in my object, the cultivation of the people, and was on the point of bringing out an extensive plan of education in Argäu when Stanz * was burnt down, and Legrand

---

* Stanz, market town, Canton Unterwalden, was destroyed by the French, Sept. 9, 1798. Jean Lue Legrand, 1755–1838, belonged with Iselin and other

at once offered me that unfortunate place for my
residence.

I went. I would have gone to the hindmost cavern
of the mountains to come nearer my end, and now I
really did come nearer it; but imagine my position—I
alone—deprived of all the means of education; I alone,
overseer, paymaster, handy man, and almost servant

---

reformers to the " Patriotic Party ". He became a
member of the Grand Council of Bern in 1783, and
President of the Swiss Directorate, 1798, but held office
for only part of a year. He became acquainted with
Oberlin, the famous pastor of Ban-de-la-Roche, in 1812,
settled near him in 1814, and devoted the remaining
years of his life wholly to popular education.

maid, in an unfinished house, surrounded by ignorance, disease, and novelty of all kinds. The number of children increased gradually to eighty, all of different ages; some full of pretensions, others wayside beggars; all, except a few, wholly ignorant. What a task! to form and develop these children! What a task!

I dared to attempt it, and stood in their midst pronouncing sounds,[7] and making them imitate them.

Whoever saw it was astonished at the result. It was like a meteor that is seen in the air, and vanishes again. No one knew its nature. I understood it not myself. It was the result of a simple psychological idea which I felt but of which I was not clearly aware.

It was exactly the pulse of the art that I was seeking; I seized it, a monstrous grip. A seeing man would never have dared; I was luckily blind, or I too had not ventured. I knew not clearly what I did, but I knew what I wanted, that was—Death, or the carrying through of my purpose.

But the means of attaining it were absolutely nothing but the direct result of the necessity with which I had to work through the extreme difficulties of my situation.

I know not and can hardly understand how I came through. In a manner I played with necessity, defied her difficulties, which stood like mountains before me. Against the apparent physical impossibility I opposed the force of a will which saw and regarded nothing but what was immediately before it; but which grappled with the difficulty at hand as if it were alone and life and death depended on it.

So I worked in Stanz until the approach of the Austrians took the heart out of my work, and the feelings that now oppressed me brought my physical powers to the state in which they were when I left Stanz. *

Up to this point I was not yet certain of the foundations of my procedure.† But as I was attempting the impossible, I found that possible which I had not expected; and as I pushed through the pathless thicket

---

* In June, 1799, the French were driven out of Uri into Unterwalden by the Austrians, and the orphanage was converted into a French hospital. On June 8, 1799, sixty children were sent away, leaving only twenty. Pestalozzi intended to return, but the Government was unfavorable and the orphanage after some time was closed.

† The first " *Letter from Stanz* " was written at Gurnigel, between June 8 and the end of July, 1799, and was printed in 1807. It will be found entire in De Guimp's Life, pp. 88–95. It should be compared with this account. At that time, he says here, " I was not certain of the foundations of my procedure." His " *Account of the Method* " to the Society of Friends of Education, June 27, 1800, is the first attempt to state his principles. (See " The Method " last paragraph.)

that no one had trodden for ages, I found footprints in it leading to the high road, which for ages had been untrodden.

I will go a little into details. As I was obliged to give the children instruction, alone, and without help, I learned the art of teaching many together; and since I had no other means but loud speaking, the idea of making the learners draw, write, and work at the same time was naturally developed.

The confusion of the repeating crowd led me to feel the need of keeping time, and beating time increased the impression made by the lesson. The utter ignorance of all made me stay long over the beginnings; and this led me to realize the high degree of inner power to be obtained by perfecting the first beginnings, and the result of a feeling of completeness and perfection in the lowest stage. I learned, as never before, the relation of the first steps in every kind of knowledge to its complete outline; and I felt, as never before, the immeasurable gaps that would bear witness in every succeeding stage of knowledge to confusion and want of perfection on these points.

The result of attending to this perfecting of the early stages far outran my expectations. It quickly developed in the children a consciousness of hitherto unknown power, and particularly a general sense of beauty and order. They felt their own power, and the tediousness of the ordinary school-tone vanished like a ghost from my rooms. They wished,—tried,—persevered,—succeeded: and they laughed. Their tone was not that of learners: it was the tone of unknown powers awakened from sleep; of a heart and mind exalted with the feeling of what these powers could and would lead them to do.

Children taught children. They tried [to put into practice] what I told them to do, [and often came themselves on the track of the means of its execution, from many sides. This self-activity, which had developed itself in many ways in the beginning of learning, worked with great force on the birth and growth of the conviction in me, that all true, all educated instruction must be drawn out of the children themselves, and be born within them.]* To this I was led chiefly by necessity. Since I had no fellow-helpers, I put a capable child between two less capable ones; he em-

---

*These brackets include additions made in the second edition. Not all have been indicated in this way. Some are very slight, and others are difficult to separate in a translation. They may be found in most German editions. Rarely words or passages in the first edition have been left out of the second. The most important omission is given in note 5. The most important additions made are to this passage, and as they give us Pestalozzi's views twenty years later, they may be considered as his last words in the book.

braced them with both arms, he told them what he knew, and they learned to repeat after him what they knew not. [They sat lovingly by each other. Joy and sympathy animated their souls, and their mutually awakened inner life led them both forward as they could only be led by this mutual self-vivification].

Dear Friend! You have heard this crowd of collective learners and seen its courage and joy. Say yourself how you felt when you saw it. I saw your tears, and in my heart arose wrath towards men who could still say, " The improvement of the people is a dream."

No; it is no dream. I will put skill into the hand of the mother, into the hand of the child, and into the hand of the innocent; and the scorner shall be silenced and shall say no more—" It is a dream."

God, I thank Thee for my necessity! Without it I should never have spoken these words, and I should not have silenced the scorner.

I am now thoroughly convinced; it was a long time before I was; but I had children in Stanz whose powers, not deadened by the weariness of unpsychological home and school discipline, developed more quickly. It was another race. Even the paupers were different from the town paupers and the weaklings of our corn and vine lands. I saw the capacity of human nature, and its peculiarities in many ways and in most open play.

Its defects were the defects of healthy nature, immeasurably different from the defects caused by bad and artificial teaching — hopeless flagging and complete crippling of the mind.

I saw in this combination of unschooled ignorance a power of seeing (*Anschauung*),[8] and a firm conception of the known and the seen of which our A B C puppets have no notion.

I learned from them—I must have been blind if I had not learned—to know the natural relation in which real knowledge stands to book-knowledge. I learned from them what a disadvantage this one-sided letter knowledge and entire reliance on words (which are only sound and noise when there is nothing behind them) must be. I saw what a hindrance this may be to the real power of observation (*Anschauung*), and the firm conception of the objects that surround us.

So far I got in Stanz. I felt my experiment had decided that it was possible to found popular instruction on psychological grounds, to lay true knowledge, gained by sense-impression at its foundation, and to tear away the mask of its superficial bombast. I felt I could solve the problem to men of penetration and unprejudiced mind; but the prejudiced crowd, like geese which ever since they cracked the shell have been shut up in the coop and shed and so have lost all power of flying and swimming, I could never make wise, as I well knew.

It was reserved for Burgdorf * to teach me more.

But imagine,—you know me,—imagine with what feelings I left Stanz. As a shipwrecked man after weary, restless nights sees land at last, breathes in hope of life, and then, swung back into the boundless ocean by an unlucky wind, says a thousand times in his trembling soul, " Why can I not die ?" and yet does not plunge into the abyss, but still forces his tired eyes open, looks around, and seeks the shore again, and when he sees it, strains every limb to numbness,— even so was I.

Gessner! imagine all this; think of my heart and my

* A town in Canton Bern. Here he resumed his interrupted work towards the end of July, 1799.

will, my work and my wreck,—my disaster, the tremb
ling of my shattered nerves, and my bewilderment.—
Such, friend, was my condition when I left Stanz and
went to Bern.

Fischer got me an introduction to Zehender of Gurnigel,* [through whose kindness] I enjoyed some restful days at that place. I needed them. It is a wonder
that I still live. But it was not my haven. It was a
rock in the ocean upon which I rested in order to swim
again. I shall never forget those days, Zehender, as
long as I live. They saved me. But I could not live
without my work. At the very moment when I looked
down from Gurnigel's height upon the beautiful,
boundless valley at my feet (I had never seen so wide
a view before), even with that view before me I thought
more of the badly taught people than of the beauty of
the scene. I could not and would not live without my
purpose.

My departure from Stanz, although I was near death,
was not a consequence of my free will but of military
measures which rendered the continuance of my plans
temporarily impossible. It renewed the old nonsense
about my uselessness and utter inability to persevere
in any business. Even my friends said, " Yes, for five

---

*A beautifully situated, much frequented bath, $\frac{3}{4}$-
hour below the summit of Mt. Gurnigel, 9 miles west
of Thun.

months it is possible for him to pose as a worker, but in the sixth 'it is no go.' We might have known it before. He can do nothing thoroughly, and is at bottom no more fit for actual life than an old hero of romance. In this, too, he has but outlived himself."

They told me to my face, " It would be ridiculous to expect, because a man wrote something sensible in his thirtieth year, that he should do something reasonable in his fiftieth." They said aloud that the very most that could be said for me was that I brooded over a beautiful dream, and like all brooding fools might now and then have a bright idea about my dream and hobby. It was obvious that no one listened to me. Meanwhile every one agreed in the opinion that things had gone wrong in Stanz, and that everything always would go wrong with me. F. . . . reported a friendly conversation in support of this view. It happened in a public assembly, but I will not describe it more particularly.

*The first* said:—" Do you see how ugly he is ? "

*The other :* " Yes, I am sorry for the poor fool."

*The first :* " And so am I; but he cannot be helped. If ever he throws out a spark one moment, so that one might think he really is capable of something, the next moment it is again dark around him; and when one comes near him, he has only burnt himself."

*The other:* " What a pity he did not burn himself to death! He cannot be helped till he is ashes. "

*The first:* " God knows we must soon wish that for him. "

That was the reward of my work in Stanz; a work that perhaps no mortal ever attempted on such a scale and under such circumstances, and of which the inner result brought me practically to the point at which I now stand.

They were astonished that I came down again from Gurnigel with my old will and former purpose, wishing and seeking for nothing but to take up the thread where I had dropped it, and to knot it together again in any corner, without regarding anything else.

Rengger and Stapfer rejoiced. Judge Schnell advised me to go to Burgdorf; and in a couple of days I was there, and found in Statthalter Schnell and in Doctor Grimm[9] men who knew the shifting sand on which our old rotten schools now stand, and thought it not impossible that firm ground might yet be found under these quicksands. I am grateful to them. They gave attention to my purpose, and helped me with energy and good-will to make the path which I was seeking.

But here, too, I was not without difficulties. Luckily they looked on me at first as casually as on any other schoolmaster who runs about seeking his bread.

A few rich people greeted me in a friendly way; a few
parsons courteously wished me, —[though I must say
evidently without confidence,]—God's blessing on my
undertaking; a few prudent men believed that something useful might come out of it for their children.
Everybody seemed to be content enough; to be willing
to wait till whatever was to peep out of it showed
itself.

But the " *Hintersassen* "[10] schoolmaster of the brisk
little town to whose school-room I was sent laid hold
of the business a little closer.    I believe he suspected
the final end of my A B C crowing was to cram his
situation, neck and crop, into my sack.    The rumor
at once spread through the neighboring street that the
" Heidelberg " * was in danger.    This is still the food
on which the youth of the lower class of the towns-
people is kept, as long as the most neglected peasantry
of the villages; and you know they are kept at it till
their betrothal day.

---

\* The Heidelberg or Palatinate Catechism was compiled and published by the Heidelberg theologians,
Zacharias Ursinus and Kasper Olevianus in 1553 by
command, and with the co-operation of Prince Elector
Friedrich III. of the Palatinate.    It was and is the
most popular elementary book of religious instruction
in the schools of the Swiss Evangelical Confession.
The little book has a preponderant doctrinal character,
and was therefore not suited for Pestalozzi's teaching.

Yet the " Heidelberg " was not the only thing.  Men still whispered in each other's ears in the streets that I could not even write, nor count, nor read correctly.

Now, my friend, that street gossip is not always entirely untrue; I could neither write, count, nor read perfectly.  But people always shut out too much of such street truths.  You have seen it in Stanz.  I could teach writing without being able to write perfectly myself; and really my ignorance of all these things was essentially necessary in order to bring me to the highest simplicity of methods of teaching, and to find means whereby the most inexperienced and ignorant man might also do the same with his children.

Meanwhile it was not to be expected of the lower classes of Burgdorf that they should accept everything beforehand, still less that they should believe in it. They did not.  They decided at a meeting that they did not wish experiments made on their children with the new teaching: the burghers might try them on their own.  But as it happened, patrons and friends brought all the influence that was needed there for that purpose, so that at last I was admitted into the lowest school in the upper town. *

---

* This was the Spelling and Reading School kept by Miss Margaretha Stähli the younger.  It was attended by 20–25 boys and girls, aged 7–8.  This must not be confused with the girls' school kept by Miss Margaretha Stähli the elder.

I considered myself happy, yet I was in the beginning very shy. Every moment I feared they would turn me out of my school-room. This made me more awkward than usual; and when I think of the fire and the life with which in the first hours of Stanz, I as it were built myself a magic temple, and then of the nervousness with which at Burgdorf I bowed myself under the yoke as a matter of business, I can hardly understand how the same man could do both.

Here was school discipline, apparently reasonable, but not free from pedantry and pretension. All this was new to me. I had never borne such a thing in my life; but now for the sake of my purpose I bore it. I crowed my A B C daily from morn till night, and I went on without plan in the empirical way which I had had to break off in Stanz.[7] I put unweariedly rows of syllables together. I wrote whole books with these rows and with rows of figures. I sought in all ways to bring the beginnings of spelling and counting to the greatest simplicity and into form, so that the child with the strictest psychological order might pass from the first step gradually to the second; and then without break, upon the foundation of the perfectly understood second step, might go on quickly and safely to the third and fourth. But instead of the letters that I made the children draw with their slate pencils, I now led them to draw angles, squares, lines, and curves.

With this work the idea gradually developed of the possibility of an " A B C of *Anschauung* " * that is now important to me; and while working this out, the whole scheme of a general method of instruction in all its scope appeared, though still dimly, before my eyes. It was long before that was clear to me.    To you it is still incomprehensible; but it is certainly true.    I [had for long months been working out all the beginning points of a path-breaking attempt at reducing the means of instruction to their elements, and] had done everything to bring them to the highest simplicity. Yet I knew not their connection, or at least, I was not clearly conscious of it; but I felt every hour that I was moving on, and moving steadily too.

While I was still in boy's shoes they preached to me that it is a holy thing to serve from below upwards; but I have learned now that in order to work miracles one must with grey hair serve from below upwards.    I

---

* We are obliged to use *Anschauung* here, so that objects seen, sense-impression, form, measurement, " intitution ", and the other meanings included in it, may retain the unity Pestalozzi intended.    It was while working out his first attempts at the A B C of *Anschauung* that the whole scheme of a united method appeared.    Here *Anschauung* is used in a wide general sense; it soon develops and differentiates.    The various meanings will be noted as they appear.

shall work none, and am in no way born or made for that[11]—I shall neither reach such heights in reality nor in any way pretend to imitate them by tricks. [If I would, I could not. I know how weak my capabilities are now;] but if men at my age, who have their whole head and unshattered nerves, would or should in a cause like mine serve from below upwards they would succeed. But no; at my age such men seek, as is fair and right, their arm-chairs. This is not my condition; I must still in my old days be glad that I am allowed to serve from below upwards. I do it willingly, but in my own way. In all I do and attempt I seek the high-roads. The advantage of these is that their straight way and open course destroy the charm of those crooked paths by which men are otherwise accustomed to reach honor and admiration.

If I could do fully what I try to do I only need to explain it and the simplest man could do it afterwards. But in spite of my clear conviction that I shall bring it neither to admiration nor to honor, I still regard it as the crown of my life; all the more since I have served this object for long years, and in my old age from below upwards.

The advantages of it strike me more every day. While I thus took in hand all the dusty school duties, not merely superficially, and while I always went on and on from eight in the morning till seven in the evening, a few hours excepted, I naturally pounced every moment upon matters of fact that might throw light on the existence of physico-mechanical laws, according to which our minds pick up arrd keep outer impressions easily or with difficulty.

I adapted my teaching daily more to my sense of such laws; but I was not really aware of their principles, until the Executive Councillor Glayre, to whom I had tried to explain the sense of my works last summer, said to me, "*Vous voulez méchaniser l'éducation.*"[1][2]

[I understood very little French. I thought by these words, he meant to say I was seeking means of bringing education and instruction into psychologically ordered sequence; and, taking the words in this sense] he really hit the nail on the head, and according to my view, put the word in my mouth which showed me the essentials of my purpose and all the means thereto. Perhaps it would have been long before I had found it out, because I did not examine myself as I went along, but surrendered myself wholly to vague though vivid feelings, that indeed made my course certain but did not teach me to know it. I could not do otherwise. I have read no book for thirty years. I could and can read none. I had nothing more to say to abstract ideas. I lived solely upon convictions that were the result of countless, though, for the most part, forgotten intuitions.

So without knowing the principles on which I was working I began to dwell upon the nearness with which the objects I explained to the children were wont to touch their senses; and so, as I followed out the teaching from its beginning to its utmost end, I tried to investigate back to its very beginning the early history of the child who is to be taught, and was soon convinced that the first hour of its teaching is the hour of its birth. From the moment in which his mind can receive impressions from Nature, Nature teaches him. The new life itself is nothing but the just-awakened readiness to receive these impressions; it is only the awakening of the perfect physical buds that now aspire with all their power and all their impulses towards the development of their individuality. It is only the awakening of the now perfect animal that will and must become a man.

All instruction of man is then only the Art * of helping Nature to develop in her own way; and this Art rests essentially on the relation and harmony between the impressions received by the child and the exact degree of his developed powers. It is also necessary in the impressions that are brought to the child by

---

* " The Art," frequently referred to hereafter, is distinguished by a capital from art generally; it is our " Science and Art of Education," which is here first put on a psychological and scientific basis.

instruction that there should be a sequence, so that
beginning and progress should keep pace with the
beginning and progress of the powers to be developed
in the child. I soon saw that an inquiry into this
sequence throughout the whole range of human knowledge, particularly those fundamental points from which
the development of the human mind originates, must
be the simple and only way ever to attain and to keep
satisfactory school and instruction books, of every
grade, suitable for our nature and our wants. I saw
just as soon that in making these books the constitu-
ents of instruction must be separated according to the
degree of the growing power of the child; and that in
all matters of instruction,[13] it is necessary to determine with the greatest accuracy which of these con-
stituents is fit for each age of the child, in order on the
one hand not to hold him back if he is ready; and on
the other, not to load him and confuse him with anything for which he is not quite ready.

This was clear to me. The child must be brought
to a high degree of knowledge both of things seen and
of words before it is reasonable to teach him to spell or
read. I was quite convinced that at their earliest age
children need psychological training in gaining intelligent sense-impressions of all things. But since such
training, without the help of art, is not to be thought
of or expected of men as they are, the need of picture-

books struck me perforce. These should precede the
A B C books, in order to make those ideas that men
express by words clear to the children [by means of
well-chosen real objects,[14] that either in reality, or in
the form of well-made models and drawings, can be
brought before their minds.]

A happy experiment confirmed my then unripe
opinion in a striking way, [in spite of all the limitations of my means, and the error and one-sidedness in
my experiments]. An anxious mother entrusted her
hardly three-year-old child to my private teaching. I
saw him for a time every day for an hour; and for a
time felt the pulse of a method with him. I tried
to teach him by letters, figures, and anything handy;
that is, I aimed at giving him clear ideas and expressions by these means. I made him name correctly
what he knew of anything---color, limbs, place, form,
and number. I was obliged to put aside that first
plague of youth, the miserable letters; he would have
nothing but pictures and things.

He soon expressed himself clearly about the objects
that lay within the limits of his knowledge. He found
common illustrations in the street, the garden, and
the room; and soon learned to pronounce the hardest
names of plants and animals, and to compare objects
quite unknown to him with those known, and to produce a clear sense-impression of them in himself.

Although this experiment led to byeways, and worked for the strange and distant to the disadvantage of the present, it threw many-sided light on the means of quickening the child to his surroundings, and showing him the charm of self-activity in the extension of his powers.

But yet the experiment was not satisfactory for that which I was particularly seeking, because the boy had already three unused years behind him.[15]   I am convinced that nature brings the children even at this age to a definite consciousness of innumerable objects.   It only needs that we should with psychological art unite speech with this knowledge in order to bring it to a high degree of clearness; and so enable us to connect the foundations of many-sided arts and truths with that which nature herself teaches, and also to use what nature teaches as a means of explaining all the fundamentals of art and truth that can be connected with them.   Their power and their experience both are great at this age; but our unpsychological schools are essentially only artificial stifling-machines for destroying all the results of the power and experience that nature herself brings to life in them.

You know it, my friend.   But for a moment picture to yourself the horror of this murder.   We leave children up to their fifth year in the full enjoyment of nature; we let every impression of nature work upon them; they feel their power; they already know full well the joy of unrestrained liberty and all its charms. The free natural bent which the sensuous happy wild thing takes in his development, has in them already taken its most decided direction. And after they have enjoyed this happiness of sensuous life for five whole years, we make all nature round them vanish from before their eyes; tyrannically stop the delightful course of their unrestrained freedom; pen them up like sheep, whole flocks huddled together, in stinking rooms; pitilessly chain them for hours, days, weeks, months, years, to the contemplation of unattractive and monotonous letters (and, contrasted with their former condition), to a maddening course of life.

I cease describing; else I shall come to the picture of the greater number of schoolmasters, thousands of whom in our days merely on account of their unfitness for any means of finding a respectable livelihood have subjected themselves to the toilsomeness of this position, which they in accordance with their unfitness for anything better look upon as a way that leads little further than to keep them from starvation. How infinitely must the children suffer under these circumstances, or, at least, be spoiled![16]

Friend, tell me, can the sword that severs the neck and sends the criminal from life to death have more effect upon his body than this change from the beautiful guidance of nature, which they have enjoyed so long, to the mean and miserable school course, has upon the souls of children?

Will men always be blind? Will they never reach the first springs from which flow our mental distraction, the destruction of our innocence, the ruin of our capacities, and all their consequences; which lead all to unsatisfactory lives, thousands to death in hospitals, and to madness.

Dear Gessner, how happy shall I be in my grave if I have contributed something towards making these springs known. How happy shall I be in my grave if I can unite Nature and Art in popular education as closely as they are now violently separated. Ah! how my inmost soul is stirred. Nature and art are not only separated, they are insanely forced asunder by wicked men!

It is as if an evil spirit had reserved for our quarter of the world and our century an infernal gift of malicious disunion, in order to make us more weak and miserable in this philosophical age than ever yet self-deception, presumption, and self-conceit have made mankind in any part of the world, in any age.

How gladly would I forget such a world! How happy I am in this state of things by the side of my dear little Ludwig, whose whims force me to penetrate ever more deeply into the spirit of beginning-books for infants. Yes, my friend, in these the fittest blow against the foolish instruction of our time must and shall be given. Their spirit grows ever clearer to me. They must start from the simplest elements of human knowledge, they must deeply impress the children with the most essential forms of all things, they must early and clearly develop the first consciousness of the relations of number [and measure] in them, they must give them words and sentences about the whole range of their knowledge and experience; and, above all, completely fill up the first steps of the ladder of knowledge by which nature herself leads us to all arts and crafts.

What a gap the want of these books makes. We want not only what we could gain by our own skill, but also what we could never gain. We want above all that spirit with whose life Nature herself surrounds us without our help. This spirit is wanting in us also, and we do violence to ourselves while we, through our miserable popular schools and their monotonous letter-teaching, extinguish within us the last trace of the burning style with which Nature would brand us.

But I return to my path. While I was thus on one side on *the track* of the first beginning-points of the practical means of psychologically unfolding human capacities and talents, which might be practicable and applicable for the development of children from the cradle upwards, I had on the other side, at the same time, to teach children who up to this time had been formed and brought up quite out of the sphere of such views and means. I naturally came while so doing in many ways in opposition to myself, and availed myself, and was forced to avail myself, of measures which seemed in direct opposition to my principles;[17] especially to the psychological sequence of knowledge of things and language, on the lines of which the ideas of children should be developed.

I could not do otherwise. I was obliged, as it were in the dark, to seek out the degree of capacity which I could not fathom in them. I set to work in every possible way and found everywhere that much further progress had intensively been made, even amidst the greatest rubbish, than seemed possible to me, considering the incomprehensible want of all knowledge of the Art. As far as men had influence I found unspeakable sleepiness; but behind this sleepiness Nature was not dead.

I have now learned and can say that it is long, inconceivably long, before human error and unreason can wholly stifle our nature in a child's [mind and] heart. There is a God who has put in our bosom a counterpoise to madness against ourselves. The life and truth of all Nature that surrounds us support this counterpoise, to the eternal pleasure of the Creator, who willeth not that the holiness of our nature should be lost in the time of our weakness and innocence, but that all children of men should, with certainty, advance to the knowledge of truth and right; until forfeiting the worth of their inner nature, *through themselves, by their own fault*, and with *full consciousness of it*, they stray into the labyrinth of error and the abyss of vice.

But [the majority of] the men [of this time] hardly know what God did for them, and allow no weight to the infinite influence of *Nature* on our development. On the contrary, they make a great fuss about any poor invention, crooked and stupid enough compared to her work, as if their skill did everything and Nature nothing for the human race; and yet Nature only does us good; she alone leads us uncorrupted and unshaken to truth and wisdom. The more I followed her track, the more I sought to unite my deeds to hers and strained my powers to keep pace with her footsteps, the more infinite this step appeared to me.

But the power of children to follow her is just as infinite. I found weakness nowhere except in myself and in the art of using what is there. I tried to drive where no driving was possible; where it was only possible to invite into a vehicle what had its own power of going in itself; [or rather, I tried to force in, where it was only possible to bring out from within the child that which lies in him, and is only to be stimulated within him, and cannot be put into him].

I now considered three times before I thought of anything: " The children cannot do it "—and ten times before I said: " It is impossible for them." They did what seemed to me impossible at their age. I let children of three years old spell the wildest nonsense merely because it was nonsensically hard.[18] Friend, you have heard children under four spell out the longest and hardest sentences. Would you have believed it possible if you had not seen it ?

Even so I taught them to read whole geographical sheets that were written in extremely abbreviated forms, and the least known words indicated only by a couple of letters, at an age when they could hardly spell the printed words. You have seen the perfect accuracy with which they read these sheets, and the unconstrained ease with which they could learn them by heart.

I even tried to make gradually clear to a few older children complicated and to them wholly incomprehensible propositions in natural science. They learned the propositions thoroughly by heart, by reading and repetition, and also the questions explaining these propositions. It was at first, like all catechisms, a mere parrot-like repetition of dull, uncomprehended words. But the sharp separation of single ideas, the definite arrangement in this separation, and the consciousness deeply and indelibly impressed of these dull words, glowing in the midst of. their dulness with a gleam of light and elucidation, brought them gradually to a feeling of truth and insight into the subject lying before them, that bit by bit cleared itself like sunlight from densest mist.

By these tentative and erring measures, blending their course with the clearest views of my purpose, these first trials gradually developed in me clear principles about my actions; and while every day it became clearer to me that in the youngest years we must not reason with children, but must limit ourselves to the means of developing their minds:

1. By ever widening more and more the sphere of their sense-impressions.

2. By firmly, and without confusion, impressing upon them those sense-impressions that have been brought to their consciousness.

3. By giving them sufficient knowledge of language for all that Nature and the Art have brought or may in part bring to their consciousness.

While, as I say, these three points of view became clearer to me every day, just as a firm conviction gradually developed within me:

1. Of the need of picture books for early childhood.

2. Of the necessity of a sure and definite means of explaining these books.

3. Of the need of a guide to names, and knowledge

of words founded upon these books and their explanations, with which the children should be
thoroughly familiar before the time of spelling.

The advantage of a fluent and early nomenclature is
invaluable to children.    The firm impression of names
makes the things unforgetable as soon as they are
brought to their knowledge; and the stringing together
of names in an order based upon reality and truth
develops and maintains in them a consciousness of the
real relations of things to each other.    The advantages
of this are progressive, only we must never think because a child does not understand anything fully that
therefore it is of no use to him.    Certain it is that
when with and by A B C learning, he has himself
made the sound and tone of the greater part of a
scientific nomenclature his own, he enjoys through it
at least the advantage that a child enjoys who in his
home, a great house of business, daily becomes acquainted from his cradle upwards with the names of
countless objects.

The philanthropic Fischer,[19] who had a similar purpose to mine, saw my course from the beginning, and
said it was wrong, so far was it removed from his own
manner and views.    The letter that he wrote about
my experiments to Steinmüller[20] is remarkable for the
view he takes of this subject at this time.    I will add
it here with a few observations.

"In judging Pestalozzi's pedagogic undertaking, everything depends on our knowing the psychological basis on which his structure rests. This may prove secure even though the outside of the building presents some ruggedness and disproportion. Many of these deficiencies are explained by the empirical course of the author and by his external circumstances, accidents, trials, and experiments. *It is almost incredible how indefatigably he makes experiments; and since he philosophizes more after these experiments than before—a few leading ideas excepted—he must certainly multiply them; but the results gain in certainty.* To bring these last into common life, that is, to adapt them to the preconceived ideas, the circumstances and claims of men, he needs liberal and sympathetic helpers to assist him to make the forms; or else a very long time to discover them gradually by himself, and through them as it were to give a body to the spirit that animates *him*. The principles on which his method rests, are the following."

(These five special points of view, which he calls the principles of my method, are only isolated views of my attempts for my purpose. As principles they are subordinate to the fundamental views which produced them in me.

But here the first view of the purpose with which I started is wanting; that is to say, I wish to remedy the deficiencies of common school instruction, particularly in lower schools, and to seek forms of instruction that have not these deficiencies.)

1. "*He wishes to raise the capacity of the mind intensively, and not merely to enrich it extensively with conceptions.*

" He hopes to attain this in many ways. While he recites words, explanations, phrases, and long sentences loudly and often to the children, and lets them repeat them, he wishes thereby (according to the distinct individual aim that each step has) to form their organs and to exercise their observation and thought. For the same reason, he allows them during the repetition exercise to draw on their slates freely, or to draw letters with colored chalk."

(I allowed them even then to draw, especially lines, angles, and curves, and to learn their definitions by heart. I proceeded in the measures that I had tried in teaching to write, from the principle founded upon experience that the children are ready at an earlier age for knowledge of proportion and the guidance of the slate pencil, than for guiding the pen and making tiny letters.)

" For this purpose he deals out thin little leaves of transparent horn to his scholars; upon these little tablets are engraved strokes and letters, and the pupils use them as models; so much the more easily since they can lay them upon the figures they have drawn, and the transparency enables them to make the necessary comparison.  A double occupation at the same time is a preparation for a thousand incidents and works in life, in which observation must *share* without *dissipating* itself.  Industrial schools, for example, are founded entirely upon this readiness."

(I had in my experiments of thirty years ago found the most decisive results.  I had already at that time brought children to a readiness of reckoning while spinning that I myself could not follow without paper.  All depends however on the psychology of the form of teaching.  The child must have perfectly in his power the handicraft which he carries on with his learning; and the task which he thus learns with the work must in every case be only an easy addition to that which he can do already.)

2.  "*He makes his teaching depend entirely on language.*"

(This should be exactly, *He holds, after the real sense-impression of Nature, language to be the first means of gaining knowledge of our race.*  I arrived at this from the principle that the child must learn to *talk* before he can be reasonably taught to read.  But I connected the art of teaching children to talk with the intuitive ideas given to them by nature, and with those given to them by art.)

" In language the results of all human progress are recorded.  It is only necessary therefore to follow its course psychologically."

(The clue to this psychological pursuit must be sought in the very nature of the development of language itself. The savage first *names* his object, then *draws* it, then *combines* it very simply, after learning its qualities, variable according to time and circumstances, with words, by terminations and combinations, in order to distinguish it more nearly. I will further unfold this view, and by so doing I will try to satisfy Fischer's demand for a psychological investigation of the course of language, under the title of *Language*.)

" He will not reason with the children until he has furnished them with a stock of words and expressions, which they bring to their places, and learn to compose and decompose. Thereby he enriches their thought with simple explanations of objects of sense, and so teaches the child to describe what surrounds him, to give an account of his ideas, and to master them, since he now, for the first time, becomes clearly conscious of those already existing in him."

(My opinion on this point is: In order to make children reasonable and put them in the way of a power of independent thought, we must guard as much as possible against allowing them to speak at haphazard, or to pronounce opinions about things that they know only superficially. I believe the time for learning is not the time for judgment; the time for judgment comes with the completion of learning; it comes with the ripening of reason, for the sake of which we judge or should judge. I believe every judgment that is supposed to have inner truth for the individual who expresses it, for this reason must of itself out of a comprehensive knowledge fall ripe and perfect, as the perfectly ripened grain falls unforced and free from the husk or shell.)

" Mechanical readiness, and a certain tact in speaking he produces by doing exercises in inflections before them."

(These inflections were limited to descriptions of well-known objects.)

" Their mental freedom gains exceedingly by this; and when they have learned, and learned to use certain forms of description by many examples, they will in future reduce thousands of objects to the same formula, and impress upon their definitions and descriptions the stamp of clear vision."

(I am now trying to find in number, measurement, and language, the primary and universal foundations for this purpose.)

3. " *He seeks to provide all operations of the mind with either data or headings or leading ideas.*"

(That is, he seeks the fundamental points in the whole compass of art and nature, the kinds of sense-impressions, the realities, which can be used through their distinctness and their universality as fruitful means for making knowledge and judgment easy upon many objects subordinate to and connected with them. So he gives the children *data* that will make them observe similar objects; he gives *headings* to sequences of analogous ideas, by defining which he separates for them the *whole sequence* of objects, and makes their essential characteristics clear to them.)

" The *data*, however disjointed they be when given, depend one upon the other. There are ideas, one suggesting the other, which for that very reason inspire the desire for inquiry through the mental necessity of completion and facility in putting together separate objects."

(The *headings* lead to the classification of the ideas to be upgathered; *they* bring order into the chaotic mass, and the set-up framework causes the child to fill up the separate shelves assiduously. That is the value of headings of Geography, Natural History, Technology, etc. Above this comes the analogy which rules in the choice of subjects for thought. The *leading ideas* lie in certain problems, which in themselves are or may be the subject of whole sciences.

When these problems, analyzed to their elements, are intelligibly put before the child, connected with data which he already has or can easily find, and are used as exercises for the observing powers, the child's mind will be led to work incessantly at their solution.

The simple question, "What can man use as clothing out of the three kingdoms of nature?" is an example of this process. The child will examine and prove much from this point of view, from which he anticipates he can contribute to the solution of a technical problem. In this way he builds up his knowledge. Truly the materials must in every case be given him. To the leading ideas belong also propositions which at first can be trusted to the memory only as practical maxims, but gradually receive force, application, and signification, and become more deeply impressed and confirmed.)

4. "*He wishes to simplify the mechanism of teaching and learning.*\*

"Whatever he picks up from his text-books and wishes to teach the children should be so simple that every mother, and later every teacher, even with the least capacity for instruction, can grasp, repeat, explain, and connect together. He particularly wishes mothers to make the earliest education of their children pleasant and important by easy instruction in speech and reading; and so, as he expresses it, gradually to

---

\* It is indisputable that the human mind is not equally susceptible to impressions aimed at in education in every form in which they may be presented. The art of finding out the methods that most readily stimulate this susceptibility is the mechanism of teaching, which every teacher should seek out in free nature, and should learn from her on behalf of his art.

cancel the need of elementary schools, and to supplement them by an improved home education. He wishes in this way to prepare experiments with mothers as soon as his text-books are printed; and it is to be hoped that the Government will help by little premiums."

(I know the difficulties of this question. People all cry that mothers will not be persuaded to undertake a new work in addition to their scrubbing and rubbing, their knitting and sewing, and all their [tiresome duties, and the distractions of their life]; and I may answer as I like: " It is no work; it is play; it takes no time, rather it fill up the emptiness of a thousand moments of depression." People have no mind for it, and answer back, " *They won't do it.*" But Pope Boniface, in the year 1519, said to the good Zwingli, " It won't do; mothers will through all eternity never read the Bible with their children, never through all eternity pray daily with them morning and evening;" yet he found in the year 1522 that they did it, and said, " *I never should have believed it.*" I am sure of my means [and I know and hope, at least, before I am buried],* that a new Pope Boniface will speak of this

---

*How steadfastly Pestalozzi hoped in mothers, appears clearly in this passage. In the first edition he wrote, " Before we get to 1803 " (p. 61). This hope was not fulfilled, and yet in the second edition he expressed it again, but this time it is " before I am buried."

matter as the old one in 1522.   I may indeed wait; it will come to the Pope.)

5. The fifth principle is connected with this, " *He would make knowledge popular.*"

(That is, he aims in all cases at that degree of insight and power of thought that all men need for an independent and wise life.   Not indeed to make the sciences as such the fallacious plaything of bread-needing poverty; but on the contrary, to free bread-needing poverty by the first principles of truth and wisdom from the danger of being the unhappy toy of its own ignorance, as well as of the cunning of others.)

" This is to be gained through the stock of textbooks, which already contain the principal elements of knowledge in well-chosen words and propositions, and, as it were, furnish the unhewn stones which later shall be easily combined to form the arch."

(I should rather have expressed myself in this way: " This should be especially aimed at through the simplification of the first steps of human instruction, and the uninterrupted progress to all that enriches the individual knowledge of every man.   The text-books themselves should be only a *skilful combination of instruction* in all branches with that which *Nature* herself does for the development of men, under all circumstances and conditions.   They should be nothing but a skilful preparation of the power that man needs, for the safe use of that which nature does in all ways for his development.)

" This shall reach further through the division and cheap sale of the text-books. Short and intelligible, they shall be issued in a series, and supplement each other; and yet be able to stand alone, and be dispersed in single numbers. For the same end he would multiply maps, geometrical figures, etc., by woodcuts, at the very lowest prices. He dedicates the profit of these works, after deducting the cost, to the improvement of his method, viz., to practically use it in an established school, institute, or orphan's home."

(This is too much to say. I am not able *to offer to the public the whole profit, merely deducting the cost of printing* of works that are the result of my whole life, and of pecuniary sacrifices that I made with this in view. But notwithstanding all the manifold sacrifices that I have already made for the sake of my aim, yet if the Government or an individual will make it possible for me to carry on an orphan's home according to my principles, I will sacrifice for this end my time and all my powers, with the greater part of the profit of my school books till I die.)

" The gain of school instruction is that the teacher with a certain minimum of skill not only does no harm but is able to make suitable progress."

(This is essential. I believe it is not possible for

common popular instruction to advance a step, so long
as formulas of instruction are not found which make
the teacher, at least in the elementary stages of knowledge, merely the mechanical tool of a method, the
result of which springs from the nature of the formulas
and not from the skill of the man who uses it.   I
assert definitely that a school-book is good only when
an uninstructed schoolmaster can use it at need [al-
most as well as an instructed and talented one.]   It
must essentially be so arranged that uninstructed men,
and even mothers, may find in its clues sufficient help
to bring them always one step nearer than the child to
that progressive development of skill to which they are
leading him.   More is not wanted; and more, at least
for centuries, the mass of schoolmasters could not give.
But we build castles in the air, and are proud of ideas
of reason and independence which exist only on paper
and are more wanting in school-rooms than even in
tailors' and weavers' rooms.   For there is no other
profession that relies so entirely on mere words; and if
we consider how very long we have been relying on
these, then the connection of this error with the cause
from which it arises startles us.)

" More could be gained in the following way.   If
many children are taught together, the emulation
aroused and the reciprocal imparting to one another of
what has been gained becomes more easy among the

children themselves; and the hitherto roundabout ways of enriching the memory may be avoided or shortened by other arts, *e. g.* by analogy of subjects, discipline, increased attention, loud repetitions, and other exercises."

So far Fischer. His whole letter shows the noble man who honors truth even in a nightgown, and when she seems to be surrounded by real shadows. He was transported by the sight of my children in Stanz; and since the impression that this sight made upon him has given sincere attention to all my doings.

But he died before my experiments had reached a ripeness in which he could see more than he really saw in them. With his death a new epoch began for me.

## II

Friend, I soon wearied in Burgdorf as in Stanz. If you know you can never lift a stone without help, do not go on trying for a quarter of an hour without this help. I did incomparably more than I was obliged, and they believed I was obliged to do more than I did. My breast was so torn from morning to night with school affairs, that I was again in danger of the worst.

I was in this condition when Fischer's death brought me into contact with the schoolmaster Krüsi,[21] through whom I learnt to know Tobler and Buss, who a few weeks later joined me. Their union with me saved my life, and preserved my undertaking from an untimely death before it was well alive. Meanwhile the latter danger was so great that there was nothing left for me to do but to risk everything, not only financially but I might almost say morally. I was driven to the point at which I despaired of the fulfilment of a dream to which my life had been devoted. This produced a state of mind and mode of acting that almost bore the stamp of madness on them; while, owing to the force of circumstances and the continuous duration of my misfortunes and undeserved sufferings that disturbed the centre of my efforts, I sank down into the depths of inward confusion, just at the moment in which I apparently began really to approach my aim.

The help that I received from these men in the whole scope of my purpose restored me financially and morally to myself. The impression that my condition as well as my work made upon them, and the consequences of their union with me, are so important in relation to my method, and throw so much light on the spirit of its psychological basis, that I cannot pass over the whole course of their union with me in silence.

Krüsi, whom I first learnt to know, spent his youth in various occupations through which he had learned much and varied manual skill, which in the lower ranks so often develops the basis of the higher mental culture, and raises men who have enjoyed it from childhood to general and comprehensive usefulness.

When only in his twelfth or thirteenth year, his father, who had a little business, used to send him several miles with six or eight dollars to buy goods; to this he added some messages and commissions. Afterwards he undertook weaving and day-laborer's work. In his eighteenth year he was employed, without any preparation, in school work in his native place, Gaiss. At that time, as he now says, he did not know even the names of the first grammatical distinctions. Anything more was not to be thought of, since he never had any instruction, except at an ordinary Swiss village school, where it was limited to reading, writing copies, learning the catechism by rote, etc. But he liked the intercourse with children, and he hoped that this post might be a means of gaining culture and knowledge, the want of which he felt keenly as a messenger. For since they distilled there, he was soon commissioned to buy prepared things, sal ammoniac, borax, and a hundred other things, the names of which he had never heard in his life, while at the same time he dared not forget the most insignificant commission, and was answerable for every farthing. It was borne in upon him how advantageous it must be for every child to be brought forward in reading, writing, counting, and all mental exercises, even in learning to speak, as far as he now felt he wished to have been brought for the sake of his poor calling.

In the first few weeks he had already a hundred pupils. But the task of occupying all these children, properly teaching them and keeping them in order, was beyond his power. He knew no art of school-keeping except *setting tasks* of spelling, reading, and learning by heart; repeating lessons by turns, *warning* and *chastising* with the rod when the tasks were not learnt. But he knew from his own youthful experience that under this method of school-keeping the majority of children sit idle for the greater part of school time, and even fall into all kinds of foolish and naughty ways; that in this way the precious time for culture passes useless away, and the advantages of learning are not balanced by the harmful consequences that such a school-keeping must necessarily have.

Pastor Schiess, who worked energetically against the old slow course of instruction, helped him to keep school for the first eight weeks. They immediately divided the children into three classes. These divisions, and the use of new reading books that were shortly afterwards introduced into the school, made it possible to exercise several children together in spelling and reading, and thus to occupy all, more than had been possible before.

He also lent him books necessary for his own culture, and a good copy-book, which he copied a hundred times in order to form his handwriting; and he was soon in a position to satisfy the highest demands of the parents. But this did not satisfy him. He wished not only to teach his scholars to read and write, but also to train their understanding.

The new reading book [that the pastor introduced into his parish] contained religious instruction in proverbs and Bible stories, passages of nature-teaching and natural history, geography, politics, and so on. At every reading lesson, Krüsi saw that his pastor asked the children questions on every paragraph to see if

they understood what they had read. Krüsi tried to
do likewise, and made most of his scholars perfectly
conversant with the contents of the reading books.
But he only succeeded in doing this, because, like the
good Hübner,[22] he fitted his questions to the answers
already standing in the books; and asked for and expected no answers except exactly those which stood in
the book, before the questions that should have preceded them were discovered. He was especially
successful, because he did not introduce into this
catechism any kind of real exercise for the understanding whatsoever. We must here notice that the
original method of instruction that we call catechizing
was far from being a real exercise of the intellect. It
was a simple verbal analysis of confused sentences
lying before the child; and has this merit, in so far as
it is a preparatory exercise for the gradual clearing up
of ideas, that it presents separate words and sentences
clearly, one by one, to the sense-impression of the
child. " Socratizing " is now for the first time blended
with this catechizing, which was originally confined to
religious matters.

The pastor put Krüsi's thus catechized children as
an example before his older pupils. But afterwards
Krüsi, [according to the fashion of the time] tried to
combine the [limited verbal analysis that we call]
catechizing with Socratizing. This latter implies a

higher treatment of the subject; but the combination, by its very nature, leads no further than the squaring of the circle that a wood cutter with the axe in his hand tries upon a wooden board; it will not do.[23] The uncultured superficial man cannot fathom the depths out of which Socrates drew spirit and truth; therefore it is natural that it should not succeed. He wanted a foundation for his questions, and the children needed a background for their answers. Further, they had no language for that which they knew, and no books that could put a definite answer in their mouths for questions understood, or not understood.

Meanwhile, Krüsi did not feel clearly yet the difference between these similar methods. He knew not yet that catechism proper, and particularly the catechism about abstract ideas, excepting the advantage of separating words and subjects into analytical forms, is nothing in itself but a parrot-like repetition of unintelligible sounds. Socratizing is essentially impossible for children, since they want both a background of preliminary knowledge and the outward means of expression—language. He was unjust to himself about this failure; he believed the cause of failure lay entirely in himself, and thought any good schoolmaster would be able to draw right and clear answers from children by questions about all sorts of religious and moral ideas.

He had fallen upon the fashionable period of Socratizing, or rather upon an epoch in which this sublime
art was [generally absorbed by an inferior art, and]
spoiled and degraded by a combination of monkish and
teachers' formulas of catechism. At that period they
dreamed of drawing out the intellect in this way, and
out of veritable nothing to call forth wonders; but I
think they are now waking from that dream.

Krüsi, however, was still fast asleep; he was locked
in it, else I should wonder if even the Appenzeller had
not observed, when half awake, that the hawk and the
eagle could take no eggs from the nest if none had
been laid. He was determined to learn an art that
seemed so essential to his calling. And as he found
in the departure of the emigrating Appenzellers an
opportuntiy of coming to Fischer, his hopes were
renewed on this subject. Fischer did everything to
make him a cultivated teacher, according to his views.
But in my opinion he has let the attempt to raise him
into the clouds of a superficial art of catechizing take
precedence of the work that should make clearer to
him the foundations of things, about which he should
catechize.

Krüsi honors his memory, and speaks only with
affection and gratitude of his benefactor and friend.
But love of truth, which bound me also to Fischer's
heart, demands that I leave no view and no circum-

stance of this subject in doubt which more or less contributed to develop views and opinions in me and my
helpers that now unite us on this subject.    Therefore
I cannot conceal that while Krüsi admired the ease
with which Fischer held a great number of questions
in readiness about a crowd of subjects, and hoped with
time and industry to gather together a sufficient number of questions for the elucidation of all the principal
subjects of human knowledge,[24] he could ever less and
less conceal it from himself that if a teachers' seminary
be a thing that must raise every village schoolmaster
to this height in the art of questioning, such a seminary
might still be a doubtful advantage.

The more he worked with Fischer, the greater seemed
the mountain that stood before him, and the less he
felt in himself the power that he saw was necessary to
climb its summit.   Since, however, he heard me talk
with Fischer of education and the culture of the
people, on the first days of his visit, and heard me distinctly declare against the Socratizing of our candi-
dates, with the expression that I was wholly against
making the judgment of children upon any subject
*apparently ripe before the time*, but rather would hold it
back as long as possible, until they really had seen with
their own eyes the object on which they should express
themselves, from all sides, and under several conditions,
and had become quite familiar with words by which

they could describe its essential characteristics, Krüsi
felt that he decidedly wanted this himself, and that he
needed just this training that I intended to give my
children.

While Fischer on his side did everything to lead
him into several departments of knowledge, in order
to prepare him for giving instruction, Krüsi felt daily
more and more that his way was not among books, so
long as he was wanting in the fundamental knowledge
of things and of words which these books presupposed
more or less.   Fortunately he became more confirmed
in this self-knowledge, by seeing before his eyes the
effect produced on the children by being taken back to
the beginning points of human knowledge, and by my
patient dwelling upon these points.   This changed his
whole view of instruction, and all the fundamental
ideas he had formed thereon.   He now saw that in all
that I did I tried more to *develop the inner capacity* of
the child than to produce isolated results by my
actions; and he was convinced, through the effect of
this principle in the whole range of my method of
development, that in this way the foundations of intelligence and further progress were laid in the children
as could never be attained in any other way.

Meanwhile Fischer's plan of founding a schoolmaster's seminary was hindered.   He was elected again to
the Bureau of Ministers of Education.   He promised

himself to wait for better times for his seminary, and meanwhile to direct the schools in Burgdorf even in his absence. They should be remodelled, and they needed it; but owing to his absence and the diverting of all his time and strength, he had not even been able to begin; and certainly would not have been able in his absence, and in the midst of varied occupations, to set it working.

Krüsi's condition was aggravated by Fischer's absence. He felt less and less capable of what Fischer expected of him without his personal presence and sympathy. Soon after Fischer's departure, he expressed to him and to me his wish to join himself and his children to my school. But though I sorely needed help I rejected it then, because I would not annoy Fischer, who showed continual zeal for his seminary and who depended upon Krüsi. But he was ill soon after, and Krüsi told him of the need of this union in the last hours that he spoke with him. An affectionate nod of the head was the dying man's answer. His memory will be always dear to me. He worked towards a like purpose to mine, energetically and nobly. Had he lived and been able to wait for the ripening of my experiment, we should certainly have entirely agreed.

After Fischer's death I myself proposed to join Krüsi's school to mine, and we now both saw our work much lightened, but the difficulties of my plan much increased. I had already from Burgdorf children unequal in age, cultivation, and manners. The arrival of children from the little cantons increased the difficulties; for beside similar inequalities, they brought into my school-room a natural independence of thought, feeling, and speech, that, combined with insinuations against my method and the want of a firm organization in my teaching, which might still be looked on as a mere experiment, made every day more depressing. In my condition I needed free play for my experiments, and yet at every moment private people sent particular orders as to how I should set to work to teach the children who were sent to me.

In one place, where they had been accustomed for ages to be content with very little in the way of instruction and teaching, they now demanded from me that a method of teaching, embracing all the elements of human knowledge, and one that was compiled for the early use of little children, should also have a great, universal, and absolute effect upon children who up to their twelfth or fourteenth year had remained in the most thoughtless mountain freedom, and had therefore become distrustful of all teaching.

It was certainly not such a method; and they said as it had not this effect it was no use. They confused it with an ordinary modification of the method of teach-

ing A B C, and.writing.   My aim of seeking firm and
sure foundations in all branches of human art and
human knowledge; my efforts to strengthen the capacities of children simply and generally for every art;
and my calm and apparently indifferent way of waiting for the results of principles that should gradually
develop out of themselves—these were castles in the
air.   They anticipated nothing from and saw nothing
in them; on the contrary, where I built up capacity,
they found emptiness.

They said: " The children do not learn to read,"
just because I taught reading properly; they said:
" They are not learning to write," because I taught
writing properly; and at last: " They do not learn to
be good," just because I did all I could to remove out
of the way the first hindrances to goodness that were in
the school, and especially opposed the idea that the
parrot-like learning by heart of the " Heidelberg " can
be the only method of teaching, by which the Saviour
of the world sought to raise the human race to reverence God and to worship Him *in Spirit and in Truth.*

It is true, I have said fearlessly, God is not a God
to whom stupidity and error, hypocrisy and lip-service
are pleasing.[25]   I have said fearlessly: Take care to
teach children to think, feel, and act rightly, to
quicken and make use of the blessings of faith and
love in themselves, before we drill the subjects of posi-

tive theology and their never-ending controversies into their memories, as a *means of cultivating their intellect*, and a *spiritual exercise*. This cannot be opposed to God and religion. But I cannot be offended at being misunderstood; they meant well; and I perfectly comprehend that, owing to the quackery of our educational methods, my rough attempts at a new way must disappoint people who, like many others, would rather see one fish in their pond, than a lake full of carp the other side of the mountains.

Meantime I took my own way, and Krüsi stood more and more firmly by me.

The principal points of which he was quickly convinced, [not however as ripe educational truths, but only as preliminary views that gradually unfolded themselves as clearly developed principles of education,] are especially these:

1. That through a well-arranged nomenclature, indelibly impressed, a general foundation for all kinds of knowledge can be laid, by which children and teacher, together as well as separately, may rise gradually but with safe steps to clear ideas in all branches of knowledge.

2. That by exercises in lines, angles, and curves, which I began to use at this time, a readiness in gaining sense-impressions of all things is produced in the children; as well as skill of hand, of which

the effect will be to make everything that comes within the sphere of their observation gradually clear and plain.

3. That by exercising children beginning to count with real objects, or at least with dots representing them, we lay the foundations of the whole of the science of arithmetic, and secure their future progress from error and confusion.

4. The descriptions that the children learnt by heart of going, seeing, standing, lying, etc., showed him the connection of the first principles with the end that I was aiming at through them, the gradual clearing up of all ideas.   He soon felt that while we make children describe *things that are so plain to them that no experiment can make them clearer*, they are checked in the presumption of wishing to describe that which they do not know, and gain the power of describing what they do know and what comes within the sphere of their observation, with brevity, clearness, and understanding.

5. A few words that I spoke about the influence of my methods in counteracting prejudice, made the deepest impression upon him.   I said: Truth that springs from sense-impression may make tiresome talk and tedious arguments superfluous (these have almost as much effect against error and prejudice as bell-ringing against a storm), because

truth so acquired generates a power in the man
that makes his soul proof against prejudice and
error; and even when through the continual chatter of our race they come to his ears, they become
so isolated in him that they cannot have the same
effect as upon the common-place men of our time,
on whom truth and error alike, without sense-
impression, with mere cabalistic words, are thrown
as through a magic lantern upon the imagination.

These expressions convinced him that it might
be possible to do more against error and prejudice
by the still silence of my method, than has yet
been done through the endless talk that we have
permitted against it, or rather have been guilty of.

6. The plant-collecting that we pursued last summer, and the conversations to which it gave rise,
particularly developed in him the conviction that
the whole circle of knowledge generated through
our senses rests upon attention to *Nature* and on
*industry* in *collecting* and *holding firm* everything
that she brings to our consciousness.

All these views, joined with his growing need of
bringing all means and subjects of instruction into
harmony with each other, convinced him of the possibility of founding a method of instruction in which
the principles of all action and knowledge should be so
united that a teacher need only learn *how to use them*, in

order by their help to raise himself and the children to any standard that can be aimed at by teaching.[26]   By this plan, not *erudition*, but only *healthy human understanding* and *practice in the method* was wanted, to lay solid foundations of all knowledge in the children, and to raise a satisfactory inner self-activity in both parents and teachers by simply using these means of gaining knowledge.

As has been said, he was six years village-schoolmaster, over a very large number of children of all ages; but with all the pains he took, he had never so developed the capacities of children, and had never seen the firmness, security, comprehension, and freedom reached, to which we had risen.

He sought the causes, and found many.

He saw first that the principle of beginning with the easiest and making this complete before going further, then gradually adding little by little to that already perfectly learnt, does not actually in the first moments of learning produce a feeling and a self-consciousness of power, but it keeps alive in the children this high witness of their unweakened natural power.

"We must never," said he, "drive the children, but only lead them by this method." Before, when he began to teach, he used to say: "Consider that. Do you not remember?"

It was inevitable, for instance, when he asked, in

arithmetic, How many times is seven contained in sixty-three? The child had no real background for his answer, and must, with great trouble, dig it out of his memory. Now, by the plan of putting nine times seven objects before his eyes, and letting him count them as nine sevens standing together, he has not to think any more about this question; he knows from what he has already learnt, although he is asked for the first time, that seven is contained nine times in sixty-three. So it is in other departments of the method.

For example, if he wanted them to write nouns with capital letters they always forgot the rule; but when he took a few pages of the methodical dictionary as a simple exercise in reading them, they began of their own accord to set down these sequences of nouns that were known to them alphabetically. This experiment presupposed an intelligent consciousness of the difference between these kinds of words and others. It is perfectly true that the method is incomplete [for the child] on any point where it needs in any way a spur to the thought; it is incomplete wherever a distinct exercise does not come by itself, and without a strain, from that which the child already knows.

He remarked further, that the words and pictures that I laid before the children singly at the reading lesson had quite a different effect upon the mind from the collective phrases that were served up in ordinary instruction. And when he now fixed his eye upon these phrases he found them of such a quality that the children could have no sensible image of the nature of the separate words; and when put together looked, not at simple well-known parts, but at a confusion of incomprehensible combinations of unknown objects, with which we lead them, against their nature, above their strength, and with many delusions, to get hold of sequences of thought which are not only wholly strange to them, but need an art of speaking, the beginning of which they have not even tried to learn.

Krüsi saw that I threw away the rubbish of our school wisdom, and, like Nature with the savage, always put a picture before the eye, and then sought for a word for the picture. He saw that this simplicity of procedure created in them no judgment and no inference while it was put before them, not as a dogma, nor in any way connected with either truth or error, but only as material for observation, as a background for future criticism and inference, and as a guide on whose track they might go further by themselves by uniting their early and future experiences.

As he learnt more, and saw deeper into the spirit of the method of reducing all branches of knowledge to the first beginning-points, and the gradual joining on of a little addition to the first step in every branch, and found that the consequence of that is a steady progress to new and further additions, he became daily more ready to work with me in the spirit of these principles; and he helped me to bring out a spelling book and an arithmetic book in which these principles are essentially followed.

In the first days of his union with me he wished to go to Basle, in order to tell Tobler,[27] to whom he was much attached, of Fischer's death, and about his present situation.   I took this opportunity of saying to him that I was indispensably in need of help in my writing work, and that I should be very glad if it were possible for Tobler to join me.   I already knew him from his correspondence with Fischer.   I told him, at the time, that I needed just as much for my purpose a man who could draw and sing.

He went to Basle and talked with Tobler, who decided almost directly to accede to my wish and came in a few weeks to Burgdorf; and since Krüsi told him that I also wanted a draughtsman, he fell in with Buss, who undertook the task directly.   Both have been here eight months; and I think it would interest you to read a precise account of their experience on this subject.   Tobler was five years tutor in an important house in Basle.

His opinion of the nature of my undertaking, comparing it with his own course in his own words, is the following:—

" After the efforts of six years, I found the results of
my instruction did not correspond to my expectations.
The intensive powers of my children did not increase
in proportion to my efforts; they did not even increase
as they should have done according to the degree of
their real knowledge.   They did not seem to perceive
the inner connection of the isolated bits of information I gave them, nor to give them the strict long-continued reflection that they needed.

" I used the best instruction-books of our time.   But
these were partly expressed in words that the children
could hardly understand, and partly so filled with ideas
that went beyond their experience and were so opposed
to their own way of looking at things at their age, that
it demanded infinite time and trouble to explain the
incomprehensible.   These explanations were themselves a continual worry, which had no more effect on
their real inner development than a single beam of
light in a dark room or in a thick fog.   This was more
the case since many of these books with their pictures
and representations descended to the deepest depths of
human knowledge, or ascended above the clouds right
up to the heaven of eternal glory, before they allowed
the children to set foot on the firm ground, on which
men must stand before they learn to fly or grow wings
wherewith to rise.

" The gloomy consciousness of all this impelled me

to try to entertain my younger pupils with pictures of objects; but to raise my elder ones to clear ideas by Socratizing. The first result was that the little ones made themselves masters of much knowledge that other children of their age do not possess. I wished to combine this kind of instruction with the formulas of teaching that I found in the best books; but all the books that I wanted to use were written in a manner that presupposed all which must first be given to the children—namely *Language*. Therefore my Socratizing with the elder scholars had the result that all word-explanations are certain to have that are not based upon a knowledge of things, and are expressed in a language which conveys no clear ideas to the children. That which they grasped to-day, in a few days vanished from their minds in an incomprehensible manner; and the more pains I took to make things clear to them, the more they seemed to lose the power of seeking it themselves, out of the mist in which Nature had placed it.

" So, on the whole, I felt insurmountable hindrances to my progress in my purpose. My conversations with teachers and educators in society strengthened my conviction that in spite of the immense educational libraries our age produces, these others were in the same perplexity in their daily work with their pupils. I felt that these difficulties were doubled and must weigh ten times heavier upon the under teachers, if a miserable kind of dabbling work did not make them wholly incapable of such a feeling.

" I lived in ardent, through misty consciousness of the gaps which I saw in the whole compass of education, and I tried by all means in my power to fill them up. I undertook to collect, partly from experience, partly from educational books, all means and advantages by which it might be possible to obviate the educational difficulties that struck me in all children of all ages.

" But I soon felt my life would not be long enough to reach this end. I had already written whole books on this subject, when Fischer drew my attention in several letters to Pestalozzi's method, and made me suspect that perhaps in other ways than mine he might reach the end I sought. I thought: My systematic scientific course perhaps creates the difficulties that do not stand in his way; and the art of our time may itself produce the gaps that he need not fill up, because he neither knows nor uses this art. Many of his means, e. g. drawing on slates,[28] etc., seemed to me so simple that I could not understand why I had not thought of them long ago. It struck me that what already lay near to hand was used by him. This principle of his method particularly attracted me—educating mothers for that to which they are so remarkably designed by nature;—because all my experiments were founded upon it.

" These opinions were confirmed by the arrival in Basle of Krüsi, who practically showed Pestalozzi's methods of teaching reading and arithmetic in the Girls' Institute. Pastor Fäsch and Von Brunn, who had organized the instruction and part of the direction of this Institute according to the first indications of Pestalozzi's method, which as yet we hardly knew, saw at once the firm impression that the drill in simultaneous reading and spelling made upon the children. The few materials that Krüsi brought with him for teaching writing and arithmetic after this fashion, as well as a few copies of a dictionary that Pestalozzi had designed as the first reading book for children, showed us that these methods had a deep psychological basis. All this made me quickly decide to accede to Pestalozzi's wish and join him.

" I came to Burgdorf, and found my expectations fulfilled at the first glance at this growing undertaking. The remarkable and general self-expressing capacity of his children, as well as the simplicity and multiplicity of means of development by which this capacity was created, filled me with astonishment. His complete disregard of all former school routine, the simplicity of the pictures he impressed, the sharp separation of the inner parts of his subject of instruction into portions that must be learnt progressively at odd times, his rejection of everything involved or confused, his silent influence upon all the inherent powers, his firm hold upon words whenever they were needed; and particularly the force with which his few means of instruction seemed to spring, like a new creation, out of the elements of art and human nature—all this stretched my attention to the utmost.

" Certainly there seemed to me a few very unpsychological things in his experiment, e. g. the repetition of difficult, confused propositions, of which the first impression must be quite vague to the child. But as I saw with what power he prepared for the gradual clearing of ideas; and how, as he told me, Nature herself wraps all sense-impressions at first in confused mistiness, but gradually clears them up, I found I had nothing more to say: and certainly less, as I saw that he set little value on the individual portions of his undertaking, but tried much only to reject it. By many of these experiments he was seeking only to raise the inner capacity of the children, and to find the explanation of the grounds and principles which occasioned the use of these various methods. I did not let myself be misled when a few of his means came upon me in the trembling weakness of isolated first experiments; the less so, as I soon convinced myself that progressive advance lay in their very nature. Certainly I saw this in arithmetic, drawing, and in the fundamental methods of language-teaching.

" Now it became clearer to me every day that his special methods, through the connection of the whole with *each*, depended especially on the susceptibility of the children to *each;* and so I saw that these methods grew ripe through his daily work, before they were spoken of as principles, which must necessarily forward the end he was seeking.   In his attempts and experiments he relied upon none of these means until *he held* it almost physically impossible to simplify their essence any further, or to penetrate deeper to their foundations.

" These steps towards simplifying the whole and completing the single parts confirmed the conviction which I before held vaguely, that all means which seek the development of the human mind through a complicated terminology carry the hindrance to their result in themselves; and that all means of education and development must be reduced to extreme simplicity of their inner being, as well as to an organization of language teaching, psychological and harmonious, if we would help Nature in that self-activity that she shows in the development of our race.

" So gradually his object in breaking up the study of language became clear to me, and also why he reduced arithmetic to the principle always to be kept in mind, that all arithmetic is only a short method of counting, and counting only a short method, instead of the tiresome expression one, and one, and one, etc., makes so much; and why he built all power of doing, —even the power of clear representation of all real objects,—upon the early development of the ability to draw lines, angles, rectangles, and curves.

" It followed of course that my conviction of the advantages of the method should be daily strengthened as I daily saw the effect produced on measurement, arithmetic, writing, and drawing, by the power universally awakened and used according to these principles. I raised myself daily more to the conviction that it might be possible to reach the end which I mentioned above as having animated my own actions, namely to educate mothers for that to which they are eminently designed by nature; and through it, even the lowest material of ordinary school-instruction might be founded upon the results of companionable motherly instruction.   I saw a universal psychological method formed, by which all fathers and mothers who found the motive in themselves might be put in a position to instruct their own children, and thereby to obviate the imaginary necessity of cultivating teachers by costly seminaries and educational libraries for a long period.

" In a word, through the impression of the whole, and through the constant similarity of my experiences,

I am restored to the faith that I cherished so warmly in the beginning of my pedagogic course, but which I nearly lost as I went on under the burden of such art and help as is provided by the age—the *faith*, namely, *in the possibility of improving the human race.*"

## III

You have now read Tobler's and Krüsi's opinion of my object. I will now send that of Buss.[29] You know my opinion of the latent capacities of the lower classes. What a proof Buss is of this! How this man has developed in six months Show Wieland his attempt at an A B C of *Anschauung*.[30] I know how interested he is in all that can throw light on the course of development of the human race; he will certainly, in this attempt, find a proof of how many apparently wasted and neglected powers can be used and increased by gentle help and stimulus.

Dear friend,—the world is full of useful men, but empty of people who can put these useful men into their places. In our time every one limits his idea of human usefulness within his own skin [or at most extends it to men who lie as near as his shirt].

Dear friend,—seriously imagine these three men and what I do with them. I wish you knew them and their way of life more exactly. Buss tells you at my request something about it himself.

Tobler's first education was sheer neglect. In his two-and-twentieth year he found himself, as by a miracle, thrown into the midst of scientific systems, and particularly in the department of education. He thought to master them; but now he sees they mastered him, and caused him in spite of a presentiment of the insufficiency of his own education trustfully to follow the way of books, without following Nature herself by the way of sense-impression, of which he dimly felt the need. He sees the danger in which he stood of losing himself in a sea of thousands upon thousands of details separately rational, without at that time finding principles of education and school-culture whose result would be, not rational words and rational books, but [through the cultivated power of reason,] rational men. He lamented that in his two-and-twentieth year, when book-study had not yet begun to lessen his native capacity, he had not already found the path that he now trod in his thirtieth year.

He felt deeply how this intervening epoch had injured him; and it does his heart and the method equal honor that he says himself that ignorant and uninstructed men could find the beginning points more easily and certainly than he, and could then go on. Meanwhile he is true to his conviction. His talents make his progress sure. When he has worked through the difficulties of the simple beginnings, these, and former knowledge which he combines with them, will make it easy for him to connect the method with the

higher points of school-instruction, to which we have
not yet come.

You know Krüsi, and have seen the power he shows
in his vocation. It is extraordinary. Whoever sees
him working is astonished. He possesses an independence in his vocation that is displeasing only to the
man who has none himself; and yet before he knew
the method he was, except in mechanical school-teach-
er's routine, far behind Buss in all branches. He now
says himself that without knowledge of the method all
his efforts towards independence would not have enabled him to stand on his own feet, but he should have
remained always dependent upon others' guidance;
and that is entirely opposed to his Appenzel spirit. He
has given up a post of 500 florins and has remained in
the most straitened circumstances of his present situation, just because he felt and saw that here he now might
indeed become a school-master, but there he could be
nothing else, and even that not satisfactorily. You
will not wonder how he came to this decision; his simplicity led him to it; he entirely lost himself in the
method. The result is natural; as Tobler truly said,
" It was easy enough for him because he had no art,
and he gained it precisely because he knew nothing
but had ability."

Friend, have I not reason to be proud of the first-
fruits of my method ? Shall men always, as you said

to me two years ago, have no mind for the simple psychological ideas on which it is founded? May all its fruits be like these three firstlings. Read Buss's opinion, too, and then hear me again.

" My father," said Buss, " held an office in a Theological college at Tübingen, and had free lodging there. He sent me from my third to my thirteenth year to the Latin school, where I learned whatever was taught at that age. At that time I lived mostly when out of school with students who were pleased to play with a lively boy. In my eighth year one of them taught me piano-playing, but as he left Tübingen in half a year my lessons were broken off, and I was left to teach myself. Steady perseverance and practice so brought me forward that I was able in my twelfth year to give lessons in this subject to a lady and a boy, with the best results.

" In my eleventh year, I enjoyed also instruction in drawing, and continued perseveringly the study of Greek and Hebrew, Logic, and Rhetoric. The aim of my parents was to devote me to study, and for this end to send me to the newly built Academy of Arts and Sciences at Stuttgart, or to the direction of the professors of the University at Tübingen.

" Up till now men of all ranks were admitted into the Academy, some paying, some free. My parents' means did not allow them to spend the least sum upon me.  For this reason a petition was sent for free admission to the Academy, but it was returned with a negative answer, signed by *Carl* himself.[31]  This, with, as far as I remember, the simultaneous notice of the closing of studies against the sons of all the *middle* and *lower* classes, had a great effect upon me.  I turned my attention entirely to drawing, but was again interrupted within the half-year; for my teacher on account of bad conduct was obliged to leave the town, and so I was left without means or prospects of being able to help myself, and soon found it necessary to bind myself apprentice to a bookbinder.

"My frame of mind had sunk almost to indifference.  I took up this trade as I should have taken any other, in order to extinguish all remembrance of my youthful dreams by constant manual labor.  This I could not do.  I worked, but I was unspeakably discontented, and nourished hasty feelings against the injustice of a power that against *precedent* shut me out, merely because I belonged to the lower classes, from any means of culture, and from the hopes and prospects to reach which I had spent a great part of my youth.  Yet I nourished the hope of earning through my trade the means of giving up my unsatisfactory handicraft, and of somehow retrieving what I had lost.

" I travelled; but the world was too narrow for me. I became melancholy, sick, had to go home again, tried anew to renounce my calling, and hoped to earn my necessary subsistence in Switzerland by means of the little I knew of music.

" I went to Basle, and hoped to find some opportunity of giving lessons. But my former position produced a certain shyness that prevented me from taking the first steps towards earning money. I had not the heart to say anything of all that must be said in order to obtain what I wanted, from people as they are. A friend who accidentally met me in this embarrassment reconciled me for the moment to my bookbinding. I went into a workshop again; but also dreamed again, from the first day I sat down in it, of the possibility of finding something else with time and opportunity, although I was almost convinced that I was too far behind in music and drawing to enable me to procure a secure independence by their means. In order to gain time to improve myself I soon changed from my first place, and gained two hours a day for myself, and found acquaintances who made my work easier.

" Among others I learned to know Tobler, who soon observed the trouble that was gnawing me, and wished to remove me from my position. He thought of me directly when Krüsi told him that Pestalozzi's newly organized method of instruction required a man who understood music and drawing.

" I knew I was backward in general culture and in drawing, and my hope of finding opportunity of advancing in both made me quickly decide to go to Burgdorf, although I was warned by several people against having any connection with Pestalozzi, because he was half an idiot, and did not know his own mind.*  This tale is still repeated with variations; how once he came into Basle with straw-bound shoes because he had given his buckles to a beggar outside the gate.  I had read ' Leonard and Gertrude ' and believed in the buckles; but that he was a fool I did not believe.

" In short, I wished to try.  I came to Burgdorf. His first appearance hardly surprised me.  He came down from an upper room with ungartered stockings, very dirty, and looking thoroughly put out with Ziemssen, who had just came to visit him.  I cannot describe my feeling at that moment; it almost approached pity, mixed with astonishment.

" Pestalozzi!—and what did I see!  His benevolence, his joy over me, a stranger, his freedom from presumption, his simplicity, and the disorder in which he stood before me, all carried me away in a moment.  No man

---

* I naturally feel that the public expression of this part of my opinion is unseemly.  But Pestalozzi wished it, and demanded an unconstrained candid statement of the impression that he and everything else had made upon me.

had ever so touched my heart, no man had ever so won my trust.

" The next morning I went into his school, and saw really nothing at first but apparent disorder, and, to me, unpleasant confusion.  But from the warmth with which Ziemssen had spoken the day before of Pestalozzi's plans, my attention was ready to be aroused beforehand, so that I soon got over this impression; and it was not long before I was struck by some advantages of this method of teaching.  I thought at first that dwelling too long upon ·a point strained the children too much; but when I saw the perfection to which he brought his children in the beginning-points of their exercises, the flitting-around and springing-about permitted by the course of instruction given in my youth appeared for the first time at a disadvantage.  It made me think that if I had been made to dwell as long and as steadily on the beginnings, *I should have been in a position to help myself in progressing towards the higher steps*, and so to conquer all the evils of life and the melancholy in which I was now plunged.

" This reflection agreed with Pestalozzi's principle *of enabling men by his method to help themselves, since, as he says, on God's earth no one helps them, or can help them.* I shuddered when I read this passage in ' Leonard and Gertrude ' for the first time.  But it is the experience of my life that no one on God's earth will or can help

him who cannot help himself.   It was now evident to
me that the gaps, which I could not fill up to attain
my end, had their origin in[32] the weakness and superficiality of the instruction I had received in the branch
of art in which I had now to work, without knowing
anything of the principles on which that art was
founded.

" I certainly now threw all my energy into the department in which Pestalozzi wanted my help, but for
a long time I could not understand a single one of his
opinions on drawing, and at first knew not what he
wanted when he said:—' Lines, angles, and curves are
the foundations of the art of drawing.'   In order to
explain himself to me he said, ' Here, too, the human
being must be raised from dim sense-impressions to
clear ideas.'   But I could not understand how that
could be done by drawing.   He said, ' This must be
obtained by the division of squares and curves into
parts, and by analyzing their parts to units that can
be seen and compared.'

" I tried to find this analysis and simplification, but
I could not find the beginning-point of simplicity, and
with all my trouble found myself in a sea of single
figures that were certainly simple in themselves but
did not make Pestalozzi's laws of simplicity clear.
Unfortunately he could neither write nor draw, though
he had brought his children by some incomprehensible

way far on in both.   In short, for months I did not
understand him, and for months did not know what
to make of the lines that he gave me as a pattern,
until at last I felt either I ought to know less than I
did, or at least must throw away my knowledge and
stand upon the simple points which I saw gave him his
power that I could not follow.

" It was hard.   At last my ripened insight compelled
me, seeing how far his children were brought by persevering upon his beginning-point, to go down to these
points.   Then was my attempt at an A B C of *Anschauung* complete in a couple of days.

" There it was, and as yet I knew not what it was;
but the first recognition of its existence had the greatest effect upon me.   I knew not before that this art
consisted of lines only.

" Now every thing that I saw suddenly stood between
lines that defined its outline.   In my representations
I had never separated the outlines from the object.
Now in my imagination they freed themselves from it
and fell into measurable forms, from which every deviation was sharply distinct to me.   But as at first I saw
only *objects*, now I saw only *lines*, and believed these
must be used with the children absolutely and to the
utmost extent before giving them real objects to imitate, or even examine.

" But Pestalozzi thought of these rules of drawing

in connection with his whole purpose, and in connection with Nature, which allows no part of the Art long to stand separate in the human mind. With this intention he had put a double series of figures before the children from the cradle upwards,—some in the book for early childhood, some in preparation for definite forms. With the first he wished to help Nature, and develop knowledge of words and things as early as possible in the children by means of a series of representations of Nature. With the second he wished to combine the rules of art with the sense-impression of art, and to support the consciousness of pure form, and of objects which fit into it, in the minds of the children by means of juxtaposition; and lastly to secure thereby a gradual psychological progress in art, so that they can use every line that they can draw perfectly for objects, the complete drawing of which is only a repetition of the measure-form that is already familiar to them.

" I feared to weaken the power of sense-impression in the children by laying down figures, but Pestalozzi wanted no unnatural power. He said once: ' Nature gives the child no lines; she gives only things, and lines must be given him only in order that he may perceive things rightly. The things must not be taken from him in order that he may see only lines.' And another time he became so angry about the danger of rejecting Nature for the sake of lines that he exclaimed: ' God forbid that I should overwhelm the human mind and harden it against natural sense-impression, for the sake of these lines and of the Art, as idolatrous priests have overwhelmed it with superstitious teaching and hardened it against natural sense-impressions.'

" Lastly, I observed and found in the plans of both books full agreement with the course of Nature, and only so much art as is necessary to make Nature have that effect upon the human mind which is essentially wanted for the development of its talents.

" Before this I had been in a dilemma. Pestalozzi said to me that the children must be taught to read these outlines like words, and to name the separate parts of curves and angles with letters, so that their combination can be as clearly expressed upon paper as any word by the combination of letters. These lines and curves should be an A B C of *Anschauung*, and thereby become the foundation of an art-language by which all varieties of forms should not only be most clearly known but distinctly expressed in words. He did not rest till I understood. I saw how much trouble I gave him; I was sorry; but it was of no use; no A B C of *Anschauung* would have been found without his patience.

" At last it was found. I began with the letter A; that was what he wanted, and one followed another,

so that I had no more trouble.   The thing already
existed in the finished drawing, but the difficulty was
that I could not express what I really knew, nor understand the expressions of others.

" It is, however, one of the essential results of the
method that this evil will be remedied.   The art of
speaking will be firmly connected with the knowledge
given us by Nature and Art, and the children will
learn to express themselves about every step of
knowledge.

" It was commonly remarked among us teachers
that we could not clearly and fully express ourselves
about matters that we thoroughly knew.   It was difficult even to Pestalozzi always to find words [for stating his views of the aims of education] that would
clearly express his meaning.

" It was owing to this want of [definite] speech that
I fumbled about so long in doubt about my department, and did not and could not see Pestalozzi's
principles.

" After I had overcome this difficulty, I recognized
the advantages of the method every day, and particularly saw how the A B C of *Anschauung* through the
definite language which it gives the children about objects and art, even in that degree, must form in them
a far more exact feeling of rightness and proportion.
I felt especially how men[33] who have been taught to

speak with art and care about their surroundings become able, merely through knowing rightly the names
of objects, to distinguish them more clearly and be
more conscious of their characteristics than can be
possible to those who have not been so taught. Experience confirmed my expectation. Children criticized
these different parts more justly than men accustomed
to measurement and drawing from their youth. Their
progress in this art was so rapid that it could not be
compared with the ordinary progress of children.

" And though I saw the whole method only through
the medium of my department and its limited effect,
yet from the energy and care with which I worked
within this limit I learnt gradually, step by step, not
only to guess its effect upon other branches but to see
and understand it. So I came to see by the limited
clue given by my lessons in drawing how it might be
possible,[34] by the psychology of language, by the
gradual progress of lessons from sound to word, from
word to speech, to attain to the formation of clear
ideas, as well as by the progress from lines to angles,
from angles to figures, and from figures to objects.

" I understood the same course in arithmetic. Till
now I had looked upon each number without any
definite consciousness of its proper value or contents,
merely as an independent entity; just as formerly I
regarded the objects of art without any discriminating

consciousness of their definite outlines or proportions, *i. e.* of their contents. Now I was sensibly conscious of the definite contents of any number; and I recognized the progress made by children who enjoyed this teaching, and saw at the same time how essential it is for every branch of knowledge that simultaneous instruction should be given in number, form, and language.

" As I had recognized the stoppage in my branch owing to want of language, so now I recognized the deficiencies owing to want of arithmetic. For example, I saw that the child cannot represent the separate parts of any form without being able to count them, just as until he distinctly knows that the number 4 is composed of four units, he cannot understand how the single number can be divided into four parts. Thus, from the clearness to which my work now brought me daily, as much *as through myself*, the conviction developed that the method, by its influence upon the human mind generally, produces in children the power of *helping themselves* further on in every branch, and is essentially a fly-wheel that needs only to be set going in order to go on by itself. But I was not the only one to find this out. Hundreds of men came, saw, and said, ' This cannot fail.' Peasant men and women said, ' I can do that with my child at home.' And they were right.

"The whole method is play for any one, as soon as he grasps the clue of the beginnings. This secures him from wandering in byways, which alone make the Art difficult to the human race, because they lead away from Nature herself, and from the firm ground upon which alone it is possible to rest its foundations. She requires nothing of us that is not easy, if we seek it in the right way and from her hands only.[35]

"I have but this to add. Knowledge of the method has in great measure restored the cheerfulness and strength of my youth, and animated my hopes for myself and the human race that I had long before this time regarded as dreams, and which I threw away in spite of the yearnings of my heart."

# IV

Friend, you have now learned to know the men who are still working with me; but I did not have them when I first came here. I did not look for them at first. After I left Stanz I was so tired and shaken, that even the ideals of my old plans for popular education began to wither up in me, and I limited my purpose at that time only to improvements of detail in the existing miserable condition of schools. It was owing simply to my needs and the circumstance that I could not even do this, and that I was forced back into the only track by which the spirit of my old purpose was attainable.

Meanwhile, I worked several months within the limits to which my own diffidence had confined me. It was a strange state of things. Ignorant and unpractical as I was, but with my power of comprehension and of simplifying, I was at the same time the lowest hedge-schoolmaster and also reformer of instruction— and this in an age, in which, since the epochs of Rousseau[36] and Basedow,[37] half the world had been set in motion for this purpose.

I really knew nothing of what they wanted and were doing. I saw only this much—the higher points of in-

struction; or rather the higher instruction itself, here
and there brought to a pitch of perfection the splendor
of which dazzled my ignorance, as sunlight dazzles a
bat. I found the middle stages of instruction raised
far above the sphere of my knowledge; and I saw even
the lowest worked here and there with an ant-like industry and fidelity the use and result of which I could
in no way mistake.

When then I looked upon the whole of instruction,
or rather on instruction as a whole, and in connection
with the real true position of the mass of individuals
who need to be instructed, the little that I could do in
spite of my ignorance seemed to me infinitely more
than that which I saw the people really received. The
more I looked upon the people, the more I found that
what seems to flow to them like a mighty stream from
books when one observes it in village or school-room,
vanishes in a mist whose moist darkness leaves the people neither wet nor dry, and gives them the advantages
of neither day nor night. I could not hide from myself that school-instruction, at least as I saw it actually
practised, was for the great majority and for the lowest
classes of no use at all.

As far as I knew it, it seemed to me like a great
house of which the upper story was bright with the
highest and best art, but inhabited by few men. In
the middle many more dwelt, but there were no steps

by which *in a human way* they could mount to the upper story; and if a few showed a desire to clamber up to the higher story, animal-fashion, whenever they were seen, sometimes a finger, here and there an arm or a leg, by which they were trying to climb, was cut off. Lastly, below lived a countless herd of men who had an equal right with the highest to sunshine and healthy air; but they were not only left in nauseous darkness, in starless dens, but by binding and blinding the eyes they were made unable even to look up to the upper stories. [3][8]

Friend, this view of things led me naturally to the conviction that it is essential and urgent, not merely to plaster over the school-evils which enervate the great majority of the men of Europe, but to heal them at the root,—that consequently half-measures in this matter will easily turn into second doses of poison, which not only cannot stop the effects of the first, but must surely double them. I certainly did not want that. Meanwhile, the consciousness began daily to develop in me that it must be absolutely impossible to remedy school-evils as a whole if one cannot succeed in reducing the mechanical formulas of instruction to those eternal laws according to which the human mind rises from mere sense-impressions to clear ideas.

This consciousness, which as I said was daily confirmed, led me also at the same time to a point of view which commanded the whole field of education. Then, though in my innermost state of mind I resembled a mouse in her hole, frightened by a cat and hardly daring to peep out, yet I was forced to see that the faint-hearted half-measures adopted in my discouragement could not only do nothing satisfactory for the needs of schools as a whole, but in circumstances that might easily arise might here and there even have the effect of making the poor children take a second dose of that opium which they were accustomed to swallow within the school walls.

But without fearing so much from the lifeless inanity of my solitary school-keeping, it displeased me more every day. I seemed in my endeavors like a seafarer, who, having lost his harpoon, tries to catch a whale with a hook. Of course it cannot be done. He must if he wants to reach shore safe and sound either take a harpoon in his hand or let the whale go. As soon as I began to comprehend what was wanted to satisfy the urgent needs of my purpose and to make the principles of instruction agree with the course of nature, I was in a like case. The claims of Nature upon my work were no longer isolated. They stood together as a connected whole before my eyes; and if, like the whale-fisher, I would reach home safe and sound, I must either give up the thought of doing anything, even the least, in my profession, or respect the unity of Nature, whithersoever it might lead me.

I did the last.   I trusted myself once and for ever
blindly to her guidance: and, after I had been knock-
ing about a will-less hedge-schoolmaster, driving the
empty A B C wheelbarrow, I threw myself suddenly
into an undertaking that included the founding of an
orphan's home, a teacher's seminary, and a boarding-
school; and  which needed in the first year an advance
of money even the tenth part of which I could not
anticipate getting into my hands.

But it succeeded.   Friend, it succeeds and it must
succeed.   Deep experience has taught me that the
human heart, even the misled government heart that
[under certain circumstances] is the hardest of all
human hearts, cannot if its fertile bud has once fully
blossomed before its eyes, resist any great and pure
effort of devotion to humanity, nor let it pine and sink
helpless away.   And, Gessner, a few of my early experiments have borne ripe fruit. [39]

Friend, man is good and desires what is good; at the
same time he desires his own welfare with it.   If he is
bad, certainly the way is blocked up *along which he
would be good.*   Oh! this blocking up is a terrible thing;
and it is so common, and man is therefore so seldom
good.   Yet I believe everywhere and always in the
human heart.   In this faith I now go on in my untrodden way as if it were on a paved Roman road.

But I wished to lead you into the confusion of ideas

through which I had to work, to gain light for myself upon the mechanical formulas of instruction and their subordination to the eternal laws of human nature.

Friend, for this purpose I will copy for you a few passages from the Report on my experiments which I made to a few friends of my Institute, six months ago.[40] They will throw much light on the progress of my ideas.

" Man," I said, in this account, " becomes man only through the Art;* but however far this guide created by ourselves goes, it must always be united with the simple course of Nature. Whatever it does, and however boldly it may lift us above the condition and even the privileges of our animal nature, yet it cannot add a hair's breadth to the spirit of that form through which our race is raised from confused sense-impressions to clear ideas. And it ought not. It fulfils its end—our ennobling—essentially in this only, that it develops us in this and in no other form; and so soon as it tries another way it throws us back into that inhuman state out of which it is destined by the Creator of our nature to raise us.

" The soul of Nature from which springs the form of development which our race requires is in itself unshaken and eternal. It is and must be the eternal and

---

* The Art, *i. e.* The art of Instruction or Education.

unshaken foundation of the Art. It also appears to the eye of every one who sees beneath the surface, in its highest splendor, only like a magnificent house that by imperceptible additions of single tiny bits has been raised upon a great everlasting rock. So long as it is inherently bound up with the rock, it rests unshakenly upon it; but it falls suddenly asunder into the tiny bits of which it was composed if the bond between it and the rock is broken in the last degree.

" So immense is the result of the Art in itself as a whole, so little and imperceptible is in every case the single thing that the Art adds to the course of Nature, or rather, builds on her foundations. Its means for the development of our faculties are limited essentially to this:—what Nature puts before us scattered over a wide area and in confusion, the Art puts together in narrower bounds and in regular sequence, and brings nearer to our five senses by associations which facilitate and strengthen our susceptibility to all impressions, and so raise our senses to present to us the objects of the world, daily in greater numbers, for a longer time, and in a more precise way. But the power of the Art depends on the harmony of its results and work, with the essential workings of Nature. Its whole action is one and the same with that of Nature.

" Man! imitate this action of high Nature, who out of the seed of the largest tree first produces a scarcely

perceptible shoot; then, just as imperceptibly, daily
and hourly, by gradual stages, unfolds first the beginnings of the stem, then the bough, then the branch,
then the extreme twig on which hangs the perishable
leaf. Consider carefully this action of great Nature,
—how she tends and perfects every single part as it is
formed, and joins on every new part to the permanent
growth of the old.

" Consider carefully how the bright blossom is unfolded from the deeply hidden bud. Consider how the
bloom of its first day's splendor is soon lost, while the
fruit, at first weak but perfectly formed, adds something important every day to all that it is already. So
quietly growing for long months, it hangs on the twig
that nourishes it until, fully ripe and perfect in all its
parts, it falls from the tree.

" Consider how mother Nature with the uprising
shoot also develops the germ of the root, and buries
the noblest part of the tree deep in the bosom of the
earth; again, how she forms the immovable stem from
the very heart of the root, and the boughs from the
very heart of the stem, and the branches from the very
heart of the boughs. How to all, even the weakest
outermost twig, she gives enough, but to none useless,
disproportionate, superfluous strength."

The mechanism of physical [human] nature is essentially subject to the same laws as those by which physi-

cal Nature generally unfolds her powers. According to these laws, all instruction should engraft the most essential parts of its subject of knowledge firmly into the very being of the human mind; then join on the less essential gradually but uninterruptedly to the most essential, and maintain all the parts of the subject, even to the outermost, in one living proportionate whole.

I now sought for laws to which the development of the human mind must, by its very nature, be subject. I knew they must be the same as those of physical Nature, and trusted to find in them a safe clue to a universal psychological method of instruction. " Man," said I to myself, while dreamily seeking this clue, " as you recognize in every physical ripening of the complete fruit the result of perfection in all its parts, so consider no human judgment ripe that does not appear to you to be the result of a complete sense-impression of all the parts of the object to be judged; but on the contrary, look upon every judgment that seems ripe before a complete observation (*Ansch.*) has been made as nothing but a worm-eaten and *therefore apparently* ripe fruit, fallen untimely from the tree."

1. Learn therefore to classify observations and complete the simple before proceeding to the complex. Try to make in every art graduated steps of knowledge, in which every new idea is only a

small, almost imperceptible addition to that which has been known before, deeply impressed and not to be forgotten.

2.  Again, bring all things essentially related to each other to that connection in your mind which they have in Nature.   Subordinate all unessential things to the essential in your idea.   Especially subordinate the impression given by the Art to that given by Nature and reality; and give to nothing a greater weight in your idea than it has in relation to your race in Nature.

3.  Strengthen and make clear the impressions of important objects by bringing them nearer to you by the Art, and letting them affect you through different senses.   Learn for this purpose the first law of physical mechanism, which makes the relative power of all influences of physical Nature depend on the physical nearness or distance of the object in contact with the senses.   Never forget that this physical nearness or distance has an immense effect in determining your positive opinions, conduct, duties, and even virtue.[41]

4.  Regard all the effects of natural law as absolutely necessary, and recognize in this necessity the result of her power by which Nature unites together the apparently heterogeneous elements of her materials for the achievement of her end.   Let the Art

with which you work through instruction upon your race, and the results you aim at, be founded upon natural law, so that all your actions may be means to this principal end, although apparently heterogeneous.

5. But the richness of its charm, and the variety of its free play cause physical necessity, or natural law, to bear the impress of freedom and independence.

Let the results of your art and your instruction, while you try to found them upon natural law, by the richness of their charm and the variety of their free play bear the impression of freedom and independence.

All these laws to which the development of human nature is subject converge towards one centre. They converge towards the centre of our whole being, and we ourselves are this centre.

Friend, all that I am, all I wish, all I might be, comes out of myself. Should not my knowledge also come out of myself ?

# V

In these several propositions I have given you threads from which I believe a general and psychological method of instruction may be woven.

They do not content me; I feel I am not in a position to state the essential laws of Nature on which these propositions rest, in all their simplicity and completeness. So far as I see they have, collectively, a threefold source.

The *first* source is Nature herself, by whose power our mind rises from misty sense-impressions to clear ideas. From this source flow the following principles, which must be recognized as foundations of the laws whose nature I am seeking.

1. All things which affect my senses are means of helping me to form correct opinions, only so far as their phenomena present to my senses their immutable, unchangeable, essential[42] nature, as distinguished from their variable appearance or their external qualities. They are, on the other hand, sources of error and deception so far as their phenomena present to my senses their accidental qualities rather than their essential characteristics.

2. To every sense-impression, perfectly and indelibly

impressed on the human mind, a whole train of
sense-impressions, more or less closely associated,
may be added easily, as it were involuntarily.

3. Now if the essential nature rather than the accidental qualities of a thing is impressed with a
force disproportionately strong upon your mind,
the organism[43] of your nature leads you of itself
in relation to this subject daily from truth to
truth.  If, on the contrary, the variable quality
rather than its essential nature is impressed with
disproportionately stronger force upon your mind,
the organism[43] of your nature leads you on this
subject daily from error to error.

4. By putting together objects whose essential nature
is the same, your insight into their inner truth becomes essentially and universally wider, sharper,
and surer.   The one-sided biased impression made
by the qualities of individual objects, as opposed
to the impression that their nature should make
upon you, becomes weakened.   Your mind is protected against being swallowed up by the isolated
force of single, separate impressions of qualities;
and you are saved from the danger of thoughtlessly
confusing the external qualities with the essential
nature of things, and from fantastically filling your
head with incidental matters to the detriment of
clearer insight.   It follows, the more a man makes

essential, comprehensive, and general views of things his own, the less can limited, one-sided views lead him astray about the nature of his object. Again, the less he is exercised in comprehensive sense-impressions of Nature, the easier can single views of an object, under varying conditions, confuse in him the essential view, and even blot it out.

5. The most complex sense-impressions rest upon simple elements. When you are perfectly clear about these, the most complex will become simple.

6. The more senses you have questioned about the nature or appearance of a thing, the more accurate will be your knowledge of it.

These seem to me the principles of the physical mechanism, which are themselves derived from the very nature of our minds. With these are connected the general laws of this mechanism itself, of which I now only say, " Perfection is the great law of Nature; all imperfection is untrue."

The *second* source of these physico-mechanical laws is the power of sense-impression intimately interwoven with the emotional side of my nature.

This wavers in all its actions between the desire of learning and knowing everything, and that of enjoying everything, which stops the impulse towards knowing and learning. As a mere physical power, the laziness of my race is stimulated by curiosity, while curiosity is lulled again by laziness. But neither the stimulus of the one nor the sedative of the other has in itself more than physical value. Yet curiosity has great value as a sense-foundation for my power of inquiry, and inertia is valuable as a sense-foundation for cool judgment. We reach all our learning through the infinite charm that the tree of knowledge has for our nature through our senses; while, owing to the principle of inertia that checks our easy superficial flitting about from one sense-impression to another, a man in many ways ripens to truth before he expresses it.

But our truth-amphibia know nothing of this ripening. They croak truth before they have an inkling of it, let alone know it. They cannot do otherwise.

They have not the power of quadrupeds to stand firm on the ground; the fins of fishes to swim over gulfs; the wings of birds to soar above the clouds. They know as little of *unbiased* sense-impressions of objects as Eve; and when like Eve they swallow the unripe fruit of truth, they share her fate.

The *third* source of these physico-mechanical laws lies in the relation of my outer condition to my power of learning.

Man is bound to his nest; and if he hangs it upon a hundred threads and describes a hundred circles round it, what does he more than the spider, who hangs her nest upon a hundred threads and describes a hundred circles round it ? And what is the difference between a somewhat larger or smaller spider ? The essence of their doing is, they sit in the centre of the circle they describe; but man chooses not the centre in which he spins and weaves; he learns all the realities of the world in their mere physical aspects, absolutely in proportion as the objects of the world that reach his sense-impressions approach the centre in which he spins and weaves [for the most part, without his help].

# VI

Friend! You see at least the pains I take to make the theory of my doings clear to you. Let this painstaking be a kind of excuse when you feel how little I have succeeded.

Since my twentieth year, I have been incapable of philosophic thought, in the true sense of the word.

Happily for the practical working out of my plan, I wanted none of that philosophy that seems to me so tiresome. I lived at the highest nerve-tension on every point in the circle wherein I worked. I knew what I wanted, took no thought for the morrow, and felt at the moment what was really necessary for the subject that particularly interested me. And if my imagination drove me to-day a hundred steps farther than I found firm ground, to-morrow, I retraced these hundred steps.

This happened thousands of times. Thousands and thousands of times I believed I was approaching my goal, and suddenly found this apparent end to be only a new mountain against which I stumbled. So I went on; particularly when the principles and laws of physical mechanism began to become clearer to me, I thought directly it needed no more than simply to use them in the branches of instruction which the experience of ages has put into the hands of the human race for the development of the faculties, and these I looked upon as the elements of all art and knowledge. *i. e.* reading, writing, arithmetic, etc.

But as I tried to do this, increasing experience gradually developed the conviction that these branches of instruction cannot be regarded as the elements of all art and of all knowledge. On the contrary, they must be subordinate to far more general views of the subject. But the consciousness of this truth, so important for instruction, which was developed by working in these branches, appeared to me for a long time in isolated glimpses only; and then only in connection with the special branch with which each separate experience was connected.

Thus I found in teaching to read the necessity of its subordination to the power of talking; and in the endeavor to find a means of teaching children to talk, I came on the principle of joining this art to the sequences by which Nature rises from sound to word, and from word, gradually to language.

Again, I found in the effort to teach writing the need of subordinating this art to that of drawing; and in the efforts to teach drawing, the combination with and subordination of this art to that of measurement. Again, teaching spelling developed in me the want of a book for early childhood, through which I trusted to raise the actual knowledge of three-and four-year-old children above the knowledge of seven-and eight-year-old school-children. These experiences that I learned practically led me indeed to isolated helps in instruction, but at the same time made me feel that I did not yet know the true scope and inner depth of my subject.

I long sought for a common psychological origin for all these arts of instruction, because I was convinced that only through this might it be possible to discover the *form*[+] in which the cultivating of mankind is determined through the very laws of Nature itself. It is evident this form is founded on the general organization of the mind, by means of which our understanding binds together in imagination the impressions which are received by the senses from Nature into a whole, that is into an idea, and gradually unfolds this idea clearly.

" Every line, every measure, every word," said I to myself, " is a result of understanding that is produced by ripened sense-impressions and must be regarded as a means towards the progressive clearing up of our ideas." Again, all instruction is essentially nothing but this. Its principles must therefore be derived from the immutable first form of human mental development.

Everything depends on the exact knowledge of this

prototype. I therefore once more began to keep my eye on these beginning-points from which it must be derived.

" The world," said I in this reverie, " lies before our eyes like a sea of confused sense-impressions, flowing one into the other. If our development through Nature only is not sufficiently rapid and unimpeded, the business of instruction is to remove the confusion of these sense-impressions; to separate the objects one from another; to put together in imagination those that resemble or are related to each other: and in this way to make all clear to us, and by perfect clearness in these to raise in us distinct ideas. It does this when it presents these confused and blurred sense-impressions to us *one by one ;* then places these separate sense-impressions in different changing positions before our eyes; and lastly, brings them into connection with the whole cycle of our previous knowledge.

So our learning grows from confusion to definiteness; from definiteness to plainness; and from plainness to perfect clearness.

But Nature, in her progress towards this development, is constant to the great law that makes the clearness of my knowledge depend on the nearness or distance of the object in touch with my senses. All that surrounds you reaches your senses, other things being equal, confused and difficult to make clear to yourself in proportion to its distance from your senses; on the contrary, everything that reaches your senses is distinct and easy for you to make clear and plain in proportion as it approaches your five senses.

You are as a physical living being nothing but your five senses; consequently the clearness or mistiness of your ideas must absolutely and essentially rest upon the nearness or distance with which all external objects touch these five senses,—that is, yourself, the centre, because your ideas converge in you.

You, yourself, are the centre of all your sense-impressions; you are also yourself an object for your sense-impressions. It is easier to make all that is within you clear and plain than all that is without you. All that you feel of yourself is in itself a *definite* sense-impression; only that which is without can be a confused sense-impression for you. It follows that the course of your knowledge, in so far as it touches yourself, is a step shorter than when it comes from something outside yourself.

All that you know of yourself, you know clearly; all that you yourself know is in you, and in itself clear through you. It follows that this road to clear ideas is easier and safer in this direction than in any other; and among all that is clear nothing can be clearer than this principle: man's knowledge of truth comes from his knowledge of himself.

Friend! Living but vague ideas of the elements of instruction whirled about my mind for a long time in this way. So I depicted them in my Report without at that time being able to discover the unbroken connection between them and the laws of physical mechanism;[45] and without being able to define with certainty the beginning-points from which the sequences of our views of the Art should proceed, or rather the form by which it might be possible to *determine the improvement* of mankind through his own essential nature. At last, suddenly, like a *Deus ex machinâ*, came the thought— The means of making clear all knowledge gained by sense-impression comes from *number, form,* and *language.* It suddenly seemed to throw a new light on what I was trying to do.

Now after my long struggle, or rather my wandering reverie, I aimed wholly and simply at finding out how a cultivated man behaves and must behave when he wishes to distinguish any object which appears misty and confused to his eyes, and gradually to make it clear to himself.

In this case he will observe three things:—

1. How many and what kinds of objects are before him?

2. Their appearance, form, or outline.

3. Their names; how he may represent each of them by a sound or word.

The result of this action in such a man manifestly pre-supposes the following ready-formed powers:

1. The power of recognizing unlike objects according to the outline, and of representing to oneself what is contained within it.

2. That of stating the number of these objects, and representing them to himself as one or many.

3. That of representing objects, their number and form, by speech, and making them unforgetable.

I also thought *number*, *form*, and *language* are, together, the elementary means of instruction, because the whole sum of the external properties of any object is comprised in its outline and its number, and is brought home to my consciousness through language.

It must then be an immutable law of the Art to start from and work within this threefold principle:

1. To teach children to look upon every object that is brought before them as a unit: that is, as separated from those with which it seems connected.

2. To teach them the form of every object: that is, its *size* and *proportions*.

3. As soon as possible to make them acquainted with all the words and names descriptive of objects known to them.

And as the instruction of children should proceed from these three elementary points, it is evident that the first efforts of the Art should be directed to the primary faculties of counting, measuring, and speaking, which lie at the basis of all accurate knowledge of objects of sense.   We should cultivate them with the strictest psychological Art, endeavoring to strengthen and make them strong, and to bring them, as a means of development and culture, to the highest pitch of simplicity, consistency, and harmony.

The only difficulty which struck me in the recogniton of these elementary points was the question: Why are *all* qualities of things that we know through our five senses not just as much elementary points of knowledge as number, form, and names ?   But I soon found that all possible objects have absolutely number, form, and names; but the other characteristics, known through our five senses, are not common to all objects. I found then such an essential and definite distinction between the number, form, and names of things and their other qualities, that I could not regard other qualities as elementary points of human knowledge. Again, I found that all other qualities can be included under these elementary points; that consequently, in instructing children, all other qualities of objects must be immediately connected with form, number, and names.   I saw now that through knowing the unity, form, and name of any object, my knowledge of it becomes *precise;* by gradually learning its other qualities my knowledge of it becomes *clear;*

through my consciousness of all its characteristics, my knowledge of it becomes *distinct*.

Then I found, further, that all our knowledge flows from three elementary powers:

1. From the power of making sounds, the origin of language.

2. From the *indefinite, simple sensuous-power of forming images*, out of which arises the consciousness of all forms.

3. From the *definite*, no longer merely *sensuous-power of imagination*, from which must be derived consciousness of unity, and with it the power of calculation and arithmetic.

I thought, then, that the art of educating our race must be joined to the first and simplest results of these three primary powers—sound, form, and number; and that instruction in separate parts can never have a satisfactory effect upon our nature as a whole, if these three simple results of our primary powers are not recognized as the common starting-point of all instruction, determined by Nature herself. In consequence of this recognition, they must be fitted into forms which flow universally and harmoniously from the results of these three elementary powers; and which tend essentially and surely to make all instruction a steady, unbroken development of these three elementary powers, used together and considered equally important. In this way only is it possible to lead us in all three branches from vague to precise sense-impressions, from precise sense-impressions to clear images, and from clear images to distinct ideas.

Here at last I find the Art in general and essential harmony with Nature; or rather, with the prototype by which Nature makes clear to us the objects of the world in their essence and utmost simplicity. The problem is solved: *How to find a common origin of all methods and arts of instruction, and with it a form by which the development of our race might be decided through the essence of our own very nature.* The difficulties are removed of applying *mechanical laws*, which I recognize as the foundation of all human instruction, to the *form of instruction* which the experience of ages has put into the hands of mankind for the development of the race; that is, to apply them to reading, writing, arithmetic, and so on.

## VII.

The first elementary means of instruction is, then,

### SOUND

This leads to the following special means of instruction:—

I. *Sound teaching*,[46] or training the organs of speech.

II. *Word teaching*, or teaching about single objects.

III. *Language teaching*, or the means whereby we are led to express ourselves accurately about well-known objects, and about all we know of them.

### 1. SOUND TEACHING

Is divided into teaching sounds spoken, and sounds sung.

#### a. Of Sounds Spoken

In regard to these, we cannot leave it to chance whether they be brought to the child's ear sooner or later, combined or separately. It is important that they reach his consciousness in their whole compass as early as possible.

This consciousness should be perfect in him before his power of speech is formed; and the power of repeating them easily should be complete before the

(150)

forms of letters are put before his eyes, or the first reading lessons begun.

The Spelling Book[47] must therefore contain all the sounds of which speech consists; and these should in every family be brought to the ear of the child in the cradle, and be deeply impressed and made unforgetable by constant repetition,[48] even before he is able to utter a single one.

No one can imagine, for it is not seen, how the utterance of these simple sounds, *ba, ba, ba, da, da, da, ma, ma, ma, la, la, la,* etc., may rouse the observation of infants and please them; nor what can be gained for the general power of learning in children by the early knowledge of these sounds.

\* In consequence of this principle of the importance of consciousness of sounds and tones before the child can imitate them, and of the conviction that the kind of objects and pictures that lie before the eyes of the infant can be as little a matter of indifference as the sounds that are brought to his ears, I have prepared a book for mothers, in which I have not only represented

---

\* These attempts were afterwards found to be superfluous, owing to a deeper knowledge of the psychological course of development and the gradation in the foundation of our knowledge, and were no longer used. This whole statement must be regarded as only a vague aspiration towards methods of education, about the nature of which I was far from clear.—Pestalozzi.

by illuminated woodcuts the beginnings of number and form, but also the other most essential characteristics in objects which our five senses make evident to us. Through a knowledge of many names, thus strengthened and enlivened by all sorts of observation, I prepare for and make his future reading easy, just as by making impressions of sounds precede letters I prepare for and make this work easy for the child, at this same age. By means of this book I make these sounds at home in his head, if I may so express myself, before he can utter a syllable.

I shall accompany these tables of sense-impression for earlier childhood with a book of methods, in which every word that the child should use about the object represented is expressed so exactly that even the most unpractised mother can work sufficiently for my purpose, because she need not add a word to what I say.

Thus, by means of the book prepared for mothers, and by constantly hearing the sounds in the Spelling Book, the child, as soon as his organs of speech are formed, must be accustomed to imitate a few of the sounds of the Spelling Book several times a day, with just the same playful ease with which he imitates purposeless sounds.

This book differs from all preceding books in this:—Its form of teaching proceeds generally from the vowels, which can be apprehended by the pupil himself.   Adding consonants one by one, before and after the syllables, evidently makes the art of reading and pronouncing more easy.

This was our way.   After every vowel we added on one consonant after another, from *b* to *z*, and so first formed the simple easy syllables, *ab ad af*, etc.; then put those consonants before these simple syllables which actually accompany them in ordinary speech.

For example—

*ab, b, g, sh, st,*   b,   ab,

g,   ab,

sh,   ab,

st,   ab, etc.

So we formed first easy syllables by simply adding consonants to all the vowels, and afterwards more difficult words by the addition of more syllables.   This ensures a constant repetition of simple sounds, and an orderly putting together of all syllables resembling each other from having a common basis.   This gives an unforgetable impression of their sound, and makes learning to read very easy.

The special advantages of this book are—

1. The children are kept so long at exercises in spelling syllables that their faculties are sufficiently formed in this direction.

2. By the use of similar sounds the repetition of the same form is made pleasant to the children,

and in this way the object of making an indelible impression is more easily attained.

3. It helps the children quickly to pronounce at a glance any new word that is formed by adding single consonants to others that are well known, without being obliged to spell it; and afterwards to be able to learn to spell these compound words by heart. This makes writing them correctly afterwards very easy.

In the short directions for using this book given in the preface, mothers are asked to pronounce to the children before they can speak these sequences of sounds several times every day, and in different ways, in order to rouse their observation and to accustom them to these sounds. This pronouncing must be carried on with redoubled zeal and be begun again from the beginning as soon as the children begin to talk, in order to induce them to imitate, and thereby teach them to talk quickly.

In order to make easy to the children the knowledge of letters, which must precede spelling, I have added large printed letters to the book, so that the children can better observe the differences between them.

These letters are, each one separately, glued upon stiff paper, and given to the child one by one. We begin with the different vowels, painted red, which they must know perfectly and be able to pronounce before we can go farther.   Afterwards they are shown the consonants one by one, but always in connection with a vowel, because they cannot be pronounced alone.

As soon as the children, partly by means of these special exercises, partly by means of real spelling (of which I will speak directly), have begun to be tolerably acquainted with the letters, we can change them for the threefold letters, also accompanying this book, on which, over the German printed letters (that may now be smaller) stand German written letters, and under them Roman letters.   Then let the child spell every syllable with the middle form already known to him, and repeat it in the other two; so without losing time he learns to read the threefold alphabet.

The fundamental rule of spelling is that all syllables are only additions, by means of consonants, to the original sound of a vowel; and that the vowel is always the foundation of the syllable.   This vowel also will be first laid down, or put on the hanging board (which should have a groove on its upper and lower edge for the letters to stand in, in which they can easily be shifted about).   This vowel will, according to the guide, gradually have consonants added before and after, $a$—$ab$—$b\ ab$—$g\ ab$, and so on.   Then every sylla- ble should be pronounced by the teacher and repeated by the children, until they cannot forget it. Then the letters are repeated in and out of their order (the first, the third, and so on); then syllables, which are hidden from them, are spelt by heart.

It is particularly necessary in the first paragraphs of the book to proceed very slowly, and never to go on to anything new until the old is indelibly impressed upon the children; because this is the foundation of all instruction in reading: all that follows is built upon it by small and gradual additions.

When the children have reached a certain readiness in spelling in this manner, we can change it for other methods. For example, we can put the letters of a word one after the other until it is complete, and let each of the letters be spoken alone and together with the next, *e. g.*, *G—Ga—Gar—Gard—Garde—Garden—Gardene—Gardener*. Then by taking away the letters one by one, we go back in the same way and repeat these again and again, until the children can spell the word perfectly by heart. We can in this way spell the word backwards.

At last the word is divided into syllables, and each is pronounced in and out of its order according to its number. One special advantage for school instruction is that the children may be accustomed *from the beginning* to pronounce all together and at the same moment every sound that is given them, or that which they are called upon to pronounce by the number of the letter or syllable, so that sounds uttered by all are heard as one sound. This makes the art of teaching quite mechanical, and works with incredible force upon the children's senses.

When these spelling exercises on the board are quite finished, the book can be put into the child's hands as his first reading book and used till he can read perfectly easily in it.

### b. *Of Sounds Sung*

So much for teaching sounds spoken. I shall now say a word about teaching singing sounds. But since song proper cannot be regarded as a means of rising from vague sense impressions to clear ideas, but rather as a faculty that must be developed at another time, and for another purpose, I will put off treating it till I take a bird's-eye view of education. I shall only say here that, according to the general principle, the teaching of singing should begin with the simplest; complete this, and only gradually proceed from one complete step to the beginning of a new exercise; and it should never tend through an unfounded belief in the stability of the foundation to check or confuse the faculties. [49]

### 2. WORD TEACHING

The second special means of instruction flowing from the power of making sounds, or the elementary

method of sound, is word or rather name teaching.  I
have already said, the child must receive his first
guidance in this direction, from the *Mother's Book*[50].
This is so arranged that the most important objects of
the world, especially those which, like *race,* and *kind,*
include a whole series of objects, should be all spoken
about, and mothers rendered able to make the child
quite familiar with their right names, so that the children are prepared from the earliest age for *name-*
*teaching;* that is, for the second special method of
instruction, founded upon the power of making sounds.

This name-teaching consists of lists of names of the
most important objects in all divisions of the kingdom
of nature, history, geography, human callings and relations.   These lists of words are given to the child
simply as exercises in reading, immediately after the
completion of his Spelling Book; and experience has
shown me that it is possible to bring the children to
learn these lists of names perfectly by heart in the
time which is given to complete their power of reading.   The gain to the children at this time of so wide
and complete a knowledge of so many and such comprehensive lists of names, is immense for making later
instruction easier, [and is only to be regarded as the
chaotic collection of materials for a house that will be
built later.]

## 3. LANGUAGE TEACHING

The third special means of instruction, based on the power of making sounds, is language-teaching proper. And here I arrive at the point at which the special form begins to disclose itself, according to which the Art, by using the special characteristic of our race, language, can keep pace with the course of Nature in our development. But what do I say? The form discloses itself by which man, according to the will of the Creator, should take the instruction of our race out of the hands of blind and senseless Nature, and put it into the guidance of those better powers which he has developed in himself for ages. The form discloses itself, independent, like the human race, by which man can give a precise and comprehensive direction to and hasten the development of these faculties for whose development Nature has given him powers and means but no guidance. This she can never give, because he is man. The form unfolds itself by which man can do all this, without destroying the loftiness and simplicity of the course of physical nature, or the harmony our physical development always has, or robbing ourselves by a single fraction of a hair of that uniform care that mother Nature confers upon our physical development.

All this must be aimed at through the perfect art of language-teaching and the highest psychology, in order

to bring the mechanism of nature's march from confused sense-impressions to clear ideas, to the greatest
perfection.   This I am far from being able to do, and
I feel verily like the voice of one crying in the wilder-
ness.

But the Egyptian who first bound the bent shovel
to the horns of the ox, and so taught it the work of
the digger, led the way to the discovery of the plough,
though he did not bring it to perfection.

Let my merit be only the bending the shovel, and
binding it to a new horn.   But why do I speak in
parables ?   I will say what I want to say straight out,
without beating about the bush.

I would take school instruction out of the hands of
the old order of decrepit, stammering, journeymen-
teachers, as well as from the new weak ones, who are
generally no better for popular instruction, and entrust
it to the undivided powers of Nature herself; to the
light that God kindles and ever keeps alive in the
hearts of fathers and mothers;  to the interest of
parents who desire that their children should grow up
in favor with God and man.

But in order to define the form, or rather, the
different methods of teaching language by which we
can attain to this purpose, that is, by which we must
be led in order to be able to express ourselves clearly
about objects that are becoming known to us, and all

that we can learn about them, we must ask ourselves:—

1. What is the end of language for man?

2. What are the means, or rather, what is the course of progress by which nature leads us to this end by the gradual development of the art of speaking?

1. The final end of language is obviously to lead our race from vague sense-impressions to clear ideas.

2. The means, by which it leads us gradually towards this end unquestionably follows in this order:—

    *a.* We recognize every object as a whole, or generally name it as a unit—*i. e.* as one object.

    *b.* We gradually become acquainted with its characteristics and learn to name them.

    *c.* We acquire through language the power of defining the qualities of things by verbs and adverbs, and of making the changes caused by change of condition clear to ourselves, by altering the words themselves and their arrangement.

    I. I have spoken above of the steps to be taken to learn to name objects.

    II. Steps to learn and to name the qualities of objects divide themselves into—

    *a.* Teaching the child to express himself clearly about number and form. Number and form, being the special elementary properties of all things, are the two comprehensive general abstractions of physical nature on which all other means of making our ideas clear depend.

*b.* Teaching the child to express himself exactly about all the other qualities of things, besides form and number (about those that we know through our five senses as well as those that we learn, not by simple sense-impression, but through our powers of imagination and judgment).

The primary physical generalizations, number and form, that we have in accordance with the experience of ages, by using our five senses, learned to abstract from the qualities of things, must be early and familiarly brought to the child, not only as inherent characteristics of special things, but as physical generalizations. He must not only be able early to call a round or a square thing, round or square, but he must as soon as possible be impressed with the idea of roundness or squareness as a unity, as a pure abstraction. This will enable him to connect all that he meets in nature round, square, simple, or complex, with the exact word that expresses this idea. Here also we see the reason why language must be considered as a means of expressing form and number, as distinguished from the way in which we may regard it as a means of expressing all the other qualities of objects that Nature teaches us through our five senses.

I therefore begin, in the book for early childhood, to lead the children to a clear consciousness of these generalizations. This book contains a comprehensive survey of the ordinary methods, as well as the simplest way of making the child understand the first properties of numbers.

Farther steps towards this end must, like the language-exercises, be reserved for a later time, and be connected with the special treatment of number and form. These, as elements of our knowledge, must be considered after a complete survey of the exercises in language.

The illustrations of the first instruction-book, the Mother's Book for infants, are in all their variety so chosen that all kinds of physical generalizations that are learnt through our five senses, are spoken of, and mothers are enabled to make the child familiarly acquainted with the most exact expressions, without any trouble to themselves.

But in whatever relates to those qualities of things that are learnt, not directly through our five senses, but through the intervention of our powers of comparison, imagination, and abstraction, I stick to my principle of making no kind of human judgment apparently prematurely ripe; but I use the unavoidable knowledge of such abstract words as children of this age possess merely as memory work, and as easy food for their fancy and power of guessing.

On the other hand, in respect to objects that can be learnt directly through our five senses, I take the following measures to enable the child to express himself accurately as soon as possible.

I take out of the dictionary substantives distinguished by striking characteristics known through our five senses, and put the adjectives that express these characteristics next to them.   For example:—

*eel,*      slippery, worm-like, leather-skinned

*carrion,*  dead, stinking

*evening,*  quiet, bright, cool, rainy

*axle,*     strong, weak, greasy

*field,*    sandy, loamy, manured, fertile, profitable, unprofitable

Then I invert the process, and find adjectives that describe the striking characteristics of objects learnt through our senses; then I put the substantive that has the characteristic described by the adjective next to it.   For example:—

*round,* ball, hat, moon, sun

*light,* feather, down, air

*heavy,* gold, lead, oak-wood

*warm,* stoves, summer days, flame

*high,* towers, mountains, trees, giants

*deep,* seas, lakes, cellars, graves

*soft,* flesh, wax, butter

*elastic,* steel springs, whalebone, etc.

I try however in no way to lessen the free play of the child's individual thought by the completeness of these illustrations, but only give a few illustrative facts that strike his mind, and ask directly:* " What else do you know like this ? " In most cases, the children find new facts within the sphere of their experience, and very often some that would not occur to the teacher. In this way the circle of their knowledge is made wider and more exact than it could ever be through catechizing, or at least only by a hundredfold more skill and trouble.

In all catechizing the child is fettered, partly by the limits of the precise idea about which he is catechized; partly by the form in which he is catechized; and lastly, but certainly, by the limits of the teacher's knowledge, and still more by the teacher's anxious care that he should not be drawn beyond the circle of his knowledge. Friend! what terrible barriers for the child; and they have been wholly removed by my method.

This done, I try to make the child, who is in many ways acquainted with the objects of the world, still more clear about the objects so far known to him by the further use of the dictionary.

For this purpose I divide this great witness of a former age under four headings:

---

* This question is repeated in Ed. I.

1. Descriptive geography.
2. History.
3. Physical science.
4. Natural history.

But to avoid unnecessary repetition of the same word, and to make the form of teaching as short as possible, I divide these principal sections into forty sub-divisions, and show the children the names of objects in these sub-divisions only.

Then I consider the principal object of my sense-impression, myself,—or rather the whole series of names that indicate myself in language; while I bring what the great witness of the ancients, language, says about men, under the following heads:

1. What does it say of man, regarded as a *mere physical being*, in relation to the animal kingdom ?
2. What does it say of him, as striving upwards through *the social state* to independence ?
3. What does it say of him as struggling upwards, through the forces of his heart, mind, and skill, to a view of himself and his surroundings higher than the animal's ?[51]

I divide these three heads into forty sub-divisions, and bring them before the children only in these sub-divisions.*

The first arrangement in these series, in both departments, about men as well as material objects,

---

* All these attempts were subsequently abandoned as the results of immature opinions.—Pestalozzi.

should be simply alphabetical, without any meaning. They are to be used simply for making things gradually clear, by putting together similar sense-impressions and ideas gained by sense-impressions.

When this is done; when the witness of the ancients has been thus used to put all that exists into simple alphabetical order, the second question arises,—

How does the Art arrange these objects later, after closer inspection? Then a new work begins. The same series of words that the child knows perfectly well up to the seventieth or eightieth row, merely alphabetically, must now be shown him anew, in all these sub-divisions and in all the classifications by which these subdivisions are further artificially divided; and he must be enabled to form sequences for himself, and to arrange them after the following plan.

The different classes into which the objects are divided are put at the head of each column, and indicated by numbers, abbreviations, or other convenient signs.

In the first reading lesson, the child must thoroughly learn the different classes of the principal divisions, and then, if he finds in the series of words the sign of the class to which it belongs, he is able at the first glance to see to which class the object belongs, and so by himself to change the alphabetical into a scientific nomenclature.

I do not know whether it is necessary to make the matter clearer by an example; it seems almost super-fluous, but I will do it in consequence of the novelty of the form. One of the sub-divisions of Europe is Germany. Now the children are first made perfectly familiar with the division of Germany into 10 circles. Then the towns of Germany are put before them, in reading, first in alphabetical order; but afterwards every town is indicated by the number of the circle to which it belongs. As soon as they can readily read these towns, they learn the connection between these num-bers and the sub-divisions of the chief headings, and in a few hours the child is able to arrange the whole series of German towns according to the sub-divisions of the principal headings.

Suppose, for example, he sees the following German towns with their numbers:—

| | | |
|---|---|---|
| Aachen, 8. | Allenbach, 5. | Altkirchen, 8. |
| Aalen, 3. | Allendorf, 5. | Altona, 10. |
| Abenberg, 4. | Allersperg, 2. | Altorf, 1. |
| Aberthran, 11. | Alschaufen, 3. | Altranstädt, 9. |
| Acken, | Alsleben, 10. | Altwasser, 13. |
| Adersbach, 11. | Altbunzlau, 11. | Amberg, 2. |
| Agler, 1. | Altena, 8. | Ambras, 1. |
| Ahrbergen, 10. | Altenau, 10. | Amöneburg, 6. |
| Aigremont, 8. | Altenberg, 9. | Andernach, 6. |
| Ala, 1. | Altenburg, 9. | |
| Alkerdissen, 8. | Altensalza, 10. | |

He uses them in this way: " Aachen is in the Westphalian circle; Abenberg in the Franconian circle; Acken in the Lower Saxon circle," etc.

So the child is enabled at the first glance at the number or sign which belongs to the heading, to determine to what class every word of this series belongs, and, as I said, to turn the alphabetical into a scientific nomenclature.

And here I find myself on the boundry where my own work ends, and where the powers of my children should have reached a point when they should be able in any kind of knowledge to which their inclination leads them to use, independently, such helps as already exist, but which are of such a nature that until now only a privileged few could use them.

*So far and no further* do I wish to come. I did not and do not wish to teach the world art and science; I know none. I did and do wish to make the learning of the first beginning-points easy for the common people, who are forsaken and left to run wild; to open the doors of art, which are the doors of manliness, to the poor and weak of the land; and if I can, to set fire to the barrier that keeps the humbler citizens of Europe in respect to that individual power which is the foundation of all true art far behind the barbarians of the south and north, because, in the midst of our vaunted and valued general enlightenment, it shuts out nine men in ten from the social rights of men, from the right to be educated, or at least from the possibility of using that right.

May this barrier burn above my grave in blazing flames. Now indeed I know that I lay only a weak coal in dank wet straw—but I see a wind, no longer afar off, and it will fan the coal; gradually the wet straw round me will be dried, will become warm, will kindle and burn. Yes, Gessner! however wet it is now round me, it will burn, it will burn!

But while I see myself so far advanced in the second special method of teaching language, I find I have not yet touched upon the third method, that should lead to the final end of education—the clearing-up of our ideas.

    *c.* Teaching the child to distinguish clearly by speech the connection of objects with each other, in their varying conditions of number, time, and proportion; or rather, to make still clearer the nature, properties, and powers of all objects that we have already learned to know by name, and have to some degree made clear by putting together their names and qualities.

Here appear the foundations on which real grammar should rest, and in this way progress will be made towards the final end of education—the clearing up of ideas.

Here also I prepare the children for the first step by a very simple but psychological instruction in speech. Without letting fall a word about forms and rules, let the mother first repeat before the child simple sentences only, as exercises. These should be imitated, as much for the sake of exercising the organs of speech as for the sake of the sentences themselves. We must clearly distinguish between these two objects—exercise in pronunciation, and learning words as language; and practise the first by itself, independently of the second. When the meaning and pronunciation are understood, the mother should repeat the following kinds of sentences: —

Father is kind.

The butterfly has gay wings.

The cow eats grass.

The fir has a straight stem.

When the child has said these sentences so often that the repetition is easy to him, the mother asks: Who is kind? What has gay wings? And then backwards: What is father? What has the butterfly? etc. And then she goes on:

*Who or what are?*

Beasts of prey are flesh-eating.

Stags are light of foot.

The roots are wide-spreading.

*Who or what has?    What has he or it?*

The lion has strength.

Man has reason.

The dog has a good nose.

The elephant has a trunk.

*Who or what have?   What have they?*

Plants have roots.

Fish have fins.

Birds have wings.

Cattle have horns.

*Who wishes?   What does he wish?*

The hungry man wishes to eat.

The creditor wishes to be paid.

The prisoner wishes to be free.

*Who wish?   What do they wish?*

Sensible people wish for what is right.

Foolish people wish for what they fancy.

Children wish to play.

Tired people wish to rest.

*Who or what can?   What can he or it do?*

The fish can swim.

The bird can fly.

The cat can climb.

The squirrel can jump.

The ox can toss.

The horse can kick.

*Who can?   What can they do?*

Tailors can sew.

Donkeys can carry.

Oxen can plough.

Pigs can grunt.

Men can talk.

Dogs can bark.

Lions can roar.

Bears can growl.

Larks can sing.

*Who or what must be?*   *What must they be?*

The draught-ox must be harnessed.

The horse must be ridden.

The ass must be loaded.

The cow must be milked.

The pig must be killed.

The hare must be hunted.

The right must be done.

Laws must be obeyed.

*Who or what must do?*   *What must they do?*

Raindrops must fall.

Fettered men must go together.

The vanquished must submit.

Debtors must pay.

Thus I go on through all the declensions and conjugations, connecting this second step immediately with the first, and particularly dwelling upon the verbs, according to a plan of which I give the following examples:

Verb and object simply connected.

*Attend*   to the teacher's words.

*Breathe*   through the lungs.

*Fell*   a tree.

*Bind*   a sheaf, etc.

Then follows the second exercise in putting verbs together.

*To tend.*   I *tend* the sheep.   I *attend* to the teacher's words, to my duty and my property;* I *attend* to my duty and my work.   I *contend* against wrong.   I do not *pretend* to be better than I am.   I *extend* my possessions.   I *intend* to buy a house.   I must *superintend* those men.   So far as a child pays *attention* to anything, he is *attentive* or *inattentive*.

*Breathe.*   I breathe hard, lightly, quickly, slowly. I breathe again, if I have lost my breath and recovered it.   I breathe air in.   The dying man breathes his last.

Then I go on to repeat these exercises with gradually extending additions, and so get to more complicated and descriptive sentences, *e. g.*—

I shall.

I shall preserve.

I shall preserve my health in no other way.

---

* Literal translation impossible; an illustration is attempted.—L. E. H.

After all that I have suffered I shall preserve my health in no other way.

After all that I suffered in my illness, I shall preserve my health in no other way.

After all that I have suffered in my illness, I shall preserve my health in no other way than by moderation.

After all that I have suffered in my illness, I shall preserve my health in no other way than by the greatest moderation.

After all that I have suffered in my illness, I shall preserve my health in no other way than by the greatest moderation and regularity.

After all that I have suffered in my illness, I shall preserve my health in no other way than by the greatest moderation and general regularity.

All these sentences should be separately repeated in all the persons of the verb, *e. g.*—

I shall preserve.

Thou shalt preserve.

He shall preserve, etc.

I shall preserve my health.

Thou shalt preserve thy health, etc.

The same sentences should be repeated in other tenses.

I have preserved.

Thou hast preserved, etc.

With these sentences, thus deeply impressed upon the children, we take care to choose those that are particularly instructive, stimulating, and suitable to their special case.

With these I give examples of descriptions of real objects, in order to strengthen and use the power given to the children by these exercises.

For example:—

*A bell* is a wide, thick, round bowl, open below, usually hanging free, growing narrower towards the top, rounded above like an egg, and having in the middle a vertical and freely hanging clapper, that by a quick movement of the bowl is knocked from side to side, thus producing a sound we call ringing.

*To walk* is to move on step by step.

*To stand* is to rest upon the legs, with the body upright or vertical.

*To lie* is to rest on something, with the body in a horizontal position.

*To sit* is to rest on something in such a position that the body makes two angles.   *To kneel* is to rest on the legs when they form an angle at the knee.

*To courtesy* is to let the body be lowered by bending the knee.

*To bow* is to bend the body forwards from an upright position.

*To climb* is to move up or down by clinging with the hands and feet.

*To ride* is to be carried sitting upon an animal.

*To drive* is to be carried in a moving vehicle.

*To fall* is to be forced to move from above downwards by one's own weight.[52]

*To dig* is to lift earth and turn it over with a spade.

I should like to conclude these exercises in language with a legacy[53] to my pupils, after my death. In this I put down as they occur to me significant verbs which at the most critical moments of my life especially attract my attention to the subjects which they indicate. By this exercise I try to connect these verbs with truths about life, living knowledge gained by sense-impression, and soul-inspiring thoughts about all that men do and suffer, *e. g.*—[54]

*To breathe.* Man! thy life hangs upon a breath. When thou snortest like a madman, and swallowest the pure air of earth like poison into thy lungs—what dost thou but hasten to make thyself breathless and to deliver from thy snorting the men annoyed by it.

*To improve the soil.* In order to improve the soil, the earth was divided. Thus property arose, the right to which is to be found only in this purpose, and can never be opposed to it. But if the State allows to the proprietor or itself an oppressive power over human nature, in opposition to this purpose, feelings are developed in the injured masses the bad consequences of which can be averted only by a wise return to the spirit of the original limitations of the purpose, for the sake of which the earth, freely given by God to man, was divided by him into special plots.[55]

*To express.* Thou art angry because thou canst not always express thyself as thou wouldst. Do not be angry that thou art forced, even against thy will, to take time to become wise.

But it is time I ended this subject.

I have dwelt long upon language as a means of gradually making our ideas clear. It is indeed the first means. My method of instruction is particularly distinguished in this:—it makes greater use of language as a means of raising the child from vague sense-impressions to clear ideas, than has ever been done before. Also it is distinguished by the principle of excluding from the first elementary instruction all collections of words presupposing actual knowledge of language or grammar.

Whoever understands that Nature leads only from clearness about individual to clearness about the whole, will understand that words must be separately clear to the child before they can be made clear to him when joined together. Whoever understands this will throw away at once all previous elementary instruction-books as such, because they all presuppose knowledge of language in the child before they have given it to him. Yes, Gessner, it is remarkable, even the best instruction-book of the past century has forgotten that the child must learn to talk before we can talk with him; this oversight is remarkable, but it is true. Since I know this, I no longer wonder that we cannot make other men than we do out of the children; for we have so far forgotten the wisdom and goodness of the ancients as to talk to them [of so many and such various things] before they can talk.

Language is an art—it is an infinite art, or rather it is the sum total of all arts which our race has reached. It is in a special sense a giving-back of all impressions that Nature, as a whole, has made upon our race. Thus I use it, and try by the associations of its spoken sounds to bring back to the child the very same impressions which these sounds formed and gave rise to in the human race. The gift of speech is infinite in itself, and becomes daily greater as it grows ever more perfect. It gives the child in a short time what Nature needed ages to give to mankind. We say of an ox, what would he be if he knew his strength ? and I say of man, what would he be if he [wholly] knew his power of speech and [wholly] used it ?

The gap is great that has arisen in the maze which we call human culture, because we have so far forgotten ourselves that we not only have done nothing to teach[56] humble folk to talk, but have made the speechless people dream their time away on abstract ideas, and while we made them learn empty words by heart, we have taught them to believe that they could in this way reach real knowledge of things, and truth.

Verily the Indians could do no more to keep[57] their lowest classes of people in everlasting idolatry, and in that way to breed a degraded race of men as sacrifices to their idols.

You may dispute the fact [that our lowest classes cannot speak, and are led astray by their apparent ability to speak]; I appeal to all clergy, magistrates, to all men who live among people who are oppressed in the midst of entire neglect by such a terribly distorted paternal, sham-careful method of teaching to speak. Let him who lives among such people come forward and bear witness if he has not experienced how troublesome it is to get any idea into the poor creatures. But every one agrees about this. " Yes, yes,"[58] say the clergy, " it is so; when they come to us to be taught, they do not understand what we say, nor we what they answer; and we get on no farther with them until they have learnt the answers to our questions by heart."

So say the magistrates; and they are right enough; it is impossible to make their justice comprehensible to these men.    When they come out of a village,

town-babblers are amazed at the want of speech of
these people, and say: " We must have them in the
house for years before they even begin to understand
orders given by word of mouth." Talkative town-folk
who have learned to talk and chatter a bit behind the
counter, think the most clever and sensible of these
people, stupid though they may be, far more stupid
than they really are. Good-for-noughts of every shade
call out, each with his own grimace, " Lucky for us
that it is so; trade would be worse if things were
different."

Friend! men of business and all kinds of people
who have much to do with the lower classes in the
country, for the sake of body and soul, express themselves alike on this subject. I might almost say, the
people of rank in our High Comedy Theatre speak
thus in their boxes and stalls about the condition of the
people in the pit. They cannot help speaking so,
because the people in the pit are to a great degree
neglected in this respect. We cannot hide from ourselves that the lowest Christian people of our continent
must in many places sink into these depths, because
in its lower schools we have for more than a century
given to empty words a weight in the human mind
that not only hindered attention to the impressions of
nature, but even destroyed man's inner suscepibility
to these impressions.

I say again—while we do this, and degrade the lower class of Europe into " word and clapper folk "[59] as hardly any people have been degraded before, *we never teach them to talk*.   It is therefore not surprising that the Christianity of this century and this continent looks as it does.   On the contrary, it is wonderful that good human nature, in spite of all the blundering of our " word and clapper " schools, has preserved so much inward strength as we often meet with in the lowest classes of the people.   But thank God! all follies and all apings find at last a counterpoise in human nature itself, and cease to be further harmful to our race when error has reached the highest point that we can bear.   Folly and error carry in every garment the seeds of their decay and death; truth alone, in every form, bears in itself the seeds of eternal life[60].

## VIII

The second elementary means from which all human knowledge, according to the nature of instruction must proceed, is—

### FORM

The teaching of form is preceded by the consciousness of the sense-impression of things having form, the artificial representations of which, for the purpose of instruction, must be derived partly from the nature of the observing powers, and partly from the definite aim of teaching itself.

All our knowledge arises:—

1. From impressions made by everything that accident brings into contact with our five senses. This kind of sense-impression is irregular, confused, and has a very slow and limited scope.

2. From all that is brought to our senses through the interposition of the Art, and the guidance of our parents and teachers. This kind of sense-impression is naturally more or less psychologically arranged, according to the degree of insight and energy of the parents and teachers [of each child], and is also more comprehensive and connected. His progress also towards the end and aim of in-

struction, *clear ideas*, is in the same degree more or less rapid and safe.

3. From my will, [based on and kept alive by the self-activity of all my faculties]; from my strong desire to obtain notions, knowledge, and ability; and from spontaneous efforts towards gaining sense-impressions. This kind of knowledge gained by sense-impression gives intrinsic value to our notions, and brings us nearer to moral self-active education by forming in us an independent vitality for the results of our sense-impressions.

4. From the results of effort, work at one's calling, and all kinds of activity, the object of which is not merely sense-impression. This manner of gaining knowledge connects my sense-impressions with my conditions and position, and brings the results into harmony with my efforts towards duty and virtue. Through the necessity of its course as well as through its results, it has the most important influence on the accuracy, continuity, and harmony of my insight, as well as on the purpose aimed at—*making ideas clear*.

5. Lastly, by analogy. Knowledge gained by sense-impression teaches me the properties of things that have not been brought to my sense-impression, by their likeness to other objects that I have observed. This mode of observation (*Ansch.*)

changes my advance in knowledge, which as the result of actual sense-impression is only the work of my senses, into the work of my mind and all its powers; and I have therefore as many kinds of sense-impression as I have powers of mind. But now " sense-impression " has a wider meaning than in common speech. It includes the whole series of feelings that are inseparable from the very nature of my mind.[6][1]

It is important to learn the difference between these two kinds of sense-impressions, in order to abstract the laws that are proper to each.

Meanwhile I return to my path.

From the consciousness of my sense-impression of the form of things arises the art of measuring. This, however, rests immediately upon the *art of sense-impression (Anschauung)*, which must be differentiated from the simple power of gaining knowledge, as well as from the simple kind of sense-impression. All divisions for measurement and their results are derived from these cultivated sense-impressions. But even this art of sense-impression leads us, through comparison of objects, beyond the rules of the art of measurement to free imitations of these proportions; that is, to the art of *drawing.* Lastly we use the power given by the art of drawing in the art of *writing.*

The Art of Measuring

presupposes an A B C of form (A B C of *Anschauung*);
that is, it presupposes an art of simplifying and defining the principles of measurement by exact separation
of all inequalities that appear to the observer.

Dear Gessner, I will again call your attention to the
empirical course that led me to this view of the subject; and for this purpose, will add an extract from a
passage in my Report.[62]   " Grant the principle," said
I, " that sense-impression is the foundation of all
knowledge, it follows inevitably that accuracy of sense-
impression is the foundation of accurate judgment.

" But it is obvious that in art education perfect
accuracy of observation must be a result of measuring
the object to be judged [or imitated], or of a power of
perceiving proportion so far cultivated as to render
measurement of the object superfluous.  Thus the
capacity of measuring correctly ranks, in the art-
education of our race, immediately after the need of
observation (*Ansch.*)  Drawing is a linear definition of
the form, of which the outline and surface are rightly
and exactly defined by complete measurement.

" The principle that the exercises and capacity of
measuring everything must precede exercises in drawing, or at least keep equal pace with them, is as
obvious as it is generally overlooked.  The usual course
of our art-education is to begin with inaccurate obser-

vation and crooked structures; then to pull down and build up again crookedly ten times over, until at last, and late, the feeling of proportion is matured. Then we come, at last, to that with which we should have begun, *measurement.* [63] That is our art-course. Yet we are so many thousand years older than the Egyptians, and Etruscans, whose drawings all depend on perfect measurement, or are at bottom nothing but [simple statements of] such measurements.

" And now comes the question:—What means have we of educating the child in this foundation of all art, correct measurement of all objects that come before his eyes ? Obviously by a series of measuring subdivisions of the square which are arranged according to simple, safe, and clear rules, and include the sum total of all possible sense-impressions.*

" True, the modern artists in spite of the want of such measurements have by long practice in their craft *acquired* methods by which they have attained more or less ability in placing any object before their eyes and

---

* Remark for the new edition. This passage is, like many another, the expression of immature, unformed opinion of the first empirical inquiry; of an idea of elementary education only mistily conceived as a whole, and now only so far interesting as it shows the first empirical course that this idea took in myself and fellow-workers.—PESTALOZZI.

drawing it as it really is in nature. It cannot be denied that many of them attained this power by toilsome and long-continued efforts. By the most confused sense-impressions, they reached a sense of proportion so far cultivated as to render actual measurement superfluous.

" But there were almost as many varieties of method as men. No one had a name for his own, because no one knew it clearly; therefore he could not properly impart it to his pupils. The pupil also was in the same state as his teacher, and was obliged, with extreme effort and long practice, to find out a method of his own, or rather the result of a method, and to acquire a correct sense of proportion. And so art staid in the hands of the few happy ones who had time and leisure to gain this sense by circuitous ways; and therefore no one could look upon it as an ordinary human business, or claim its cultivation as an ordinary human right.

" Yet it is one; at least he cannot be contradicted who asserts that every man living in a cultivated State has a right to learn to read and write. Then, evidently, the wish to draw and the capacity of measuring, which are developed naturally and easily in the child (as compared to the toil with which he is taught reading and writing) must be restored to him with greater art or more force, if we would not injure him more than the reading can ever be worth.

" But drawing, as a help towards the end of instruction, *making ideas clear*, is essentially bound up with the measurement of forms. When to a child an object is given to draw, he can never use his art as he should, that is as a means of rising through vague sense-impression to clear ideas in all his education, until he can represent the proportions of the form, and express himself about them; nor can his art have that real value that it might and should have, were it in harmony with the great purpose of education."

Thus in order to found the art of drawing, we must subordinate it to the art of measuring, and endeavor to organize as definite measuring forms the divisions into angles and arcs that come out of the fundamental form of the square, as well as its rectilinear divisions. This has been done; and I think I have organized a series of such measuring-forms,[64] the use of which makes the learning of all measurements and the proportions of all forms easy to understand, just as the A B C of sounds makes the learning of language easy.

* This A B C of form (A B C of *Anschauung*), however, is an equal division of the square into definite measure-forms, and requires an exact knowledge of its foundation—the straight line in a vertical or horizontal position.

---

* I must here remark that the A B C of *Anschauung* appears to be the only essential and true method of

These divisions of the square by straight lines produce certain forms for defining and measuring all angles, as well as the circle and all arcs. I call the whole " The A B C of *Anschauung* ".

This should be presented to the child in the following way.

We show him the properties of straight lines, unconnected and each by itself, under many conditions and in different arbitrary directions, and make him clearly conscious of the different appearances, without considering their further uses.   Then we begin to name

---

instruction for the just appreciation of the forms of things.   But until now, this method has been entirely neglected and ignored, though we have a hundred such methods for arithmetic and language.   Meanwhile the want of such a method of instruction about form is to be regarded not only as a defect in the structure of human knowledge, but as *the* defect in the foundation of all knowledge.   It seems to me a defect in knowledge, at the very point where language and number should be subordinate to it.   My A B C of *Anschauung* will remedy this deficiency, and secure instruction a basis on which other methods of instruction must be built.   I beg the men of Germany who feel themselves entitled to judge to look upon this point as the foundation of my method.   The value or worthlessness of my attempt rests upon the rightness or wrongness of this foundation.—Pestalozzi.

the straight lines as horizontal, vertical, and oblique; describing the oblique lines first as rising or falling, then as rising or falling to right or left. Then we name the different parallels as horizontal, vertical, and oblique parallel lines; then we name the principal angles formed by joining these lines, as right, acute, obtuse. In the same way we teach them to know and name the prototype of all measure-forms, the square, which arises from joining together two angles, and its divisions into halves, quarters, sixths, and so on; then the circle and its variations, in elongated forms, and their different parts.

All these definitions should be taught to the children as results of measuring with the eye, and the measuring-forms named in this course as square, horizontal, or vertical oblong (or rectangle); the curved lines as circle, semi-circle, quadrant; first oval,[65] half-oval, quarter-oval, second, third, fourth, fifth, and so on. They must be led to use these forms as means of measuring, and to learn the nature of the proportions by which they are produced. The first means of obtaining this end is—

1. To endeavor to make the child know and name the proportions of these measure-forms.

2. To enable him to apply and use them independently.

The child will be already prepared for this purpose

by the Mother's Book; and many objects have been shown him that are square, round, oval, broad, long, narrow. Soon after the divisions of the A B C of *Anschauung* will be cut out in cardboard and shown him as quarter, half quarter, sixth of the square, and so on; and then again as circle, half and quarter circle, oval, half and quarter oval.

In this way a dim consciousness will be produced beforehand of the clear idea that must hereafter be developed by learning the artistic appearance and the use of these forms. For this, too, they are prepared by the Mother's Book, in which are given the beginnings of a definite language of the forms, as well as the beginnings of number, which presupposes measurement.

For this purpose they are led through the A B C of *Anschauung*, since the methods of this art, language and number, of which they are made dimly conscious by the Mother's Book, are, in this A B C, made clear for the precise purpose of measuring; and they are enabled to express themselves clearly about number and measure in every form.

3. The third means of attaining this end is by drawing these forms themselves, by which the children (combining this with the other two methods) not only gradually gain clear ideas about every form, but gain accurate power of working with every

form. In order to attain the first end, we show them also the proportions of the forms that are recognized in the first course as horizontal and vertical rectangles, and described in the second course as *e. g.*, "the horizontal rectangle 2 is twice as long as it is high: the vertical rectangle 2 is twice as high as it is long," and so on through all the divisions. Here, too, the oblique lines of several rectangles must be seen and described by ratios for the sake of the different directions: *e. g.*: "horizontal rectangle, $1 \times 1\frac{1}{2}$, vertical rectangle, $1 \times 2\frac{1}{3}$, $3\frac{1}{4}$, $1\frac{1}{6}$." For the same purpose the different angles of the oblique lines, acute or obtuse, must be defined, as well as the divisions of the circle, and the ovals arising from dividing the rectangle.

The power of measuring, thus developed in me by the recognition of such definite forms, raises my feeble observing power to an art subordinated to definite rules, from which arises that just appreciation of all forms that I call the art of sense-impression (*Anschauung*). This is a new art that should precede the usual, old-fashioned, well-known ideas of art-culture, and serve as their general and essential foundation. By this means, every child in the simplest way is enabled to judge rightly and express himself clearly about every object in nature, according to its external * proportions and

---

* Ed. 1, internal.

its relationto others.   By this art-guidance he is enabled
whenever he looks at a figure to describe and name not
only the proportion of height to breadth, but the proportion of every single deviation of its form from the
square, in oblique lines and curves, and to apply the
names which denote these deviations in our A B C of
*Anschauung.*

The means of attaining this power lie in the art of
measuring; and will be still further developed in the
child by the art of drawing, particularly the art of
drawing lines.   He will be brought to a point when he
will be so familar with the measure-forms that they
will become a kind of instinct.   After perfecting the
preliminary exercises, he need no longer put them before his eyes as an actual means of measuring the most
complex objects; but without the help of [special]
measurement, he can represent all their proportions,
and express himself clearly about them.

We cannot say to what results the developed power
may raise every child, even the weakest.   No one shall
say it is a dream.   I have led children on these principles, and my theory is for me entirely the result of
my decided experience.   Any one may come and see.
Certainly my children are only at the beginning of this
guidance, but these beginnings show, so far, that it
needs a peculiar species of man to stand near my children and not be convinced; and this is no less than
extraordinary.

## THE ART OF DRAWING

is the power of representing to oneself the sense-impression made by any object, its outline and the characteristics contained within the outline, by means of similar lines, and of being able to imitate these lines accurately.

This art will become beyond comparison easier by the new method, because in every way it appears to be only an easy application of the forms that have not only been observed by the child already, but by practice in imitating have developed in him a real power of measuring.

This is done in this way. As soon as the child draws readily and correctly the horizontal line, with which the A B C of *Anschauung* begins, out of the whole chaos of objects seen and shown we try to find him figures whose outline is only the application of the familiar horizontal line, or at least offers only an imperceptible deviation from it.

Then we go on to the vertical line, then to the right angle, and so on. As the child by easy application of these forms becomes stronger, we gradually vary the figures. The results of these measures (which agree with the natural physical mechanical laws) on the art of drawing are as remarkable as those of the A B C of *Anschauung* upon the art of measuring. While in this way the children before they proceed farther bring to perfection every drawing, even the first-beginning drawing, a consciousness of the result of perfected power is already developed in them, in the first steps of this art; and with this consciousness are also developed an effort towards perfection and a perseverance towards completion, which the hurly-burly caused by the folly and disorder of our unpsychological men and methods of art-education never attempts or can attempt.

The foundation of progress in children so taught is not only in the hand; it is founded on the intrinsic powers of human nature. The exercise-books of measure-forms then give the sequence of means by which this effort, used with psychological art and within physical-mechanical laws, raises the child step by step to the point on which we have already touched, when having the measure-forms actually before him becomes gradually superfluous, and when of the guiding lines in art none remains but art itself.

## The Art of Writing

Nature herself has subordinated this art to that of drawing; and all methods by which drawing is developed and brought to perfection in children must then be naturally and specially dependent upon the art of measuring.

The art of writing can as little as drawing be begun and pursued without preceding developing exercises in measured lines, not only because it is a special kind of linear drawing and suffers no arbitrary deviation from the fixed direction of its forms, but also because if it is made easy to the child before drawing, it must necessarily spoil the hand (for drawing), by stiffening it in particular directions before the universal flexibility for all the forms which drawing requires has been sufficiently and firmly established. Still more should drawing precede writing because it makes the right forming of the letters incomparably easier, and saves the great waste of time spent in making again and again crooked [and incorrect] forms. The child enjoys this advantage in his whole education; from the very beginning of the art he is made conscious of its power of perfection; and therefore from the first moment of learning to write, it creates the will to add nothing inharmonious, incorrect, and imperfect to the first steps already brought to a certain degree of accuracy, precision, and perfection.

Writing, like drawing, should be tried first with the slate pencil on a slate, until the child is *old enough* to make letters with a certain degree of accuracy with the pencil,—an age at which it would be extremely difficult to teach him to guide a pen.

Again, the use of the pencil before the pen in writing and in drawing is to be recommended, because, in any case, mistakes *can be easily erased* from the slate; while,

on the contrary, one wrong word remaining on paper
often leads to a whole tribe of still worse mistakes
than the first, and almost from the beginning of a line
or page of writing to the end there is a remarkable
kind of progression from the mistaken deviation set
up at the beginning of the line or page.

Lastly, I consider it an essential advantage of this
method that the child rubs out the perfectly good
work also from the slate.   No one can believe how
important this is if he does not generally know how
important it is for the human race that man should be
educated without conceit, and not come to set a ficti-
tious value on his own handiwork too soon.

So I divide learning to write into two stages.

1. That in which the child becomes familiar with
   the forms of the letters and their combinations,
   independently of the use of the pen.

2. That in which his hand is practised in the use of
   the proper writing instrument, the pen.

In the first stage I put the letters in exact proportions before the child, and have prepared a copy-book
by which the child, in harmony with this whole method
and its advantages, may educate himself in the power
of writing almost alone and without further help.   The
advantages of this writing-book are:—

1. It dwells long enough on the beginning and fundamental forms of the letters.

2. It gradually joins the parts of the combined forms of letters to each other, so that the completion of the more difficult letters is to be regarded only as a gradual addition of new parts to the already practised beginnings of letters.

3. It exercises the child in combining several letters from the moment that he is able to copy one correctly, and he rises step by step to the combination of such words as consist simply of those letters which he can copy correctly at that time.

4. Lastly, it has this advantage; it can be cut up into single lines, and so laid before the child that the lines to be imitated by eye and hand stand immediately over the letters of the copy.

In the second stage, when the child must be led to use the special writing instrument, the pen, he has already been exercised in the forms of the letters and their combinations, and is tolerably perfect. The teacher has then nothing further to do but to complete the power of drawing these forms by the use of the pen, and make it the real art of writing.

Meanwhile the child here too must join on the further progress to the point up to which he has already practised. His first writing with the pen is merely his pencil progress over again; and with the first use of the pen he should begin with writing the letters just the same size as he drew them at first, and only gradually be exercised in copying the ordinary small writing.

All branches of instruction demand essentially psychological analysis of their methods, and the age should be exactly fixed at which each may and ought to be given to the child.   As I work on this principle in all subjects, so in the art of writing, by always following it and by using a slate pencil copy for children from four to five, I have come to the conclusion that by this method even a bad teacher, or a very untrained mother, may be able to teach the children accurate and beautiful writing up to a certain point, without being able to do it herself.   The *essential* purpose of my method here and elsewhere is to make home instruction possible again for people neglected in this respect; and to raise every mother whose heart beats for her children, step by step, till at last she can follow my elementary exercises by herself, and be able to use them with her children.   To do this, she need in every case be but a little step in advance of the children.

My heart beats high with the hopes to which these views lead me; but, dear friend, ever since I began to express any suggestion of the kind, men cry out at me from all sides, " *The mothers of this country will never do it.*"   And not only men of the people, but even men who teach the people, men who teach the people Christianity, say scornfully to me, " You may run up and down our villages,—you will find no mothers who will do what you ask them." [They are quite right. It *is* so; but it *should* not be so; it *shall* not be so. Of a hundred men, who make this objection hardly one knows why it is so, and still fewer know how to make it different.]

Meanwhile I can answer these people with the utmost calmness: " *I will, with the means that are in my hand, enable heathen mothers* in the far north *to do* what I want; and if it is really true that *Christian mothers* in temperate Europe—that Christian mothers in *my fatherland* cannot be brought so far as I will bring heathen mothers in the wild north, at any time "=— then I would cry out to these gentlemen who *now in this way slander* the people of our fatherland, whom they and their fathers have taught, instructed, and guided hitherto: " You should wash your hands, and say aloud: ' We are guiltless of this monstrous barbarism of the people of temperate Europe. We are guiltless of this monstrous barbarism of the best natured, most docile of all European people, the Swiss.' Say out loud, ' We and our fathers have done what we ought to have done, to remove the unutterable misery of this barbarism from our country and our fatherland, and to prevent this unspeakable ruin of the first principles of morality and Christianity in our country and fatherland.' "

I would answer the men who dare to say, " Run up
and down the country, *the mothers of the land* will not
do it or wish to do it," and say, " You ought to cry
out to these unnatural mothers of our fatherland as
Christ once cried to Jerusalem, ' Mothers! mothers!
we would have gathered you together under the wings
of wisdom, humanity, and Christianity, as a hen
gathereth her chickens, *but ye would not.*' "

If they dare do this, I will be silent and believe in
their word and in their experience—and not in the
mothers of the land, not in the heart that God has put
into their breast.    But if they dare not do this, I will
not believe in them, but in the mothers of the land,
and in the heart that God has put in their breast.    I
will declare the wretched talk, in which they throw
away the people of the land as if they were the produce of a lower order of creation, a slander against the
people, against nature and truth.

I go on my way like a wanderer who hears the wind
in a distant wold but feels it not.    I go on my way for
all this talk.    Throughout my whole life, I have seen
and known all kinds of such wordy men, wrapped up
in systems and theories, *knowing nothing and caring
nothing for the people;* and the individuals who to-day
slander the people in this way about this matter of
education are more in this state than any others that
I know.    Such men think themselves upon a height,

and the people far below them in the valley; but they are mistaken in both; and are like poor apes hindered and by the conceit of their miserable nature made incapable of judging rightly about the pure worth of real animal powers, or about true human talents.   The brilliant polish, which these wordy men owe to their unnatural way of living, makes them incapable of understanding that they are mounted on stilts, and therefore *must come down from their miserable wooden legs,* in order *to stand as firmly as other folk, upon God's earth.*

I pity them.   I have heard many of these wretched wordy men say, with a mixture of nun-like innocence and rabbinical wisdom: " *What can be more beautiful for the people than the Heidelberg Catechism and the Psalter?* " —and I must take humanity into account even here, and recall to mind the causes of this error.

Yes, friend!  I will excuse them this error of the human mind; it has always been and will ever be so. Men are alike; the scribes and the disciples were so too.   Then I will not open my mouth again against the verbosity of their social dogmas, against the tinkling cymbals of their ceremonies, and the loveless and foolish frame of mind that they must, by their very nature, produce; but, with the greatest man who ever declared the cause of truth, of the people, and of love victorious against the errors of the scribes, I will only say, " *Father, forgive them; for they know not what they do.*"

But I return. Learning to write appears to be, thirdly, a kind of learing· to talk. In its nature it is only a peculiar and special exercise of this art.

As writing, considered as form, appears in my methods, in connection with measuring and drawing, and in this connection, enjoys all the advantages that are produced by the early development of these faculties, so it appears again as *a special kind of learning to talk* in connection with the very exercises which have been used from the cradle upwards for the development of this power.

The child enjoys just the same advantages that he has had already in the development of his speech, a faculty that has been developed and firmly fixed in him by the Mother's Book, the Spelling and the Reading Books.

A child taught by these methods knows the spelling and first reading book almost by heart. He knows the fundamentals of orthography and language as one great whole, and when he has practised the forms of the letters by means of the slate pencil and the first writing exercises, and is quite familiar with the individual features of the letters and their combinations, he needs for his further writing lessons *no more special copies*. He has the essence of copies in his head, by his readiness in speech and orthography; he writes from his own experience, on the lines of the spelling and reading books, lists of words by which he confirms his knowledge of language and uses his powers of memory and imagination.

The advantages of these graduated exercises in writing, connected with those used in learning to talk, are especially these:—

1. They confirm the grammatical facility that the child already possesses, and impress its principles indelibly upon him. It must be so, since, following the direction of the reading book, in which nouns, verbs, adjectives, adverbs, etc., are arranged in separate columns, he is exercised in putting these words into their places; and so he learns to know at once to which column any given word belongs, and to make for himself rules which are applicable to these sequences.

2. In the same way his power of gaining clear ideas generally is strengthened by speech (still according to the method); while as a writing-exercise, he can with his dictionary make lists of headings and signs of subdivisions and some generalizations collected by himself on the relationships of all things.

3. The means of gaining clear ideas by writing-exercises is confirmed: for not only is he exercised by writing as by speaking in *putting together* nouns, verbs, and adjectives; but by these exercises he

gains independent power of discovering and adding his own knowledge or ideas to the many sequences the chief contents of which he has made his own in learning to talk.

For example, in the writing-exercise he not only adds what in the reading book he has learned to call high and pointed, but he is taught, and is pleased with the task, to think and add what objects within his own circle of knowledge have this form.

I give an example, which shows the children's power of discovering such illustrations.

I gave them the word *three-cornered* and they used it, with the help of a country schoolmaster, on the following examples:

*Three-cornered:* the triangle; the plummet; half a handkerchief; the joiner's rule; a kind of file; the bayonet; the prism; the beechnut; the scraper of an engraver; the wound made by a leech; the sword blade; buckwheat seed; the legs of the compass; the lower part of the nose; Good Henry's leaf;* the spinach-leaf; the ovary-of the tulip; the figure 4; and the ovary of the shepherd's purse.

They found several more three-cornered figures in tables, and windows with round panes, for which however they knew no names.

---

* Chenopodium, Bonus Henricus, Goosefoot.

The same thing is done when they add adjectives to nouns. They add for example not only all the adjectives which they have learned from the reading book to eel, carrion, evening, etc., but also those adjectives that their experience has shown them to be suitable. So in the simplest way, by collecting the characteristics of things, they make themselves acquainted and familiar with the nature, essence, and properties of all things within their knowledge. Verbs also are treated in the same way. When, for example, they wish to explain *to observe* by adding nouns and adverbs, they will not only explain it or support it by those which they find in the reading book, but will do as before.

The results of these exercises are far-reaching. They enable the children from the descriptions learned by heart, *e. g.* the bell, to go, to stand, to lie, eye, ear, etc., which are fixed and general leading-strings for them, to express themselves clearly about every possible thing whose form or substance they know either by word of mouth or by writing. But of course it must be understood that this result is attained, not by isolated special writing-exercises, but by connecting these with the whole series of means by which the method raises the pupils gradually to clear ideas.

This must be understood throughout the whole course of this teaching, when I say that learning to

write is perfected not only as an art but also as a calling; and that the child in this way may be enabled to
express itself in words as easily and as naturally by
this art as by speech itself.

## IX

The third elementary means of gaining knowledge is
NUMBER.

Now while sound and form lead us by several subordinate methods to the clear ideas and mental independence which we aim at through them, arithmetic
is the only means of instruction which is connected
with no subordinate means. Wherever it applies it
appears only as a simple result of that elementary faculty by which we make ourselves clearly conscious of
the relations of more or less in all seen objects (*Ansch.*),
and are enabled to represent these ratios with infinite
accuracy.

Sound and form very often carry seeds of error and
deception in themselves — number never. It alone
leads to certain results; and if measurement makes
the·same claim, it can only support it by the help of
arithmetic and in union with it. That is, it is sure
because it calculates.

Now arithmetic is to be considered the means that
aims most directly at the end of instruction, *clear ideas*,
the most important of all means. It is obvious therefore that this subject should always be pursued with

special care and skill.   It is extremely important that it should be put into such forms as will enable us to use all the advantages afforded to instruction by deep psychology and a comprehensive knowledge of the immutable laws of the physical mechanism.

I have therefore taken especial trouble to make arithmetic evident to the child's sense-impression as the clearest result of these laws.   I have tried not only to reduce its elements to that simplicity in which they appear in actual, natural sense-impressions, but also to connect accurately and uninterruptedly its further steps and all its variations with this simplicity of the beginning-points.   I am convinced that even the extreme limits of this art can be means of true enlightenment (that is a means of gaining clear ideas and pure insight) only in so far as they develop these in the human mind in the same gradation with which nature herself goes on from the first beginning-points.

## ARITHMETIC

arises entirely from simply putting together and separating several units.   Its basis, as I said, is essentially this: *One and one are two, and one from two leave one.* Any number, whatever it may be, is only an abbreviation of this natural, original method of counting.   But it is important that this consciousness of the origin of relations of numbers should not be weakened in the human mind by the shortening expedients of arithmetic. It should be deeply impressed with great care on all the ways in which this art is taught; and all the future steps should be built upon the consciousness, deeply retained in the human mind, of the real relations of things which lie at the bottom of all calculation. If this is not done, this first means of gaining clear ideas will be degraded to a plaything of our memory and imagination, and will be useless for its essential purpose.

It cannot be otherwise. When, for example, we just learn by heart " three and four make seven " and then build upon this seven, as if we really knew that three and four make seven, we deceive ourselves; for the inner truth of seven is not in us, since we are not conscious of the meaning behind it which alone can make an empty word a truth for us. It is the same with all branches of human knowledge. Drawing too, for want of being connected with its basis, measurement, loses the inner truth of its being, by which alone it can be raised to a means of leading us to clear ideas.

In the Mother's Book I begin my efforts to give the children an impression of the relations of numbers as actual changes of more and less; these can be found in the objects before their eyes. The first tables of this book contain a series of objects that give the child a clear sense-impression of one, two, three, etc., up to ten.   Then I let the children look for those objects that are represented on these tables as units, pairs of units, threes of units, and so on.

Afterwards I let them find these same relations on their fingers, or with peas, stones, or other handy objects, and I renew the knowledge hundreds and hundreds of times daily.   For as I divide words into syllables and letters on the spelling-board, I throw out the question, " How many syllables has this word ?   What is the first, second, third ? " and so on.   In this way the beginning of calculation is deeply impressed upon the children, and they become familiar with its abbreviations, and with numbers, with full consciousness of their inner truth before they use them without the background of sense-impression before their eyes.

Independently of the advantage of *in this way* making calculation the foundation of clear ideas, it is incredible how easy the art itself may be made to the child by this firmly based preparation through sense-impressions.   Experience shows that the beginnings are difficult only because these [necessary] psychological methods are not so widely used as they should be.   Therefore I must be somewhat circumstantial in my description of the methods to be applied here.

Besides the means already indicated, we use after them the spelling-board also for counting.   We put upon it each tablet as a unit; and when the children are learning their letters, we begin to make them learn the relations of numbers also. We take a particular tablet and ask the child, " Are there many tablets? " The child answers, " No; only one." Then we add another and ask, " One and one—how many? " The child answers, " One and one are two." Thus we go on, adding only one at a time; afterwards we add two, three, and so on.

When the child understands the addition of one and one, up to ten, perfectly, and can express himself with absolute ease, we put the letter-tablets in the same way upon the board, but alter the questions, and say: " When you have two tablets how many times *one* tablet have you? " The child looks, counts, and answers rightly: " If I have two tablets, I have twice one tablet."

When by exact and often repeated counting of the parts, he has become clearly conscious how many units are in the first numbers, we change the question again and say with a similar arrangement of tablets: " How many times one is two? How many times one is three? " etc.; and then again: " How many times is one contained in two? In three? " etc.

Then when the child is acquainted with the simple beginnings of addition, multiplication, and division, and is perfectly familiar with the nature of these forms of reckoning through sense-impression, we try to make him acquainted and familiar with the beginnings of subtraction, in the same way, through sense-impression.

This is done in this way. From the ten tablets collected together, we take away one, and ask: "When you have taken one away from ten how many are left?" The child counts, finds nine, and answers, "When I take one away from ten, nine are left." Then we take a second tablet away, and ask: "One less than nine, how many?" The child counts again, finds eight, and answers: "One less than nine is eight." So we go on to the last.

This kind of explanation of arithmetic may now be set down in writing in the following way in rows.

| | | | | | | etc.

| | | | | | | | | | etc.

| | | | | | | | | | etc.

As the counting of each row is finished, the separate numbers will be taken way in like manner; as follows:—

If, for example, we add 1 and 2 are 3, and 2 are 5, and 2 are 7, etc., up to 21, then we take two tablets away and say, "2 less than 21, how many?" and go on till no more are left.

The consciousness of many or few objects that is produced by laying real, movable, actual things before the child, is then confirmed in him by counting-tables, by which he is shown similar sequences of reiations by means of strokes and dots. These tables, like real objects, will be used as guides to counting, as the Spelling-Book is used for putting up the words on the spelling-board.

When the child is accustomed to count with real objects, and with the dots and strokes put in their place, as far as these tables (that are founded entirely on sense-impression) go, the knowledge of the real relations of numbers will be so confirmed in him that the short methods by means of ordinary numbers, without sense-impression, will be incredibly easy to him, because his mental powers have not been dissipated [so far as arithmetic goes] by confusion, discrepancies, and guessing. We can say in a special sense that such counting is an exercise for the reason, and not memory or routine work. It is the result of the clearest, most exact sense-impression; and leads safely to clear ideas about these relations.

But as increase and decrease of all objects does not consist only of more or fewer units, but also in the division of units into several parts, a second form of counting arises; or rather a path is opened by which every separate unit may be the foundation of endless divisions of itself, and endless divisions of the units contained in it.

As in the first kind of counting, that is of many or few whole units, we have considered the number *one* as the beginning point of all calculation; and as the foundation of the *art of sense-impression* and all its changes; so now in the second kind of counting a figure must be found which does the same for this kind of counting as the number one does for the other.

We must find a figure that is infinitely divisible and that in all its divisions is like itself; a figure by which a kind of sense-impression may be given of infinitessimal fractions, either as parts of a whole or as independent undivided units. This figure must put before the child's eyes every relation of a fraction in relation to the whole, as clearly and as exactly as by our method in simple arithmetic the number one is shown in the number three exactly three times.

There is no possible figure that can do this except the square.

By this we can put sensibly before the child's eyes the proportions of the divisions of the unit or the fraction, in their progressive sequences from the common beginning-point of all notions of more or less,—the number one: just as we showed him the increase or decrease of undivided units. We have prepared a table of sense-impressions of fractions that has 11 rows, each consisting of ten squares.*

---

* For this purpose Pestalozzi used three tables. (1) Table of Units, which is not referred to here, consisting of twelve rows of twelve rectangular spaces; in

PESTALOZZI'S TABLE OF COMPOUND FRACTIONS

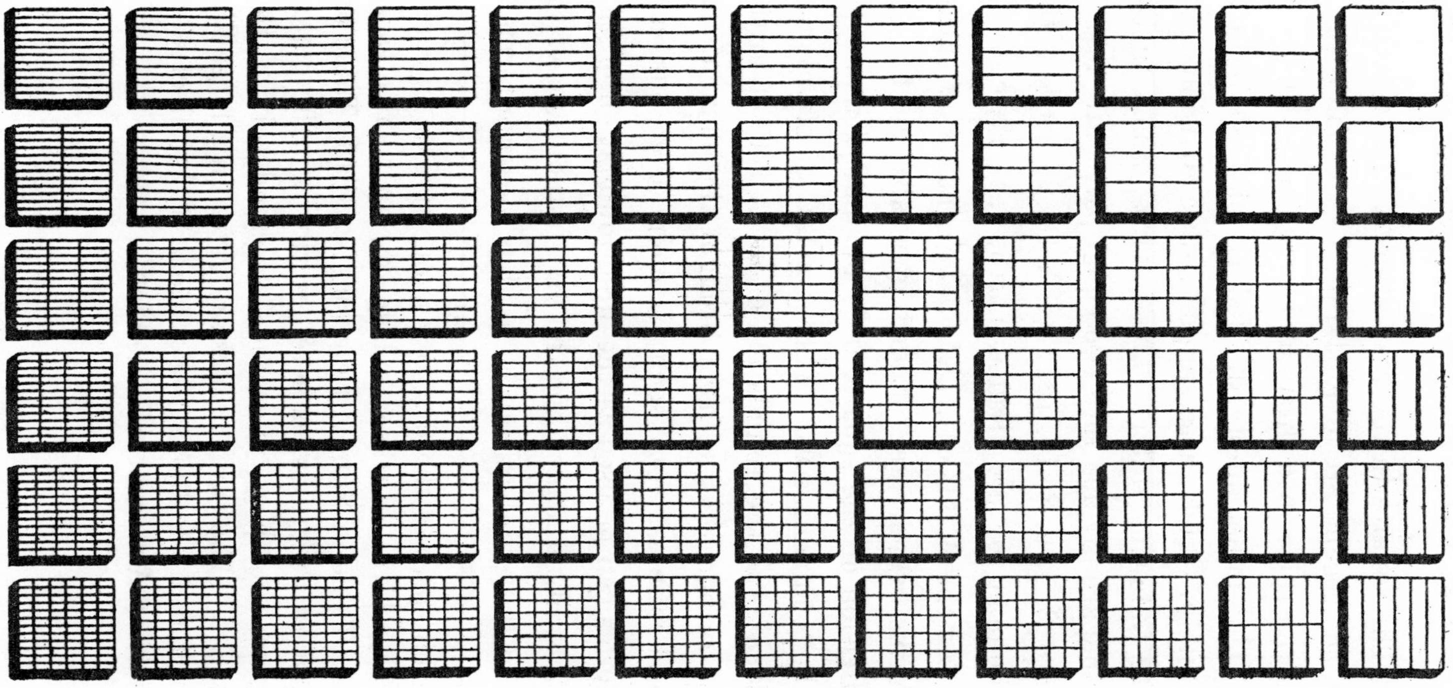

The squares in the first row are undivided. Those in the second are divided into two equal parts; those in the third into three, and so on up to 10.

This table simply divided is followed by a second table in which these simple visible divisions go on in the following order. The squares, which in the first table are divided into two equal parts, are now divided into 2, 4, 6, 8, 10, 12, 14, 16, 18, 20 parts ; those in the next row are divided into 3, 6, 9, 12, etc.

As the A B C of *Anschauung* consists of measuring forms which are founded generally on the ten-fold division of the square, it is obvious that we can use the common basis of the A B C of *Anschauung*, the square, as the foundation of an A B C of arithmetic; or rather, that we have brought the elements of form and number into such harmony that our measure-forms can be used as the first foundation of the relations of numbers; and the first foundations of the relations of numbers can be used as measure-forms.

---

each space of the first row is one stroke, in each of the second two strokes, and so on, up to twelve strokes. (2) Table of Simple Fractions; and (3) Table of Compound Fractions, as here described. The plate on the preceding page gives the left hand half of the third table. The three tables are given in a large sheet inserted in Pullen's " Pestalozzi's Intellectual or Intuitive Arithmetic ", London, 1821.

So we have reached this: By our method we can teach children arithmetic only by using the very same A B C that at first we used as the A B C of *Anschauung* in a narrow sense,[66] that is, as the foundation of measure, drawing, and writing.

The child will be made so fully conscious of the visible relations of all fractions by the use of these tables, that exercises in fractional arithmetic, in ordinary numbers, will be as incredibly easy as arithmetic with undivided units. Experience shows that by this method children attain readiness in these exercises three or four years sooner than is possible without it. By these, as by the former exercises, the child's mind is preserved from confusion, discrepancies, and useless guesses; and here too we can say with decision:—The calculating power of such children is the result of the clearest, most exact sense-impression, and leads by its clearness to truth, and susceptibility to truth.[67]

# X

Friend! When I now look back and ask myself: What have I specially done for the very being of education, I find I have fixed the highest supreme principle of instruction in the recognition of *sense-impression as the absolute foundation of all knowledge.* Apart from all *special teaching* I have sought to discover the *nature of teaching itself;* and the *prototype,* by which Nature herself has determined the instruction of our race. I find I have reduced all instruction to three elementary means; and have sought for special methods which would render the results of all instruction in these three branches absolutely certain.

Lastly, I find I have brought these three elementary means into harmony with each other; I have made instruction in all three branches in many ways harmonious not only each with itself but also with human nature; and I have brought it nearer to the course of Nature in the development of the human race.

But while I did this I found of necessity that the instruction of our country, as it is *publicly and generally* conducted *for the people,* wholly and entirely ignores sense-impression as the supreme principle of instruction; that throughout it does not take sufficient notice

(220)

of the prototype, within which the instruction of our race is determined by the necessary laws of our nature itself; that it rather sacrifices the *essentials of all teaching* to the hurly burly of *isolated teaching of special things*, and kills the spirit of truth by dishing up all kinds of *broken truths;* and that it extinguishes in the human race the power of self-activity which rests upon it. I found, and it was clear as day, that this kind of instruction reduces its particular methods neither to elementary principles nor to elementary forms; that by the neglect of sense-impression as the absolute foundation of all knowledge, it is unable by any of its unconnected methods to attain the end of all instruction—clear ideas; and even to make those limited results, at which it solely aims, absolutely certain.

* This educational[68] position in which at least nine men in every ten are to be found in Europe, as well as the actual quality of that instruction which they enjoy, appears almost incredible at the first glance of the subject; but it is not only historically correct, it is

---

* Even the good Lavater, caring for an honoring the positive condition of the world as nobody else did, knew and confessed this. He answered the question: What simple element can be found for the Art and particularly for the observation (*Ansch.*) of all things ? *He knew none,* and it surpassed all belief how groundless the Art (of education) in Europe was.—PESTALOZZI.

psychologically inevitable; it could not be otherwise. Europe, with its system of popular instruction, was bound to sink into the error, or rather insanity, that really underlay it. It rose on the one hand to a gigantic height in special arts and sciences, and lost on the other all foundations of natural teaching for the whole race. No country ever rose so high on the one side, nor sank so low on the other. Like the image of the prophet, it touches the clouds with its golden head of *special arts and sciences;* but popular instruction, that should be the foundation of this *golden head,* is, like the feet of this gigantic image, the *most wretched, most fragile, most good for nothing clay.*

This disproportion, ruinous for the human mind, between the advantages of the upper and the misery of the lower classes, or rather the beginning-point from which this striking disproportion in the culture of our country dates, is the invention of the art of printing. The country, in its first astonishment about this new and boundless influence, this making of word-knowledge easy, fell into a kind of dizzy, quack-like trust in the universality of its effects. This was natural in the first generation after the discovery; but that the country after so many ages still lives in the same dizzy state, and has let it grow to a soul-and-body-destroying nervous fever without feeling ill! really this could have happened in no country but ours.

But it needed another influence, interwoven of monkish, feudal, Jesuit, and government systems, in order to produce through this art *the result* it has had on Europe. With these surrounding circumstances, it is then really not only comprehensible how it came to take a positive position together with our arts and our popular instruction, but it is even clear that under given circumstances it could produce no *inferior* art but also no *better* instruction than it has actually produced. It is quite clear how it was *forced* to narrow the five senses of the country, and so to bind particularly that instrument of sense-impression, the eye, to the heathen altar of the new learning, letters and books. I might almost say it was forced to make this universal instrument of knowledge a mere letter-eye, and us mere letter-men.

The Reformation [by the weakening of its original spirit and the necessary resulting deification of dead forms and thoughts] completed what the art of printing began. Without putting its heart under the obvious stupidity of a monkish or feudal world, it has opened its mouth generally only to express abstract ideas.[69] This still more increased the inner atrophy of the world, making its men letter-beings; and brought it to such a point that the errors of this condition cannot be dissolved by progress in truth, love, and faith; but on the contrary, they can only be strengthened,

while they seem to be dissolved, by the still more dangerous errors of infidelity, indifference, and lawlessness.

As a devastating flood, checked in its career by a
fallen rock, takes a new course and spreads its devastation from generation to generation, so European popular education, having once forsaken the even road of
sense-impression, owing to the influence of these two
great events, has taken generally a baseless, visionary
course, increasing its human devastation year by year,
from generation to generation.

Now after ages it has culminated in the general
*word-twisting*[70] of our knowledge. This has [led to
the word-twisting of infidelity. This profound vice of
word and dream is in no way fitted to raise us to the
still wisdom of faith and love, but on the contrary to
lead as to the word-twisting of sham and superstition
and its indifference and hardness. In any case it is
undeniable that this devouring word and book nature
of our culture has] brought us to this—we cannot any
longer remain as we are.

It could not be otherwise. Since we have contrived
with deeply founded art and still more deeply founded
measures for supporting error, to rob our knowledge
and our methods of instruction of all sense-impression,
and ourselves of all power of gaining sense-impressions,
the gilded, giddy pate of our culture could not possibly
stand on any feet but those on which it does actually

stand.  Nothing else was possible.  The drifting haphazard methods of our culture could in no subject
attain the final end of public instruction, *clear ideas*,
and *perfect facility* in what is essentially necessary for
the people to know and to learn of all these subjects.

Even the best of these methods, the abundant aids
for teaching arithmetic, [mathematics,] and grammar
must under these circumstances lose power, because
without finding any other foundation for all instruction they have neglected sense-impression.  So these
means of instruction, word, number, and form, not
being sufficiently subordinated to the one only foundation of all knowledge, sense-impression, must necessarily mislead our generation to elaborate these means
of instruction unequally, superficially, and aimlessly,
in the midst of error and deception; and by this elab-
oration, weaken our inmost powers, rather than
strengthen and cultivate them.  We become necessarily
degraded to *lies and folly*, and branded as miserable,
weak, unobservant, wordy babblers, by the very same
powers and the very same organism * with which the
Art, holding the hand of Nature, might raise us up to
*truth and wisdom*.

Even the knowledge gained by observation (*Ansch.*),
forced upon us by our circumstances and our business,

---

* Ed. 1 Mechanism.

in spite of our folly (because it is impossible for any error in the Art to snatch this wholly from mankind) —even this kind of knowledge, being isolated, becomes one-sided, illusory, egotistic, and illiberal.   There is no help for it.   Under such guidance we are forced to rebel against whatever is opposed to this one-sided, illiberal kind of observation (*Ansch.*), and to become insensible to all truth that may be beyond the limited range of our untrained senses.   There is no help for it. We are forced under these circumstances to sink ever deeper from generation to generation into the unnatural conventionality, the narrow-hearted selfishness, the lawless, ambitious violence resulting from it, in which we now are.

Dear Gessner! thus and in no other way can we explain how in the past century, during the latter part of which this delusion rose to its greatest height, we were plunged into a dreamy or rather raving condition of baseless, frantic presumption.   This prevented all our ideas of truth and justice.   Yielding to the violent agitation of our wild and blind natural feelings we sank down, and a general overturning spirit of sansculottism took possession of us all in one way or another, resulting, as it must needs result, in the inner disorganization of all pure natural feelings, and of all those means of helping humanity which rest upon those feelings.   This led to the disappearance of all *humanity* from political systems; this again to the dissolution of a few political systems which had ceased to be human. But unfortunately this did not work to the advantage of humanity.

This, dear friend, is a sketch of my views on the latest events. Thus I explain the measures both of Robespierre and Pitt, the behavior of the senators and of the people. And every time I reconsider it I come back to the assertion that the deficiencies of European instruction,—or rather, the artificial inversion of all natural principles of instruction,—has brought this part of the world *where it is now ;* and that there is no remedy for our present and future overturn in society, morality, and religion except to turn back from the superficiality, incompleteness, and giddy-headedness of our popular instruction, and to recognize that *sense-impression is absolutely the foundation of all knowledge ;* in other words, *all knowledge grows out of sense-impression and may be traced back to it.*

## XI

Friend ! sense-impression, considered as the point at which all instruction begins, must be differentiated from the art of sense-impression (*Ansch.*) which teaches us the relations of all forms. Sense-impression, as the common foundation of all three elementary means of instruction, must come as long before the art of sense-impression as it comes before the arts of reckoning and speaking. If we consider sense-impression as opposed to the art of sense-impression (*Ansch.*) separately and by itself, it is nothing but the presence of *the external object before the senses* which rouses a consciousness of the impression made by it. With it Nature begins all instruction. The infant enjoys it, the mother gives it him.

But the Art has done nothing here to keep equal pace with Nature. In vain that most beautiful spectacle, the mother showing the world to her infant, was presented to its eyes; *the Art has done nothing, has verily done nothing for the people,* in connection with this spectacle.

Dear Gessner, I will here quote for you the passage that expressed this feeling about our Art more than a year ago.[7][1]

" From the moment that a mother takes a child upon her lap, she teaches him. She brings nearer to his senses what nature has scattered afar off over large areas and in confusion, and makes the action of receiving sense-impressions, and the knowledge derived from them, easy, pleasant, and delightful to him.

" The mother, weak and untrained, follows Nature without help or guidance, and knows not what she is doing. She does not intend to teach; she intends only to quiet the child, to occupy him. But neverthe-of less in her pure simplicity she follows the high course Nature without knowing what *Nature* does through *her;* and Nature does very much through her. In this way she opens the world to the child. She makes him ready to use his senses, and prepares for the early development of his attention and power of observation.

" Now if this high course of Nature were used; if that were connected with it which might be connected with it; if the helping Art could make it possible to the mother's heart to go on with what she does instinctively for the infant, wisely and freely with the growing child; if, too, the heart [and disposition] of the father were also used for this purpose; and if the helping Art made it possible for him to link with the disposition and circumstances of the child all the activities he needs, in order by good management of his most important affairs to attain inner content with himself throughout his life, how easy would it be to assist in raising our race and every individual man in any position whatever, even amid the difficulties of unfavorable circumstances, and amid all the evils of unhappy times, and secure him a still, calm, peaceful life. O God! what would be gained for men. But we are not yet so far advanced as the Appenzell woman, who in the first weeks of her child's life hangs a large many-colored paper bird over his cradle, and in this way clearly shows the point at which the Art should begin to bring the objects of Nature firmly to the child's clear consciousness."

Dear friend! Whoever has seen how the two- and three-weeks old child stretches hands and feet towards this bird, and considers how easy it would be for the Art to lay a foundation for actual sense-impressions of all objects of Art and Nature in the child by a series of such visible representations, which may then be made gradually more distinct and extended—whoever considers all this and then does not feel how we have wasted our time on Gothic monkish educational rubbish, until it has become hateful to us,—truly cakes and ale are wasted on him.

To me the Appenzell bird, like the ox to the Egyptians, is a holy thing, and I have done everything to begin my instruction at the same point as the Appenzell woman. I go further. Neither at the first point nor in the whole series of means of teaching do I leave to chance what Nature, circumstance, or mother-love may present to the sense of the child before he can speak. I have done all I could to make it possible, by omitting accidental characteristics, to bring the essentials of knowledge gained by sense-impression to the child's senses before that age, and to make the conscious impressions he receives unforgetable.

The first *course in the Mother's Book* is nothing but an attempt to raise sense-impression itself to an art, and to lead the children by all three elementary divisions of knowledge, *form, number,* and *words,* to a comprehensive consciousness of all sense-impressions, the more definite concepts of which will constitute the foundation of their later knowledge.

This book will contain not only representations of those objects most necessary for us to know, but also material for a continuous series of such objects as are fit, at the first sense-impression, to rouse a feeling in the children of their manifold relationships and similarities.

In this respect the Spelling Book does the same thing as the Mother's Book. Simply bringing sounds *to the ear* and rousing a consciousness of the impression made *through the hearing,* is as much *sense-impression* for the child as putting objects *before his eye,* and rousing a consciousness of the impression made *through the sense of sight.* Founded on this, I have so arranged the Spelling Book that its first course is nothing but *simple sense-impression :* that is, it rests simply on the effort to bring the whole series of sounds that must afterwards serve as the foundation of language *to the child's sense of hearing*, and to make the impression made by them permanent *at exactly the same age* at which in the Mother's Book I bring before his sense of sight the visible objects of the world, the clear perception of which must be the foundation of his future knowledge.

This same principle, of raising sense-impression to an art, has a place too in our third elementary means of knowledge. Number in itself, without a foundation of sense-impression, is a delusive phantom of an idea, which our imagination certainly holds in a dreamy fashion, but which our reason cannot grasp firmly as a truth. The child must learn to know rightly the inner nature of every form in which the relations of number may appear, before he is in a position to comprehend one of these forms as the foundation of a clear consciousness of few or many. [72] Therefore in the Mother's Book I have impressed the first ten numbers on the child's senses (*Ansch.*) even at this age in many ways, by fingers, claws, leaves, dots, and also as triangle, square, octagon, etc.

After I have done this in all three branches, and have made sense-impression the absolute foundation of all actual knowledge, I again raise sense-impression in all three subjects to the art of sense-impression (*Ansch.*), that is, a power of considering all objects of sense-impression as *objects for the exercise of my judgment and my (Fert.) skill.*

In this way I lead the child, with the first elementary means of knowledge, *Form*. After I have made him acquainted in the Mother's Book with manifold sense-impressions of the objects and their names, I lead him to the A B C of the art of sense-impression (*Ansch.*). By this he is put in a position to give an account of the form of objects, which he *distinguished* in the Mother's Book, but did not *clearly* know. This book will enable the child to form clear ideas on the forms of all things by their relation to the square, and in this way to find a whole series of means within the compass of subjects of instruction, by which he may rise from vague sense-impressions to clear ideas.

With regard to the second primary means of knowledge, *Number*, I go on in the same way. After I have tried by the Mother's Book to make the child clearly conscious, before he can speak, of the ideas of *the first ten numbers*, I try to teach him these expressions for few or many things, by gradually adding *one unit to another*, and making him know the nature of *two*, and then of *three*, and so on. And thus I bring the beginning of all reckoning to the clearest sense-impression

of the child, and at the same time make him unforget-
ably familiar with the expressions which stand for
them.

Thus I bring the beginnings of arithmetic in general
into sequences which are nothing but a psychological,
certain and unbroken march onwards from deeply
impressed judgments, resting on sense-impression, to
a little additional new sense-impression, but mounting
only from 1 to 2 and from 2 to 3.   The result of this
course, ascertained by experience, is that when the
children have wholly understood the beginning of any
kind of calculation, they are able to go on without
further help.

It is generally to be noticed with respect to this
manner of teaching that it tends to make the principles of each subject so evident to the children that
they can complete every step of their learning, so that
in every case they may be absolutely considered [and
used] as teachers of their younger brothers and sisters,
as far as they have gone themselves.

The most important thing that I have done to simplify and illustrate number teaching is this: I not only
bring the consciousness of the truth within all relations
of numbers to the child, by means of sense-impression;
but I unite this truth of sense-impression with the
truth of the science of magnitudes, and have set up

the square as the common foundation of the art of sense-impression and of arithmetic.

The third primary means of knowledge, *speech*, considered as an application of my principles, is capable of the greatest extension.

If knowledge of form and number should precede speech (and this last must partly arise from the first two), it follows that the progress of grammar is quicker than that of the art of sense-impression (*Ansch.*) and arithmetic. The impression made on the senses (*Ansch.*) by form and number *precedes* the art of *speech*, but the art of sense-impression and arithmetic *come after* the *art of speech* (*grammar*). The great peculiarity and highest characteristic of our nature, *Language*, begins in the power of making sounds. It becomes gradually developed by improving *sounds* to *articulate words;* and from *articulate words* to *language*.

Nature needed ages to raise our race to perfect power of speech, yet we learn this art, for which Nature in respect to this subject needed ages, in a few months. [In teaching our children to speak] we must then follow exactly the same course that Nature followed with the human race. We dare not do otherwise. And she unquestionably began with sense-impression. Even the simplest sound by which man strove to express the impression that an object made on him, was an expression of a sense-impression.

The speech of my race was long only a *power of mimicry and of making sounds* that imitated the tones of living and lifeless nature. From *mimicry* and *sound-making* they came to *hieroglyphics* and *separate words*, and for long they gave *special* objects *special* names. This condition of language is sublimely described in the first book of Moses, ii. 19, 20: "The Lord God brought to Adam all the beasts of the earth, and all the birds under heaven, that he might *look upon them* and *name* them. And Adam gave every beast his name."

From this point speech gradually went further. Men first *observed* the striking differences in the objects that they *named*. Then they came to name properties; and then to name the differences in the *actions* and *forces* of objects. Much later the art developed of *making single words mean much*, unity, plurality, size, many or few, form and number, and at last to express clearly all variations and properties of an object which were produced by changes of time and place, by modifying the form and by joining words together.

In all these stages, speech was to the race a *means* produced by art, not only of *representing* the actual process of making manifold ideas (*Intuitionen*) clear by the power of sound, but also of *making impressions unforgetable*.

Language-teaching is, then, in its nature, nothing but a collection of psychological means of expressing impressions (feelings and thoughts); and of making all their modifications that would be else *fleeting* and *incommunicable, lasting* and *communicable* by uniting them to words.

But in consequence of the constant likeness in human nature, this can be done only through the harmony between language-teaching and the original course by which Nature herself developed our power of speaking to that art which is now ours.    That is, all instruction in language must be founded on *sense-impression*.    It must make mimicry superfluous through the art of sense-impression (or observation) and *number-teaching*. It must supersede imitation of the *sounds of animate and inanimate nature* by a series of *conventional sounds.* Then it must gradually pass from *sound-teaching,* or rather from general *exercises of the organs* in all human sounds, to *word-teaching,* to *names,* to *speech-teaching,* to grammatical declensions, inflections, and composition. But in ·this class of gradation the child must maintain the slow progressive step which Nature has foreshown in the development of the grammar of the race.

But now come the questions: How have I *held firmly* to *this course of Nature* in the three stages into which Nature and experience have divided the development of language, in respect to *sound-teaching, word-teaching,* and *speech-teaching?* How have I brought the forms of my method of instruction in these subjects into harmony with the aforesaid stages ?

I have given the highest scope of which it is capable to *sound-teaching*, by firmly holding and distinguishing the *vowels*, as the special roots of all sounds, and by gradually adding single consonants before and after the vowels. In this way I have made it possible for the child in the cradle to become conscious of all these speech-sounds and their sequences. I have even made it possible in the infant to let an *inner* sense-impression precede the *outer*, by means of this instruction, which shows the child arbitrary signs of sounds. In this way I insure that the impression on the ear should have the same start of the impression on the eye that it has in Nature's teaching of sound.

Again, I have made this subject easier to teach by arranging the sequences of sounds in this book in such a way that every succeeding sound is as like as possible to the preceding, and is only differentiated from it by the addition of a *single* letter. Thus I rise from complete familiarity with syllables to *word-teaching*, to names; and give the child a word in the first reading book, in the " word-book " and again in sequences, which by the greatest possible similarity of form makes the further steps of the reading book the easiest play, since this word has been deeply impressed and made familiar by a constant addition of a few new letters to those already known. Thus many-sided sense-impression lies at the base of the Mother's Book, of its speech-teaching, and of the meaning of the words which the child has to speak.

The infinite range of knowledge gained by sense-impression that nature brings to the child's consciousness at the earliest age is, in this book, psychologically arranged and concentrated; and the supreme law of Nature, by virtue of which the *near* is always more firmly impressed upon the child than the *distant*, is connected with the principle, which is just as important for instruction, of letting the *essential nature* of things make a far deeper impression on the children than their varying properties. In this book, by concentration and psychological arrangement of objects, the boundless range of speech and knowledge gained by sense-impression, it is made easy to the child to get a general view. The separate objects of Nature only are countless, their essential characteristics are not. Therefore, when the objects are arranged according to these characteristics, it can be made easy for the child to get a general view.

I subordinate special language-teaching to this principle. My[73] grammar is only a series of methods for enabling the child to express himself accurately about all knowledge gained by sense-impression, and its rela-

tions with number and time.  I even use for this purpose the art of writing, so far as it can be considered
as language-teaching, and have, generally, tried to use
for this same purpose all the means that Nature and
experience have put into my hand for the clearing up
of ideas.

The empirical attempts I have contrived have chiefly
served to show me that our monkish instruction, by its
neglect of all psychology, has not only driven us in all
subjects from this final end of instruction, but has
even robbed us of those methods which Nature offers
to us, without the help of the Art for making our
ideas clear; and has made the use of these means impossible for us by its pernicious effects on our minds.

Friend!  The annihilation of all real power in our
country by this unnatural monkish instruction and all
the misery of its unconnected teaching, is incredible.
Incredible, also, is the degree in which all natural means
of rising through sense-impression to true knowledge,
and all enticement to strengthen ourselves for this purpose, have vanished from our midst; because this unconnected teaching has dazzled us with the charm of a
language which we speak without having knowledge,
founded on sense-impression of the ideas which we let
fall from our mouths.  I repeat:—The mass of our
public schools not only give us nothing, but on the
contrary they quench all that in us which humanity

has without schools, that which every savage possesses, to a degree of which we can form no conception.

This is a truth which is applicable to no part of the world and no age but ours.    A man who is instructed with monkish art to this wordy foolishness is so far less susceptible to truth than a savage, and more unfit than he to make use of the guidance of Nature, and of what she does herself to make our ideas clear. These experiences have convinced me that the public school-coach throughout all Europe not only must be driven better, but must be turned round and put on quite a new road.    I am convinced of this by experience, that its fundamental error, the empty speech of our age, and our one-sided [superficial, thoughtless, senseless] jabbering must be *brought to death and laid in the grave,* before it will be possible, by *instruction* and *language* to bring forth *truth* and *life* in our race.

Verily this is a hard saying, and I am inclined to say: ". Who can hear it ? "    But I am convinced by experiments that lie at the base of this statement, that in elementary language-teaching we must reject all half measures; we must set aside all instruction-books (on this subject) which are based on the supposition[74] that a child can talk before he has learned to talk. All instruction books, the words of which bear the evidence of a complete grammar in their terminations, their prefixes, and their combinations, as well as in the composition of phrases and sentences, are in this way rendered unfit to develop clearly in the child's mind a consciousness of the causes and means which led to this completion.    Therefore I would if I had influence take apparently pitiless measures with these instruction-books in the school libraries; or give up the attempt to bring language teaching into harmony with the course of Nature. [7 5]

Dear friend! It is generally known that Nature in the first stages of the development of language in the race wholly and entirely ignores the complicated and artificial combinations of the complete grammar; and the child understands these combinations as little as the barbarian.    Only gradually, by continuous practice in simple combinations, does he gain the power of understanding the *complicated*.    Therefore my exercises in language, from the first putting aside all science and all knowledge that can only be aimed at through complete grammar, inquire into the elements of language; and give the child the advantages of forming speech in *exactly the same gradual way* in which Nature gave it to the human race.

Dear friend! Will men misunderstand me here too? [7 6] Will there be even a few who wish with me that I may succeed in checking and putting an end to the mad faith in words that from the very nature of the subject, as well as from their artificial construction and

combination, bear the stamp of incomprehensibility
for the child; and being void of all sense-impression,
by their inner emptiness work towards the devastation
of the human mind ?   May I succeed in making noise
and sound unimportant by language-teaching itself;
and again give sense-impression the preponderating
influence which is due to it; by which alone speech
may become the true basis of mental culture and of
all real knowledge, and of the power of judgment
resulting from it ?

Yes, friend.   [77]I know that for a long, long time
there will be but few who do not misunderstand me,
and who recognize that dreams, sound, and noise are
absolutely worthless foundations for mental culture.
The causes for this are many and deep-seated.   The
love of babble is so closely connected with respect for
what is called *good society*, and its pretension to wide
general culture, and still more with the livelihood of
many thousands among us, that it must be long, very
long, before the men of our time can take with love
into their hearts that truth against which they have
hardened themselves so long.

But I go on my way and say again :  All science-
teaching that is dictated, explained, analyzed, by men
who have not learnt to think and to *speak in accordance
with the laws of Nature;* all science-teaching of which
the definitions are forced as if by magic into the minds

of children like a *Deus ex Machinâ,* or rather are blown
into their ears as by a stage-prompter,—so far as it
does this must necessarily sink into a miserable bur-
lesque of education.   For where the primary powers of
the human mind are left asleep, and when words are
crammed upon the sleeping powers, we make dreamers,
who dream unnaturally and inconstantly in proportion
as the words, crammed into these miserable gaping
creatures, are big and pretentious.   [78]Such pupils
dream of anything in the world except that they are
asleep and dreaming; but the wakeful people round
them feel all their presumption; and those who see
most consider them night wanderers, in the fullest
and clearest sense of the word.

The course of Nature in the development of our
race is unchangeable.   There are and can be no *two
good* methods of instruction in this respect.   There
is but *one*—and this is the one that rests entirely upon
the eternal laws of Nature.   But of *bad* methods there
are *infinitely many;* and the badness of every one *increases* in proportion as it *deviates from* the *laws of
Nature,* and *decreases* in proportion as it *approaches* to
following these laws.

[79]I well know that this one good method is neither
in my hands nor in any other man's; that we can only
approach it.   But its completion, its perfection must
be the aim of him who would found human instruc-

tion upon truth, and thereby content human nature and satisfy its natural claims. From this point of view, I declare I pursue this method of instruction with all the powers that are in my hands. I have one rule for judging my own action, as well as the actions of all those who strive for this end—*by their fruits ye shall know them.*[80] Human power, mother-wit, and common sense are to me the only evidence of the inner worth of any kind of instruction. Any method that brands the brow of the learner with the stamp of completely stifled natural powers and the want of common sense and mother-wit, is condemned by me, whatever other advantages it may have. I do not deny that even *such* methods may produce good tailors, shoemakers, tradesmen, and soldiers; but I do deny that they can produce a tailor or a tradesman who is *a man* in the highest sense of the word.

Oh! if men would only comprehend that the aim of all instruction is, and can be, nothing but the development of human nature, by the harmonious cultivation of its powers and talents and the promotion of manliness of life. Oh, if they would only ask themselves, at every step in their methods of education and instruction,—" Does it further this end ? "[81]

I will now again consider the influence of clear ideas upon the essential development of humanity. *Clear ideas to the child are only those to which his experience*

*can bring no more clearness.*   This principle settles, first,
the order of the powers and faculties to be developed,
by which the *clearness* of all ideas can gradually be arrived at; secondly, the *order* of *objects* by which exercises
in definitions can be begun and carried on with the
children; lastly, the *exact time* at which definitions of
*any kind* contain real truth for the child.

It is evident that *clear ideas* must be worked out or
cultivated in the child by teaching, before we can take
for granted that he is *able* to understand the result of
such training—the clear idea, or rather its statement
in words.

The way to *clear ideas* depends on making all objects
clear to the reason in their proper order.   This order
again rests on the *harmony* of all the arts, by which a
child is enabled to express himself clearly about the
properties of all things, particularly about the measure, number, and form of any object.   [8][2] In this way,
and no other, can the child be led to a comprehensive
knowledge of the whole nature of any object, and become capable of defining it; that is, of stating in words
its whole nature, with the utmost precision and brevity.   All definitions,—that is, all such clear statements in words of the nature of any object,—contain
essential truth for the child only so far as he has a
clear, vivid background of sense-impression of the object.   Where thorough clearness in the sense-impres-

sion of the object to be defined is wanting, he only learns to play with words; to deceive himself; and to believe blindly in words whose sounds convey no idea to him, or give him no other thought than that he has just given out a sound.

HINC ILLÆ LACRYMÆ.

In rainy weather toadstools grow fast on every dung-heap; and in the same way definitions not founded on sense-impression produce, just as quickly, a fungus-·like wisdom, which dies just as quickly in the sun-light, and which looks upon the clear sky as poison to it. The baseless, wordy show of such baseless wisdom produces men who believe they have reached the end in all subjects, because their life is a tiresome babble about this end. They have never reached it, never pur-sued it, because all their life it has not had that attrac-tive charm for their observing powers (*Ansch.*) which is generally necessary to produce a manly effort.

Our generation is full of such men. They lie sick of a kind of wisdom that leads us *pro formâ* to the goal of knowledge, like cripples on the race course, without being able to make this goal their goal until their feet are cured. The power of describing generally pre-cedes definition. I can describe what is quite clear to me, but I cannot on that account define it. That is, I can say exactly what its properties are but not

what it is.  I only know the object, the individual ;
I cannot yet point out its relations or its kind.  Of
that which is not clear to me, I cannot say exactly
what its properties are, let alone what it is.  I cannot
describe it, much less define it.  When a third person,
to whom the matter is clear, puts words into my
mouth with which he makes it clear to *people in his own
condition*, it is not on that account clear to me, but it
is and will remain his clear thing, not mine, inasmuch
as the words of another cannot be for me what they
are to him—the exact expression of his own idea,
which is to him perfectly clear.

This purpose of leading men, with psychological art
and according to the laws of their physical mechanism,
to clear ideas, and to their expression, definitions, demands a gradation of statements about the physical
world before definitions.  This gradation proceeds
from sense-impressions of separate objects to their
names, from their names to determining their characteristics, that is the power of describing; and from the
power of describing to the power of *specializing*, that
is, of defining.  Wisdom in guiding sense-impression
is obviously the beginning-point on which this chain
of means for attaining clear ideas must depend; and it
is obvious that the final fruit, the end of all instruction, the clearness of all ideas, depends essentially on
the complete power of its first germination.

Wherever in the whole circle of all-working Nature anything is imperfect in the germ, there it has lost the power of becoming perfect in its complete ripeness. Everything that is imperfect in the germ will be crippled in its growth, in the outward development of its parts. This is as true of the products of your mind as of the products of your garden. It is as true of the results of a single idea gained by sense-impression, as it is certain of the condition of a grown cabbage.

The most important means of preventing confusion, inconsequence, and superficiality in human educaton, rests principally on care in making the first sense-impression of *things most essential* for us to know, as clear, correct, and comprehensive as possible, when they are first brought before our senses, for contemplation (*Ansch.*). Even at the infant's cradle we must begin to take the training of our race out of the hands of blind, sportive Nature, and put it into the hands of that better power which the experience of ages has taught us to abstract from the eternal laws of our nature.

[83]You must generally distinguish between the laws of Nature and her course; that is, her single workings, and statements about those workings. In her laws she is eternal truth, and for us, the eternal standard of all truth; but in her modifications, in which her laws apply to every individual and to every case, her truth

does not satisfy and content our race. The positive truth of the condition and circumstances of any individual case claims the same equal right of necessity, by virtue of eternal laws, as the common law of human nature itself. Consequently, the claim of necessity of both laws must be brought into harmony, if they are to work satisfactorily on men. Care for this union is essential for our race. The accidental is, by its existence and its consequences, as necessary as the eternal and unchangeable; but the accidental must, from its very existence and its inevitable consequences, be brought into harmony with the eternal and unchangeable in human nature by means of the freedom of the human will.

Nature, on which the inevitable laws of the existence and consequences of the accidental are based, seems only devoted to the whole, and is careless of the individual that she is affecting externally. On this side she is blind; and being blind, she is not the Nature that comes or can come into harmony with the seeing, spiritual, moral nature of men. On the contrary, it is only simple and moral nature that is able to bring itself into harmony with the physical—and that can, and ought to do so.

The laws of our senses, by virtue of the essential claims of our nature, must be subordinated to the laws of our moral and spiritual life. Without this subordination it is impossible that the physical part of our nature can ever influence the actual final result of our education, the production of manliness. Man will become man only through his inner and spiritual life. He becomes through it independent, free, and contented. Mere physical Nature leads him not hither. She is in her very nature blind; her ways are ways of darkness and death. Therefore the education and training of our race must be taken out of the hands of blind sensuous Nature, and the influence of her darkness and death, and put into the hands of our moral and spiritual being, and its divine, eternal, inner light and truth.

All, all that you carelessly leave to outer blind Nature sinks. That is true of lifeless nature as of living. Wherever you carelessly leave the earth to Nature, it bears weeds and thistles. Wherever you leave the education of your race to her, she goes no further than a confused impression on the senses that is not adapted to your power of comprehension, nor to that of your child in the way that is needed for the best instruction.

In order to lead a child in the most certain way to correct and perfect knowledge of a tree or plant, it is not by any means the best way to turn him without care into a wood or meadow where trees and plants of all kinds grow together. Neither trees nor plants here come before his eyes in such a manner as is calculated to make him observe their nature and relationships, and to prepare for a general knowledge of their subject by the first impression. In order to lead your child by the shortest way to the end of instruction, clear ideas, you must with great care first put before his eyes, visibly and distinctly, those objects (in every branch of learning) which bear the most essential characteristics of the branch to which this object belongs, and which are therefore fitted to strike the eye with the essential nature rather than the variable qualities. If you neglect this, you lead the child at the very first glance to look upon the accidental qualities as essential, and in this at least to delay the knowledge of truth, and miss the shortest road of rising from misty sense-impressions to clear ideas.

But if this error in your method of instruction is avoided, if the sequences of subjects in all branches of your instruction are brought to the child's sense-impression so arranged from the very beginning that at the very first observation (*Ansch.*) the impression of the essential nature of an object begins to overpower the impression of its qualities, the child learns from the very first to subordinate the accidental properties of an object to its essential nature. He is undoubtedly moving on the safe path, in which his power develops daily, of connecting in the simplest manner all accidental qualities with his full consciousness of the essential nature of all objects and their inner truth, and so to read all Nature as an open book.

As a child, left to itself, peeping into the world without understanding, sinks daily from error to error, through the confusion of separate scraps of knowledge which he has found while so groping; so, on the contrary, a child who is led on this road from his cradle rises gaily from truth to truth. All that exists, or at least all that comes within the range of his experience, unites itself clearly and comprehensively with the power already existing in him, and there is no error behind his views. No bias to any kind of error has been artificially and methodically organized in him, and the *nihil admirari*, which has hitherto been considered the privilege of old age, becomes, thanks to this training, the portion of innocence and youth. Having arrived at this, if he possesses fair average abilities the child will necessarily reach the final goal of instruction, clear ideas,—it matters little for the time being whether thse lead him to the conclusion that we know nothing, or that we understand everything.

In order to reach this high end, to organize the means and secure them, and especially to give the first sense-impressions of objects that breadth and accuracy which they demand in order to avoid deficiencies and error at the foundation and to build our sequences of methods of gaining knowledge on truth, I have kept all these objects fully in view in the Mother's Book.

Friend, I have succeeded; I have so far confirmed my powers of gaining knowledge through my senses by this book that I foresee that children trained by it may throw away the book and find in Nature and all that surrounds them a better guide to my goal than that which I have given them.

Friend, the book as yet is not; yet I already see it superseded by its own action.

### Note for New Edition

The Mother's Book, of which this is a dreamy account, never existed. At that moment I thought it easy to complete it. Its non-appearance is explained by the erroneous views in which I was then involved. This suggests a closer examination into the exact degree of truth I had then attained with regard to my bold ideals, and the glaring deficiencies which were caused by immature judgment. It is now twenty years since these utterances, and yet I am hardly beginning to be able to give myself a clear account of the views here expressed. I must ask myself, "How have these twenty years passed in regard to these ideals?" and I rejoice to be able to say at last: However much they appeared to hinder my attempts to develop the vague ideas I then held, in that same degree they actually favored this development, so far as it was attainable by a man of my character. Time has quenched my hopes, and I no longer stretch out my hand to pluck the moon from heaven, as a child does in his nurse's lap.

# XII

Dear friend! The statement with which I ended my last letter is important, and I now repeat more emphatically, the training for the purpose of instruction which I spoke of just now is only adapting the course of nature for that end; but there is a higher means possible of attaining it, a completion of this adapted course of nature, a course of pure reason. A training of pure reason is possible. It is possible for my nature to raise all that is uncertain in human sense-impression to the most definite truth. It is possible for my nature to separate sense-impression itself from the uncertainty of its origin in mere sensation, and to make it the work of the higher power of my being, that is of my reason. It is possible for the Art, thus ennobled by the hand of Nature, to make the wild man's living power of observation more than the mere mechanism of the senses. It is possible to add to this living power of observation my power of reason. It is possible to unite the restoration of this living power of observation with the most sublime study of my race, the study of absolute infallible truth.

Dear friend! If my life has any value, it is that I have raised the square to the foundation of a system that the people never had before of teaching by sense-impression. Through it I have prepared a series of methods for the *basis of our knowledge* such as only existed before for speech and number, which are means of instruction subordinate to it and which had never been worked out for form itself. In this way I have brought *sense-impression* and *judgment, sense-mechanism* and *the course of pure reason* into harmony with each other; and while, through this method, I have put aside the variegated hurly burly of thousands of separate truths, I have turned instruction back to truth.\*

Friend! For upwards of twenty years I hardly knew to what the following passage, in the preface of "Leonard and Gertrude", would lead: "I take no share in all the strife of men about their opinions, but whatever makes them good, brave, true, and honest; whatever can bring love of God and love of one's neighbor into the heart, and happiness and blessing into the house,—that, I think, is above all strife, and is put into every heart for us all."

Now the course of my attempts makes me see that this is very true of the kind of instruction the knowledge and introduction of which I am striving after; in this too I take no part in all the disputes of men.

---

\* This beginning is omitted in Ed. 2, probably by an oversight.

Purely as a means of developing all our powers and talents, by its *very nature* it extends its influence and its results not one step beyond that which is incontestable. Purely as a means of developing our powers, it is not the teaching of truths, but of truth. It is not a combatant against error; it is the inner development of moral and mental powers that are opposed to error. It is purely a guide to the faculty of recognizing truth and error. The very nature of its effort is only to base the good cultivation of this faculty on psychological grounds, and to supply all its needs.

Friend! I see both how far this expression leads, and how far distant I am from it. I recognize only the tracks of the means by which it may be possible to reach this end as a whole. Yet faith in the possibility of reaching this end lives, undying, in my soul. But how, when, and through whom my anticipations can or will be fulfilled, I really know not. There is no presumption in my soul. In all my efforts, the results of which lead me to these expressions, I have sought only to make easier and more simple the methods of instructing the lowest classes in my immediate neighborhood, whom I saw to be unhappy, discontented, and dangerous, in consequence of their wrong training. My heart was inclined to this effort from my youth up. From my youth up I have had opportunities, granted to few, of learning the causes of the moral, mental, and domestic degradation of the people, and the suffering, deserved or not, intimately con-- nected with it. You may believe me I have borne some suffering and some wrongs with the people.

I say it to excuse the apparent boldness of some of my assertions, for in my inmost soul lies only the ard- ent desire to help the people in the sources of their backwardness and the misery arising from it,—not the least presumption, no thought of *being able* to do it. I pray you, consider all my apparently bold expressions in this light.

When, for instance, I say distinctly the development of all human powers proceeds from an organism the action of which is absolutely certain, I do not say that the laws of this organism are clearly known by me, nor that I recognize their whole scope. When I say there is a course of pure reason in instruction, I do not say I have proved and practised these laws in their full per- fection. In the whole account of my doings I have tried far more to make the truth of my principles clear, than to bring my very restricted action to the standard of what might and must come for the human race from the complete development of these princi- ples. I do not know myself; and I feel daily more and more how much I do not know[84].

Whatever theory and judgment exist in my whole statement are absolutely nothing but the result of a

limited, very laborious, and I must add seldom successful, series of experiments.  I ought not to and I will
not conceal that if a man who had long ago sunk into
weariness, and become a poor tired creature,—who,
until his hair turned gray, had been considered everywhere absolutely impracticable by practical men,—
had not finally succeeded in becoming a schoolmaster,
and if *Buss, Krüsi* and *Tobler* had not come with a
power of helping his utter helplessness in all arts and
activities (*Fert.*), as I never dared to hope, my theories
on this subject would have died within me, like the
glow of a burning mountain that can find no outlet.
I should have sunk into my grave like a dreaming fool,
on whom no charitable judgment would be passed,
misunderstood by the good, and despised by the bad.

My only merit, my desire, my incessant ever-grow-
ing desire for the *salvation of the people,* my laborious
days, the sacrifice of my life, the murder of myself
would have been given over to the mockery of rogues.
I should not have had a friend who dared to do justice to my despised shade.  I could not have defended
myself; I could not have done it.  I should have sunk
into the grave, angry with myself and despairing at my
own misery and that of the people.  Friend! sinking
thus, I should only have retained the miserable power
of complaining against my fate.  I should,—I could
not have helped it,—I should have imputed the guilt

of my ruin to myself alone. The awful ideal of my life would have stood before my eyes, all in shadow, without any mitigating beam of light.

Friend! Imagine my feelings, my despair, this ideal of shadow, and the thought that in my ruin I should [myself] have ruined the purpose of my life; and verily by my own fault I should have lost it. There is a God who gave it me again, after I had lost it. I failed over and over again like a child, even when it seemed that the means thereto were given into my hands. Ah! I behaved long like nobody else, and things went with me as with no one else. Not only did my utter want of developed practical skill, and the entire incompatibility between the scope of my will and the limits of my power, impede from my childhood the attainment of my goal; but each year I became more unfit for everything that could really help towards its outward attainment, for that which was essentially necessary for the outward attainment of my end.

But is it my fault that the course of a life constantly crushed did not let me go on one bit of the way with an unbroken heart? Is it my fault that all signs of interest on the part of the happy, or at least the not miserable, have been erased long ago from my soul, as the traces of an island sunk in the deep? Is it my fault that men around me, around me so long! have seen nothing in me but a bleeding creature, crushed and thrown on the wayside, without consciousness,—in whom the aim of life, like an ear of corn among thorns, thistles and marshy reeds, budded up very slowly, in constant danger of death and suffocation ? Is it my fault, that the aim of my life now remains like a bare rock in the flood, from which the wasting waters have washed away every trace of the beautiful earth that once covered it ?

Yes, friend; it is my fault. I feel it deeply, and bow myself to the dust, not indeed before the judgment of bad men, buzzing round me like a disturbed nest of wasps, but before the ideal of myself, and of the inner worth to which I might have risen, if in the midst of the everlasting night of my forlorn life I had been able to rise above my fate, and above the horror of days in which all that cheers and elevates human nature vanished; while all that confuses and degrades it pressed round me unceasingly and constantly, falling with all its weight on the weakness of my heart, that found no support in my head against the blows that broke on it.

But it is my fault, friend. All my misfortune is my own fault. I could have done it; I ought to have done it; I might say I determined to do it. I did determine to raise myself above my fate—if that can be called a determination which I did not carry out. This much is true. I have grown old; the misery of my days has brought me near my grave, before the whole shattering of my nerves has completely destroyed my balance, and before the last revolt within me finally made me throw away myself and my sympathy with the human race.

Friend! A woman greater than any man,—a woman, who was only ennobled, never degraded by the misfortunes of a life that far outweighed my misery,— saw long ago my despair of myself and answered my distracted words, " *It does not matter,*" with—" O Pestalozzi! if a man once utters that word of despair may God help him; he can help himself no more."

I saw the glance of sadness and anxiety in her eyes as she spoke the word of warning; and, friend, if I had no more guilt in the final disappearance of my better self than that I could hear this word and forget it again, my guilt would be greater than that of all men who have never seen this virtue and never heard this word.

Friend! Let me now forget my action and my purpose for a moment, and give myself wholly up to the feeling of sadness that overwhelms me, because I still live and am no more my *self*. I have lost all; I have lost my *self*. Yet hast Thou, O Lord, preserved the desire of my life in me; and hast not destroyed the object of my pains before my eyes, as Thou hast destroyed the aim of a thousand men who ruined their own way before their eyes and mine.  Thou hast preserved the work of my life in the midst of my ruin, and hast cast an evening glow over my hopeless, dying old age; the lovely sight outweighs the sorrows of my life.  Lord, I am unworthy of the faith and mercy that Thou hast shown me.  Thou, Thou alone hast pitied the crushed worm.  The bruised reed Thou hast not broken, and the smoking flax Thou hast not quenched.  Till my death Thou hast not turned Thine eyes away from the offering which from childhood I wished to make, and have never been able to make, to the forsaken in the world!

### Note for the New Edition

I read this letter, written twenty years ago, with heartfelt sorrow.  It expresses my depression and my despair at the course of my life and the annihilation of my hopes, at the very moment when a new, living path for my purpose was opened.  I cannot say how my heart beats, and how the impression of feelings long ago subdued and raised again, is renewed.  The words of self-accusation shake my soul, as the mitigation of these accusations confuse it.  Gladly would I fall on my knees and pray, as I read this letter again, at a time when after twenty years I again see a new, living path opened for my purpose.  Reader! how I should feel encouraged, when after so many years I stand again at the point at which I stood then.  I must repeat, speaking of my efforts and hopes, that without the almost miraculous assistance of Providence, without the co-operation of friends (in whom I recognized almost heroic power), I should undoubtedly again have come to a state in which my laborious days, the giving up of my life, and the sacrifice of my family would to-day have been given over to the mockery of a blind crowd!

Reader! How I gain fresh courage, as after so many years I read again the passage: " Friend, imagine my feelings, my despair, and this ideal of shadow, and the thought that in my ruin I had ruined the aim of my life." Then, reader, imagine how my heart soars up in thankfulness to God, who has preserved the desire of my life in me, and has not wholly destroyed the object of my pains before my eyes.

And yet, reader, if this had been, if I had really sunk into, and had not only been nearly brought to despair but wholly conquered by it, I should yet bear witness to-day, as in that letter, half accusing myself of my misfortunes, and sink forbearing, forgiving, thanking, and loving into the grave. But, reader, how my heart beats high when I can say, as twenty years ago, " The Lord hath helped." How my heart beats as I repeat the words of that letter: " Thou, O Lord! hast preserved the desire of my life, and hast not destroyed the object of my pains before my eyes, as Thou hast destroyed the desire of thousands who spoilt their own path, before their eyes and mine. Thou hast preserved the work of my life in the midst of my ruin. Thou hast cast an evening glow over my hopeless old age, and the sight of its beauty compensates for my sufferings. Lord, I am unworthy of Thy loving kindness and faithfulness. Thou, Thou alone hast had pity for the crushed worm; Thou, Thou alone hast left the bruised reed unbroken, and the smoking flax unquenched. Thou hast not rejected the sacrifice that from childhood I would have made for the poor and forsaken in the land, and have never made."

Reader, forgive the repetition of the same words in the same page. But the ardent desire of my heart will not permit me to oppose this new feeling of salvation and happiness that must be expressed and put down in words, that I wrote twenty years ago. I must use them to express the feelings of the present hour with the words of to-day. You will, I know, willingly forgive this repetition.

# XIII

In my last letter my feelings would not allow me to say more. I put my pen away, and I did well. What are words when the heart bows itself in dark despair, or rises in highest rapture to the clouds?

Friend, what are words even apart from these heights and depths!

In the eternal nothingness of the most sublime characteristic of our race, human speech, and then again in its sublime power, I see the mark of the external limitation of the shell in which my cramped-up spirit pines. I see in it the ideal of the lost innocence of my race; but I see in it also the ideal of the shame which the memory of this lost holiness always awakens in me, so long as I am not wholly unworthy. This feeling, so long as I have not sunk in the depths, ever revives within me the power of seeking what I have lost, and of saving myself from ruin.

Friend, so long as man is worthy of the sublime characteristic of his race, speech, so long as he uses it as a powerful means of expression and for the maintenance of his human superiority, with a pure desire to ennoble himself and humanize himself by it, it is a high and holy thing. But when he is no longer worthy;

when he no longer uses it as a powerful expression of his human superiority, and with no pure desire to humanize himself, it will be nothing but a natural inexhaustible source of illusion, the use of which will lead to the loss of his manliness, to effeminacy and brutality.   It will be to him the first and most powerful means of completely ruining his moral and spiritual nature, and the first source of his domestic misery, civil wrong-doing and wrong suffering, and the public crime arising from it.

Meanwhile he most skilfully makes it into a cloak for all this ruin and crime.   It is incalculable how deeply the depravity of our language has spread; how deep a hold it has on all the aspects of the world of our time; how its tone is to be found in good society, at court, in the law courts, in books, in comedies, in periodicals, in daily papers,—in short, it is everywhere in our midst, with all its dissolute force.   It is notorious that now, more than ever before, it is encouraged from the cradle; it is inspired by the school; it is strengthened through life; I might even say it speaks from the pulpit and the council-chamber, down to the tavern and the beershop; it is heard among us everywhere.   All the sources of human depravity and sensuality find a centre in it, in which they collect and unite for their common interest, and become infectious.

By this, and this only, can we explain the terrible fact

that the depravity of language grows with the depravity of men. Through it the wretched become more wretched; through it the night of error becomes still darker; through it crimes of the wicked still increase. Friend! the crimes of Europe are still increasing through idle talk. It is connected with over-civilization, and its results are influencing the condition of all our feelings, thoughts, and actions. It is connected with the far-reaching increase of our *slavery*. It is intimately connected with the equally far-reaching loss of independence, not only in the common, lower classes of the country, but of our so-called gentry, notables, and persons of importance; and it is also connected with the increasing degeneration of our middle class, the recognized first and most essential support of all true political power and civil happiness.

The daily increasing list of publications is only an insignificant symptom of this great evil of our time. But the public and private placards on the corners of our walls, increasing daily in number and size, are often more significant indications of this evil than the swollen list of publications. Yet in any case we cannot guess to what this chattering degeneracy will lead a generation which has already reached the state of so many countries in our part of the world by its weakness, confusion, violence, and inconsequence.[85]

But I return to my path. In my experimental inquiries into the subject, I started from no positive notion of teaching—I had *none*—I ask myself simply, " What would you do, if you wished to produce in a single child, all the *knowledge* and *ability* (*Fert.*) that it needs, in order *by wise care of its essential concerns to attain to inward content ?*"

But I see now that in the whole series of my letters to you, I have only considered the first portion of the subject, the training of the child's *judgment* and *knowledge;* but not the training of his *activities* (*Fert.*), so far as these are not especially activities brought out by instruction [in knowledge and science]. And yet the activities that a man needs to attain inner content by their possession are not actually limited to the few subjects that the nature of instruction forced me to touch upon.

I cannot leave these gaps untouched. Perhaps the most fearful gift that a fiendish spirit has made to this age is *knowledge without power of doing* (*Fert.*) *and insight without that power of exertion or of overcoming* that makes it possible and easy for our life to be in harmony with our inmost nature.

Man! needing much and desiring all, thou must to satisfy thy wants and wishes *know* and *think*, but for this thou must also [*can* and] *do.* And knowing and doing are so closely connected that if one ceases the other ceases with it.[86]. But there can be this har-

mony between thy life and thy inmost nature only if
the *powers of doing* (*Fert.*) (without which it is impossible to satisfy thy wishes and wants) are cultivated in
thee with just the same art, and raised to the same
degree of perfection, as thy insight into the objects of
thy wants and wishes.   The cultivation of these activities rests then on the same organic[87] laws as the cultivation of knowledge.

The organism[87] of Nature is one and the same in
the living plant; in the animal, whose nature is merely
physical; and in man, whose nature is also physical,
but who possesses will.   In the threefold results which
Nature is capable of producing in me, she is always the
same.   Her laws work either physically upon my physical nature, in the same manner as upon animals generally; or, secondly, they work upon me so far as they
determine the *sensuous basis of my judgment and will.*
In this respect they are the sensuous basis of my opinions, my inclinations, and my resolutions.   Thirdly,
they work upon me so far as *they make me capable of that
practical skill* (*Fert.*), the need of which I *feel* through
my instinct, 1 *recognize* through my insight, and the
learning of which I *command* through my will.   But in
this respect also, the Art must take the cultivation of
our race out of the hands of Nature, or rather from
her accidental attitude towards each individual, in
order to put it in the hands of knowledge, power, and

methods, which she has taught us for ages to the advantage of the race.

Certainly men never lose the feeling for the necessity of being cultivated in the activities required in ordinary life, even in the deepest decadence caused by over-refinement and artificial training. * Still less does the individual man lose this consciousness.

Natural instinct, in all moral, mental, and practical things, drives him with his whole force into paths of life in which this consciousness of need increases and develops daily. This tends in every way to take his improvement out of the hands of blind Nature, and out of the one-sided, over-refined, and artificial training of his senses, in this case intimately connected with the blindness of Nature, and put it into the hands of those intelligent powers, methods, and arts which have been raising our race of ages.

But in every case bodies of men succumb to the claims of sensuous nature and its over-refined and artificial training, far, far more than individuals. This is true even of governments. They succumb as bodies, masses, or corporations to the claims of our sensuous nature and its atrophy, far more than individuals, or

---

*Abrichtungsverderben*, degeneracy or decadence caused by artificial or circus training; that is, training possible but not in harmony with the true nature of the creature trained.

even the individual members of the corporations. It is certain, in matters in which a father would not easily act wrongly towards his son, or a teacher towards his pupils, a government may very easily act wrongly towards its people.

It cannot well be otherwise. Human nature acts with far greater gentleness and purer power on each individual than it ever can on masses, corporations, or communities of men, whatever they may be. The first common instinct of human nature remains, and keeps itself infinitely purer and more powerful, in the individual, than in any corporation or community. Instinct stimulates no body or community of men as it can and does stimulate the individual. It loses the basis of harmony from which its influence on the whole compass of human powers may and should start and aspire. It is undeniable that whatever is holy and divine in instinct expresses itself in the individual by its harmonious influence on all natural powers. This holy and divine quality in instinct becomes crippled and ineffectual (whatever form its one-sidedness may take) in every case where it influences any mass or body of men in their collective capacity, and by this very influence produces in them an *esprit du corps* with its deadening influences. Instinct affects masses of men of whatever kind with the same deadening force that every kind of union among men produces in itself; and wherever this is the case, there its influence on truth and justice, and in consequence on national enlightenment and national happiness, is inevitably hindered.

This distinction between the effect of instinct upon individuals and upon bodies of men is of the highest importance, and deserves far more attention than it gets. It throws, when we understand it, decided light on many phenomena of human life, particularly on many actions of governments which else would be incomprehensible. It also explains why we must not expect too much of governments with regard to the care of the individual, of the education of the people. and everything on which the common weal depends—things which can only be accomplished by individuals.

No, it is an eternal truth, easily explained by human nature, and shown in all the history of the world, that what can be done by the life and energy of individuals in the state, that is by the people, cannot be done so well by the government. We cannot expect it, much less demand it. The only thing we can ask is that the individual should not be allowed to sink down into want of power and will. Governments ought to try to guard against this want of power in the individual, in those matters in which he could accomplish and contribute anything himself to forward the public good; and should neglect nothing that every individual needs for the cultivation of his intelligence, disposition, and abilities, in order as an individual to be able to do his part for the public good.

But it grieves me to say that the governments of our time are not strong and living enough for the practical skill required for this end.   It is undeniable that the people of our part of the world do not enjoy the practical help that each man needs for the cultivation of his intelligence, disposition, and ability (*Fert.*), in order, on the one hand, by wise care of his own business to attain inner self-content; and on the other to facilitate, provide, and secure to the state all that it needs, in order as a state to find help and assistance in its millions of individuals, for that which it can only maintain through the good condition of the moral, mental, and practical powers of these individuals. [88]

HERE IS A GREAT GAP *

---

* Much as I have wished and resolved to leave the original edition of this work unaltered, and to give free course to the stream of my opinions and thoughts at that time, I have here suppressed a long passage that expressed my feelings about the position of the people and our country at that time, although the *horrible events* of the twenty years between the first and second edition have in many ways confirmed these opinions.   I was obliged to suppress them.   I now regard the condition of the people with more sorrow than zeal; and my views of remedies for the evils of

All ability (*Fert.*), on the possession of which depend all the powers of knowing and doing that are required by an educated mind and a noble heart, comes as little of itself as the *intelligence* and *knowledge* that man needs for it.  As the cultivation of mental powers and faculties presupposes a psychologically arranged gradation of means, adapted to human nature, so the cultivation of the faculties which these powers of doing (*Fert.*) presuppose, rests on the deep-rooted mechanism of an A B C of *Art;* that is on universal laws of the Art, by following which the children may be educated by a series of exercises, proceeding gradually from the simplest to the most complicated.  These must result, with physical certainty, in obtaining for them a daily increasing facility in all that they need for their education.

But this A B C is anything but *found*.  It is quite natural that we seldom find anything that nobody looks for.  But if we would seek it with all the earnestness with which we are wont to seek any small advantage in the money-market, it would be easy to find, and when found would be a great blessing to mankind.  It must start from the simplest manifestations of physical pow-

---

the time tend rather to more sorrow than to the eloquence of youthful zeal, the shrill expressions of which, with whatever reserve of love, truth and justice, rather extinguish than kindle the holy, eternal, inner nature of love.—Pestalozzi.

ers, which contain the foundations of the most complicated human practical ability[89] (*Fert.*). Striking and
carrying, thrusting and throwing, drawing and turning, encircling and swinging, etc., are extremely simple
expressions of our physical powers. In themselves
essentially different, they contain, all together and
each separately, the foundations of all possible actions
(*Fert.*), even the most complicated, on which human
callings depend. Therefore, it is obvious that the
A B C of actions must start altogether from early psychologically arranged exercises in these actions, all and
each. This A B C of limb exercise must, naturally,
be brought into harmony with the A B C of sense exercises, and with all the mechanical practice in thinking, and with exercises in form and number-teaching.

But as we are far behind the Appenzell woman and
her paper bird in the A B C of *Anschauung*, so are we
far behind the greatest barbarians in the A B C of actions, (gymnastics) (*Fert.*), and their skill in striking
and throwing, thrusting and dragging.

We want a graduated series of exercises, from their
simplest beginning to their highest perfection; that is,
to the utmost delicacy of nerve power which enables
us to perform with certainty and in a hundred different
ways the actions of thrusting and parrying, swinging
and throwing. We want, too, actions exercising hand
and foot in opposite as well as in the same directions.

All these, as far as popular instruction is concerned, are castles in the air. The ground is clear. We have spelling schools, writing schools, catechism (Heidelberger) schools only, and we want—*men's schools.*

⁹⁰ But these can be of no use to those whose whole idea is to keep things as they are, to the jobbery and injustice that are so readily maintained by this idea; nor to the nervous state of the gentry whose interests are involved in this contemptible state of *laissez-faire.* [But I almost forget the point at which I began.]

The mechanism of activities takes the same course as that of knowledge, and its foundations with regard to self-education are perhaps still more far-reaching. In order to *be able,* you must *act;* in order *to know,* you must, in many cases, *keep passive;* you can only see and hear. Hence in relation to your activities you are not only the centre of their cultivation, but in many cases you determine their ultimate use—always within the laws of the physical mechanism. As in the infinite range of lifeless nature, its situation, needs, and relations have determined the special characteristics of every object; so in the infinite range of living nature that produces the development of your faculties, your situation, needs, and relations determine the sort of power (*Fert.*) that you specially need.

⁹¹ These considerations throw light on the mode of developing our activities, and also on the character of

the activities when developed. Every influence that in the development of our powers and activities turns us away from the centre point on which rests the personal responsibilitiy of everything that man is bound throughout his life to do, to bear, to attend and provide for, must be regarded as an influence opposed to wise manly education. Every influence leading us to apply our powers and activities in a way that turns us away from this central point, and thus weakens or robs the activities of the special character which our duty towards ourselves requires of us, or puts us out of accord with them, or in some way or other makes us incapable of serving our fellow-men or our country, must be regarded as a deviation from the laws of nature, from the harmony with myself and my surroundings. Therefore it is a hindrance to my self-culture, to the training for my calling, and to my sense of duty. It is a delusive and self-destructive deviation from the pure and beautiful dependence of my relations in life on my real character.

92 Every kind of instruction or education, every kind of life, every use of our trained powers and talents in life, which bears in itself the seeds of such discord between our education and our actions, and the real character of our being, our relations and our duties, must be guarded against by all fathers and mothers who have their children's life-long peace of mind at heart; for

we must seek the sources of the infinite evil of our baseless *sham-enlightenment*, and the misery of our *masquerade revolution*, in errors of this kind ; since both find a place alike in the instruction and in the life of our educated and uneducated people.

The necessity of great care for the psychological manner of developing and cultivating our powers of doing (*Fert.*), as well as the psychological training for the development of our power of knowing, is obvious. This psychological training for the development of our powers of knowing is based on an A B C of *Anschauung*, and must lead the child by this fundamental clue to the fullest purity of clear ideas.   For the cultivation of the activities, on which the sense-foundation of our *virtue* rests, we must seek for an A B C for developing this power; and on its lines a sense-cultivation, a physical dexterity of those powers and activities which are needed for the life-duties of our race,[93] which we must recognize as *leading strings in the nursery of virtue*, until our senses, ennobled by this training, need the leading-strings no longer.

In [94] this way can be developed a general kind of education, suitable to the human race, for training those practical abilities which are necessary for the fulfilment of the duties of life.   It goes from *complete power of doing to the recognition of law*, just as the education of intelligence goes from *complete sense-impression to clear ideas,* and from these to their expression in words, to definitions.

Therefore it is that as *definitions before sense-impression* lead men to presumptuous chatter, so word-teachings about virtue and faith, preceding the realities of living sense-impressions, lead men astray to similar confusion about them.  It is undeniable that the presumption of these confusions, by virtue of the inner profanity and impurity that lie at the bottom of all presumption, leads even the virtuous faithful generally to the common vice of presumption.  I believe also (experience speaks loudly on this view, and it must be so) that gaps in the early sense-cultivation of virtue have the same consequences as gaps in the early sense-cultivation of knowledge. [95]

But I see myself at the beginning of a far greater problem than that which I think I have solved.  I see myself at the beginning of this problem:—

" How can the child, considering the nature of his disposition, and the changeableness of his circumstances and relations, be so trained that whatever is demanded of him in the course of his life by necessity and duty may be easy to him, and may if possible become second nature to him ? "

I see myself at the beginning of the task of forming in the child in its baby clothes a satisfactory wife, the helpmeet of her husband, a good and vigorous mother,

who fulfils her duties well.   I see myself at the beginning of the task of making the child in its baby clothes
the satisfactory husband of the woman, and a strong
father, filling his place well.

What a task, my friend !   To make the spirit of his
future calling a second nature to the son of man.
And what a still higher task to bring the sense-means
of facilitating the virtuous and wise disposition of mind
into the blood and veins, before the hot desires for
sensual pleasures have so infected blood and veins as
to make virtue and wisdom impossible.

Friend!   This problem is also solved.   The same
laws of the physical mechanism that develop in me the
sense-foundations of knowledge are also the sense-
means of facilitating my virtue.   But, dear friend, it
is impossible for me to go into the details of this solution now.   I reserve it for another time.

## XIV

Friend! As I said, it would have led me too far to enter into details of the principles and laws upon which the cultivation of the practical abilities (*Fert.*) in life depend. But I will not end my letters without touching on the keystone of my whole system, namely this question,—How is religious feeling connected with these principles which I have accepted as generally true for the development of the human race?

Here also I seek the solution of my problem in myself, and I ask: How is the idea of God germinated in my soul? How comes it that I believe in God, that I throw myself in His arms, and feel blessed when I love Him, trust Him, thank Him, follow Him?

I soon see that the feelings of love, trust, gratitude, and readiness to obey, must be developed in me before I can apply them to God. I must love men, trust men, thank men, and obey men before I can aspire to love, thank, trust, and obey God. For whoso loveth not his brother whom he hath seen, how can he love God whom he hath not seen?

Then I ask myself: How do I come to love, trust, thank, and obey men? How come those feelings in my nature on which human love, human gratitude, human confidence rest, and those activities by which obedience is formed ?   And I find: *That they have their chief source in the relations that exist between the baby and his mother.*

The mother is forced by the power of animal instinct to tend her child, feed him, protect and please him. She does this.   She satisfies his wants, she removes anything unpleasant, she comes to the help of his helplessness.   The child is cared for, is pleased.   *The germ of love is developed in him.*

Now put an object that he has never seen before his eyes; he is astonished, frightened; he cries.   The mother presses him to her bosom, dandles him, and diverts him.   He leaves off crying, but his eyes are still wet.   The object appears again.   The mother takes him into her sheltering arms and smiles at him again.   Now he weeps no more.   He returns his mother's smile with clear unclouded eyes.   *The germ of trust is developed in him.*

The mother hastens to his cradle at his every need. She is there at the hour of hunger, she gives him drink in the hour of thirst.   When he hears her step he is quiet; when he sees her he stretches out his hands.   His eye is cast on her breast.   He is satisfied. Mother, and being satisfied, are one and the same thought to him.   *He is grateful.*

The germs of love, trust, and gratitude soon grow.

The child knows his mother's step; he smiles at her shadow.   He loves those who are like her; a creature like his mother is a good creature to him.   He smiles at his mother's face, at all human faces; he loves those who are dear to his mother.   Whom his mother embraces, he embraces; whom his mother kisses, he kisses too.   *The germ of human love, of brotherly love is developed in him.*

Obedience in its origin is an activity whose driving-wheel is opposed to the first inclinations of animal nature.   Its cultivation rests on art.   [96] It is not a simple result of pure instinct, but it is closely connected with it.   Its first stage is distinctly instinctive. As *want* precedes love, *nourishment* gratitude, and care trust, so *passionate desire* precedes obedience.   The child screams before he waits; he is impatient before he obeys.   Patience is developed before obedience; he becomes obedient only through patience.   The first manifestations (*Fert.*) of this virtue are simply passive; they arise generally from a consciousness of hard necessity.   But this, too, is first developed on the mother's lap.   The child must wait until she opens her breast to him; he must wait until she takes him up.   *Active* obedience develops much later, and later still the consciousness that it is good for him to obey his mother.

*The developement of the human race begins* in a strong passionate desire for the satisfaction of physical wants.

The mother's breast stills the first storm of physical needs and creates *love;* soon after *fear* is developed. The mother's arm stills *fear.* These actions produce the *union* of the feelings of love and trust, and develop the first germ of *gratitude.*

Nature is inflexible towards the passionate child. He beats wood and stone; Nature is inflexible, and the child *ceases to beat* wood and stone. Now the mother is inflexible towards his irregular desires. He rages and roars—she is still inflexible. He *leaves off crying;* he becomes accustomed to subject his will to hers. *The first germs of patience, the first germs of obedience are developed.*

Obedience and love, gratitude and trust united, develop the first germ of conscience, the first faint shadow of the feeling that *it is not right* to rage against the loving mother; the first faint shadow of the feeling that the mother is not in the world *altogether for his sake;* the first faint shadow of a feeling that everything in the world is not altogether for his sake; and with it is also germinated the feeling that *he himself* is not in the world for *his own sake* only. The first shadow of duty and right is in the germ.

These are the first principles of moral self-development, which are unfolded by the natural relations between mother and child. But in them lies the whole essence of the natural germ of that state of mind which

is peculiar to human dependence on the Author of our
being. That is, the germ of all feelings of dependence on God, through faith, is in its essence the same
germ which is produced by the infant's dependence on
its mother. The manner in which these feelings develop is one and the same.

In both, the infant hears, believes, follows; but in
both at this time it *knows* not what it believes and *what
it does.* Meanwhile, at this time, the *first grounds* of its
faith and actions begin to vanish. Growing independence makes the child let go his mother's hand. He
begins to become conscious of his own personality, and
a secret thought unfolds itself in his heart,—" *I no
longer need my mother.* " She reads the growing thought
in his eyes; she presses her darling more firmly to her
heart, and says, in a voice he has not yet heard:
" Child, there is a God whom thou needest, who
taketh thee in His arms when thou needest me no
longer, when I can shelter thee no more. There is a
God who prepares joy and happiness for thee when I
can no more give them thee."

Then an inexpressible something rises in the child's
heart, a holy feeling, a desire for faith, that raises
him above himself. He rejoices in the name of God as
soon as he hears his mother speak it. The feelings of
love, gratitude, and trust that were developed at her
bosom, extend and embrace God as father, God as

mother.   The practice (*Fert.*) of obedience has a wider field.   The child, who believes from this time forwards in the eye of God as in the eye of his mother, does right now for *God's sake*, as he formerly did right for his *mother's sake*.

Here, in this first attempt of the mother's innocence and the mother's heart to *unite the first feeling of independence with the newly developed feeling of morality through the inclination to faith in God*, the foundations are disclosed on which education and instruction must cast their eyes if they would aim with certainty at ennobling us.

As the first germination of love, gratitude, trust, and obedience was a simple result of the *coincidence of instinctive feelings* between mother and child, so the *further development* of these germinated feelings is a *high human art*.   But it is an art the threads of which will be *lost* in your hands if for one moment you lose sight of the origin from which the web springs.   The danger of this loss to the child is great, and comes early.   He lisps his mother's name, he loves, thanks, trusts, and follows.   He lisps the name of God, he loves, thanks, trusts, and follows.   But the motives of gratitude, love, and trust vanish with the first appearance of the idea: *He needs his mother no more.*   The world that now surrounds him appears to him in a new light, and entices him with its pleasure, saying, " *You are mine now.* "

The child cannot but hear this voice. The instinct of the infant is quenched in him; the instinct of *growing powers take its place;* and the germ of morality, *in so far as it begins in feelings that are proper to the infant,* suddenly withers up, and must wither if at this moment no one attaches to the golden spindle of creation the thread of his life that is the first throbbing of the higher feelings of his moral nature.

Mother, mother! the world is now beginning to wean your child from your heart; and if at this moment no one connects his nobler nature with the new revelation of the world of sense, it is all over. Mother, mother, your child is torn from your heart. The new world becomes his mother, *the new world* becomes his god, *sensual pleasure* becomes his god, *self-will* becomes his god.

Mother, mother! he has lost you, he has lost God, he has lost himself. The touch of love is quenched for him. The germ of *self-respect* is dead within him. He is going towards destruction, striving only after sensual enjoyment.

Mankind, mankind! now with this transition when the feelings of infancy vanish in the first consciousness of the charm of the world, independent of the mother —now when the ground in which the noblest feelings of nature germinate begins for the first time to tremble under the child's feet; now when the mother begins to

be no more what she once was to her child; now when
the germ of trust in the new aspect of the world is developed in him, and the charm of this new manifestation begins to *stifle and devour* his trust in his mother,
who is no more what she once was to him, and with it
his trust in an unseen and unknown God—as the wild
web of tangled roots of the poisonous plant stifle and
devour the finer web of roots of the noblest plants,—
now, mankind! now at this moment of transition between the feelings of trust in mother and God, and
those of trust in the new aspect of the world and all
that therein is,—now at this parting place, you should
use all your art and all your power to keep the feelings
of love, gratitude, trust, and obedience pure in your
child.

God is in these feelings, and the whole power of your
moral life is intrinsically connected with their preservation.

Mankind! at this time when the physical causes of
the germination of these feelings in the infant cease,
your Art should do everything to bring to hand *new
methods of stimulating them, and to let the attractions of
the world come before the mind of your growing child only in
connection with them.*

Now for the first time you *cannot trust Nature*, but
must *do everything* to *take* the reins out of her blind
*hands* and put them into the hands of principles and

powers in which the experience of ages has put them. The world that appears before the child's eyes is not God's first creation; it is a world spoilt alike for the innocent enjoyment of the senses and for the feelings of his inner nature. It is a world full of war for the means of gratifying selfishness, full of contradiction, full of violence, presumption, lying, and deceit.

Not God's first creation but *this* world decoys the child to the giddy dance of the whirlpool of the abyss whose depths are the home of lovelessness and moral death. Not God's creation, but the brute force and art of bringing about its own ruin, is what *this* world puts before the child's eyes.

Poor child! your dwelling-room is your world; but your father is bound to his workshop, your mother is vexed to-day, has company to-morrow, and has whims the next day. You are bored; you ask questions; your nurse will not answer. You want to go out; you may not. Now you quarrel with your sister about a toy.—Poor child! what a miserable, heartless, heart-corrupting thing your world is! But is it anything more when you drive about in a gilded carriage under shady trees? Your guide deceives your mother. You suffer less, but you become worse than all sufferers. What have you gained? Your world is become a heavier load to you than any pain.

This world is so rocked to sleep in the ruin of a perverse and oppressive opposition to the laws of Nature that it has no mind for being the means of preserving purity in the heart of man; on the contrary, it is as careless at the critical moment of the innocence of our race as a heartless second wife of her step-child: a carelessness that in a hundred cases to one *causes and must cause* the wreck of the last means that is left us for ennobling our race.

At this time the child has no counterpoise that can be opposed to the phenomena of the world and the one-sided charm of its impressions on the senses; and so its conceptions, both through their one-sidedness and through their vividness, maintain a decided preponderance over the impressions of *experiences* and *feelings* which *lie at the base* of the moral and spiritual improvement of our race. Henceforth an infinite and infinitely living field is opened up for selfish and degraded passions. On the other hand, the way to that state of mind on which the powers of his intelligence and enlightenment rest is lost; that path to the narrow gate of morality is blocked up; the whole sensuousness of his nature must take a direction separating the *path of reason* from that of *love,* and the *improvement of the mind* from the *impulse towards faith in God,*—a way that more or less makes selfishness the one driving wheel of all his actions, and thereby determines the result of his culture to his own destruction.

It is incomprehensible that mankind does not recognize this *universal source of ruin.* It is incomprehensible that it is not the one *universal aim of their Art* to stop it, and to *subordinate* the education of our race to *principles* which do not destroy the *work of God,* the feelings of love, gratitude, and trust already developed in infancy, but which must at this dangerous time tend specially to care for those *means of uniting our moral and spiritual improvement* implanted in our nature by God Himself, and of bringing education and instruction into harmony on the one side with those *laws of the physical mechanism* according to which our God raises us from vague sense-impressions to clear ideas ; and on the other with *those feelings of my inner nature* through the gradual development of which my mind rises to recognize and venerate the *moral law.*

It is incomprehensible that mankind *does not begin to bring out a perfect gradation of methods of developing the mind and feelings,* the essential purpose of which should be to use the advantages of instruction and its mechanism for the preservation of moral perfection; to prevent the selfishness of the reason by preserving the purity of the heart from error and one-sidedness; and, above all, to *subordinate* my sense-impressions to my convictions, my eagerness to my benevolence, and my benevolence to my righteous will.

The causes which make this subordination necessary,

lie deep in my nature. As my physical powers *increase*, their *preponderance*, by virtue of the laws of my development, *must vanish*, that is they must be *subordinated* to a higher law. But every step of my development must be completed before it can be subordinated to a higher purpose. This subordination of that which is already complete to that which is to be completed, requires above all pure *holding fast* to the *beginning-points* of all knowledge, and the most exact continuity in gradual progress from these beginning-points to the final *completion*. The primary law of this continuity is this: the first instruction of the child should never be the business of the *head* or of the *reason ;* it should always be the business of the senses, of the *heart*, of the *mother*.

The second law, that follows it, is this: human education goes on slowly from exercise of the senses to exercise of the judgment. It is for a long time the business of the *heart*, before it is the business of the *reason*. It is for a long time the business of the *woman* before it begins to be the business of the *man*.

What shall I say more ?—With these words the eternal laws of nature lead me back to your hand, *mother !* Mother! I can keep my innocence, my love, my obedience, the excellences of my nobler nature with the new impressions of the world, *all, all* at *your side* only. Mother, mother! while you have still a hand, a heart

for me, let me not turn away from you.    If no one
has taught you to know the world as I am forced to
learn it, *then come, we will learn it together*, as you ought,
and I must.    Mother, mother! we will not *part from
each other* at the moment when I run into danger of being drawn away from you, from God, and from myself,
by the new phenomena of the world.    Mother, mother!
*sanctify the transition from your heart to this world by the
support of your heart.*

Friend! I must be silent.    My heart is moved, and
I see tears in your eyes.    Farewell!

# XV

Friend! I go further now and ask myself: What have I done to work against the evils that affected me throughout my life, from a religious point of view? Friend! If by my efforts I have in any way succeeded in preparing the road to the goal at which I have been aiming, that is to take human education out of the hands of blind Nature, to free it from the destructive influence of her sensual side and the power of the routine of her miserable teaching, and to put it into the hands of the noblest powers of our nature, the soul of which is faith and love; if I can only in some slight degree succeed in making the Art of education begin in the sanctuary of home, more than it now does, and to put new life into the religious instinct of our race, from this tender side; if I should only have partly succeeded in bringing nearer to my contemporaries the withered rootstock of mental and spiritual education, and an Art of education in harmony with the noblest powers of heart and mind: if I have done this, my life will be blessed, and I shall see my greatest hopes fulfilled. [97]

I will dwell a moment longer on this point. The germ out of which spring the feelings that are essential to religion and morality, is the same from which the whole spirit of my method of teaching arises. It begins entirely in the natural relation which exists between the infant and its mother, and essentially rests on the Art of connecting instruction from the cradle upwards with this natural relation, and building it with continuous Art upon a state of mind that resembles our dependence on the Author of our being.

When the physical dependence of child on mother begins to vanish, my method uses all possible means to prevent the germ of the nobler feelings that arose from this dependence from withering away ; and as the physical causes cease, it supplies new sources of vitality.

At the important moment of the first separation of the feelings of trust in mother and God, and of reliance on the phenomena of the world, it applies all possible power and Art so that the charm of the new phenomena of the world shall always appear to the child in connection with the nobler feelings of his nature.

It uses all its power and Art to let these phenomena come before his eyes as God's *first creation*, not merely as a world full of lying and deceit. It limits the one-sided charm of the new phenomena by stimulating dependence upon mother and God. It limits the boundless free play of selfishness, to which the destructive phenomena of the world lead my animal nature, and

does not allow the path of my reason to divide absolutely from the path of my heart, nor the improvement
of my mind to separate me absolutely from my impulse
of faith in God.

The whole spirit of my method is not only to renew
the bond between mother and child, with the disappearance of its physical cause, but to put a methodical
series of means, that is an Art, into her hand by which
she can give permanence to this relation between her
heart and her child, until the sense-methods of making
virtue easy, united with the sense-methods of acquiring knowledge, may be able by exercise to ripen the
independence of the child in all that concerns right
and duty.

It has made it easy for every mother whose heart is
her child's to keep him not only at the critical period
from the danger of being drawn away from God and
love, to save his soul from dreadful withering, and
himself from being given up to unavoidable bewilderment, but also to lead him by the hand of her love and
with pure, supporting, noble feelings into God's best
creation, before his heart is spoilt for the impressions
of innocence, truth, and love by all the lying and deceit of this world.

For the woman who makes my method her own, her
child is no longer confined within the miserable and
limited sphere of her own actual knowledge. The

Mother's Book opens to her for her child the world which is God's world. The purest love opens her mouth for all that the child sees through her. She has taught him to lisp the name of God on her bosom; now she shows him the All-loving in the rising sun, in the rippling brook, in the branches of the trees, in the splendor of the flower, in the dewdrops. She shows him the All-present in himself, in the light of his eyes, in the flexibility of his joints, in the tones of his voice,—in everything she shows him God; and wherever he sees God his heart rises, wherever he sees God in the world he loves the world. Joy in God's world is interwoven with joy in God. He includes God, the world, and his mother in one and the same emotion. The torn bond is joined together again. He loves his mother more now than when he lay upon her breast.

He stands now a step higher. He is now raised through the very same world by which he would have been bewildered if he had not learned to know it through his mother. The mouth that smiled on him so often from the day of his birth, the voice that from the day of his birth has so often foretold joy to him, this voice now teaches him to talk. The hand that pressed him so often to her heart now shows him pictures whose names he has often heard. A new feeling germinates in his breast. He becomes conscious by words of what he sees. The first step of the gradation of the union of his spiritual and moral improvement is open. The mother's hand opens it; the child learns, knows, and names; he wishes to know more, to name more. He forces the mother to learn with him; she learns with him, and both mount daily to knowledge, power, and love.

Now she attempts with him the elements and grounds of art, straight and curved lines. The child soon out-steps her—the joy of both is equal, new powers develop in his mind, he *draws, measures, reckons.* The mother shows him God in the aspect of the world; now she shows him God in his drawing, measuring, reckoning, in all his powers. He now sees God in his self-perfection. The law of perfection is the law of his training. He recognizes it in the first perfect drawing, in one straight or curved line—yes, friend, with the first perfect drawing of a line, with the first perfect pronunciation of a word, the first idea of the high law: " Be ye also perfect, as your Father in heaven is perfect " is developed in his breast. And since my method rests essentially on constant efforts towards the perfection of single things, it works powerfully and constantly to impress the spirit of this law *deeply* in the child's breast from the cradle upwards.

To this first law of your inner perfection a second is united, intrinsically interwoven with the first. This is,—Man is not in the world for his own sake only; he can perfect himself only through the perfection of his brethren. My method seems exactly fitted to make these two laws, united, second nature to the children, almost before they know right from left. The child of my method can hardly talk before he is his brother's teacher and his mother's helper.

Friend! It is not possible to join the bonds of the feelings on which true reverence for God rests more tightly than it is done by the whole spirit of my method. By it I have preserved the mother for the child, and procured permanence for the influence of her heart. By it I have united God's worship with human nature, and secured their preservation by stimulating those emotions from which the impulse of faith is germinated in our hearts. Mother and Creator, mother and Preserver, become through it one and the same emotion for the child. By it the child remains longer *his mother's child;* by it he remains longer *God's child.* The gradual development of his mind and heart united rests longer on the pure beginning-points from which their germs sprang.

The path of his love of man and his wisdom is familiarly and sublimely opened. By it I am the father of the poor, the support of the wretched. As my mother *leaves* her healthy children and *clings* to the sickly, and *takes double care* of the wretched because she *must, being the mother*, because she stands in God's place to the child, so must *I, if the mother is in God's place* to me, and God fills my heart in the *mother's place.*

A feeling like the mother's feeling impels me.   Man is my brother, my love embraces the whole race; but I cling to the *wretched,* I am *doubly* his father; to act *like God* becomes my *nature.*   I am a child of God; I believed in my mother, her heart showed me God.   God is the God of my *mother,* of *my heart* and *her heart.*   I know no other God.   The God of my *brain* is a *chimœra.* I know no other God but the God of my *heart.*   By faith in the God of *my heart* only I feel a man.   The God of my *brain* is an *idol.*   I ruin myself by worshipping him.   The God of my *heart,* is my God.   I perfect myself in His love.   Mother, mother! you showed me God in your *commands,* and I found Him in *obedience.* Mother, mother! when I forget *God* I forget *you,* and when I *love* God I am in *your place* to your infant.   I cling to your *wretched ones,* and *those who weep* rest in my arms as in their *mother's.*

Mother, mother! as I love you so I love God, and duty is *my highest good.*   Mother! when *I forget you, I forget* God, and the wretched ones *no longer* rest in my arms, I am *no longer* in God's place to the sufferer. When I forget you I forget *God.*   Then live I like the lion for *myself,* and in self-confidence use my powers for *myself against my own race.*   Then is there no sense of fatherhood in my soul; then no *sense of God* sanctifies my obedience; and my apparent *sense of duty* is a vain deception.

Mother, mother, as I love you, so love I God. *Mother and obedience, God and duty* are one and the same to me—*God's will,* and the *best* and *noblest* that I can imagine are one and the same to me. I live then no more for *myself;* I lose myself in *my brethren,* the children of my God—I live *no more for myself,* I live for Him who took me in my mother's arms, and *raised* me with a father's hand above the dust of my mortal coil to His love. And the more I love Him, the Eternal, the more I honor His commandments, the more I *depend on Him,* the more I *lose myself and become His,* the more does my nature become *divine,* the more do I feel in harmony with my inner nature and with my whole race. The more I love Him, the more I follow Him, the more do I hear on all sides the voice of the Eternal: "Fear not, I am thy God, I will never forsake thee; follow My commandments; My will is thy salvation." And the more I follow Him, the more I love Him and thank Him; the more I trust the Eternal, the more I know Him *who is and was and was and shall be evermore,* the Author of my being, needing me not.

I have recognized the Eternal *in myself.* I have *seen* the way of the Lord, I have *read* the laws of the Almighty in the dust, I have *sought* out the laws of His love in my heart—I *know* in whom I *believe.* My trust in God becomes infinite through my self-knowledge, and through the insight germinated in it of the laws of the moral world. The idea of the Infinite is interwoven in my nature with the idea of the Eternal. I hope for eternal life, and the more I love Him, the Eternal, the more I hope for eternal love. The more I trust, the more I thank and follow Him. The more faith in His eternal goodness becomes a truth to me, the more does my faith in His eternal goodness become a witness of my immortality.

I am silent again, Friend!—What are words to express a certainty that springs from the heart ? What are words on a subject in which a man whose head and heart alike deserve my respect thus expressed himself: " There is no perception of God from mere knowledge; the true God lives only for faith, for childlike faith.

> " What is dim to the wisdom of the wise
> Is clear and simple unto childlike eyes.

" Then only the heart knows God, the heart that rising above care for its own finite being embraces mankind, be it the whole or a part.

" This pure human heart requires and creates for its love, its obedience, its trust, its worship, a personified type of the highest, a high, holy will, which exists as the soul of the whole spiritual world.

" Ask the good man,—Why is your duty your high-

est good ?    Why do you believe in God ?    If he gives
proofs, only the schools are speaking in him.    A more
skilful intellect beats all these proofs down.    He trembles a moment, but his heart cannot deny the Divine;
he comes back to Him, blessing and loving, as to his
mother's bosom.

" Then  whence  comes  the  good  man's  conviction  of
God ?    Not from the intellect, but from that inexplicable impulse which cannot be comprehended in any
word,  or  any  thought,  the  impulse  to  glorify  and
immortalize his being in the higher imperishable being
of the whole.—*Not me, but the brethren.*—*Not the individual, but the race.*    This is the unconditional expression
of the divine voice within the soul.    In comprehending and following it lies the only nobility of human
nature."[98]

# THE METHOD

A REPORT BY PESTALOZZI

# PREFATORY NOTE

" The Method, a Report by Pestalozzi," was published by Niederer, with other posthumous works by Pestalozzi, in the *Allgemeine Monatschrift für Erziehung und Unterricht*, edited by J. P. Rossel, *Aix-la-Chappelle*, 1828, Vol. ix., pp. 66–80, 161–174.—This book is in the Library of the Teachers' Guild, London.—These papers were also published separately under the title of *Pestalozzische Blätter*, of which one volume and part of another were published. A copy is in the *Musée Pédagogue*, Paris.

Niederer says, in the Introduction: " The following original treatise, hitherto unprinted, contains Pestalozzi's report to a Society which had been formed to support his efforts for education at the time of his return from Stanz to Burgdorf. It is Pestalozzi's own work, and he signed the copy from which this is taken with his own hand.

" This precious document takes us back again to Pestalozzi's standpoint when he created the method. In this his views are fully expressed, and it contains the germ which developed later into the theory of elementary human education ; but it also contains the errors and mistakes which hindred the progress of his work."

Seyffarth, who publishes it, Vol. 18, says : "It seems that Niederer made no alteration in this treatise, for he has added notes to the text, which he did not do when he made alterations." But there is reason for thinking that it has been touched by Niederer. See pp. 313, 314.

The Society of Friends of Education was founded by Stapfer, in June, 1800, to make Pestalozzi's views better known. A commission was appointed from among its members to examine and report. At their request he gave them " An Account of the Method ". They visited his school and presented their Report at a general meeting of the Society, Oct. 1, 1800.

The " Report or Account of the Method ", which Pestalozzi made for this Society, is the first systematic statement of his views. When he left Stanz, he was not sure of his principles. In this Report, Anschauung and his great principles first appear; but the A B C of Anschauung is not here. That and his Elements first appear in How Gertrude, as well as his attempts to correlate and unite them.

When he wrote this Report, he was quite alone. It is entirely his own work: it gives us the condition of his mind a year after he left Stanz. The observations made there have germinated and developed: this is their first expression. It comes between the *First Letter from Stanz*, and *How Gertrude Teaches her Children;* these three works complete his writings at this important period of his own development. After this, until we come to the *Swan's Song*, there is nothing of equal value,—nothing quite free from the influence of helpers who had never been at Stanz.

The Report is quoted several times in *How Gertrude;* it is the germ of that work; to add it here is necessary to complete the work of this period, and also to show how the idea " germinated " in him. " It presents," says DeGuimps, " the doctrine of Pestalozzi with a clearness and fairness which have hardly been surpassed in anything the author wrote later." (P. 106). He forgets that he has only just said, overleaf, " He was not yet clear as to what *was* his method; he was unable to explain it; he was seeking it. He was, in fact, seeking a principle." These statements can be reconciled if applied to 1799, but not to 1800.

" This memoir, unfortunately left unpublished," says DeGuimps, " remained almost unknown. It was at last printed by Niederer in his Pestalozzian Pamphlets, Aix-la-Chapelle, 1828, but this book is not now to be had." But DeGuimps is mistaken. The first edition of his Life of Pestalozzi was published in 1874. Seyffarth had reprinted *The Method* only the previous year, 1873, while Niederer had published it in 1828 in the *Allgemeine*

*Monatschrift für Erziehung und Unterricht,* with other works of Pestalozzi. These works had also been published separately, but DeGuimps did not know this in 1874, when his first edition was published; in Edition 2 he adds an appendix, but does not correct the text, and his note is not quite accurate. He says, that Seyffarth (vol. 18) contains some special works here first published; among them " *The Method* ". This is the Report presented by Pestalozzi to the Society of the Friends of Education in 1800, referred to by us in its proper place.

Now this Niederer version of the Method referred to in the appendix is not the same as that quoted by De-Guimps. He has not discovered this. He gives the *conclusion* of the Report, but his last two paragraphs are at the *beginning* of Niederer's version, its second and third paragraphs. There are other differences. There is evidently then another copy. This is confirmed by *How Gertrude;* some of the quotations given there are not to be found in this version of Niederer's. In Letter VII. there is a long quotation beginning, " Grant the principle " (p. 116). This is not in Niederer's version; so that, although it is signed by Pestalozzi, is in his own handwriting, and is undoubtedly genuine, it is not the version quoted in *How Gertrude* nor by DeGuimps. It may be the first draft. The question arises, If no account was published, how did

DeGuimps obtain an abstract and quotations for his first edition? This is answered by referring to Morf, vol. I. p. 228. Morf has given an abstract and quotations, and DeGuimps has copied them. The one quotation he gives, which is not in Morf, is taken from *How Gertrude*, Letter IV.

Seyffarth also has not seen that there are *two* versions of the " *Account of The Method* ". He says in the Preface to *How Gertrude*, Pestalozzi made " a Report which was afterwards published by Niederer, 1840, in the *Pestaloggische Blätter*—unfortunately with Niederer's revisions. Morf gives a summary of it." Seyffarth does not know apparently that Morf's version is entirely different from Niederer's. It is strange that this first *Account of the Method* is not known to Pestalozzi's editor and biographer, and has never been, so far as we can learn, reprinted.

It seemed probable to us that Pestalozzi's version of *The Method* might have been published at the time it was presented. Dr. Schnell, Perfect of Burgdorf, published a pamphlet in 1800 which gave a more complete exposition of Pestalozzi's views than the Report contained. The Society also appealed publicly for subscriptions. Possibly the Report was printed and circulated. Mr. Morf evidently knew; we wrote to him and he replied:

" In answer to your letter of June 23d, allow me

first to remind you that in dealing with those portions of Pestalozzi's work which he edited, Niederer left nothing untouched; he gave his own color to everything. He lived in the firm belief that he understood Pestalozzi better than Pestalozzi understood himself. The quotations that I give, i. 228 and seq., are taken from the original document of June, 1800. It was printed in the newspapers of that date.''

At present, we have not been able to get at these newspapers, but we may suggest to the editor of *Pestalozzi-blätter* that it would be well to reprint it. The *Augsburger Zeitung* and *Deutscher Merkur* (Wieland editor) took up his cause.

Mr. Morf does not settle one point of importance. Did the diagram of (Buss's) *A B C der Anschauung* (see page 330) appear in the newspapers? Seyffarth excludes it, and the sentence preceeding it. If this diagram is really Buss's, it could not have existed when Pestalozzi wrote the Report. If it is not in the versions from which Morf copies, it seems clear that Niederer has not left this untouched. The A B C is probably not Pestalozzi's own production, for Buss says (page 116) he could not draw, and that for months he could not understand him. But he gave Buss some lines as a pattern.

# THE METHOD

I am trying to psychologize the instruction of mankind; I am trying to bring it into harmony with the nature of my mind, with that of my circumstances and my relations to others. I start from no positive form of teaching, as such, but simply ask myself:—

" What would you do, if you wished to give a single child all the knowledge and practical skill he needs, so that by wise care of his best opportunities he might reach inner content ? "

I think to gain this end the human race needs exactly the same thing as the single child.

I think, further, the poor man's child needs a greater refinement in the methods of instruction than the rich man's child.

Nature, indeed, does much for the human race, but we have strayed away from her path. The poor man is thrust away from her bosom, and the rich destroy themselves both by rioting and by lounging on her overflowing breast.

The picture is severe. But ever since I have been able to see I have seen it so; and it is from this view that the impulse arises within me, not merely to plaster over the evils in schools which are enervating the people of Europe, but to cure them at their root.

But this can never be done without subordinating all forms of instruction to those eternal laws by which the human mind is raised from physical impressions on the senses to clear ideas.

I have tried to simplify the elements of all human knowledge according to these laws, and to put them into a series of typical examples that shall result in spreading a wide knowledge of Nature, general clearness of the most important ideas in the mind, and vigorous exercises of the chief bodily powers, even among the lowest classes.

I know what I am undertaking; but neither the difficulties in the way, nor my own limitations in skill and insight, shall hinder me from giving my mite for a purpose which Europe needs so much. And, gentlemen, in laying before you the results of those labors on which my life has been spent, I beg of you but one thing. It is this:—Separate those of my assertions that may be doubtful from those that are indisputable. I wish to found my conclusions entirely upon complete convictions, or at least upon perfectly recognized premises.

The most essential point from which I start is this:—

Sense-impression of Nature is the only true foundation of human instruction, because it is the only true foundation of human knowledge.

All that follows is the result of this sense-impression, and the process of abstraction from it. Hence in every case where this is imperfect, the result also will be neither certain, safe, nor positive; and in any case, where the sense-impression is inaccurate, deception and error follow.

I start from this point and ask:—" What does Nature itself do in order to present the world truly to me, so far as it affects me ? That is,—By what means does she bring the sense-impressions of the most important things around me to a perfection that contents me ? " And I find,—She does this through my surroundings, my wants and my relations to others.

Through my surroundings she determines the kinds of sense-impressions I receive. Through my wants she stimulates my activities. Through my relations to others she widens my observation and raises it to insight and forethought. Through my surroundings, my wants, my relations to others, she lays the foundations of my knowledge, my work, and my right-doing.

And now I ask myself:—" What general method of the Art* has the experience of ages put into the hands of humanity to strengthen this influence of Nature in developing intelligence, energy, and virtue in our race ? " And I find these methods are speech, the arts of drawing, writing, reckoning and measuring.

And when I trace back all these elements of the

---

* The Art of Teaching : our Science and Art of Education.

human Art to their origin, I find it in the common basis of our mind, by means of which our understanding combines those impressions which the senses have received from Nature, and represents them as wholes, that is, as concepts.

It is evident from this statement that in any case where systematic training does not keep pace with the actual sense-impressions of Nature, the Art by its over-hasty work upon the human mind becomes a source of physical atrophy, which must inevitably result in one-sidedness, warped judgment, superficiality, and error. Every word, every number, is a result of the understanding that is generated by ripened sense-impression.

But the gradations by which physical impressions on the senses become clear ideas reach the limits of the spontaneous working of the intellect, independent of the senses, along a course in harmony with the laws of the physical mechanism.

Imitation precedes hieroglyphics; hieroglyphics precede cultivated language, just as the individual name precedes the generic.

Further, it is only through this course, in harmony with the mechanism of the senses, that culture brings up before me the sea of confused phenomena (*Ansch.*) flowing one into another, first as definite sense-impressions, and from these forms clear concepts.

Thus all the Art (of teaching) men is essentially a

result of physico-mechanical laws, the most important of which are the following:—

1. Bring all things essentially related to each other to that connection in your mind which they really have in Nature.

2. Subordinate all unessential things to essential, and especially subordinate the impression given by the Art to that given by Nature and reality.

3. Give to nothing a greater weight in your idea than it has in relation to your race in Nature.

4. Arrange all objects in the world according to their likeness.

5. Strengthen the impressions of important objects by allowing them to affect you through different senses.

6. In every subject try to arrange graduated steps of knowledge, in which every new idea shall be only a small, almost imperceptible addition to that earlier knowledge which has been deeply impressed and made unforgetable.

7. Learn to make the simple perfect before going on to the complex.

8. Recognize that as every physical ripening must be the result of the whole perfect fruit in all its parts, so every just judgment must be the result of a sense-impression, perfect in all its parts, of the object to be judged. Distrust the appearance of precocious ripeness as the apparent ripeness of a worm-eaten apple.

9. All physical effects are absolutely necessary; and

this necessity is the result of the art of Nature, with which she unites the apparently heterogenous elements of her material into one whole for the achievement of her end. The Art, which imitates her, must try in the same way to raise the results at which it aims to a physical necessity, while it unites its elements into one whole for the achievement of its end.

10. The richness of its charm and the variety of its free play cause the results of physical necessity to bear the impress of freedom and independence. Here, too, the Art must imitate the course of Nature, and by the richness of its charm and the variety of its free play try to make its results bear the impress of freedom and independence.

11. Above all, learn the first law of the physical mechanism, the powerful, universal connection between its results and the proportion of nearness or distance between the object and our senses. Never forget that this physical nearness or distance of all objects around you has an immense effect in determining your positive sense-impressions, practical ability, and even virtue.

But even this law of your nature converges as a whole towards another. It converges towards the centre of our whole being, and we ourselves are this centre. Man! never forget it! All that you are, all you wish, all you might be, comes out of yourself. All must have a centre in your physical sense-impressions, and this again is yourself. In all it does, the Art really only adds this to the simple course of Nature. That which Nature puts before us, scattered and over a wide area, the Art puts together in narrower bounds and brings nearer to our five senses, by associations which facilitate the power of memory and strengthen the susceptibility of our senses; and make it easier for them by daily practice to present to us the objects around us in greater numbers, for a longer time and in a more precise way.

The mechanism of Nature as a whole is great and simple. Man! imitate it. Imitate this action of great Nature, who out of the seed of the largest tree produces a scarcely perceptible shoot; then, just as imperceptibly, daily and hourly by gradual stages, unfolds first the beginnings of the stem, then the bough, then the branch, then the extreme twig on which hangs the perishable leaf.

Consider carefully this action of great Nature: how she tends and perfects every single part as it is formed, and joins on every new part to the permanent life of the old.

Consider carefully how the bright blossom is unfolded from the deeply hidden bud. Consider how the bloom of its first day's splendor is soon lost, while the fruit, at first weak but perfectly formed, adds something important every day to all that it is already. So, quietly growing for long months, it hangs on the twig that nourishes it; until, fully ripe and perfect in all its parts, it falls from the tree.

Consider how Mother Nature with the uprising shoot also develops the germ of the root, and buries the noblest part of the tree deep in the bosom of the earth; then how she forms the immovable stem from the very heart of the root, and the boughs from the heart of the stem, and the branches from the very heart of the boughs. How to all, even the weakest, outermost twig she gives enough, but to none useless, disproportionate strength.

The mechanism of physical human nature is essentially subject to the same laws by which physical Nature generally unfolds her powers. According to these laws, all instruction should graft the most essential parts of its subject firmly into the very being of the human mind; then join on the less essential gradually but uninterruptedly to the most essential, and maintain all the parts of the subject, even to the outermost, in one living proportionate whole.

I now go further, and ask:—How has Europe applied these laws of the physical mechanism to all matters of popular education? What has Europe done to bring the elementary means of human knowledge that the work of ages has put into our hands into harmony with the real nature of the human mind, and the laws of the physical mechanism? What use has this generation made of these laws in the organization of its teaching institutions; in its speaking, drawing, writing, reading, reckoning, and measuring?

I see none. In the existing organization of these institutions, at least so far as they affect the poorer classes, I see no trace of any regard for the general harmony of the whole and for the psychological gradations required by these laws.

No, it is notorious! In the existing methods of popular instruction these laws are not only ignored, but generally rudely opposed.

And when I ask again:—What are the unmistakable consequences of thus rudely despising these laws, I cannot conceal from myself the physical atrophy, one-sidedness, warped judgment, superficiality, and presumptuous vanity that characterize the masses in this generation, are the necessary consequence of despising these laws, and of the isolated, unpsychological, baseless, unorganized, unconnected teaching, which our poor race has received in our lower schools.

Then the problem I have to solve is this:—How to bring the elements of every art into harmony with the very nature of my mind, by following the psychological mechanical laws by which my mind rises from physical sense-impressions to clear ideas.

Nature has two principal and general means of directing human activity towards the cultivation of the arts, and these should be employed, if not before, at least side by side with any particular means. They are singing and the sense of the beautiful.

With song the mother lulls her babe to sleep; but here, as in everything else, we do not follow the law of Nature. Before the child is a year old, his mother's song ceases; by that time she is, as a rule, no longer a mother to the weaned child. For him, as for all others, she is only a distracted, over-burdened woman. Alas! that it is so. Why has not the Art of ages taught us to join the nursery lullabies to a series of national songs, that should rise in the cottages of the people from the gentle cradle song to the sublime hymn of praise? But I cannot fill this gap. I can only point it out.

It is the same with the sense of the beautiful. All Nature is full of grand and lovely sights, but Europe has done nothing to awaken in the poor a sense for these beauties, or to arrange them in such a way as to produce a series of impressions, capable of developing this sense. The sun rises for us in vain; in vain for us he sets. In vain for us do wood and meadow, mountain and valley spread forth their innumerable charms. They are nothing to us.

Here, again, I can do nothing; but if ever popular education should cease to be the barbarous absurdity it now is, and put itself into harmony with the real needs of our nature, this want will be supplied.

I leave these means of directing the Art generally, and turn to the forms by which special means of education, speaking, reading, drawing, and writing should be taught.

Before the child can utter a sound, a many-sided consciousness of all physical truths exists already within him, as a starting-point for the whole round of his experiences. For instance, he feels that the pebble and the tree have different properties; that wood differs from glass. To make this dim consciousness clear, speech is necessary. We must give him names for the various things he knows, as well as for their properties.

So we connect his speech with his knowledge, and extend his knowledge with his speech. This makes the consciousness of impressions which have touched his senses clearer to the child. And the common work of all instruction is to make this consciousness clear.

This may be done in two ways. Either we lead the children through knowledge of names to that of things, or else through knowledge of things to that of names. The second method is mine. I wish always to let sense-impression precede the word, and definite knowledge the judgment. I wish to make words and talk unimportant on the human mind, and to secure that preponderance due to the actual impressions of physical objects (*Ansch.*), that forms such a remarkable protection against mere noise and empty sound. From his very first development I wish to lead my child into the whole circle of Nature surrounding him; I would organize his learning to talk by a collection of natural products; I would teach him early to abstract all physical generalizations from separate physical facts, and teach him to express them in words; and I would everywhere substitute physical generalizations for those metaphysical generalizations with which we begin the instruction of our race. Not till after the foundation of human knowledge (sense-impressions of Nature) has been fairly laid and secure would I begin the dull, abstract work of studying from books.

But even my A B C book is only a collection of easy stories by which every mother is enabled with the sound of the letter to make her child acquainted with the most important facts of his physical nature.

Supplement No. 1 contains the letter T of this A B C book.

Before the child knows the forms of the letters by sight, before his organs begin to make articulate sounds, I let the root-forms of all German syllables be repeated so often and so carefully before his developing organs, that he learns to imitate them easily and distinctly. When this is done, I let him see first single letters, then two or three together, letting him hear the sound as he looks at them; and when he has fixed the

order in which they are placed in his memory, he pro-
nounces two, three, or four together like one.

The examples of the series by which this is done are
in Supplement No. 2. I also depend here on the
physical effects of completeness, and have given this
stage of sense-impression a fulness that it has never
had before.

Words of one or more syllables are placed letter by
letter on the board. For instance, take the word
Soldatenstand. We first put:—

| | | S and ask, How do you say that? Answer, S |
|---|---|---|
| then | O | " " " now ? " SO |
| " | L | " " " " " SOL |
| " | D | " " " " " SOLD |
| " | A | " " " " " SOLDA |
| " | T | " " " " " SOLDAT |
| " | E | " " " " " SOLDATE |
| " | N | " " " " " SOLDATEN |
| " | ST | " " " " " SOLDATENST |

and so on.

Frequent repetition of building up the same word is
absolutely necessary to make the formation and pronunciation perfectly fluent to the child.

When the children can form and pronounce the word
with ease, it should be shown them in syllables, and
imitated by them until they feel, themselves, which
letters on the board belong to each syllable. I number
the syllables, and ask: What is the first, the second,

and so on ? and out of the order of their sequence—
the sixth, the first, the fourth, and so on ? Then, for
the first time, I let them spell it. Changing the letters of a word to be spelled, taking one or more of them
away, adding others, and dividing it up into false syllables, strengthen the observation of the children, and
their increased power enables them to re-arrange the
very hardest words by themselves.

By this method the formation of words becomes evident to children; their organs of speech are exercised
to pronounce the hardest words easily; in a short time
they reach an incredible facility in this business, usually
so tiresome; and from one word often learn a number
of independent words, as in the above example.

Lastly, we use the separate letters as a basis for beginning arithmetic, according to a systematic series of
number-relationships, which is shown in Supplement
No. 3.

Regardless of confusion and error, Nature lays her
whole wealth before the eyes of the inexperienced
child, and the child in her great warehouse hears the
whole wealth of language before he has an idea of a
single word. But sound and tone are deeply impressed
upon him, and the connection in which he daily hears
the words soon gives him a vague sense of what they
mean.

Here, too, I imitate the course of Nature. My first

reading book for the child is the dictionary: the sum of our ancestors' testimony about all that exists. Language, as one great whole, is in this first reading book, that rises through a serious of repetitions, of imperceptible grammatical additions, to be an encyclopedic register of facts. No. 4 contains a specimen of this reading book in its original simplicity. No. 5 contains a specimen of sample grammatical additions.

No. 6 contains the classification of words according to the similarity of their meaning.

No. 7 contains exercises in language-teaching, in the use of verbs and substantives together.

Writing is only a kind of linear drawing applied to certain arbitrary forms, and must be subject to the general laws of linear drawing. Nature confirms this principle. The child is able to make the elements of linear drawing his own, two years before he is in a position to guide well that delicate instrument, the pen. Therefore I teach the children to draw before thinking of writing, and by this means they form the letters more perfectly than they would otherwise do at this age.

The success depends entirely on the very simple principle that whoever can divide an angle accurately and draw an arc round it, has already the foundations for the accurate drawing of all letters in his hand.

The following figure contains the characteristic lines of the art of writing. *

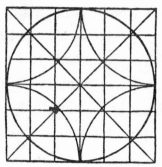

The principle from which I start is this:—

Angles, parallels and arcs comprise the whole art of drawing. Everything that can possibly be drawn is only a definite application of these three primary forms. We can imagine a perfectly simple series arising out of these primary forms, within which an absolute

---

* Seyffarth omits the last sentence and diagram; he may have good reasons. It is supposed to be Buss's A B C of *Anschauung*—Form. See Note 30, page 356. If it really occurs here in the original text, Pestalozzi must have made it. When this Report was written he had not met Buss. I cannot yet satisfactorily trace its origin. Biber calls it the alphabet of form, and uses it to illustrate Buss's account; he says " it was never published, and soon superseded " (p. 205). He evidently did not know Niederer had published it three years before. Although he had his information through Krüsi and Niederer, we follow Rossel. Seyffarth apparently thinks that Niederer has added it, and therefore leaves it out.

standard is to be found for all drawing; and the æsthetic beauty of all forms can be evolved from the nature of these primary forms.

No. 9 contains a few drawings, mathematical and æsthetic.

No. 10 contains mathematical definitions of the primary forms of all the letters.

No. 11 contains graded exercises in writing with the slate pencil. The beginnings of geometry are closely connected with these.

No. 12 contains examples of the way in which I try to sharpen the child's eyes.

No. 13 contains attempts to make clear to them the principles of this subject.

Numbers are abstractions from magnitudes; therefore it is necessary that the elements of geometry should precede the first principles of arithmetic, or, at least, should be taught at the same time.

Here, too, I begin with sense-impressions, and make the divisions of numbers by showing first few or more real things; then groups of dots so that the child does not take arbitrary forms as numbers, but can revise and test by the actual dots the actual relations of numbers.

In No. 14 are a few examples of this method of calculating.

In this way, gentlemen, I try to follow in elementary

instruction the mechanical laws by which man rises from sense-impression to clear ideas.

All Nature is bound to this course of action. She is bound to rise step by step from the simple beginning.

I follow in her path. If the child knows simple bodies—air, earth, water, fire,—I show him the effects of these elements on bodies that he knows; and as he learns the properties of several simple bodies, I show him the different effects obtained by uniting one body to another, and lead him always by the simplest course of sense-impression to the boundaries of the higher sciences. Everything must be put into forms that make it possible and easy for any sensible mother to follow this instruction. But I would also wish that my children, taught in this way, should not let themselves be led astray by the presumptuous ignorance of schoolmasters.

I maintain that my method will lead them as early as their seventh year to seek the man who is master of any branch of knowledge, and to be able to judge about it independently and freely.

But we know neither what education is, nor what the child is.

The details of human sense-impression from which his knowledge arises are in themselves imperceptible, and left to Nature, unarranged, they are chaotically confused. But the important part of this boundless chaos is small in each department, and when accurately arranged can easily be surveyed. On the other hand the child's power of apprehension when used psychologically is infinite; but we must in all subjects use the work of our forefathers, which has not only brought the details of our sense-impressions nearer to our consciousness through language, but has arranged their infinite details, and has brought them for definite purposes into orderly sequence.

It is obvious that we must not neglect the preliminary work of former ages, as if we were apes and never meant to be men. Here my course rises to the final destiny of the child; but I look on it only within the limits of physical mechanism, the scope of which I would inquire into and try to follow, and I find myself once more at Nature's law, that my sense-impressions, my efforts, and my ends are closely connected with the physical nearness or distance of the objects that determine my will.

It is true that a child, who runs about for an hour, looking for a tree that grows before his door, will never know a tree. The child, who in his dwelling-room finds no stimulant to effort, will scarcely find any in the wide world ; and he who finds no stimulus to human love in his mother's eyes may travel the world through and find no motive for benevolence in human tears.

The natural man becomes an angel when he avails himself of the incentives to wisdom and virtue that naturally and closely surround him. He becomes a devil when he neglects them, and ranges over all mountains to seek them at a distance. It must be so. When the objects of the world are removed from my senses they are, so far, sources of deception and error, and even of crime. But I say again, this law of the physical mechanism revolves about a higher one; it revolves about the centre of your whole being, that is yourself. Self-knowledge, then, is the centre from which all human instruction must start.

But this has a double nature.

No. 15 shows, (1) how much I try to use the knowledge of my physical nature as the foundation of human instruction.

(2) How much I try to use the knowledge of my inner individuality; the consciousness of my will to further my own welfare; and of my duty to be true to my inner light. But in the sphere of the child's physical experience, there are not enough motives for standpoints. Therefore, Nature has inspired him with trust in his mother, and upon this trust has founded willing obedience, within the limits of which the child has acquired those habits the possession of which will make the duties of life easier.

Nourished on his mother's breast, reading love in her every glance, dependent for each want of his life upon her, obedience in its first origin is a physical necessity for him, its performance an easy duty, and its result the source of his pleasure.

Even so is man.   He finds in the whirl of existence and in his material experiences no sufficient motives for subjecting himself to that alone which the duties of his life require of him.

To fill this gap Nature has implanted in his bosom trust in God; and upon this trust has founded willing obedience, within the limits of which he daily acquires those habits the possession of which alone makes a lasting effort towards inner nobility possible.   He, too, is nourished at the bosom of Nature, and finds all his joys resting on her lap; but just as much is he dependent on stern necessity.   Therefore for him obedience to truth and justice, obedience to the Author of his being, who has no need of him, is also in its origin a physical necessity of his condition, its fulfilment an easy duty, and its result the source of all his joy.

I, then, lay the keystone of my instruction upon the early development of the natural motive to fear God; for though I am thoroughly convinced that religion is badly used as an exercise for the understanding and as a subject of instruction for children, yet I am equally convinced that as the affair of the heart it is a necessity for my nature even at the tenderest age; that as such it cannot too early be awakened, purified or elevated. From Moses to Christ all the prophets have tried to connect this sentiment with the innocence of the child-like mind, and to develop and nourish it through sense-impression of all Nature.

I follow their path. My whole instruction is nothing but a series of illustrations of the wisdom and greatness of my nature in so far as it has not been degraded by me.

Through an eye, opened by infinite preparation of the Art, I show the child the world, and he no longer dreams of God, he sees Him; he lives in contemplation (*Ansch.*) of Him. He prays to Him.

Supplement No. 16 contains an example of my series of verbs, from the simple combination of which every process and action of Nature that specially concerns man is made clear,—what he does in common with inanimate Nature and what he does in common with the brute.

I do not think it possible to find illustrations by which the natural man can be more surely raised to worship God and to reverence himself and his own worth. It is my honest wish, too, to found my instruction on this foundation of human tranquillity. For I am convinced that a child brought up without trust in God is a motherless waif; that a child out of tune with this trust is an unhappy daughter who has lost her mother's heart.

But it is time I ended. Gentlemen, this is the first sketch of my principles and method of instruction, and I offer it to your free criticism.

PESTALOZZI.

BURGDORF, *June 27th,* 1800.

# SUPPLEMENTS TO THE METHOD

The supplements omitted are not necessary, as their character can be inferred from the book, nor have we given all Pestalozzi's examples.

Supplement No. 2. A collection of words almost alike, which receive a variety of changes by small additions. These must have the effect of giving certainty to spelling—a result that could hardly be so easily gained in any other way. All combinations of letters, grammatically possible, have been used as series of syllables and words. Here is an example:—

| ein | eint | eine | einen | einet | einern |
|------|---------|-------|--------|--------|----------------|
| bein | meint | deine | deinen | meinet | beinern |
| dein | neint | meine | meinen | weinet | steinern |
| sein | scheint | seine | seinen | scheinet | kleinern, etc. |

The use of these words in language may at the same time be learnt in a way pleasant to the children and adapted to their intelligence.

For instance, *ine* (*ein*) is put upon the board as the principal sound, and while I add to it I say, " What I have bought is ? *mine* (*m-ein*). But with a *w :* " What do we squeeze out of grapes ? " *W*ine (*W-ein*), etc.

No. 3 is a guide to lessons upon the relations of numbers according to regulated steps.

The various relations of the numerical system must be brought home to the sense-impression of the children by means of real objects. I find the letters on the reading-board the handiest.

At first, I put one letter on the board, and ask, "How many are there?" The child says 1. I add another, and ask—

$$1 \text{ and } 1 \text{ are? } 2$$
$$2 \text{ '' } 1 \text{ '' ? } 3$$
$$3 \text{ '' } 1 \text{ '' ? } 4$$

Only very few are wanted at first, until by very easy exercises the increased power of the child demands gradually more and different numbers. Then we take the added letters away one by one, and ask—

How much is 1 less than 20? Ans. 19.
"        "   1 "   "   19?     "   18.

I go on with—What are 1 and 2?   3.
                  "   "   3 "   2?   5.
                  "   "   5 "   2?   7, etc.

Then back again.   2 less than 99 are ?   97.
                   2 "   "   97 "   ?   95.

Then 1 and 3 are?   4.
      4 "   3 "   ?   7 up to 100 and back again.
Then 2 "   3 "   ?   5.
      5 "   3 "   ?   8 up to 100 etc.
Then 1 "   4 "   ?   5.
      5 "   4 "   ?   9 up to 100 etc.

Then 2 and 4 are ?   6 etc.

Then 3  "   4  "  ?   7 etc.

Then 1  "   5  "  ?   6 etc.

I go on further to

   2 and 2 are ?   4.   How many times 2 make 4 ?

   4  "  2  "  ?   6.   How many times 2 make 6 ?

   6  "  2  "  ?   8.   How many times 2 make 8 ?

And so on up to 100 and then backwards.

2 less than 100 are ?  98.   How many times 2 make 98 ?

2  "   "    98  "  ?  96.   How many times 2 make 96 ?

In the same way I go on—

   3 and 3 are ?   6.   How many times 3 make 6 ?

   4  "  4  "  ?   8.   How many times 4 make 8 ? etc.

No. 4.   Gold-finch       Silver-gilt       Almond-tree.

       "   mine           "   mine            "     scent.

       "   dust           "   ware            "     flavor.

       "   fish           "   plate            "     oil.

(A selection from many examples.)

No. 8.   To make signs is to make something understood by gestures without words.

To extend is to make longer.

To stretch is to make longer.

To spread is to make broader.

(All the other examples, " to go ", etc., are in Letter VII.)

# NOTES

(G) Refers to Roger DeGuimps's *Pestalozzi*, His Aim and Work, Syracuse, C. W. Bardeen, 1889.

**1** (p. 18)—Ith, J. von, wrote *Official Report of the Pestalozzian Institute and the New Method of Teaching.* Bern and Zürich, 1802. This was one of the first works published on the new method of Burgdorf.

Johannsen published a *Criticism of the Pestalozzian Method.* Jena and Leipzig, 1804.

Niederer, editor of Pestalozzi's collected works, was one of Pestalozzi's principal fellow-workers at Yverdun, and had great influence over him. His first work, *The Pestalozzian Institute and the Public,* with a preface by Pestalozzi, was published at Yverdun in 1811; *Pestalozzi's Educational Undertaking in its Relation to the Culture of the Age,* 2 vols., Stuttgart and Tübingen, 1812–13.

**2** (p. 18)—Gruner published *Letters from Burgdorf about Pestalozzi, his Method and his Institute.* 1804, Ed. 2, 1806, Frankfort.

Von Türk was of a noble family in North Germany. He gave up a good position in the magistracy of Oldenburg, and went to Yverdun to study Pestalozzi's work and methods. He was the author of *Contributions to Information about German Elementary Schools* and *Letters from München-Buchsee on Pestalozzi and his Educational Method,* 2 vols., Leipzig, 1806. He was appointed Counsellor of State at Potsdam, and worked zealously for thirty years in propagating and applying Pestalozzi's method. (G., p. 162.)

Chavannes, D. A. *An Account of the Elementary Method of H. Pestalozzi, with an account of the works of this celebrated man, his Institute, principles, and fellow-workers.* Paris, 1805. Ed. 2, 1809.

**3** (p. 29)—Lavater, Johann Kasper, Zürich, 1741–

1802. Died Jan. 2, from effects of a bullet-wound received on Sept. 22, 1799, when the French entered Zürich, while he was helping wounded soldiers in the street. Preacher, philosopher, poet, and prose writer. Best known to us by his w o r k o n physiognomy.

JOHANN KASPER LAVATER, 1741–1802 Member of Patriotic Party; warm friend of Pestalozzi. His *Views on Eternity*, in Letters to J. G. Zimmermann, was published, Zürich, 1768, 4 vols. See G., p. 306.

Zimmermann, Johann Georg, Brugg, Canton Aargaü, 1728–95. Physician and philosophical writer. His *Observations on Solitude* is well known.

**4** (p. 30)—Isaak, Iselin, author and publisher, Basle, 1728–82, published a journal entitled *Ephemerides of Humanity.* In 1776, Pestalozzi published in it *A Prayer to the Friends and Well-wishers of Mankind for Kind Support of an Establishment for giving Poor Children Education and Work in the Country.* Iselin warmly supported the appeal. Pestalozzi's *Evening Hour of a Hermit* also appeared first in this journal, May, 1780. Iselin especially directed the attention of the readers of the

*Ephemerides* to Pestalozzi's efforts, and tried to support him in every way. Pestalozzi always remembered him gratefully. "In the good hot working days, when apparently I was wasting my strength, he was the only one upon whom I could lean, covered as I was with dust and sweat, and find refreshment in my pains. Oh, my friend! perhaps without you I should have sunk in the depths and been lost in the mire of my life." (*Beck;* and G., p. 39.)

**5** (p. 32)—Ed. 1, pp. 3, 4, instead of "But I was young", etc., has the following beginning with the oft-quoted passage, not in Ed. 2. "Long years I lived surrounded by more than fifty beggar children. In poverty I shared my bread with them. I lived like a beggar in order to learn how to make beggars live like men," etc. (See G., chap. v. pp. 26–38, for account of the experiment at Neuhof, which began in the winter of 1774.)

**6** (p. 33)—The first volume of this work appeared 1781, and was a great success. In the form of a story Pestalozzi shows how the people in Bonal were reformed by education. Gertrude, the mother of seven children, wife of Leonard, a mason, is the educator. But these things are an allegory: Bonal is the world, and Gertrude the typical mother-educator. Pestalozzi likes to connect his work, and Gertrude here is only a name for the ideal mother who educates, as in his previous work. We forget sometimes, perhaps Pestalozzi himself forgets, that this work is "a guide to mothers in educating their children". Few mothers can undertake the entire education of their children; but the mother is the child's first teacher and guide; her natural methods of teaching, prompted by sympathy and love, are adapted to the little child, and her influence is generally stronger than any other. "The mother, untrained, follows nature in pure simplicity without knowing what nature does through her, and nature does very much through her. She opens the world to the child, she makes him ready to use his senses, and prepares for development of attention and observation." Two women, both servants, are said to have been models for Gertrude,—Babeli, servant to Pestalozzi's mother (G. pp. 2–4), and Elizabeth Naef, who found Neuhof in disorder and worked hard to provide for Pestalozzi and his family. Of her Pestalozzi said, "She is an image of Gertrude" (G., pp. 37, 38).

7 (p. 41)—Herbart, as early as May, 1801, promised his friend Halem, who was planning a literary journal under the name *Irene*, an article on Pestalozzi. The letter accompanying the article is dated Dec. 24, 1801, and the article appeared early in 1802.

Herbart met Pestalozzi for the first time at Zürich.

JOHANN FRIEDRICH HERBART,
(1776-1841)

"In Zürich I met neither Lavater nor Hegel, but chance brought me in contact with the celebrated Pestalozzi." (Letter, Jan. 28, 1798.)

The second time he visited him was at Burgdorf; but Pestalozzi says that here " he crowed his A B C daily from morn till night, and went on the same empirical way " that he had followed at Stanz.

Herbart says: " I saw him in his schoolroom. A dozen children, from five to eight years old, were called into school at an unusual hour in the evening. I feared they would be sulky, and that the experiment which I had come to see would be a failure. But the children came with no signs of reluctance; a lively activity lasted continuously to the end. The noise of the whole school speaking together—no, not the noise—it was a pleasant harmony of words, quite intelligible, in measured time, like a chorus, as powerful, and as firmly united, and so clearly arising from what had been learned, that I had some difficulty not to change from a spectator and observer into a learner and child. I went around among them to hear if any were silent or speaking carelessly ; I found none. The children's pronunciation did my ears good, although their teacher has the most incomprehensible organ in the world, and their tongues cannot be well trained by their Swiss parents." (Herbart, *Päd. Schriften*, 1880, i. 88.)

Herbart's " *Pestalozzi's Idee eines A B C der Anchauung als ein Cyklus von Vorübungen im Auffassen der Gestalten wissenschaftlich ausgeführt* " was published at Göttingen in 1804. A translation was published in New York, 1898.

8 (p. 46)—See pp. 7–16.

9 (p. 50)—Rengger, Albert, 1764–1835, educated as a theologian; became tutor to Emanuel von Fellenberg, afterwards studied medicine. After some years abroad he settled in Bern, 1789. Became Minister of the Interior, 1798.

Stapfer, Phillipe Albert, 1766–1840, Professor of

Philosophy and Philology, Bern, Minister of Arts and Sciences. He alone remained steadfast to Pestalozzi when he left Stanz, and exerted himself to find a place where he might carry on his experiments. Stapfer wished to found a Teachers' Institute. Fischer submitted his plans to him, and Stapfer proposed to the Directorate that they give up the castle of Burgdorf to him. In July, 1799, Fischer went to Burgdorf as superintendent of the schools and institutes that he had just organized. Stapfer opened a new field of work to Pestalozzi at Burgdorf; he sent a report to the Directory, July 23, 1799; on the same day they granted him part of Castle Burgdorf as a dwelling, and a fixed position as a teacher, with a salary of Livres 160. (Seyffarth, *Introduction.*) He founded the Society of Friends of Education, June, 1800; in July, 1800, a further grant was made to Pestalozzi through his efforts, of as much of the Castle of Burgdorf as he needed, a garden and wood (G., pp. 98–160). Sept., 1800, was ambassador to Paris. At the end of the Republic, 1803, he retired into private life, and lived in France 37 years.

Schnell, J., Prefect of Burgdorf. He published a pamphlet, perhaps the first on the subject, giving a complete exposition of Pestalozzi's views, about October, 1800. Reprinted in *Pestalozzi Blätter*, Zurich, 1888. (G., p. 102.) The first edition of *Wie Gertrud* closed with an extract from a letter of Dr. Schnell.

Dr. Grimm, an influential citizen of Burgdorf, and a warm friend of Pestalozzi.

**10** (p. 51)—*Hintersassen,* or *Hintersedler,* were non-burgesses, who possessed, besides a house, a garden or a bit of field. They were also small suburban peasants. Their children attended the school of a worthy shoemaker, Samuel Dysli, who carried on his trade in his spare time as well as when with the children. His instruction consisted in teaching the children to read in a mechanical, tedious manner, and in hearing the Heidelberg Catechism. The room belonged to him, and he worked at his trade in it. His teaching apparatus consisted of the *Spelling and Name Book* (Fibel), *The Beginnings of Christian Doctrine* (Siegfried), *The Heidelberg Catechism*, and the usual *Psalter*. The school contained seventy-three scholars of all ages. (G., p. 99.)

Morf obtains much information about the wretched condition and entire absence of culture among Swiss teachers in Pestalozzi's time from the official list of questions which teachers had to answer in writing, about their personal relations, their former occupations, their future work, their nomination, etc. One teacher, Meyer of Schöfflesdorf, could not answer the questions because he " could not write very well ". Another, Meyer of Kloten, " in summer, when he has no school, earns his bread by bricklaying. He used to be a watchman in the town; he now works in the garden, and is a rope-maker."

" We find hardly any trace of a proper schoolroom. The choice of a teacher often depended, not on his ability, but on his having a room; his family remained in it and carried on their domestic duties during school hours. Often neighbors brought their spinning wheels, finding more warmth and entertainment there than at home. . . . Reading and learning by heart were the pupils' only tasks. The big ones were learning aloud, so there was a constant hubbub in the school. Class teaching was not thought of. One report says: —' The vanity of parents makes them wish their children to appear clever. A child is considered clever if he can shout the whole catechism without a blunder. If he knows the 119th Psalm and can rattle off a few chapters of the Bible (never mind the sense), he is a wonder. To read the Bible through is the highest point.' " See also Seyffarth, *Introduction to " Wie Gertrude"*, Vol. XI.

Schools of this kind were not confined to Switzerland. Possibly some exist still, changed it may be in appearance, but unchanged in principle. Psalm and catechism are gone, but mere word memory work remains.

**11** (p. 55)—Ed. 1, p. 30. " I shall work none. I am not pre-ordained for this. I will have nothing to do with miracles, real or pretended."

**12** (p. 56)—Ed. 1, p. 32. " ' *Vous voulez méchaniser l'éducation.*' He hit the nail on the head, and put the word into my mouth that exactly described the nature of my purpose." Pestalozzi soon afterwards found that he had not quite understood Gleyre.

In the second edition the word " mechanical " is sometimes changed to " organic ". He altered this word as he thought and knowledge became *clear*, as scientific terms are altered with additional knowledge. " Mechanical " became sometimes " psychological ", then " organic ". In " *Anschauung* " he retains his first word, but various meanings develop from and are included in it. DeGuimps says whenever he speaks of *mechanism* he means *organism*. " That the mind and heart of man no less than his body develop according to organic laws, is indeed the fundamental principle of his doctrine;" but he uses *mechanical* sometimes with its own meaning.

**13** (p. 58)—Ed. 1, p. 35. "And all three branches." An interesting little slip. Pestalozzi anticipates the elements, number, form, and language, which he describes later; in Ed. 2 he corrects this.

**14** (p. 59)—Ed. 1, 36. " In order to make those ideas, which are to be imparted by language, clear to the children beforehand by well-chosen, well-executed drawings."

Pestalozzi here says *drawings*, but in the second edition " *real things*, models and drawings." The paragraph bears evidence of revision. *Anschauung* or *picture*-books should precede A B C books to make ideas clear by means of well-chosen *real* objects. At first he showed the children large drawings for them to observe and describe. This is one of his A B C's of *Anschauung*. " I made much progress in what was called the A B C of *Anschauung*," says Ramsauer. DeGuimps adds this note: " Exercises in which the children made their own remarks on the object placed before them ", our " object-lesson ". At Burgdorf it is an A B C of *Anschauung*, the foundation of *all* studies. The observation, thought, and expression are all the child's; with us the object lesson is isolated, and in this way, almost

obsolete.   We *tell* what should be seen, thought, and
said.   This A B C of *Anschauung* involves expression
by words as " observation " is sometimes used by us.
It includes *expression by the child* of what *it see and thinks.*

One day at Burgdorf, when they were looking at a
drawing of a window, a child said, " Could we not
learn as well from the window itself ? "   Another time
a similar remark was made.   " The child is right,"
said he, and put the drawings away, and studied from
objects, but he does not exclude drawings.

Some have naturally supposed that as objects are the
sources of ideas and knowledge, objects only should
be given for drawing studies.   In Belgium " they
reject absolutely the practice of drawing from prints.
.   .   .   .   As soon as a child can draw lines, he is set
to produce geometrical forms, plane surfaces, and
solid bodies."   (M. Couvreur, Minutes of the International Conference, 1884, ii. 259.)   But the child's nature should be considered also, and children prefer to
draw from copies, even the usual dead copies; but copies
made with them, by the living teacher or the mother
are the best.   Historically, direct imitation of objects
comes later.   Possibly drawings may have value as well
as objects.   If they are useful as copies for drawing,
they may be useful as helps to observation.

**15** (p. 60)—Ed. 1, p. 37.   " All came soon to know
the hardest names of the least known animals in Buf-
fon's *Natural History*, and to notice and distinguish
clearly points in them as well as in plants and men.
But yet this test was not decisive for the beginning

point of instruction. This boy had already three un-used years behind him, and I am convinced," etc.

**16** (p. 61)—Ed. 1, p. 39. " I cease describing, lest I should come again upon the picture of the school-master, and the terrible contrast between their nature, their action, their state, and their misery, and that of lovely nature. But, friend, tell me," etc.

**17** (p. 64)—Ed. 1, p. 42. " While I was thus on the track of the first beginning points of all instruc-tion for the children who should be educated by it from the cradle, and all power for the method itself, I took means with the school children who fell into my hands, not having been formed by it in direct opposition to my principles," etc.

**18** (p. 66)—Pestalozzi came in many ways into oppo-sition with himself; he tried to cram in when he ought to have " drawn out ". Nature's method alone is right, he says; and then gives this unnatural parrot-like repetition of " dull, uncomprehended words or wildest nonsense, absurdly hard, complicated and en-tirely incomprehensible." We must always remember he has only really reached clear ideas about his princi-ples within this year, and it is not wonderful that he opposes himself; the habits and thoughts of his life are not all reformed and regenerated at once. Pos-sibly, too, something may be said in favor of such test exercises.

**19** (p. 68)—Fischer, 1772–1800, was a pupil of Salzmann, in Schnepfenthal. Was appointed Secretary of Science and Art Department by Stapfer in 1798. In 1799, with Stapfer's consent, he attempted to organize a course of training for teachers in Castle Burgdorf, but failed. In 1800 he left Burgdorf, and went back to his post as secretary. He died on the 4th of May, 1800.

Fischer's letter was printed in full by Steinmüller, to whom it was addressed in his *Helvetischer Schulmeisterbibliothek*, vol. i. pp. 216, seq. St. Gallen, 1801.

**20** (p. 68)—Steinmüller took great interest in Pestalozzi, and applied to Fischer to learn more of his method of teaching. Fischer answered, Dec. 6, 1799. On Dec. 31, Steinmüller wrote to thank him, and said: " Oh, how true it is that the teacher without psychology does his work as badly as an old woman doctoring." Steinmüller in 1803 criticized Pestalozzi's views and methods in a small pamphlet, *Remarks upon Pestalozzi's Method of Instruction*. It is especially directed against exaggerated praise of the method, and disputes to some degree the claim of novelty of Pestalozzi's ideas.

Morf publishes a collection of his letters to Fischer taken from the Swiss Archives at Bern, giving an account of his life.

**21** (p. 81)—Krüsi's career from an errand boy to a fellow-worker with Pestalozzi is given in the text. His situation in Gais brought him plenty of work, and 2½ gulden a week. For self-culture, he zealously studied the works of Basedow, Salzmann, and others, and tried to use in school what he learned this way, as well as by his own observations and experiences from nature and life. He was an active, thoughtful teacher, with a lovable disposition, the effects of which were soon

recognized. At Steinmüller's suggestion he went to
Fischer at Burgdorf, 1799, with the orphans from Gais,
and after Fischer's death he joined Pestalozzi, with
whom he worked out the sense-impression-teaching of
word and number (*Sprach-und-Rechenunterricht*). He
accompanied him to Münchenbuchsee, and also to
Yverdun. He parted from him with great regret in
1817, and founded an educational establishment of his
own, which soon became known. In 1822 he undertook the direction of Hans Karl Zellweger's school in
Trogen, and in 1833 the direction of the Teachers'
Seminary in Gais. He died there, after successful
work, July 25, 1844. Gruner says he was " a man
whose unassuming soul and quiet talent was formed by
much experience. He has a gentle disposition, is calm,
indefatigable, active and firm. He knows his pupils
and child-nature generally, and how to treat children."
(G., pp. 110–120.)

His son, Hermann Krüsi, taught in Dr. Mayo's
school at Cheam, in the Home and Colonial School,
London, and in the Oswego Normal from 1862 to 1887.

**22** (p. 85)—Johann Hübner, rector, Hamburg,
1688–1731, wrote a Biblical History, 1714,—*Twice Two
and Fifty Selected Bible Stories*. Each story was followed
by " plain questions ". These questions were so compiled that they fitted in with the words of the story,
and could only be answered in the same words. Pestalozzi called this *Catechizing* as opposed to *Socratizing*.
He makes a great distinction between them. " Catechisms, a mere parrot-like repetition of dull uncomprehended words; " " Socratizing, real development of

thought, mental power, and expression by means of questions." He objected to Fischer's Socratizing because it was not prepared for and preceded by sense-impression or observation of objects, at this time new to him. " Consider no human judgment ripe that is not clearly the result of complete sense-impression of all parts of the object to be judged " (p. 132). He would rather hold back the judgment until the child had *really seen with its own eyes* the object about which he should express himself *from all sides and under different conditions*. But he believes even now strongly in Socratizing. " I found weakness nowhere except in myself and in the art of using what already exists. I tried to force in where it is only possible to draw out from within the child that which is in him and is only to be developed from what is within him and cannot be put into him." (Letter I.) Later he is not less than Fischer its supporter. " All true, all real educative instruction must be drawn out of the children." (Letter I.)

**23** (p. 86)—Ed. 1, p. 74. " Aftewards Krüsi tried to combine Socratizing and catechising. But this combination by its very nature leads no further than the squaring of the circle ·that a wood-cutter," etc.

**24** (p. 88)—Ed. 1, p. 77. " With time and industry, it is possible to ask many questions easily about many subjects."

**25** (p. 92)—Ed. 1, p. 84. " I have said, fearlessly, that it is not opposed to God or religion to lead up to clear ideas, and endeavor to teach children to talk before we cram their memories with the affairs of positive theology and its never-to-be-settled disputes."

**26** (p. 96)—Ed. 1, p. 88. "All these views, .connected with the harmony daily becoming clearer between my methods of instruction and nature, fully convinced him that all knowledge lay in the union of these methods, so that a teacher need only *learn how to use them* in order to raise himself and his pupils by their means to all knowledge that can be aimed at by teaching."

**27** (p. 99)—Tobler, Johann Georg, 1769–1843, from Trogen, in Appenzell, Ausserhoden, went to Basle, 1792, to be trained for the Church, but soon gave up theology for teaching. He was a tutor for five years, and became director of a girls' school in Basle, 1799. In 1800 his friend Krüsi introduced him to Pestalozzi, with whom he stayed seven

JOHANN GEORG TOBLER, 1769-1843

years. In 1807 he founded an industrial school at Mühlhausen, that soon numbered 600 scholars; this was closed in 1811. In 1812 he became master of a private school in Glarus, but left in 1817, on account of the famine. After again being a tutor for three years he became director of an educational institute founded by himself; this he gave to his eldest son in 1831. His last years were spent in Basle, where he died at the house of his youngest son, who had a boy's school at Nyon. Tobler helped Pestalozzi in his writing. His written works consist chiefly of children's and popular books.—*Riegel*.

**28** (p. 102)—Slates. Pestalozzi was led by his limited means to use slates and slate pencils. This very practical invention made writing, drawing and arithmetic common subjects of instruction at a time when the more expensive paper could not have been used. He speaks first of using slates at Burgdorf. They were of great service, but he never mentions the invention or application as his own. Tobler's statement here is allowed to stand, and is therefore sanctioned by Pestalozzi. Chalk too was used. "For drawing we were given only slates and red chalk." (Ramsauer's account; G., p. 104.)

**29** (p. 108)—Buss, of Tübingen, tells his own history in the text. Afterwards he taught drawing in Bern; Gruner thus describes him. "Buss has extraordinary talents, particulary for art. He is born to teach by sense-impression. He has indefatigable zeal, energy and skill. Like Krüsi he has absolute authority over his pupils, and manages them well, showing admirable patience in teaching them."—*Riegel*.

**30** (p. 108)—Ed. 1, p. 107. "Show Wieland the *A B C der Anschauung* and ask him if he ever found stronger proofs of powers thrown away."

Wieland, author of *Oberon*, was friendly to Pestalozzi. His *German Mercury*, Dec., 1801, contains the first notice of *Wie Gertrud*. It is warmly recommended. In it he says, "Pestalozzi promises much, but judging from the first fruits lying before us, he is a man to keep his word."

Buss's A B C of *Anschauung* is an A B C of Form, of linear form. He gives us in the text its purpose. " Children should read outlines of forms as they read words, and name the parts, curves and angles, with letters, so that lines combined in the outline of an object may be as clearly expressed as words by letters." This he did not reach. Biber gives a diagram, p. 205, " for the better understanding of what is said," and says " it was never published, for it was soon superseded by more matured labors," but this diagram (p. 330) was published, 1828, by Niederer. It is incorporated in his version of the Report; but if it is Buss's A B C, it could not have existed when Pestalozzi made that Report of the Method. In Letter VIII the ellipse is included (p. 191), but it is not even mentioned here. The smaller squares or chequers for measurement became hereafter an A B C of measure-forms. They are the origin of the chequers in the Kindergarten, and are now used in English schools for various purposes of design. Fragments of the unity he sought and strove for are used for the unconnected teaching, that he protested against, and yet they are applied at last to the hand-training he from first to last earnestly worked to establish.

**31** (p. 112)—Duke Carl Engen of Würtemburg founded a military training school at Castle Solitude in 1771—" the Carl's School ". In 1775 this was removed to Stuttgart, enlarged and made into an academy. Schiller was educated here.

**32** (p. 116)—Ed. 1, p. 119. " In the weakness and superficiality of the instruction I had received in art.

For this reason I failed to grasp its principles. I threw all my energy into the special department in which Pestalozzi wanted my help."

**33** (p. 120)—Ed. 1, p. 126. "How men have language, in order by knowing the names of objects to be able more easily to distinguish one from another."

**34** (p. 121)—Ed. 1, p. 127. "However, I estimated the whole method only through the medium of a department and its effects upon it. In this way I came step by step to see and understand its effects upon other branches. I found now by the clue given by my art-teaching how it might be possible," etc.

**35** (p. 123)—Ed. 1, p. 129. "Which alone make the Art difficult to the human race because they undermine the foundation which it has in man and lead him away from Nature, who asks nothing of us that is not easy, if we only seek it in the right way from her hands only."

Richter says, "We see, even this account of one of Pestalozzi's fellow-workers is altered in the second edition in one or two places. Did Pestalozzi do this? It is doubtful. It is more likely that Jos. Schmid, who brought out 'the collected works', made these changes, for he has been proved to have made arbitrary alterations sometimes. Some other changes in the second edition are due to Schmid. But that Pestalozzi did sometimes make alterations appears from the preface, in which he says that he left the book 'almost unaltered', in fact *most* of the alterations are limited to forms of expression. In some, however, and particularly in the more important alterations, Pestalozzi's authorship is undoubted, as is evident from their character."

This note of Richter's illustrates the way in which the best editors speak of Schmid, while the latter part neutralizes the beginning, "most of the alterations are limited to forms of expression." Yes, they are often so slight that we could not well represent them in translation. For instance, "villages in Bohemia" become "castles in Spain" in the second edition; "*dem Auge*" becomes "*in dem Auge*," etc., etc. Some are evidently corrections. But if the more important additions are evidently Pestalozzi's own, the lesser alterations and corrections may also be his; besides the original communication of Buss may have been written under circumstances which justified these slight alterations by Pestalozzi. No Schmid theory is needed to explain them.

**36** (p. 124)—Rousseau, Jean Jacques, 1712–1787. The Revolution last century began a new era. It was not like the Renaissance—a return to an older civilization, with its art and literature, but a return to nature. A new faith was growing, and the need was felt for cultivating the in-

JEAN JACQUES ROUSSEAU, 1712-1787

tellect instead of subjugating it to priestly authority. It was a struggle for liberty of thought, speech, and inquiry. Rousseau was the man of his time, prepared by special education and mental condition for it. " It was his work more than that of any other man that France arose from decay and found irresistible energy," says Mr. Morley. " For twelve years," he says himself, " his heart made hot within him by the idea of the future happiness of the human race and the honor of contributing to it," he wrote those works which, Mr. Morley says, " gave Europe a new gospel " and a new education. One of these works, perhaps the best, is *Emile*. By some means he had the very education himself that he suggested for Emile, that of nature. All his life he was outside the rules of civilization, " an untamed natural man," a vagabond, Quick says. For extracts both in the original and translated that give an excellent view of *Emile*, see Quick's " Educational Reformers " (Syracuse edition), pp. 141–182.

These quotations will give some idea of the new education founded by Rousseau, and worked out by Pestalozzi, Froebel and others. Strangely enough, it agrees with the Renaissance in the place given to the child. We must study the child, learn its nature, if we would teach it. " We must conquer nature by obeying her." Employ the child's activity. Let it learn from things, not books; it is an observer and a doer. Self-activity helps self-teaching. Knowledge comes by the action of our mind, not from what it is told. The real teacher is within. Teach the method of acquiring knowledge. Exercise faculty, and by so doing develop it.

**37** (p. 124)—Basedow, John Bernard (1723-1790),
was one of the earliest to
feel Rousseau's influence and
to apply his principles. Kant
had said that revolution, not
reform, was wanted in education, and Basedow attempted
it. " Everything according
to nature " is his great principle. Treat children as

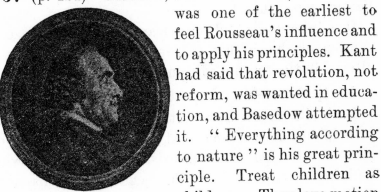

John Bernard Basedow, 1723-1790 children. They love motion
and noise, here is a hint from nature. Even in play
children may learn names of things. (Both Rousseau
and Basedow are here at one with Froebel.) They
should be acquainted with the world through the
senses first—should learn from nature. Reduce mere
memory work. Educate the whole being—the body
by gymnastics, the mind by study of things. Coercion
is wrong; children should be free. Educate the natural
desires and direct them, but never suppress. In 1774
he opened an Institute at Dessau, called the Philan-
thropin. At first it was successful; but, owing to
disputes with his associates, he withdrew in 1778 to
Magdeburg, where he taught privately till his death,
1790. His method had considerable influence in Germany. (Räumer, *Geschichte der Pädagogik;* Quick's
*Educational Reformers,* pp. 183-202.)

**38** (p. 126)—Ed. 1, p. 134. " But they violently
put out the eyes of those who dare to raise their heads
to peep at the splendor of the highest story."

**39** (p. 128)—Ed. 1, p. 138. " And, Gessner, my

experiments went further: they have thriven and become ripe fruit.''

It is interesting and significant of Pestalozzi's conception of the subject to see how the expression is altered in the second edition.

**40** (p. 129)—This Report is given in full, p. 309.

In it Pestalozzi first states his great fundamental principle of *Anschauung*.   At first he limited his purpose to *improving* details in existing schools, and when he left Stanz, he says at the beginning of his letter that even his old plans for educating the people began to wither.   But this Report marks a new epoch.   He is now a *Reformer of Education*, not an *Improver of Instruction*.   What he observed at Stanz had germinated and developed, and the first printed expression of the method of Burgdorf is this Report.   The next is *Wie Gertrud*.

**41** (p. 133)—Ed. 1, p. 145. '' This physical nearness or distance determines all that is positive in your sense-impression, in your technical training, and even in your virtue.''

**42** (p. 135)—Pestalozzi's frequent use of the word *wesentlich*, '' *essential* '', is due to scientific and philosophical ideas now no longer held.   From Plato downwards the qualities of objects were divided into two classes, essential and accidental.   To some extent this corresponds to the distinction drawn by Mill between connotative and nonconnotative qualities, *i. e.* those qualities which help to decide the classification, and so are implied in the use of the name, and those that do not.   (F. C. T.)

**43** (p. 136)—Ed. 1, p. 150.   "This mechanism of your nature."

In two places in this paragraph "mechanism" has been altered in the second edition to "organism".

**44** (p. 142)—*Form* is one of the key-words in Kant's

philosophy.   To put the matter simply, the manner in which we think is determined by the nature of our minds, and it is impossible for us to think of any object except as in time and space.   Time and space, therefore, are not to us properties of the external world, but the form in which

IMMANUAL KANT, 1724–1804

alone it can be thought.   Although Pestalozzi does not use the word strictly in the Kantian sense, his use of it is colored thereby.   Following Grimm, we get those meanings that have any bearing on the use of the word in *Wie Gertrud.*

1. Outline of figure, shape.
   " A just appreciation of all form."   (*P.*)
2. As opposed to matter.
3. The vessel or mould in which a work is made.
5. (Technical.)   The frame in which type is set.
   (*Metaph.*) "Must be fitted into *forms.*"   (*P.*)
6. The form of a legal process (rel. to 2).
   " *Ein Widerspruch in der besten Form.*"   (*Kant.*)
   A contradiction in the best form.
8. General for *manner.*
   " *Aber in den heitern Regionen*

*Wo die reinen Formen wohnen*
*Rauscht des Jammers trüber Sturm nicht mehr."*

—*Schiller.*

9. Visualization, sense representation of phenomena.
" The Kingdom of God can be represented in the visible form of a church."

Pestalozzi's special meanings, which do not exactly correspond to any of the above, though they follow immediately upon them, are—

(*a*) Model, type.  *Urform*, prototype.
" The form discloses itself independent like the human race."   (*P.*)
" All instruction is nothing but this; it is derived from the typical form of human development."   (*P.*)
" Everything depends on the exact knowledge of this prototype."   (*P.*)

(*b*) Method imposed by the facts of human nature.
" The Art leads us no further than the spirit of that *form* by which the race is raised from vague sense-impressions to clear ideas."   (*P*)
" The *form* or rather the different methods of teaching languages.   (*P.*)                    F. C. T.

**45** (p. 145)—The Elements were not reached when *The Method* was written.

**46** (p. 150)—His natural means of teaching at Stanz was the living voice; and here he begins with *sounds*, not with *names*, or *forms* of letters.  The child should be able to repeat the sounds easily before the forms are put before his eyes.  Phonetics he had not reached. " Always connect a consonant with a vowel, because it cannot be pronounced alone."   " We here see," says

Seyffarth, " the beginning of the method of teaching by sound, instead of the more difficult method of spelling."

**47** (p. 151)—*Spelling Book.* "Hints on Teaching Spelling and Reading," published 1801. Pestalozzi calls this the "Spelling Book". It consists of syllables and words, from which other words can be made by adding letters or syllables before or after. "But when Pestalozzi more fully comprehended the *method of spelling*, he felt it was deficient and unnatural, and tried to improve it. He combined sentences about real objects with the spelling course, exercised the children in spelling by ear before he taught them the symbols in writing, and arranged the letters in groups, which he used by degrees. Movable letters, pasted on cards, spread through his influence. But he fell into the error of putting a certain number of letters together in the most complicated manner, without troubling himself whether the words thus produced were used in speaking or not; and by so doing encouraged the use of sounds without meaning, against which he so strongly protests. For instance, he put O T I N together in the following ways: *nito, toin, into, onit, toni, tino, tion*" (Schindler, *Theoretical and Practical Handbook for First School Teaching. Quoted by Beck*).

**48** (p. 151)—Ed. 1, p. 171. "These should be repeated daily by the child who is learning to spell, in the presence of the child in the cradle, that the latter may become conscious of these sounds through constant repetition," etc.

**49** (p. 157)—*Singing.* This method was soon applied to singing by Nägeli and Pfeiffer. In England his influence has been greater or his method used more effectively in teaching singing than any other subject. The Rev. John Curwen, founder of the Tonic Sol Fa method, said in a discussion on Pestalozzi at the Education Society, that he came on purpose to testify how much and how deeply he was indebted to him; and Mrs. J. S. Curwen tells me he was always ready to acknowledge it, and that before he attempted to teach singing he was familiar with Pestalozzi's method, and used it.

**50** (p. 158)—*The Mother's Book* never existed, so Pestalozzi himself says (p. 254). That is, not as he conceived it. One of his elementary books, published 1803, was called *The Mother's Book or Hints to Mother's on Teaching their Children to Observe and Talk.* But this book was nearly all of it written by Krüsi, and its fundamental idea—that of using the human body as the basis for the first lessons in sense-impression—Krüsi owed to Basedow. Parts 1–6 are by Krüsi; part 7 and the introduction are by Pestalozzi; 10 parts were proposed, but only 7 were published. The separate parts —called " Exercises " in the book—are:—

1. Observation, and naming the parts of the body; 2. Their position ; 3. Their connection; 4. Which parts are single, double, etc.; 5. Characteristics of each separate part; 6. Comparison of parts; 7. Function.

The three remaining exercises were to have been:—

8. What belongs and is necessary to the *care* of the body; 9. Various uses of the special parts—5; 10. Summary and description.

Pestalozzi seems to have thought that his fellow-workers understood his ideas better, and were more capable of carrying them out than he was himself. But he saw later they were not, as the note in Letter XI (p. 254) and Preface to Ed. 2 (pp. 17–28) show. " We were too different," he says. None had had his experience; none followed so heartily his way of experiment and observation. This, then, is not his conception of the *Mother's Book;* it is only a part, and an unsatisfactory part, of what he proposed. He often indicates his notion of it, especially in Letter XI.— " The first course in the *Mother's Book* is an attempt to raise sense-impression to an art, and to lead the child by form, number, and speech to a comprehensive consciousness of all sense-impression, the more definite concepts of which will constitute the foundation of his later knowledge." " I have impressed the first ten numbers on the child's senses," etc. These quotations show the difference between his conception of the *Mother's Book* and the portion published.

This book was attacked and criticised more than any other of his elementary books, and perhaps justly. However, it probably suggested to Froebel his *Mutter und Koselieder.* But the idea of his own *Mother's Book* is most nearly carried out in his " Letters on Early Education, addressed to J. P. Greaves ", first published in 1827 and recently (1898) reprinted in America.

**51** (p. 166)—Ed. 1, p. 196. " What does it say of him as a reasonable being struggling upwards towards inner independence and self-ennoblement ? "

**52** (p. 177)—Ed. 1, p. 212. " To fall is to move downwards without or against your will."

**53** (p. 177)—"*A legacy.*" Pestalozzi left a work in MS. called *The Natural Schoolmaster*, written between 1802–1805, which contains several exercises of the kind referred to. He gave it to Krüsi, who published it, or a selection from it and other works, under the title of *A Father's Lessons on the Customary Use of Words, a Legacy from Father Pestalozzi to His Pupils*, 1829. The manuscript, in Pestalozzi's handwriting throughout, is in Morf's possession. It is printed in Seyffarth's Ed., vol. 16. Pestalozzi began this before the *Mother's Book* was published. After talking to the child about his physical impressions, he thought it would be well to talk about his moral impressions, and he took words for his text.—The " moral lesson " and its Socratizing was as regular with us as the " object lesson ", but I never hear of it now.

**54** (p. 177)—Ed. 1, p. 212. " I should try to connect truth, correct sense-impressions, and pure feelings with every word describing human action or condition."

**55** (p. 178)—Ed. 1, p. 213. " But if the state allows the proprietor or itself a power opposed to this purpose, then special actions of the rich and powerful, springing from this, will rouse, as far as they are felt, feelings never to be quite extinguished in the human breast, of its original equal rights in the division of the land; and if they become universal, will produce revolutions, so long as men are men. The evils of this cannot be mitigated or remedied except by turning them back to the limits of the purpose for the sake of which," etc.

**56** (p. 180)—Ed. 1, p. 216. " To teach the humble

folk to talk, but have made the speechless people
learn isolated, abstract words by heart."

**57** (p. 180)—Ed. 1, p. 216.   "To keep their lowest
classes always lowest and always stupid."

**58** (p. 180)—Ed. 1, p. 217.   "'Yes! yes!' say the
clergy. 'When they come to us they understand not
a word of our teaching.' 'Yes! yes!' say the magistrates, 'even when they are right it is impossible for
them to make their rights intelligible to man.' The
lady complains loudly and piteously, 'They are hardly
a step higher than cattle; they can be used for no service.' Thick-heads that cannot count five find them
stupider than themselves, and rogues of many kinds
call out, each with his own gesture: 'Well for us that
it is so; were they different, we could neither buy so
cheap, nor sell so dear at the market.'

"Friend! this is the way all the people in the stalls
of the Great European Christian Theatre talk of the
people in the gallery, and they cannot speak in any
other way, because, for more than a century, those in
the gallery have been made by them soulless, as no
Asiatic and heathen people ever were. I once more
explain it. The Christian people of our part of the
world have sunk so low because for more than a century, in our lower schools, empty words have been given
an importance to the human mind that not only over-
powered attention to the impressions of nature, but
even destroyed the inner susceptibility to such impressions in men. I say again, while men did that, and
degraded the Christian people of Europe to a people
of words and chatter, as no people have ever yet been

degraded, they *never taught them to talk.* It is no wonder that the Christianity of this century and this land looks as it does; on the contrary, it is wonderful that good human nature, in spite of all the bungling arts that are tried in our own word and clapper schools, has still preserved so much inward strength as we always find in the midst of the people. Yet, praised be God! the stupidity of all these ape-like arts finds at last a counterpoise in human nature itself, and ceases to be harmful to our race when its apeings have reached the highest point that we can bear. Folly and error," etc.

Karl Riedel's comment on this is worth repetition, even here where we are so often told that we have got beyond Pestalozzi and need his method no more:—

" Seldom has all word-teaching, all weakness in school teaching been so boldly and frankly criticised as here by Pestalozzi with all justice and noble wrath. Parents, teachers, teachers' trainers, and school inspectors should never forget for one instant that only by instruction founded upon the Pestalozzian principle of sense-impression and self-activity that avoids every uncomprehended or superfluous word can ' word and clapper ' schools be set aside. This cannot be too often repeated."

**59** (p. 182)—" Word and clapper folk "; words and empty phases; " sounding brass and tinkling cymbals."

**60** (p. 182)—Seyffarth ends Letter VII. here; his Letter VIII. begins with *Form*. We follow his numbering, as that most commonly used. (See G. 145.)

**61** (p. 185)—A summary of Pestalozzi's meanings of *Anschauung* is given on pp. 7–14.

**62** (p. 186)—The five paragraphs which follow are not in Niederer's version of *The Report of the Method.*

**63** (p. 187)—" Measurement." Compare this with what Prof. Ruskin says on our public schools of art system. " The first error in that system is the forbidding accuracy of measurement, and enforcing the practice of guessing the size of objects. . . . the student finishes his inaccurate drawing to the end, and his mind is thus during the whole process of his work accustomed to falseness of every contour. Such a practice is not to be characterized as merely harmful—it is ruinous." *Laws of Fésole*, Preface, pp. vii., viii. Pestalozzi, however, carried measurement to extremes, until form was lost. The author of *The Two Paths* would not agree to this. One of Pestalozzi's strong points is that in teaching the child we should follow the natural course of the race. The *Laws of Fésole* are so called because they are " founded on principles established by Giotto in Florence, he receiving them from the Attic Greeks through Cimabue, the last of their disciples." Pestalozzi's principle is admitted here as the foundation of teaching art. It is not generally admitted, and is applied less frequently, perhaps not even in these *Laws of Fésole.*

**64** (p. 189)—These measuring-forms are the squares in Buss's A B C of Form, (*The Method*, page 330:) " measuring sub-divisions of the square " are those underlying the general form. The child is to be so familiar with the measure-forms that they become a kind of instinct. Then they are needed no longer; without this help he can represent all proportions and express himself clearly about them. Froebel adopts these measured squares to get over the difficulty children have of measuring for invention, but we hear nothing about abandoning them later.

**65** (p. 191)—" First oval, half oval," etc. In Letter III ovals or " elongated forms of the circle " are not mentioned at all. What he means by " oval " is not clear, but Herbart explains it. " Pestalozzi also has taken up the ellipse in the *A B C der Anschauung*. He calls it somewhat erroneously the oval " (Herbart, *Päd. Schriften*, ii. 142). Pestalozzi has not understood or appreciated this form or its allies, nor its parts. His description " elongated form of the circle " shows this. He mentions it and leaves it. It seems to me that the oval is the fundamental form of all living things, and until some line of graduated curvature, such as the quadrant of the ellipse, is added to elementary lines, and the ellipse or oval, to our general forms, an A B C of Form is impossible, useless, injurious. Pestalozzi's failed partly because he did not see this, as I have tried to show in a paper on " *Neglected Elements in Art Teaching* " (Trans. Teachers Guild, 1887).—I did not know when that was published that Pestalozzi recognized the ellipse or oval at all. Biber says nothing about it. The entire absence of satisfactory accounts of Pestalozzi's work drives us to the original works.

**66** (p. 219)—Pestalozzi's " narrow sense " seems wider than this. He has reduced *form* to the square only. He never really saw the value of the oval and ellipse.   He can teach number by these measure-forms, but he cannot reverse the process and teach *form* by them, nor by number nor by words.   His " Elements " have not the same foundation as his " *Anschauung,* Psychology, and Prototype ".   What value there is in them rests on these principles, not on the harmony which he endeavors to establish between these elements.

**67** (p. 219)—Ed. 1, p. 271.   " Here too we can say with decision, this reckoning is an exercise for the reason only, and is in no way a mere work of memory and no routine-like help to trade.   It is the result of the clearest, most definite sense-impressions, and leads easily, by simple evidence, to truth."

**68** (p. 221)—" Educational " here should be " Instructional ".

Except in this case we have translated *Unterricht* by instruction.   It is Pestalozzi's usual term.   *Erziehung* (education) he made the current term it is now, but it often has not his meaning.   Instead of " drawing out ", it frequently means " cramming in ".

**69** (p. 223)—Ed. 1, p. 277.   " Because it opened the mouth of the obvious stupidity of a monkish and feudal world to express abstract ideas, that the most perfect wisdom of the most intellectual life of our race can never solve."

**70** (p. 224) — *Zungendrescherei,* literary tongue-threshing.   Tongue-twisting  or  turning  sophistry; twisted words or twisted talk.

This is one of his many characteristic words, not easily translated, like *Maulbrauchen,* Letter I.

**71** (p. 228)—If this passage is from *The Method* it is not to be found in the Niederer version. When he referred to the Report in Letter I, he said, "six months ago," here "more than a year ago". But *Wie Gertrud* was not published till October, 1801.

In this letter we have said "the art of sense-impression (or *observation*)", to distinguish it from sense-impression, but Pestalozzi uses "art of sense-impression" only. "What Pestalozzi meant," says J. H. Fichte, is "that only can become the pupil's, or even the man's, true mental possession which he has raised for himself to a perfectly clear mental picture (*Ansch.*), that is, has thought out and has reproduced out of himself from his own knowledge through the self-activity of his mind. It is only then that it becomes one with his consciousness. It is become evident, real, to him a conviction which is theoretically and practically at his command at any moment of his life" (*Deutsche Vierteljahrsschrift*, No. 127, 1869). "This is really what Pestalozzi meant by his art of sense-impression," Richter adds (*Exkurse Wie Gertrud*, p. 187).

**72** (p. 232)—Ed. 1, 289. "Number also in itself, without a foundation of sense-impression is a phantom for our mind. The child must know its *form* before he is in a position to consider it as a *number-relation*, *i. e.*, as the basis of a clear consciousness of few or many."

**73** (p. 239)—Ed. 1, p. 301. "My grammar is only a series of methods for leading the child by every kind or change of word-combination from vague sense-impressions to clear ideas."

**74** (p. 241)—Ed. 1, p. 303. "But I am convinced by experiments, which lie at the base of this statement, and have come with decision to reject all half measures, and to put aside all text-books for elementary instruction which are based on the supposition," etc.

**75** (p. 242)—Ed. 1, p. 304. "And since all instruction books which are written in the usual grammatical way assume this, I would, had I influence, act quite mercilessly towards school libraries, or at any rate towards those elementary books which are meant for the youngest children."

**76** (p. 242)—Ed. 1, p. 305. "Will there be even a few who wish, with me, that I may succeed in checking and putting an end to the mad trust in empty words that is enervating our generation, by making word and sound unimportant to the imagination of men, and in restoring to sense-impression that preponderance over word and sound in instruction that obviously belongs to it?"

**77** (p. 243)—Ed. 1, p. 305. "Yes, friend, there will long be few, very few. The babble of our time is so closely connected with the bread-getting, and the ordinary association of tens and hundreds of thousands together, that it must be long, very long, before the men of our time can take that truth" etc.

**78** (p. 244)—Ed. 1, p. 306. "Such pupils never dream that they are dreaming and sleeping; but all wakeful men round them feel their presumption, and —if they are kind—look on them as night wanderers," etc.

**79** (p. 244)—Ed. 1, p. 307. "I well know that the one good method is neither in my hands nor in any other man's, but with all the power lying in my hands I try to approach this one true good (method)."

**80** (p. 245)—Ed. 1, p. 307. "I have one rule in judging all others. ' *By their fruits shall ye know them.* '"

**81** p. 245)—Ed. 1, p. 308. "Can be nothing but developed faculties and clear ideas. Oh, if starting from this point of view, they would ask themselves at every step, ' Does it really further this end ? '"

**82** (p. 246)—Ed. 1, p. 310. "In this way and no other can the child be led to definitions which give him ideas of the thing to be defined. For definitions are only the simplest and purest expression of clear ideas, but, for the child, definitions contain actual truth only so far as he has a clear, vivid background of sense-impression."

**83** (p. 249)—Ed. 1, pp. 314–316. "You must distinguish the laws of nature from her course, that is, from special workings and statements about these workings. In respect to her laws she is eternal truth, and for us the eternal standard of all truth. But in respect to her course and the statements about her course she is not satisfactory to the individual of my race; she is not *all-satisfying truth.* Careful of the whole, she is careless of the single creature and particularly of man, whose self-dependence she will lessen by no kind of guardianship.

" In this aspect and no other, be it understood that she is careless and blind, and that she requires that the guidance of our race should be taken out of our hands.

But in this respect it is quite true and urgent for my race.  When you leave the earth to nature, she bears weeds and thistles, and when you leave the training of your race to her, she carries it on no further than to a confusion of sense-impressions, necessary for your first lessons, but now unfit either for your own power of comprehension or for that of your child.  Therefore it is neither to the forest nor the meadow that the child must go to learn herbs and trees.  Trees and herbs stand not there in the orders which are most suitable to make the essentials of every relationship visible (*anschaulich*) to him, and through this first impression of the thing itself to prepare him for general knowledge of the subject.''

84 (p. 259) — Ed. 1, pp. 322–324.  '' Now my method gives this passage a kind of truth which I could not imagine then; it is now incontestable.  In it I take no share in all this strife of men, I teach through it neither truth nor error.  It spreads its influence not one step beyond what is undeniable, it touches on no opinion that is disputed among men, it is not the teacher of *truths*, it is the teacher of *truth;* and combines the results of physical necessity, at which the mechanism of my Art is aiming, with the complete certainty of my judgment.

'' Friend, there is no presumption in my heart. Throughout my life I have wished for nothing but the salvation of the people, whom I love, and whose misery I feel as few feel it, bcause I have suffered with them as few have done before.  However, when I say there is a mechanism which results from physical necessity,

I do not therefore say I have developed all its laws; and when I say there is a rational course of instruction, it does not follow that I have fully stated this course. In the whole account of my doings, I have tried far more to make the security of my principles clear than to set up the very limited action of my own little individuality as a standard of what may and must come from the full development of these principles for the human race. I do not know myself, and I feel daily more and more how much I do not know."

**85** (p. 269)—Ed. 1, p. 332. "I see in it the ideal of the lost innocence of my race, but I see in it also the ideal of the shame which the memory of this lost holiness always awakens in me, so long as I am worthy, and so long as I am worthy ever revives within me the power of seeking what I have lost and of saving myself from ruin. Friend, so long as man is worthy of the sublime characteristic of his race, speech, so long as he uses it with a pure desire to ennoble himself through it, it is a high and holy thing. But when he is no longer worthy, when he uses it with no pure desire to ennoble himself, it will be to him and for him the first cause of ruin, a wretched promoter of much misery, an inexhaustible source of unspeakable illusion, and a lamentable cloak for his crimes. Friend, it is true— terribly true—the depravity of language grows with the depravity of man. Through it the wretched become more wretched; through it the night of error becomes still darker; through it the crimes of the wicked still increase. Friend, the crimes of Europe are still increasing through idle talk. We cannot guess to what this ever-increasing list of publications will lead a generation whose weakness, confusion, and violence have already reached the stage we see."

This passage has been extended but not much altered in the second edition.

**86** (p. 270)—Ed. 1, p. 335. " Thought and action should stand in such close relation to each other, that, like spring and stream, if one cease the other ceases with it."

**87** (p. 271)—Ed. 1, p. 336. " Mechanical laws." " The mechanism of nature."

**88** (p. 275)—This entire passage and the beginning of the next is altered in the later edition. We give it here as it stands in the first edition, and also fill up the " great gap " once more.

Ed. 1, p. 324. " The individual man has not lost the consciousness of these important requirements for his development. His natural instinct, together with the knowledge he possesses, drives him to this path. The father does not leave his child wholly to Nature, still less the master his *apprentice, but governments make infinitely more mistakes than men.* No corporation is influenced by instinct, and where instinct does not act truth enjoys but half its right.

" It is a fact that no father is guilty towards his son, no master towards his apprentice, of that which the government is guilty towards the people. The people of Europe do not enjoy in regard to their culture in skill (*Fertigkeit*=technical education) a vestige of that public and general help from government that each man needs in order by wise care of his own business to attain inward satisfaction. In no way do they enjoy the cultivation of their *practical abilities*, except indeed for the purpose of human slaughter ; for military organization devours all that is due to the people, or rather what they owe to themselves. It devours all that is ground out of the people, all that can be ground out of them in an ever-increasing ratio. Their practical abilities are neglected because the government does not fulfil the promises which were made in order to grind the people. But this which the government withholds from them is of such a nature that if it were only granted the extortion would become just; and the misery of the people, as a consequence of this justice, would be changed into contentment and happiness. But now they snatch the bread from the widow, who is taking it out of her own mouth to give it to her babe. They snatch it, not intending to use it for the people, but in order to make their injustice and worthlessness lawful and legal. In the same spirit, at one time, they snatch bread from the widow and orphan to make jobbery ecclesiastical and canonical. The same methods served for both: for the jobbery, spiritual extortion, and for the injustice, worldly taxation, both in the name of the public welfare—the one for the salvation of the soul, the other for the happiness of the body— both notoriously work against salvation and against happiness.

" The people of Europe are fatherless and wretched. Most of those who stand near enough to help them have something else to do than to think of their welfare. In the stable, and with dogs and cats, you will be led to believe that many of them are humane, but they are not humane to the people; they have no heart for them. They live on the revenues from land, but in constant forgetfulness of the conditions that produce these revenues. They do not realize how the people are degraded by the ever-increasing extortion and the *confusion caused by it*, nor how *practical honesty* is constantly decreasing, as well as a *want of a sense of responsibility* in using public property. They are responsible for the dreadful increase of physical enervation of men and classes who are *de facto*, if not *de jure*, free from responsibility. They, receiving revenues, wash their dirty hands. It is this which degrades and preplexes human nature and robs it of its power of enjoyment and its true humanity. They do not realize how great the universal pressure of work has become. They do not realize how the difficulty increases day by day of getting through the world with religion and honor, and of leaving the children behind provided for according to their circumstances. Least of all do they realize the disproportion between that which they grind from the poor of the land, and that which they leave in his hands wherewith to earn what they grind from him. But, dear friend, whither is my holy simplicity leading me ? ''

**89** (p. 277)—Ed. 1, p. 341. '' The culture of the physical faculties, that the state should assiduously and might easily give to the people, like the culture for special purposes, depends, like all culture, on a profound mechanism—on an A B C of the Art; that is, on general rules of art by following which the children can be trained by a series of exercises, proceeding gradually from the simplest to the most complicated. These exercises must certainly result in affording daily increasing ease in those faculties (*Fert.*) which needed improvement.   But this A B C is *not found*.   Of course we seldom find what nobody seeks.   It was so easy to find.   It must begin with the simplest expressions of the physical powers, which contain the principles of the most complicated human practical ability (*Fert.*)."

**90** (p. 278)—Ed. 1, p. 343.  " But these are of no use to the principles of jobbery and injustice that form the basis of our public revenues, and are not easily compatible with the distinctly nervous state of the gentry, who *take the biggest slice* of the results of the jobbery and injustice."

**91** (p. 278)—Ed. 1, p. 345.  " These considerations must determine the power of applying our activities. Every influence that in the application of our powers and faculties turns us away from the centre point."

**92** (p. 279)—Ed. 1, p. 346.  " Every kind of in-struction that bears within itself the seeds of such evil for short-lived men must cause the more terror to every father and mother who have their children's life-long peace of mind at heart, since we must seek the sources of the infinite evil of our *sham enlightenment* and the misery of our *masquerade revolution* in errors of this kind, since they have existed for generations both in the *instruction* and *non-instruction* of our people."

**93** (p. 280)—Ed. 1, p. 347  " And on its lines a sense-preparation for physical instinct will be laid, which will promote the wisdom and virtue of our race."

**94** (p. 280)—Ed. 1, p. 347.  " In this way the only

form of education suitable to the human race is developed which can be recognized as a means of training virtue."

**95** (p. 281)—Ed. 1, p. 347. " Therefore it is that as definition before sense-impression makes men presumptuous fools, so explanations about virtue before the exercise of virtue make them presumptuous villains. I do not believe I am contradicted by experience. Gaps in the sense-cultivation of virtue cannot well have other results than gaps in the sense-cultivation of knowledge."

**96** (p. 285)—Ed. 1, p. 353. " It is not a simple result of natural instinct, but yet it follows the same course of development."

**97** (p. 296)—Ed. 1, p. 370. " Friend, if my method here satisfies a want of my race, its value surpasses my every hope, and it does."

**98** (p. 305)—Ed. 1, p. 370. Here the second edition ends. In the first edition a long passage follows from a letter addressed to Pestalozzi by Dr. Schnell, of Burgdorf.

# INDEX

EDUCATIONAL CLASSICS

*General Editor :* Prof. J. W. ADAMSON

# PESTALOZZI'S
# EDUCATIONAL WRITINGS

EDITED BY

## J. A. GREEN, M.A.

PROFESSOR OF EDUCATION IN THE UNIVERSITY OF SHEFFIELD

WITH THE ASSISTANCE OF

## FRANCES A. COLLIE, M.A.

NEW YORK

LONGMANS, GREEN & CO.

LONDON : EDWARD ARNOLD

1912

# GENERAL PREFACE

THE belief which inspires the editors of the volumes included in this series is one which should find a ready adherence from all who accept the doctrine of development. That belief may be summed up in the assertion that the present is both the child of the past and the parent of the future. Hence the high value of all forms of historical study. The educational theory and practice of a community are not things which arise *e nihilo* ; they are the result of the thoughts, activities, conditions, and circumstances, which constituted the community's past life, especially as these were more directly related to the upbringing of the young. This is so far true that an intelligent and effective comprehension of any existing educational system can only be attained when its antecedent conditions are known and appreciated.

Educational history furnishes a key to the understanding of many of the problems of aim, administration, organization, and method, which confront the student to-day. It will also help him to assume a just attitude towards the future, dispose him to avoid routine, to beware of prejudice, and to keep an open mind with reference to suggested change. History is the true prophylactic against the fogeydom which besets the schoolmaster, the committeeman, and the official.

The influence exerted by the lives or writings of individual thinkers is one of many factors of the protracted development of education. But many have written, and written well, on education, whose effect upon practice has been negligible. The aim of the present series is to present only such authors as have shaped subsequent educational history, or who at least have depicted with authority the educational ideals and practice of their own time.

Many German thinkers hold that the educational system of their country fails because it takes insufficient account of personality and of the duty of social service; they are turning to Pestalozzi for aid in attaining these ideals. The latest Swiss educational reformers are only trying to adapt Pestalozzi's counsels to the new conditions of to-day. A writer who thus retains vital heat over a century, so full of change as the last, has an unquestionable right to a place in such a series as the present.

J. W. A.

# PREFACE

THE problem of making a representative selection from Pestalozzi's voluminous writings presents considerable difficulty. Only one of his books has hitherto been completely translated into English, *How Gertrude Teaches her Children*. Selected portions of his romance, *Leonard and Gertrude*, have appeared in book form, but, for the rest, we have only had such selections as his various biographers, in particular Biber and de Guimps, have incorporated into their work.

I have tried, in the present case, to bring together those parts of his writings which show the essentials of Pestalozzian doctrine, and which exhibit the broad movements of his mind from the vague but germinal *Evening Hours of a Hermit* to the preciser discussions of great educational problems in the *Swansong*. The *Diary*, the *Stanz Letter*, and the *Report to Parents*, which deal with Pestalozzi's actual educational practice, have been omitted. They will, however, be found complete in my *Life and Work of Pestalozzi* (Clive and Co.).

With certain exceptions (the *Letters to Greaves*, of which the original text has never been published and is probably lost, chapter xxxi. of *Leonard and Gertrude*, and the

vii

chapter from *Christopher and Elizabeth*) the translations are new. Only those who have tried to put Pestalozzi's clumsy German into readable English can realize the difficulty of the task, and whilst it is hoped that the author's meaning has been faithfully rendered, it has often been necessary to clear up his paragraphs by shortening them. Actual omissions are indicated thus ( . . . ) or by a note in the text.

The titles of the letters in *How Gertrude Teaches her Children*, in the *Views and Experiences*, and in the Greaves series, and the headings of sections throughout the book, are introduced to facilitate cross reference. Where paragraphs are numbered, they follow the numbers in Mann's *Pestalozzi's Ausgewählte Werke*.

Whilst the responsibility for the selection and editing has rested entirely with me, the work could not have been done in the midst of other duties without the invaluable assistance of my old pupil and former colleague, Miss F. A. Collie, in the labour of translation. My indebtedness to various Swiss and German editors of Pestalozzi, and in particular to Seyffarth, Mann, and Hunziker, will be obvious to all who know the literature.

J. A. GREEN.

THE UNIVERSITY,
SHEFFIELD.

# CONTENTS

* Because the entire text of *How Gertrude Teaches Her Children* is reprinted in the first half of the present volume, Chapter II's selections from *Gertrude* have not been reprinted here. [1977 note]

# CHRONOLOGICAL TABLE

1746. Born at Zurich.

1751-1765. At school and college in his native town.

1762. Rousseau's *Emile* published.

1765. His first journalistic efforts appeared in a weekly newspaper, *Der Erinnerer*, devoted to social and literary subjects.

1769. Went to learn farming in the Emmenthal.

1769. Married Anna Schulthess ; settled at Neuhof.

1774. The fragments of his diary referring to the education of his son belong to this year.

1774-1779. Industrial School at Neuhof.

1780. Wrote the *Evening Hours of a Hermit*.

1781. Wrote *Leonard and Gertrude* (vol. i.). Succeeding volumes appeared in 1783, 1785, and 1787.

1782. Conducted a newspaper—*Ein Schweizer-Blatt.*

1797. Published *Enquiries Concerning the Course of Nature in the Development of the Human Race.*

1798. Took charge of orphanage at Stanz at the request of the Government.

1799-1804. Schoolmaster at Burgdorf. Worked at the problem of Method in Teaching. Published *How Gertrude Teaches her Children*, and inspired the A B C books.

1804-05. Short-lived project of school at Münchenbuchsee. Wrote *Views and Experiences.*

1805. Settled at Yverdun. School there won European reputation.

1807-1810. A weekly journal, *Wochenschrift für Menschenbildung*, was issued from the school. In it appeared the letter describing Pestalozzi's work at Stanz, and the *Report to Parents.*

1819. School for poor children opened at Clendy, but united with that of Yverdun the next year.

1825. After some years of struggle against internal discord, the school at Yverdun was given up.

1826. The *Swansong* and the *Life's Destiny* published as one book.

1827. Pestalozzi died.

# REFERENCES IN THE TEXT

M = Mann's *Pestalozzi's Ausgewählte Werke.* 4 Bde.

S = Seyffarth's *Pestalozzi's Sämtliche Werke.* 12 Bde.
(Edition, 1899.)

G = Green's *Life and Work of Pestalozzi.* (Clive and Co.) 1912.

# PESTALOZZI'S
# EDUCATIONAL WRITINGS

## INTRODUCTION

PESTALOZZI may fairly be regarded as the starting-point of modern educational theory and practice. Although he had not freed himself from the faculty psychology that was current in his day, and although his practical efforts at school-work were not as clear of the error of mere words as he tried to make them, yet it was from him that twentieth-century schoolmasters have directly or indirectly learned that the problem of education is that of an undivided soul developing spontaneously in contact with the issues of life. He taught us that life is the great educator, and that our chief business is to learn the secret of life's method, and apply it to the problems of the classroom.

We shall, however, best understand his position if we consider briefly that of those educational reformers to whom he is most nearly related—Comenius, Francke, Rousseau, and Basedow.

Whether Pestalozzi was more than superficially acquainted with the doctrines of Comenius is doubtful, yet the pedagogy and the career of the two men have many points in common. Both men were in advance of their time; both men were for a long time neglected or forgotten. But whilst Comenius is mainly concerned with externals, Pestalozzi strove to reach the deeper places of the human soul. Both men were especially

1

interested in the education of a small people. For the Bohemians, Comenius outlined an educational organization, and a scientifically ordered doctrine which has become a classic. Pestalozzi had a less well-organized mind than Comenius. He was stirred by the degraded condition of the Swiss poor, and saw the only hope of the future in their moral elevation. This was for all time the ultimate object of popular education, and he discussed, not external machinery, but the spiritual conditions on the basis of which the problem could be solved. Comenius says many beautiful things about moral education, but his interest lay chiefly in the Baconian revolt against verbalism. Hence his *Orbis Pictus*, his demand that the study of the mother-tongue should precede that of Latin, and his call for examples before rules. His principles of method are, however, not based upon the nature of men, but upon citations from the Bible or upon analogy with external Nature.

" Comenius' title to fame rests on the discovery, application, and embodiment in a large-minded treatise on Didactic, of the fundamental principles—

" 1. That all instructions must be carefully graded.

" 2. That, in imparting knowledge to children, the teacher must, to the utmost, appeal to the faculties of sense-perception."

So Mr. Keatinge writes in his scholarly edition of the *Great Didactic*, and so far it is true to say that Comenius anticipated Pestalozzi; but, as we shall see, Pestalozzi had a sounder grip of both principles, and his claim to fame must be put on much higher ground, in spite of the " ineptitude " with which he often expressed his ideas.

But Comenius' educational ideas were in effect a dead letter almost as soon as they were written. The main current of education both in England and abroad continued along the old lines of a decadent humanism, although the eighteenth century witnessed a gallant fight for classical studies in Germany, thanks especially to the labours and enthusiasm of J. M. Gesner (1691-1761) and F. A. Wolf (1759-1824). The waning interest in classical studies had, however, been helped on by the work and influence of the Pietists. Their pedagogical leader, Heinrich Francke (1663-1727), was chiefly interested in religious education, not in the formal sense of the stricter Lutherans, for whom "learning the catechism" was the chief end of school life, but in a deeper spiritual sense which brings him into close relation with Pestalozzi. But how differently it worked in practice will be best understood by comparing the following account of the discipline of Francke's Institution in Halle with the spirit and practice of Pestalozzi :[1]

" Many complaints were made of the offensive names which the teachers hurled at their pupils : Oxen, Donkeys, Fools, Calves, Beasts, Ruffians. Sticks, canes, and whips, were often used on their bared person in full view of the school. To make the punishment worse, the teachers would use the butt end of their whips, and strike them on their shoulders, arms, and heads, in such a way that lumps, and often sores, resulted : they used to seize the lads by the hair and strike them with their fists in their faces, making nose and mouth bleed profusely. They were ordered not to allow the consolation of loud crying ; and in order to prevent scandal, punishments in the rooms which faced the street were expressly forbidden ; nor was it allowed to punish the children when strangers were being shown over the school. It was a rule that the teacher must not have the cane in his hand when visitors were in the room. It must be put away, that it might not be seen, and the children were not to be spoken to harshly."

How different all this from the discipline at Stanz and Yverdun ! It was not that Pestalozzi disapproved of corporal punishment, but he insisted that it should leave no sense of injustice behind. It must be given in love. The punishments of parents do not usually create ill-will, neither did his. " How pleased my children were

[1] Quoted by Seyffarth from a report by Dr. Eckstein ( *V. S.*, vol. i., p. 21).

when I offered them my hand a moment after I had been obliged to whip them !"[1]

In another respect Francke and his followers approached, at least externally, the pedagogical position of Pestalozzi. They revived and gave new meaning to the old idea, *Non scholæ, sed vitæ discendum*, and Christopher Semler, a colleague of Francke's at Halle, gave it form by organizing what he called a *Realschule*, in which Latin was not taught, but emphasis was laid on mathematics, geography, science, agriculture, and the like. Twice he started such a school (1708 and 1738), but each time it only lasted two years ; this was due the second time to Semler's death. The idea was not dead, however, and more successful efforts to give it practical shape were made in Berlin in 1747 by pupils of Francke and by others. It is therefore not without justification that the Pietists are usually credited with starting a movement out of which the so-called " modern school " has sprung. It was Semler who first used the term *Realschule ;* but the resemblance to Pestalozzi does not go below the surface. There is all the difference in the world between the principle *Life educates* and that which insists upon the school curriculum being determined by the needs of the future. Of course Pestalozzi said that the school must take into account the probable future of the child, but for him it is the life the child is living now—what he feels, what he does in the light of what he knows, what he seeks to know in order that he may do—it is these things that are educative. Yet " the poor must be trained to poverty," and to surround them with an establishment in which everything is done for them is a profound educational blunder.[2]

Any resemblances which we may discover between Pestalozzi and his predecessors are for the most part accidental. It is not very likely that he had read the

---

[1] *Cf.* Pestalozzi's letter on his work at Stanz, G., pp. 77-8.
[2] *V.* his letter on the *Education of the Children of the Poor ;* G. : pp. 286 f.; *cf.* also *Swansong*, pp. 320-1; and his *Address of 1818*, pp. 199 f. in this book.

*Great Didactic* or that he was acquainted with the educational ideas of the Pietists. This cannot, however, be said of Pestalozzi's relations with Rousseau. He tells in the *Swansong*[1] of the effect which Rousseau's writings had upon the students of Zurich and upon himself. His political and educational outlook was profoundly and permanently affected by them. His earliest educational activity and his comments thereon[2] are constantly reminiscent of the *Émile*. There we find him enlarging upon the dangerous familiarity with " words," which are implicit judgments, and therefore often premature. Jacqueli is to gain ideas through actions ; he is to keep his eyes and ears open, but to keep his mouth closed ; he is to discover all he can ; his teacher is to remember that Nature is the best teacher. He should take the child to Nature, and leave him there, free as possible. All this is Rousseau pure and simple, but even in those early pedagogic efforts Pestalozzi showed his independence of mind. He made experiments of his own (*e.g.*, teaching his four-year-old boy Latin by the " direct " method), and he deliberately abandoned Rousseau on the question of children's obedience. Rousseau would abolish such words as " command," " duties," and " obedience," from the child's vocabulary. Pestalozzi saw that freedom and obedience were essential to childish experience. He would unite what Rousseau had separated.

But Rousseau's influence upon Pestalozzi was not exhausted in this practical effort. Throughout his writings we hear the echo of Rousseau's " natural man." " The way of Nature," " the book of Nature," " the natural man," are characteristically Pestalozzian expressions. But here again the disciple is better than his master. His conception of the relation between primitive man and moral man, and of the transition from one to the other, differ fundamentally from that of Rousseau.[3]

[1] *V. S.*, vol. xii., pp. 414-5. These are the opening paragraphs of the biographical parts of the *Swansong*.

[2] *The Diary*, in which he records for a brief period his educational experiences in connection with his own son (*V. G.*, pp. 28 ff.).

[3] *Cf.* Section I., p. 57.

Again, although both recognized the social roots of education, and both accepted the social aim of education, Pestalozzi was not a dreamer in the same sense as Rousseau. At least, he was not an idle dreamer. Instead of writing dream books, he established orphanages at Neuhof and Stanz and conducted great educational experiments at Burgdorf and Yverdun.

Pestalozzi was as profoundly convinced of the rottenness of society as Rousseau, but more clearly, or at any rate more consistently, than Rousseau, perhaps, he saw salvation in education, and in education promoted by the State.[1] From youth upwards, Pestalozzi had been a keen politician, in the best sense of that word. Whilst anything but a man of the world, he saw the evils from which the world was suffering, and especially that part of it which was less articulate in those days than it is now. He understood thoroughly the point of view of the Swiss labouring man of that day. *Leonard and Gertrude* brings that out admirably. He saw above all things his want of independence. The old social order was that of an agricultural community—landlord, farmer, labourer—in which the personal tie was commonly more marked than the mercenary one. But the luxurious

---

[1] The fact that Émile was separated from society, and educated by a tutor in isolation, suggests an antisocial point of view. If Rousseau were inspired by such a feeling at the moment of writing, it was inconsistent with views expressed by him both before and after his educational romance was written. Compare, for example, the educational part of his article on " Political Economy," written for the *Encyclopædia* (1755), and his *Considerations on the Government of Poland* (1773). May it, in fact, not be that he severed Émile from society as he saw it, as he took his education out of the hands of parents as he saw them ? It was a powerful protest against the corruptions of society and of parenthood, and not intended as a model procedure. As Mr. Boyd points out, if even Rousseau himself was inclined to accept a literal interpretation of his book, any doubt he may have had on the matter was not long-lived. " You remark very truly that it is impossible to make an Émile," he wrote in 1764, " but surely you do not think that that was my object." Whether or not it is worth while to try to defend Rousseau against the charge of inconsistency, this is hardly the place to undertake the task.

artificiality of the wealthier classes was bringing ruin upon the country people, who were left to the tender mercies of unscrupulous agents. Moved by the wretchedness and degradation which he saw around him, he tried to improve the lot of the villagers in two ways—(1) by education (in its fullest sense) ; (2) by introducing one or other of the new industries (*e.g.*, cotton-spinning) into the villages.

But for him education was not concerned with instruction simply, or even primarily. He was concerned to raise men from their present degradation to the level of humanity. It was not the poverty which he saw around him which stirred his soul to its depths ; it was the degraded lives the poor people led. Their shiftlessness, their want of purpose and initiative, their utter lack of human dignity, hurt him. All these things could be cured by a properly-devised system of education. The problem was at bottom an individual and a moral one : " Help the people to help themselves " ; " Teach them the worth and dignity of honest labour." He would make the people happy and contented, not by showering charitable doles upon them, but by making them feel and prize their independence.[1]

Nothing is more characteristic of Pestalozzi than the motives which stirred his educational activities. His vision was never shut in by the walls of his class-room. Education and life for him were only two ways of regarding the same process of experience. In *Leonard and Gertrude* the vocational aspect of the educational problem was perhaps too strongly emphasized ; but even there he did not lose sight of the need for men first, and specifically trained artisans afterwards. In *How Gertrude Teaches her Children* the vocational problem is in the background, but in the *Swansong* the proper balance is restored.

To save the people was Pestalozzi's leading motive. How was this to be done ? Social amelioration in the shape of better housing and juster laws could be of little effect without education, but it must be an education in

[1] *Cf.* pp. 46 f., 200 f., 320 f., and elsewhere.

close relation to the facts and needs of life. A schooling "which gave knowledge without practical power" had no charm for him.

It is commonly said that Pestalozzi was not a psychologist, and in the strictly scientific sense of that word we may accept the judgment. Yet who can read the letters entitled *Views and Experiences* without realizing what an intelligent observer of children Pestalozzi was? The modern psychologist would write the fifth and sixth of these letters, shall we say, in less popular terms, but we may doubt whether he would succeed in producing a truer account of the mental life of early infancy. There are similar passages in all his writings which reveal a psychological insight far surpassing that of many of his successors. Nor was his knowledge of human nature in maturer form less profound—using the word "knowledge" to cover "feelings, instincts, and intuitional methods of arriving at conclusions," such as the French philosopher, Henri Bergson, has defended so powerfully. We may push aside the *Enquiries and Researches* and the *Evening Hours of a Hermit* as being unphilosophical, but there is more humanity in them than in many a more reasoned treatise on education and sociology.

In his own time, Pestalozzi was often accused of stealing the ideas of Basedow and the Philanthropinists. He vigorously defended himself against the accusation in a polemic which Morf describes in great detail. That there were points in common between them must be admitted, but, again, the resemblance is more superficial than fundamental. Basedow's educational work was in the first place confined to the well-to-do classes. He was interested only in them. His aims were utilitarian in the broad sense of the word, but his methods were external and mechanical rather than internal and spiritual. "Induction" not "education" was the keynote of his method. He would have his pupils lead useful, patriotic, and happy lives, and he would attain this by giving them useful knowledge, founded on acquaintance with things rather than words. The needs of the present day were dominant in his mind. Classical learning had nothing to offer in that direction ; it had therefore no countenance in his school. Learning was to be made easy ; effort and strain were to be abolished from school life ; work should be transformed into play whenever possible. Art and poetry had little place in his scheme of things. Campe, one of his most distinguished followers, said " the inventor of a new spinning-machine was a greater benefactor to humanity than Homer and all his poetry." As to religion, they thought that whilst it was not the only way of making children virtuous, yet it was the quickest and most effective ; moreover, a man who is professedly religious is more honoured in the world than the irreligious—they must therefore teach it.

The attitude of the Philanthropinists towards religion brings into strongest relief the contrast between them and Pestalozzi,[1] but it only illustrates a difference that extended right through their pedagogy. Pestalozzi's originality was more frequently challenged in reference to " teaching through the senses." In its bald form, this principle is of course much older than Pestalozzi. As we have seen, it was a cardinal feature of the pedagogy of Comenius, and it was certainly proclaimed again by Basedow. But " teaching through the senses " is only a very partial way of describing Pestalozzi's position. It is only a very superficial way of describing his *Anschauungs-Prinzip*, the full force of which is perhaps best expressed by the " principle of concreteness." Scores of visitors went away from Burgdorf and Yverdun without piercing the veil of imperfect practice which they saw there, and arriving at the real mind behind it. It was not altogether their fault, for Pestalozzi was misled partly by his mistaken analysis of the fundamental activities of the mind, and partly by a view of words themselves which was current in his day.[2] The word itself is for the child a thing that is sensed ; and just as the objects that

[1] *Cf.* pp. 33 f., 142 f.
[2] *V. How Gertrude Teaches her Children*, pp. 109 and 116.

are sensed by the eye may, even apart from experience
of them, be supposed to suggest their own meaning and
a more or less appropriate response (*e.g.*, children will
often shrink from a dog the first time they see one), so
the sounds of words awaken a sort of racial memory
which gives them initial values in the mental life of the
child.

But *Anschauung* (concreteness) means something much
more. It went down into the deeper places of the mind,
and was not satisfied with a sensory veneer. The word
suffers by its wide connotation, for Pestalozzi uses it of
" inner feelings " as well as of " inner intellectual processes." It does not in the least follow that a teacher
who is giving an object lesson with a complete equipment of objects is fulfilling what Pestalozzi understood
by this principle. The *whole* mind of the children may
not be called into play. It is not a question of inattention, but the quality of attention, so to speak, which is
being given by the children. They may be thinking of
nothing else as they enumerate the sensory qualities of
the object exhibited to them, in response to their teacher's
questions, and yet their whole beings are not engaged.
There is a want of recognized purpose in their work
which makes it formal and abstract instead of human
and living. It is not " concrete " (meaningful) in the
Pestalozzian sense.

The depth of Pestalozzi's insight lifts him head and
shoulders above Comenius and Basedow, however much
we should honour them for their work on " realities " in
education. Sense reals are, however, only half reals—
a truth which has still to penetrate the practice of the
schools. Pestalozzi saw this, but at Burgdorf, at any
rate, his practice was misleading. In Yverdun he more
nearly realized his theoretical views.

His point of view comes out, perhaps, more clearly in
his defence of the home as the place of education *par
excellence*, and of the good mother as the eternal type of
educator. Why was this ? Precisely because the home
is the child's fundamental " reality." His activities there

have a " real " setting ; the mutual services, the personal relationships, the whole of his experience, in fact, is concrete in the full sense of that word. It is life that reigns there, and it is life that educates. There, inner affections are transformed into acts of kindly service, and the whole environment builds up within the child that sacred love for home which remains with most of us the great " real " of life. Inner is made Outer, and Outer is made Inner, to use the words which Pestalozzi himself used[1] before Fröbelian mysteries were put into them.

Pestalozzi, however, won his fame as a schoolmaster through that badly-named book *How Gertrude Teaches her Children*, in which he is mainly occupied with the problem of instruction. What was called the " Pestalozzian Method " was a more or less faithful imitation of teaching devices which, when separated from the spirit of the master, quickly degenerated into the verbalism against which Pestalozzi waged war ; indeed, he and his assistants often fell into practices which could hardly be defended against the charge of formalism which critics were not slow to hurl at them—charges which were made especially against the *Mother's Book*, for which Pestalozzi was himself only partially responsible.

If we would understand Pestalozzi's permanent contribution to the educational thought and practice, we must look deeper than his ABC books, which, as he himself acknowledged, were only the first attempts to give practical shapes to ideas which he felt were unassailable. They were the outcome of his effort to reduce education to a simple " mechanical " process which ignorant mothers might make use of. All these have long since been superseded, for no other reason than that they were themselves not conceived in the true spirit of the master. They were nothing more than a mechanical interpretation of the least satisfactory features of the " Elementary Method "—continuous gradation in scarcely perceptible steps from simple to complex, from the near to the more

---

[1] *Cf. Address to my House,* p. 207; *How Gertrude Teaches her Children,* p. 128.

remote.   The principle that *Life educates* was forgotten.

The more fundamental features of his method are
brought out in the *Address of* 1818 and in the *Swansong.*
There he states in unmistakable terms the principle of
spontaneity.   The teacher's business is like that of the
gardener, who may protect and nourish his plants,
securing for them the most suitable environment, but he
can do no more.[1]   " The impulse to development lies
within."   This is as true of intellectual as of moral power,
and equally true of practical capacity, though it is
especially characteristic of morality.   The feelings (*innere
Anschauungen*) which are the germs of moral development
we recognize as peculiarly intimate and self-originating.
We must not, however, suppose the germs of our intellectual development less spontaneous in origin.   Time,
space, and number, are themselves contributions which
mind makes to experience, thereby reducing its mul-
tifarious impressions to order.   The impulse and the
capacity to organize his experiences are already in the
child ; it is the teacher's business so to arrange his environment and his needs that the impulse and the capacity
are brought into activity.

Similarly, in the same two essays, Pestalozzi insists
upon the harmonious development of the child's threefold capacity.   He had a horror of one-sidedness in any
direction,[2] and the test of success was social efficiency.
It is in the first two letters of the *Views and Experiences*
that this test is most clearly applied, but the social principle is a conspicuous feature of his writings and of his
practical work from the Neuhof days to the days of his
death.   Home life is the great social teacher, and school

[1] The analogy of gardener and teacher is one that cannot be
pressed very far.   Pestalozzi himself saw the great difference
between the plant and the child.   The child has a will which is free.
Men are masters of their circumstances.   *Cf. Address of* 1818, p. 190,
and *Enquiries and Researches*, p. 58.   The spiritual element in
man's environment makes the gardener analogy also misleading
if it is at all pressed.

[2] *Cf.* p. 157, and pp. 268-9.

is more likely to fulfil its functions the more nearly it approaches the spirit and temper of the home. It is the life of the school at Yverdun which constitutes the deepest note of the *Report to Parents*.

The services of Pestalozzi to the development of educational thought and practice are hardly to be over-estimated. The eleven Prussian students sent by the State authorities to Yverdun—the Prussian " eleven " they were called— became educational administrators on their return; and if Moltke could say that it was the schoolmaster who triumphed at Gravelotte, not a little success was due to Pestalozzi. Hardly a country in Europe was not affected by him. Educational activity in England was occupied in the main with the struggles between the supporters of Bell and Lancaster, or with the question whether education was at all an affair of the State, and to what extent. Yet the Pestalozzian method was represented in the activities of Dr. and Miss Mayo, and in books for parents and teachers which Biber and others inspired or wrote.

Amongst the visitors to Burgdorf were Herbart and Fröbel, both of whom acknowledged their indebtedness to Pestalozzi. Herbart remained a diligent interpreter and friendly critic of Pestalozzi. He was, of course, a psychologist and philosopher, as well as a mathematician. He could pierce the husk of formalism into which Pestalozzian practice had fallen, and reduce to logical system the sound intuitions which lay behind them. But Herbart's point of view was alien to the spirit of Pestalozzi, who always had in mind a living and growing soul, in place of which Herbart gives us an external and mechanically-formed mind.

In a still greater degree the secret of Fröbel will be found in Pestalozzi. Fröbelian *self-activity* is neither more nor less than Pestalozzian *spontaneity*. The very phrases which are peculiarly associated with the name of Fröbel were used by Pestalozzi: " Learn by doing "; " Live for our children "; " Making the Inner Outer." Fröbel was a mystic by temperament. He could not have written so simply of children as Pestalozzi does in the *Views and Experiences* (Letter VI.), and his psychology of childhood loses enormously by the mysteries with which it is involved.

Yet both Herbart and Fröbel have made an impression upon the professional teachers of the last fifty years apparently far more striking than Pestalozzi. This is due in part to the practical form into which they or their followers have reduced their teaching. Fröbelian " gifts " and Herbartian " steps " were formulæ of direct and easy application to class-room practice. Whether in use they represented the spirit of the master was another matter. Pestalozzi's attempts to " mechanize " instruction were too clumsy for wide appreciation, and he was represented chiefly by the " object lesson " which the Mayos popularized in this country.

Pestalozzi's principles were, however, too fundamental ever to form a school of practice. He stands outside and above party. His ideas are the very breath of all later idealistic and practical educational work. " Back to Pestalozzi " is a common cry in modern German pedagogy. Thanks largely to Professor Natorp and Drs. Wiget and Leser, the deeper Pestalozzian message has been heard. From whatever side we approach him, with whatever problems we confront him, Pestalozzi reveals a pedagogical insight and breadth of view which belongs to no school, but will be fruitful for all time.[1]

[1] For a fuller exposition of Pestalozzian Doctrine, I am permitted to refer to my *Life and Work of Pestalozzi* (Clive and Co.).

# I.—EARLY WRITINGS

## "EVENING HOURS OF A HERMIT"

[*These detached thoughts on education were published in the* Ephemerides, *a journal devoted to literary, social, and philosophical subjects, in* 1780. *It was reprinted with some changes in the* Wochenschrift *in* 1807, *and again in* 1815. *Pestalozzi describes the aphorisms himself, in a letter to Iselin, as the preface to all that he should write in the future. For that reason he suggested their being reprinted. He would have them better known. They do in fact contain his whole philosophy of life and education. The text is complete and is translated from the edition of* 1807.]

WHAT is man in essence? Apart from differences of station—king and cottager—what is the nature of the manhood which king and cottager alike enjoy? Why do not our wise men examine this question? Does the farmer not study his oxen? Does the shepherd not consider the nature of his sheep?

And you who teach men to regard you as their shepherds, do you take as much trouble to understand your flock as the farmer does in respect of his cattle, or the shepherd in respect of his sheep? Does your claim to honour rest on your special knowledge of mankind, and does your reputation depend on the enlightened way in which you shepherd your people? In any case, it surely should be so. To know what man in himself is like, what his needs are, what elevates and what depraves him, that is obviously necessary to the self-styled shepherds

15

of the people. So much indeed should all men know, however humble their station.

Everywhere this need is felt. Everywhere men are struggling painfully and spasmodically upwards. Generations pass away, and the goal is no nearer. The only result is to hand on still further the unmistakable tale of incomplete lives. For such men the end was not the autumn of life, with its ripening fruit followed appropriately by the winter's rest — their destiny fulfilled.

Why, then, does man continue this struggle for truth so aimlessly? Why does he not set himself to find out the fundamental needs of man, the foundation on which lives of joy and blessedness might be built? Why does he not seek after truth which would satisfy him in his heart, develop his powers, brighten his days and bring blessings upon his years?

The satisfaction of the human heart, the strength and purity of our common human nature, the blessedness of human existence—these things are no dream! To seek and to find them is surely man's real vocation. Therein at least lies the desire of my own heart; my whole nature drives me to take a part in that search.

### The Means whereby Human Nature may find Satisfaction—Educational Foundations.

Where must man seek the truth on which the perfection of his nature depends? Driven by his needs, he will find it ultimately in his own inmost depths.

Man's capacity for happiness is dependent neither on artifice nor on chance circumstance. It lies in himself, bound up with his fundamental aptitudes. We must of all things realize this truth first.

Life itself as the individual himself lives it is Nature's book. Therein lies the secret of the power of a wise education, and schools whose work is not based on this foundation only mislead.

The happy nursling learns in this way what his mother means to him. Thus love and gratitude are planted as *realities* in his mind before he knows anything of *words* like " duty " or " thanks." In the same natural way the son who eats his father's bread and warms himself at his hearth finds happiness in the discharge of his filial duties.

At bottom all men are alike ; there is only one way to their happiness. Sooner or later the truth which has its source in the depths of their common nature will be recognized everywhere, thereby uniting the thousands who are now at variance over mere externals.

It is man himself, his sense of power, that is the concern of natural education.

## The Aim and the Sphere of Education.

That all men, even the humblest, should attain this level of human wisdom in all its simplicity is the object of a *general* education. To adapt that wisdom, by practical exercises, to the particular circumstances of life is vocational education. But the latter must always be subordinate to the wider aim.

Whatever the station in life, however humble it may be, wisdom and strength based on simplicity and innocence of life have a blessed influence ; similarly, these qualities are indispensable in the ruling classes. He who is not first of all a man with all his humanity fully developed lacks even the first essential of an education which is designed for a special position in the world, and no external greatness can dispense with it. Between the father of a family and the prince, between the poor burdened with the cares of poverty and the rich perhaps more burdened with the anxieties of his position, between the ignorant mother and the famous scholar, between the lazy sluggard and the genius of world-wide influence, there is a wide gulf fixed. But if the great of the earth have, with the growth of their dignities, lost their simple human feelings, then will dark and gloomy clouds

surround them in their heights, whilst cultivated human
nature in the cottager lives in the sunshine of true human
worth, lofty, contented, and pure.

Thus it is that a prince who is anxious that justice
and righteousness should be dealt out to offenders against
the law vainly offers liberal monetary rewards to secure
it.  If he will have judges who shall discharge their duties
wisely, who shall deal with wrongdoers in the fashion
of fathers of the people, let him encourage humaner views
in the council of war and in the estate office, and let his
own household be penetrated by the family spirit.  Otherwise the talk of enlightened laws is as empty as that of
neighbourly love among heartless people.

It may be that you, prince, are thus far from the
blessedness of the truth which you vainly seek.  Meanwhile there are fathers in the dust under your feet who
are dealing wisely with their troublesome children.  In
the tears of their night watches, and in the way they bear
their daily burden, learn, prince, how to deal wisely with
those who offend.  Entrust the right of life and death
to men who seek wisdom on this same road.  O prince,
the most blessed theory in the world is a humane spirit ;
only through that have laws any effect in spreading light,
wisdom, and happiness, amongst the people.

### The Course which Nature must follow in the Development of Man.

Any method of opening up man's powers which claims
to be natural must be open and easy, and education
which aims at leading men to true and restful wisdom
must be simple and of general application.

The natural way of cultivating power is to put it to
use, to give it exercise.

That power comes from putting knowledge, gifts, and
capacities, to use is Nature's secret for the education
of man.

Therefore the man of simple character and unstained
life, who quietly, diligently, and with all docility, makes

good use of his knowledge and of his finer powers, is educated according to Nature; whilst the man who puts this natural ordinance to confusion in his own heart, by weakening the simplicity and adaptability of his requirements, grows unfit to enjoy the blessedness of truth.

Parents should not hurry their children into working at things remote from their immediate interests. Let them first attain the strength that comes from dealing efficiently with matters near at hand. Be fearful of sternness and strain. By anticipating the ordinary course, they diminish the powers of their children, and disturb profoundly the equilibrium of their nature. This is what happens when teachers hurry children into lessons that are concerned chiefly with words, before they have passed through the discipline of actual encounter with real things. Yet it is out of such experience that wisdom and truth develop. The teacher's course lays the foundations of intellectual growth and power in empty words instead of in the solid truths that come from contact with realities.

The artificial methods of the school which prefers the order of words to the free though slow sequence of Nature may make men superficially brilliant, hiding in this way their want of native power and satisfying times like ours.

The perverse and exhausting pursuit of the mere shadows of truth; the desire for talk about truth in which there is no genuine interest and for which there is no possible application; the devotion of the developing powers of youth to teachers who are one-sided and inelastic in their views; the manifold artifices employed in this commerce of words which is the basis of contemporary education—all this shows how pitiful is our departure from Nature's way.

Yet there is nothing hard and compulsory in the methods of Nature. If it were so, one-sidedness would follow, and truth would not fall softly and freely, nor would it penetrate human nature to its depths. If truth were difficult of access, its attainment would not make for the gentle service of humanity ; it would not make good and tender mothers, whose joy and wisdom is the happy necessity of their children.

The forces of Nature, although they lead infallibly to their end (which is truth) show no stiffness (or difficulties) in their working.  The nightingale's song vibrates through the darkness, and all natural objects move in thrilling freedom — not a sign of intrusive compulsion anywhere.

Man loses the equilibrium of his power, the strength of his wisdom, in proportion as his mind is compulsorily given up to the pursuit of an object.  Hence the natural way of teaching is not coercive.

## Intellectual Education.

To lead men to the truth is nothing more than to train them to that knowledge of themselves which brings repose.                    *Or,*

To lead men to the truth (to reality) is to educate their nature to rest-bringing wisdom.

If men seek the truth as Nature defines it, then will they find it as they need it for their particular point of view and their particular career.  Just as it is needful to man's rest and peace, just as it is a guiding star in his immediate affairs, just as it is the very support of his life, so is it full of blessedness.  Individual men in their individual positions could make no use of the whole field of knowledge.  The range of knowledge through which man is blessed in his station is narrow, and it is in the beginning narrower still, centred entirely about himself and his immediate neighbourhood.  Gradually the range is widened, but every extension derives its usefulness from its connections with this intimate beginning.

The direct feeling for reality is formed only in those narrow circles, and true human wisdom has for its bed-rock an intimate knowledge of the immediate environment, and trained capacity for dealing adequately with it.

Wisdom which is called into play by the needs of our particular situations increases and strengthens our effectiveness, and the type of mind which it engenders is simple and clear-sighted ; formed by actual contact with uncompromising realities, it is adaptive to future situations. In action it is firm, sensitive, and sure. Nature's sublime road leads straight to reality, which is none other than strong and active human nature itself ; this is at once the source, the means of training, and the ultimate end.

Surely it is men we are educating, not brilliant mushroom growths. The child of Nature is limited (and recognizes the fact) ; he speaks only when his knowledge is adequate. The scattered confusion which comes from knowing many things is not the natural type. Similarly, the man who hovers lightly about every branch of knowledge, without putting his knowledge steadily and unobtrusively to use, loses the feeling of reality which is expressed in the steadfast glance of quiet solid joy.

The way of men who in the medley of their manifold knowledge find much opportunity for talk is uncertain and wavering ; they never attain the reposeful feeling that belongs to true wisdom. For them, in all their noisy pride, their immediate surroundings are a dark and dreary desert, whereas it is there that the power of the blessedly wise shines most brightly.

Similarly, the dreary wastes of gloomy ignorance lead from Nature's path. Want of knowledge of our own nature puts narrower limits upon wisdom than actual circumstance. The perversion of the fundamental notions concerning our place in the world, oppressive tyranny, unnatural want of general rational enlightenment in the most essential needs and relationships of humanity, increase the obscurity, as the shades of night darken the earth.

## The Education of the Heart.

Conduct which is contrary to our inner feeling of right undermines our capacity for knowing reality, destroys the purity and simplicity of our fundamental ideas and feelings. Human wisdom is founded on the strength of a good heart which is obedient to truth, and human blessedness on the rock of simplicity and innocence. To preserve in men this simplicity and innocence is the first care of the fatherhood of humanity, in order that on the foundation of an unpolluted heart the right intellectual structure may be assured.

Man must be educated to internal peace. To teach him to be contented with his lot and its attainable joys, to be patient, to be ready to give honour, and to have faith in his Father's love in times of trial—that is what man needs in his education. Unless he is at peace with himself, he wanders hither and thither on unknown ways. His longing for the impossible robs him of the pleasure to be got from his immediate surroundings, and of that strength which belongs to the wise, the patient, and the adaptable. If he has not peace in his heart, the foundations of his manhood are undermined, and he is harassed by dark fears at times when the wise man laughs in joyousness of spirit.

The discontented man worries himself in his home circle, because he did not distinguish himself in the dance, in the orchestra, or in the political assembly. Restfulness and quiet pleasure are the first objects of human education; they are the greatest need of the time. Knowledge and ambition should be subordinate to these; otherwise they become a source of torment and growing disappointment.

## Home Education.

Man does not live for himself alone. Nature educates him for and by means of his external social relations. In proportion to the intimacy of the relations into which man enters, are they important as factors in educating him for his future destiny (walk in life). The power that comes from dealing with the things about him is always the source of capacity for the wise handling of things more remote. The experience of fatherhood is the best training for the governor; good brothers make good citizens; from both sources spring order in the home and in the state. The family relationship is the first and foremost of natural relationships. Man works at his calling, and bears the burden of citizenship in order that he may enjoy in quiet the blessings of home.

Thus, the education of men for this or that occupation or for a particular social rank must be subordinate to an education which aims primarily at the purity and happiness of family life. For this reason the home should be the foundation of any natural scheme of education. Home is the great school of character and of citizenship. Man is first of all a child, and then the apprentice of his calling. The virtues of childhood bear fruit in the days of apprenticeship; establishing those virtues is the first preparation for the blessings of the future life. Whoever departs from this natural order and hurries forward an education specialized with reference to the needs of the state or of a special calling, whether that of ruler or that of servant, draws men from the enjoyment of their natural blessings on to a sea fraught with unknown dangers.

Surely all recognize and lament the fact that the ruling classes are losing their natural advantages through their education. Is it not clear that in departing from the wise order of Nature their education is bringing disappointment and decay upon them, and is thus adversely affecting the welfare of the people? Do we not all feel how the men of all nations are abandoning the simple joys of home life for unprofitable and glittering shows, in which they may advertise their accomplishments and gratify their lust of praise? Men are wandering far astray and losing sight altogether of their bearings.

## Religious Education.

Man's relationship to God is the nearest of all his relationships. Neither home nor wise enjoyment brings repose at all times. His gentle nature, however well and sympathetically trained, has not without God the strength to withstand authority and death. God as the Father of his house—God as the Source of all happiness, God as his own Father—in this faith man finds rest and power which neither authority nor the grave can destroy. Faith in God is in accord with the highest human feelings; it is the attitude of trustfulness which God's children assume towards their Father in heaven. Faith in God gives the peace on which social order depends, on which, again, depends that undisturbed use of our power which is essential to its increase and its development towards wisdom, and wisdom is the source of all human blessedness. Thus, faith in God is the beginning of wisdom and blessedness—Nature's simple provision for the education of men. Faith in God is graven deep in man's nature; as his sense of right and wrong is indestructible, so is this, the unchangeable foundation of human education, to be found in the innermost recesses of his nature. Faith in God is ever the people's portion, however humble the circumstances; it is the source of true power in the highest station, and of its strength in the lowest. Faith in God is *not* the consequence of training and education; it is the consciousness of the pure and the simple, who with innocent ear listen to Nature's voice and know that God is their Father. Childlike obedience is *not* the result of a finished education; it is the very beginning, the foundation thereof.

The awe of the learned who contemplates the wonders of creation, his researches into the mysteries of the Creator—this is not the way to the faith of which we speak. Such an inquirer may easily lose himself in the bottomless depths of the creation, and dive hither and thither in their waters, far astray from the Source of this unfathomable sea.

God my Father, the God who is there in the humblest cottage—the God of my inmost being—God, Giver of His gifts and of my life's joys—to lead men to realize these things, that is the way education should take; only when faith is based on joy and personal experience can it attain to its natural power.

Or I call loudly to the people, Does this story of overwhelming goodness not touch you, O men? Do you find consolation in the doctrine that it is mere chance whether good or ill predominates in life? When the flames of distress burn over your heads and threaten destruction, do you find consolation in this sort of wisdom?

But when your Father strengthens you in your inmost parts, brings joy to your days, fortifies you in suffering, and makes you certain of the overwhelming preponderance of good, then have you found Nature's way of establishing faith in God.

The bread which my child eats from my hand gives shape to his childish feelings—not his astonishment over my night watches, not my care for his later years. His judgments over my actions are unthinking; they may mislead him and turn his ear from me.

Simplicity and innocence, pure human gratitude and love, is the source of faith. In his childlike simplicity man feels the hope of eternal life, and without that hope the simple faith of men in God loses its primitive force.

The footsteps of the tyrant, trampling upon his brothers, the children of his God, shatter the hopes of men to their foundations. The crowds of dead victims, their widows and orphans, cry aloud, tremble, hunger, believe, and die.

If God is the Father of men, then in the day of their death their destiny is not accomplished.

Hast thou any sense of truth left in thee, O man? Speak! Canst thou believe that God is the Father of man, and that He would allow that day to be the end of the matter for such sufferers? Either God is the Father of man or death is the end of all things.

O man, that inner feeling of thine is a safe guide to

truth and to duty; and dost thou doubt whether that sense tells thee of a life everlasting ?   Believe in thyself, give ear to the teachings of thine own heart; then wilt thou believe in God and in eternal life.

God is our Father, and His children live for ever.   There comes from the depths of thy nature, O man, a voice which truth, innocence, and simplicity, hear with reverence and faith.   But innocence and simplicity do not fall to all men.   To many this inner sense of human nature is a dream-play, and faith in God and eternal life that is built upon it is a contemptible motive of man's art.

O God, who teachest me so powerfully the lesson of truth, happiness, faith, and eternal life—God, whom all His children hear—God, whom all gentle, sensitive, simple, loving folk understand, and all in the same measure—God, did I not give ear to Thy voice which speaks the eternal truth to my inmost nature—did I not believe, what should I be, what should I do ?

Belief in God divides men into children of God and children of the world; it is belief in the Fatherhood of God, belief in eternal life.   God the Father of man, man the child of God, that is the simple message of the faith. Paternal feeling, filial feeling—this common household blessing is also the result of faith.

The enjoyment of my rights as father, the blissful devotion of my wife, the deep and elevating gratitude of my children—this is the result of my faith in God.   Belief in my father, who is God's child, is the root of my faith in God, and, conversely, my belief in God is the guarantee of my faith in my father and of the fulfilment of every household duty.

## EDUCATION FOR CITIZENSHIP.

In the sublime education of Nature duty and enjoyment are united; in her hands man passes from his present blessings to new duties.   All men, be they rulers or subjects, lords or vassals, are prepared for the special duties of their position in the course of enjoying their earliest natural relations. The prince is at once the child of God and the child of his father. The prince is both the child of his father and the father of his people. The subject is at once the child of God and the child of his father. The subject is both the child of his father and the child of his prince. A prince as such is comparable with God. He is the father of the nation. His subjects are his children, and, with him, they are the children of God. How delicate, and yet how strong and beautiful, is this complex relationship of mankind! But men of great station should realize how vain is their dignity in the presence of a nation that is depraved.

I may not name a father's rank. What is a father, and what might he be ? An ox at the manger, a lord of his house. A very prince in his cottage, however humble his lot. O Lord and Father of all, the humblest dependent is in essence the equal of his master, and the satisfaction of his natural needs is his due. To raise the people to the full joy of which their nature is capable is the aim of the ruler who calls himself the father of his people. That the people should enjoy the blessings of home, confident as children in the fatherhood of their prince ; that they should expect to fulfil their paternal duty to bring up and train their children to the joys of manhood : is this a dream ? Is such childlike hope at bottom a sign of sleep ? Not so ; faith in God is the force behind this hope. Princes who believe in God and in the brotherhood of man find here stimulus to the duties of their position. They are God's vicegerents ; they were trained for their people's good. Princes who deny the Fatherhood of God and the brotherhood of men destroy thereby all faith in their duties. They are men of terror, whose power devastates the earth. In recognizing the ultimate Fatherhood of God, princes insure the obedience of their people, for then it is God's own affair. And the prince who refuses to recognize his responsibilities to God is building his throne on the treacherous sand of fear.

Faith in God is in this respect the bond between prince

and people, the bond which unites men in happy human relationships. Unbelief, denial of brotherhood and brotherly duties amongst men, disregard of God's paternal rights, contemptuous and impudent misuse of power, is the bursting of all the bonds that make for human happiness.

Priests tell us of the Fatherhood of God and of the brotherhood of man; their profession brings man's natural relations into union with his blessedness through faith in God. Faith in God is the origin of the feelings of fatherhood and brotherhood amongst men—the source of all righteousness. Righteousness without fatherly and brotherly feeling is a glittering absurdity with no power of blessedness. The disdainful righteousness of the oracle who has sown his wild oats, the sort of thing on which lawyers and courts of justice flourish, is a masquerade of reality, and not a source of popular blessing.

Sincerity, innocence, and fearlessness, that inspire simple popular virtues, and the wise and fatherly administration of justice, spring from faith.

Reckless and passionate outcry against innocence, right, and truth—these proofs of the absence of a strong and pure administration of the law—spring from unbelief. Tyrannous action and daring insolent encroachment upon the law and upon purity weaken the national spirit; again unbelief is at the root of the mischief.

But, on the other hand, the sense of brotherhood and fatherhood gives rise to all unsullied national joys. Popular belief in God is the source of national virtues, national blessing, and national strength.

Sin is both the cause and the consequence of unbelief. It is man's active opposition to the teachings of his conscience concerning right and wrong. It brings confusion into our fundamental notions and sullies the purity of our primitive feelings. It means loss of faith in self and in the teachings of conscience, loss of faith in God, loss of the childlike attitude towards Him. Public sinfulness is man's presumption against God.

Horror of sin, the purity of our childlike attitude

towards God—these are the express results of man's faith in God's revelation. Horror of public misdeeds should be like the feeling of a child towards him whom his parents despise.

National horror of national wrongdoing is a sure sign of national faith and of the childlike attitude of the people towards God on high.

National horror at the manifest insolence of their princes towards God is a proof of national virtue. Should that diminish, quiet confidence in God will diminish also.

Unbelief destroys all social bonds. The unbelief of the ruling classes leads their subjects to rebel. Fatherly virtues in the rulers insure the obedience of the ruled. Unbelief destroys obedience at its source. Under the rule of one who is not their father, the popular mind does not develop a sentiment of simple gratitude and childlike obedience. The consequences of unbelief—burdens that increase daily, daily diminishing patrimony, arbitrary and unprofitable action, odd and undignified buffoonery in the palace, oppressive officialdom, money bled from the people, an impoverished nation—are unavoidable in a state where unbelief reigns and the rights of God and man are not respected.

Popular resentment of the unnatural use of paternal rights weakens the strength and purity of the bond between prince and people. Kindly maternal human nature tightens the bonds of citizenship through a sense of blessings mutually enjoyed. The national sense of these blessings consecrates the ties of prince and people through gratitude, love, and faith. Herein is the sacred source of patriotism and civic virtue.

I am touching strings that are loose and out of tune. The music of the dance will drown them; the song of the insolent will shout them down. We care no more for truth and human purity. Human power is only blessed through faith in God, and the paternal attitude of the prince—the sole source of his people's happiness— is the consequence of his faith in God. Man, humble as is thy station, if thy prince is a child of God, then is his power the power of a father.

The hard, arrogant use of royal rights does not come from fatherly feelings nor from faith in God. It is the destruction of the highest concerns of the prince and of his land ; it is the destruction of the simple childlike attitude of the people towards the prince.

Nevertheless I may not call this widespread custom of intelligent officials high-treason.

But what else is it, if it represents the paternal right of the prince as a right to do good or evil as he pleases ?

What is it else if in the name of the prince it destroys domestic happiness, attacks private property, and heaps insult and calumny upon the innocent ?

The bond which unites men in happiness, the faith of the prince and his people in the Lord on high, faith in God, that alone can insure mankind from being wrecked upon this rock.

All unbelief is arrogant, but faith in God, the childlike attitude of man towards the Godhead, is quiet confidence in the Divine influence.

Brilliant, dazzling exhaustion of his nature, bold, careless courage in the midst of danger and destruction, is man's strength when he forsakes his childlike attitude towards God. Earnest, economical use of every small capacity, and a desire to increase his strength, is Nature's provision for the training and improvement of our powers, and in times of difficulty and weakness it is man's innocent tendency to turn to God.

To be attracted by unworthy appearances, to be induced to show off one's capacities and powers, to hide one's weaknesses, is the tendency of the lowest and weakest of men who is drawn away from this educative way of Nature. Man in his noblest expression, trained in this natural way, shows a father's care against these lower powers and aptitudes.

Man, in thy fulness apply thyself to this end.

Set a father's sense of lofty powers against the weak and undeveloped crowd.

O pure blessedness of humanity, thou art the strength and the consequence of faith.

O joy around my cottage, thou also art a consequence of this faith. Be my salvation and that of my house.

That man may believe in God, I remain under this humble roof.

The belief of the people in God's true priests is the source of rest in life. God's priests represent the simple paternal relation of man. Thy power, O consecrated one, is God's means of illumination.

God's means of illumination is love, wisdom, and the paternal sense.

Would that I might throw a shadow of God's power on whomsoever wanders about my doors!

O sun, thou type of His power, thy daily course is finished. Thou goest down behind my mountain.

O day of my destiny, O hope of the coming morning, O power of my faith!

I build all freedom on justice, but I see in this world no certain justice except in a manhood devoted to and inspired by simplicity, piety, and love.

The justice of family life, which is the greatest, purest, and most universally enjoyed, rests solely upon love; its blessings are widespread, while the peoples retain their simplicity.

As all justice rests on love, so freedom rests on justice. Simple childlike confidence is the true source of the freedom which rests on justice, and the paternal spirit in its purity is the secret of such state power as maintains righteousness of action and love of freedom.

And the source of justice and of world blessedness, the source of brotherly love amongst men, comes from the great religious idea that we are God's children, and that belief in this is the sure foundation of human well-being. In this great religious principle lies the secret of all true statesmanship which aims at the people's happiness, for all inner moral power, all power of illumination, all wisdom, is based on man's faith in God.

And forgetfulness of God, neglect of man's childlike relations to God, is a disintegrating force under which morality, inspiration and wisdom disappear. No greater misfortune could come upon man than this, that he should lose his childlike faith in God; for then the education which God as Father gives would be impossible, and the restoration of this lost attitude to God is the only means of rescuing His terrestrial children.

The Man of God who through His suffering and death restored that lost childlike feeling towards God, is the Saviour of the World; He is the sacrificed Priest of the Lord, He is the Mediator between God and His forgetful people. His teaching is pure justice, educative, popular philosophy; it is the revelation of God the Father to the lost generation of His children.

## "LEONARD AND GERTRUDE"

### (*Part I., Chapter XXXI.*)

[*In 1780 Pestalozzi published a simple story of village life. Its aim was to show how carelessness (or worse) on the part of landowners and officials might bring about the moral degradation of a whole community. The village of Bonnal had suffered terribly at the hands of a man who combined the office of land-agent with the business of an innkeeper. With one exception, every home in the village was ruined by this unscrupulous rascal. The household of the stone-mason Leonard had withstood both his threats and his wiles, thanks to the nobility of Gertrude, Leonard's wife. She is Pestalozzi's model mother, and the influence she exerts upon her children is precisely the influence which he regards as the fundamental basis of all education. The chapter is given because it offers in the concrete what Pestalozzi describes more generally in the thirteenth and fourteenth letters of* How Gertrude Teaches her Children *and in the eighth of the* Views and Experiences.]

### EVENING BEFORE A FESTIVAL DAY IN THE HOUSE OF A PIOUS MOTHER.

" GERTRUDE was yet alone with her children. The events of the week and the thoughts of the festival Easter morning filled her heart. In silence she prepared the supper, took from the closet the Sunday clothes for her husband, herself and her children, and laid them all ready for to-morrow, that no earthly care should distract her mind on the holy day. And when she had completed it all, she assembled her children round the table to pray with them.

" It was her custom on Saturdays to remind the children, in the hour of evening prayer, of their faults, and of such occurrences as were calculated peculiarly to interest and to edify them.

" And this day especially she remembered the loving-kindness of God towards her during the past week, and she wished, as far as possible, to impress deeply and indelibly upon the minds of her children the marks which she had received of the goodness and mercy of God.

" The children sat round her in silence, with their little hands folded for prayer, and the mother said to them :

" ' Children, I have to tell you of good things. Our dear father has had this week very excellent work given him, by which he will earn much more than he could do before ; and we may hope, my children, to eat our bread in future with less care and sorrow.

" ' Give thanks, therefore, unto God, our loving Father in heaven, for His goodness towards us, and remember often the old times, when I was obliged to portion out to you every mouthful of bread with care and anxiety. Oh! it grieved my heart many a time that I could not give you sufficient, but our kind Heavenly Father knew that He would help us, and that it was better for you, my dears, to be accustomed to poverty and patience, and to learn to conquer your own desires, than to live in plenty. For man, when he has whatever he likes, is liable to grow thoughtless, and to forget God, and not to do what is best and most beneficial for himself.   Oh! remember, as long as you live, my children, our days of poverty, and the distress and the sorrows which we have endured; and if we be better off henceforth, my children, be mindful of those who are suffering in want, even as you have been suffering.   Never forget what it is to be visited by want and hunger, that you may always be merciful towards the poor; and that you may be willing, if you have a morsel to spare, to give it to those that have not. Yes, you are willing; are you not, my children?'

"'O yes, dear mother!' replied the children, 'surely we will do it.'

"*Mother.*—' Well then, Niclas, whom do you know that suffers most from hunger?'

"*Niclas.*—' Mother! 'tis Rudeli.   You were yesterday with his father.   He is almost starving; he eats grass off the ground.'

"*Mother.*—' Should you like to give him your supper now and then?'

"*Niclas.*—' O yes, mother! may I to-morrow?'

"*Mother.*—' Yes, you may.'

"*Niclas.*—' That's very nice.'

"*Mother.*—' And you, Betty! to whom would you give your supper now and then?'

"*Betty.*—' I can't think just now to whom I should like to give it.'

"*Mother.*—' Can you not think of a child, then, that must go without food sometimes?'

"*Betty.*—' O yes, I can, mother!'

"*Mother.*—' Why, then, can you not tell to whom you would give?   You are always so scrupulous, Betty.'

"*Betty.*—' Well, mother, I know now.'

"*Mother.*—' To whom?'

"*Betty.*—' To Marx's Beteli.   I saw her to-day digging out rotten potatoes from the bailiff's dunghill.'

"*Niclas.*—' O yes, mother! and I saw her too; and I looked in all my pockets for bread, but I had not a mouthful left: if I had but kept it a quarter of an hour longer.'

" The mother then asked, in the same way, the other children; and they were all delighted at the idea of giving their suppers to poor children to-morrow.

" The mother let them enjoy their delight for a while, and then she said to them : ' That's enough, my children ; now think what beautiful presents his lordship has made you.'

" ' O yes, the new bright pennies—will you show them to us, mother ?' said the children.

" ' Yes, after prayers,' said the mother.

" And the children shouted with joy.

" ' You are too noisy, children,' said the mother. ' If something good comes to you, always think on God, who gives us all things. If you do that, children, you will not be wild and boisterous in your joy. I like to be cheerful with you, my dears ! but when people are loud and violent in their joy or their sorrow, evenness of temper and peace of heart are lost ; and a man who has not a still, quiet, and glad heart cannot be happy. Therefore we ought always to have the fear of God before our eyes. Your morning and evening prayers are on purpose that you should not forget this : for people that thank God and pray to Him are neither immoderate in their joys nor comfortless in their sorrows. And therefore, my children, we should try, especially in the hour of prayer, to be still and quiet. You see, children, if you thank your father for anything, you do not shout and make a noise ; you fall round his neck silently or with a few words, and when it goes near to your hearts the tears come into your eyes. So it is with God, my dear children. If you are very much rejoiced at the good He does you, and if you have it in your heart to thank Him, I am sure you will not make many words or much noise, but the tears will come in your eyes when you think how kind your Heavenly Father is. That is the good of praying, you see ; one's heart should always remain thankful towards God and man ; and if you pray aright, you will do aright alikewise, and you will be in favour with God and man all your lives.'

"*Niclas.*—' We shall be in favour with the good lord at Arnburg, too, if we do right; did not you say so yesterday, mother?'

"*Mother.*—' Yes, children, he is a very good and pious man. May God reward him for all that he has done for us! I hope he will be pleased with you, Niclas, by-and-by!'

"*Niclas.*—' I'll do all he would wish me to do; I will do anything for him, just as for you and for our father, because he is so very good.'

"*Mother.*—' That's right, Niclas. Always think so, and you may be sure he will like you.'

"*Niclas.*—' Oh, how I should like to talk to him some day!'

"*Mother.*—' Well, what would you say to him?'

"*Niclas.*—' I would thank him for that fine new penny.'

"*Anne.*—' Should you be bold enough to thank him?'

"*Niclas.*—' Why not?'

"*Anne.*—' I should not, I am sure.'

"*Betty.*—' No, nor I either!'

"*Mother.*—' Why should not you, my children?'

"*Betty.*—' Oh, I should be laughing!'

"*Mother.*—' What, laughing! O fie! Betty, to say beforehand that you would be silly! If you had not a great many foolish things in your brains, you could never think or talk thus.'

"*Anne.*—' I should not laugh, but I should be afraid.'

"*Mother.*—' He would take you by the hand, Anne, and would smile upon you, as your father does when he is well pleased. Then you would not be afraid, I suppose?'

"*Anne.*—' Oh no, not if he did that.'

"*Jonas.*—' No, no more should I.'

"*Mother.*—' Well, but, my dears, how is it about your goodness this week?'

"The children look at one another and say nothing.

"*Mother.*—' Anne, have you been a good girl this week?'

"*Anne.*—' No, mother! you know about my little brother.'

" *Mother.*—' O yes, Anne, the poor child might have been very much injured ; poor babes that have been left in that way have sometimes died. Besides, only think if you were shut by yourself in a room, and left to cry, and to suffer hunger and thirst. Poor little children get angry when they see that nobody cares for them, and cry so dreadfully that they may hurt themselves for their whole lives. Really, Anne, I should not be able to leave the house for one moment with comfort, if I was not sure that you would take good care of the baby.'

" *Anne.*—' Trust me, dear mother ! I will not leave him again for a single moment.'

" *Mother.*—' Well, I hope that you will not give me such another fright. And now, Niclas, how has it been with you this week ?'

" *Niclas.*—' I know of nothing wrong.'

" *Mother.*—' Have you forgotten that you threw down Kitty on Monday last ?'

" *Niclas.*—' I did not mean to do it, mother.'

" *Mother.*—' To be sure you did not mean it. To do such a thing on purpose would be fine indeed. Are you not ashamed to make such a speech ?'

" *Niclas.*—' I am sorry for it, dear mother. I'll not do it again.'

" *Mother.*—' If you should be so careless when you grow bigger, you will have to learn better at your own expense. Even among boys the thoughtless and careless ones get into a great many scrapes and quarrels ; and I am afraid you will bring great misfortune and sorrow upon me, some day, by your careless ways.'

" *Niclas.*—' I am sure, mother, I'll be more careful.'

" *Mother.*—' Be sure not to forget it, my dear : believe me, that your carelessness would certainly make you unhappy.'

" *Niclas.*—' I know it and believe it, my dear, dear mother ; and I promise you I shall be careful in future.'

" *Mother.*—' Well, and you, Betty, how have you behaved this week ?'

" *Betty.*—' I am sure I can't think of anything out of the way this week, mother.'

" *Mother.*—' Are you quite sure ?'

" *Betty.*—' I am indeed, mother—as much as I can recollect. I should not mind telling of it if I knew.'

" *Mother.*—' It's very odd that, even when you have nothing to tell, you answer always with as many words as another who has got a great deal to say.'

" *Betty.*—' Well, what have I said then, mother ?'

" *Mother.*—' You have said nothing, I know ; but you have given me a long answer. 'Tis what we have told you a thousand times, that you are too forward : you never think what you should say, and yet you will always be talking. For instance, what business had you, the day before yesterday, to tell the bailiff you knew that Arner was coming shortly ?'

" *Betty.*—' I am sorry for it, mother.'

" *Mother.*—' We have often told you not to talk about things which don't belong to you, particularly before strange folks, and yet you must always do it. Now, suppose it had been wrong for your father to let it be known that he knew of it, and suppose your gossip had brought him into trouble ?'

" *Betty.*—' I should be sorry for it, but neither you nor he have said a word of its being a thing not to be known.'

" *Mother.*—' Very well, I'll tell your father, when he comes home, that to whatever we say in this room we must always add : Now, this is a thing which Betty may gossip about at the neighbours' doors and at the fountain, but not this and this ; but of this, again, she may prate ;" and then you will always know what you may chatter about.'

" *Betty.*—' I beg your pardon, mother ; I did not mean to do it so.'

" *Mother.*—' You have been told, once for all, that you are not to talk of anything that is no business of yours ; but it is all in vain : there is no getting you of that habit except by severe means ; and the very first time that I overtake you again in any such idle gossip, I shall take to the rod.'

" The tears burst from poor Betty's eyes when her mother mentioned the rod. The mother saw it, and said to her : ' The greatest mischief, Betty, often arises out of idle gossip, and you must be cured of that fault.'

" Thus the mother discoursed with them all ; even to little Kitty she said : ' You must not be so impatient again in asking for your soup, or I shall make you wait still longer, and, after all, give it to someone else.'

" All this being over, the children said their usual evening prayers, and after them the Saturday night's prayer which Gertrude had taught them.

" And after this the mother and children sat yet a little while in that silence which a true prayer always imposes.

" Betty interrupted this silence. ' You will now show us our new pennies,' said she to her mother.

" ' I will,' replied the mother ; ' but you are always the first to speak, Betty.'

" Niclas now jumped up from his seat, and pushed forward that he might be nearer the candle and see the new pennies better ; in doing so he hurt the little baby so that it began to cry aloud.

" Then said the mother : ' Niclas, this is very bad. You promised not more than a quarter of an hour ago that you would be more careful, and now you see what you have done again.'

" *Niclas.*—' O mother, I am very sorry for it; it shall not happen any more.'

" *Mother.*—' That is what you just now promised to God Almighty, and yet you have done it again. You are not in earnest.'

" *Niclas.*—' O yes, my dear mother ! I am quite in earnest. Forgive me ; I am so very, very sorry.'

" *Mother.*—' So am I, my dear ! but you will not remember it unless you are punished. You shall go to bed now without your supper.'

" And so saying she led him away from the others into

his chamber.   His brothers and sisters were all standing about grieved, for they were sorry that poor Niclas should go without his supper.

"'What a pity it is that you will not be governed by kindness!' said the mother when she came back.

"'Let him come out again this once,' said the children.

"'No, my dears; he must be got out of his thoughtless habits,' was the mother's reply.

"'Well, then, we will not see the pennies till to-morrow, that he may see them with us,' said Anne.

"'Well spoken, Anne! said the mother; 'he shall see them with you.'

"After this she gave the children their suppers, and then she led them to the chamber where Niclas was still crying.

"'Be very careful another time, my dear Niclas,' said the mother to him.

"And Niclas: 'Do pray forgive me, dear, dear mother; do forgive me, and kiss me.   I do not want any supper.'

"And Gertrude kissed her Niclas, and a burning tear flowed down her cheek upon her face, when she said to him: 'O Niclas, Niclas, do try to become more careful.' And Niclas threw both his arms round her neck, and said: 'O mother, mother, forgive me!'

"And Gertrude once more blessed her children, and then she returned to her room.

"She was now quite alone.   A small lamp shed its feeble rays through the apartment, and her heart was still in silent prayer, which, without words, inexpressibly moved her soul.   The feeling of God and of His goodness, the hope of life everlasting, the sense of that internal joy and peace which dwells in those who trust in their Heavenly Father—all this stirred her soul, and she sank down on her knees, and a stream of tears flowed down over her cheeks."

## "CHRISTOPHER AND ELIZABETH"

[*The* Leonard and Gertrude *story was a great success, but the people were more interested in the tale than in the moral. In order to make the moral clear, Pestalozzi published a commentary in the shape of evening conversations in the family of a farmer, where* Leonard and Gertrude *was read chapter by chapter and talked about. This chapter (the fourteenth evening) is typical. Perhaps it should also be said that nobody read* Christopher and Elizabeth, *much to its author's disappointment.*]

" ' This is my chapter, father !' said Elizabeth, when Christopher had finished the twelfth chapter of our book ;[1] ' a pious mother who herself teaches her children seems to me to be the finest sight on earth.'

" ' It is a very different one from a schoolroom, at all events,' said Josiah.

" *Eliza.*—' I did not mean to say that schools are not very good.'

" *Christopher.*—' Nor would I allow myself to think so.'

" *Josiah.*—' Well, and it is true, after all, that nothing of what the schoolmaster can say will ever reach the children's hearts in the same way as what their parents teach them ; and, generally speaking, I am sure that there is not in school-going all the good that people fancy there is.'

" *Christopher.*—' I am afraid, Josiah, we must say to thee as to the old cobbler, " Stick to your last." We ought to thank God for all the good there is in the world ; and as for the schools in the country, we can't thank Him enough for them.'

" *Josiah.*—' Well spoken, master. It is well that there are schools, and God forbid that I should be ungrateful

---

[1] This chapter represents Gertrude in the midst of her children, teaching them at the same time that they are engaged in spinning.

for any good that is done to us. But, with all this, I think
that he must be a fool who, having plenty at home, runs
about begging ; and that is the very thing which our
village folks do, by forgetting all the good lessons which
they might teach their children at home, and instead
thereof sending them every day to gather up the dry
crumbs which are to be got in our miserable schools. I
am sure that is not quite as it ought to be.'

" *Christopher.*—' Nor is it, perhaps, quite as you have
put it.'

" *Josiah.*—' Nay, master ! but look it in the face, and
thou'lt surely see it the same as I do. That which
parents can teach their children is always what they
stand most in need of in life ; and it is a pity that parents
should neglect this, by trusting in the words which the
schoolmaster makes them get by heart. It is true they
may be good and wise words, and have an excellent meaning to them, but, after all, they are only words, and,
coming from the mouth of a stranger, they don't come
half as near home as father's or mother's words.'

" *Christopher.*—' I cannot see what thou wouldst be at,
Josiah.'

" *Josiah.*—' Look, master ! The great point in bringing up a child is that he should be well brought up for his
own house ; he must learn to know and handle and use
those things on which his bread and his quiet will depend
through life ; and it seems to me very plain that fathers
and mothers can teach it much better than any schoolmaster can do it in his school. The schoolmaster, no
doubt, tells the children of a great many things which
are right and good, but they are never worth as much in
his mouth as in the mouth of an upright father or a pious
mother. The schoolmaster, for instance, will tell the
child to fear God, and to honour his father and mother,
for such is the word of God ; but the child understands
little of what he says, and mostly forgets it again before
he comes home. But if at home his father gives him
milk and bread, and his mother denies herself a morsel,
that she may give it to him, the child feels and under-

stands that he ought to honour his father and mother, who are so kind to him, and he will not forget his father's word, which tells him that such is the word of God, as easily as the empty word of the schoolmaster. In the same way, if the child is told at school to be merciful, and to love his neighbour as himself, he gets the text by heart, and perhaps thinks of it for a few days, till the nice words slip again from his memory. But at home he sees a poor neighbour's wife calling in upon his mother, lamenting over her misery, her hunger, and nakedness; he sees her pale countenance, her emaciated and trembling figure, the very image of wretchedness; his heart throbs, his tears flow; he lifts up his eyes full of grief and anxiety to his mother, as if he himself was starving; his mother goes to fetch some refreshments for the poor sufferer, in whose looks the child now reads comfort and reviving hope; his anguish ceases, his tears flow no longer, he approaches her with a smiling face; at last his mother returns, and her gift is received with sobs of gratitude, which draw fresh tears from the child's eyes. Here, then, he learns what it is to be merciful and to love one's neighbour. He learns it, without the aid of words, by the real fact; he sees mercy itself, instead of learning words about mercy. . . .'

" *Christopher.*—' I must own I begin to think you are not quite mistaken in saying that too much value is put upon the schoolmaster's teaching.'

" *Josiah.*—' Of course, master! If you send your sheep up into the mountain, you rely upon their being well kept by the shepherd who is paid for it, and you do not think of running about after them yourself; but if you have them at home in your own stables, you look after them yourself. Now, it is just the same thing with the school; only there is this difference, that it is easy to get for the sheep, pasture which is infinitely better than the food they have in the stable; but it is not so easy to find a school in which the children are better taught than they might be at home. The parents' teaching is the kernel of wisdom, and the schoolmaster's business is

only to make a husk over it, and that even is a great
chance whether it turn out well.'

" *Eliza.*—' Why, Josiah, you make one's brains whirl
all round, about one's children.   I think I see now what
you are at ; and I fancy many a poor ignorant mother
who now sends her children to school, without thinking
anything about it, merely because it is the custom to do
so, would be very glad to be taught better.'

" *Josiah.*—' There is yet another part of the story,
master.  What helps the common people to get through
the world, you know, and to have their daily bread
and a cheerful heart, is nothing else but good sense and
natural understanding ; and I have never found in all
my life a useful man who was what they call a good scholar.
The right understanding with the common people is, as
it were, free and easy, and shows itself always in the
proper place and season ; so that a man's words don't
fit but at the very moment when they are spoken, and a
quarter of an hour before or after they would not fit at
all.  But the school understanding brings in all manner
of sayings which are fit at all times, in summer and
winter, in hot and cold, in Lent and at Easter ; and that
is the reason why this school understanding does not do
any good to common people, who must regulate themselves according to times and seasons ; and that is the
reason, again, why their natural understandings which
are in them ought to be drawn out more.  And for this
there are no better teachers than the house, and the
father's and mother's love, and the daily labour at home
and all the wants and necessities of life.  But if the
children must needs be sent to school, the schoolmaster
should at least be an open-hearted, cheerful, affectionate,
and kind man, who would be as a father to the children—
a man made on purpose to open children's hearts and
their mouths, and to draw forth their understandings as
it were from the hindermost corner.  In most schools,
however, it is just the contrary : the schoolmaster seems
as if he was made on purpose to shut up children's mouths
and hearts, and to bury their good understandings ever

so deep underground. That is the reason why healthy and cheerful children, whose hearts are full of joy and gladness, hardly ever like school. Those that show best at school are the children of whining hypocrites or of conceited parish-officers ; stupid dunces, who have no pleasure with other children ; these are the bright ornaments of schoolrooms, who hold up their heads among the other children like the wooden king in the ninepins among his eight fellows. But if there is a boy who has too much good sense to keep his eyes for hours together fixed upon a dozen letters which he hates ; or a merry girl, who, while the schoolmaster discourses of spiritual life, has all kinds of fun with her hands under the desk, the schoolmaster, in his wisdom, decides that these are the goats who care not for their everlasting salvation. . . .

" Thus spoke good Josiah, in the overflowing of his zeal, against the nonsense of village schools, and his master and mistress grew more and more attentive to what he said."

### "LEONARD AND GERTRUDE"
#### (*Part III., Chapters XIX. and LXIV.*)

[*Pestalozzi turned his hand to the continuation of his story. Three further volumes appeared, the last two being concerned with projects of reform—educational and legislative. The squire has dismissed his agent. A friend of his volunteers to become schoolmaster. It is first necessary for him to understand the life of the village. To that end, he and the squire visit the employers and the homes of the people. The chief employers of labour are farmers who combine agriculture with spinning. Meyer is a case in point. The visit to Gertrude's house and the first day of the new school are described in the text which form Chapters XIX. and LXIV. of Part III. of* Leonard and Gertrude.]

## The Guiding Principles in a Good School.

" The squire, since his return from his visit to the farmer, has passed every minute which he could steal from his other duties with the lieutenant, in order to talk over arrangements which they wished to make in connection with their new school. They both thought that the best education on earth which a child could receive was one which would teach him to look after and manage methodically those things which would most likely be his when he was grown up. It would teach him how to use these things for his own good and for the welfare of those dear to him. This excellent aim of all education seemed to them, without more ado, the very first thing to be considered in establishing a school on common-sense principles.

" In this connection they saw clearly that the lieutenant, and everyone who wished to establish a suitable school for farmers and cotton-spinners, must themselves know and understand what farmers and cotton-spinners ought to know and ought to be able to do—*i.e.*, if they are to be satisfactory farmers and cotton-spinners. If the would-be schoolmasters do not possess this knowledge themselves, they must be ready to go and ask for instruction from those people who do know and are able to help them. They naturally thought first of all of the farmer spinner, and went to see him immediately after the meal at which this conversation had taken place. ' This is the man I have talked to you so much about,' said the squire to the lieutenant ; then, turning to the farmer, he said : ' And this is a gentleman who, I hope, will be able to comfort you concerning your school.' The cotton-spinner did not understand the meaning of this speech, but the squire explained matters to him, and said that the gentleman was going to be their schoolmaster. The cotton-spinner could not find words to express his astonishment at this, but said that, if the gentleman was really willing to take so much trouble, they would never be able to thank him sufficiently ; but it would need time before he would be able to get a thorough understanding of the manners and customs of their village life. ' I can quite believe that,' said the lieutenant; ' but one must begin some time, and I will spare no trouble in trying to find out what is really necessary for your children, and what they ought to learn, in order to fulfil their duties as farmers or cotton-spinners in a thoroughly satisfactory way.'

" *The Farmer.*—' That is a fine thing for you to do, to wish to begin in that way.'

" *The Lieutenant.*—' I had no notion of beginning in any other way. Moreover, whenever I have an occasion, I shall try to get some idea of every sort of domestic and outdoor work, in order that I may really understand on what sort of pattern your children should be turned out, if they are to be properly educated for their work and position in life.'

" Marelli was quite at home with him ; he pointed out to him everywhere in the house, in the cowsheds, and all round about, what the children must be taught, and what they must do, if they were to learn to manage everything properly ; he got them to hoe the garden, dig up the ground, climb on to the platform,, make food for the animals. The more the lieutenant saw, the more questions he asked. He even wanted to know how they computed the tithes, how they estimated the wages for the cotton-spinning, what difference there was between the returns made by cotton and by wool, and a hundred other similar matters. They explained everything as well as they could. Finally he wished to have the children taught spinning, too, but Marelli said to him : ' We only take in some few hundredweights of yarn during the year, and I have never succeeded in getting the children to spin really well : in truth, I cannot altogether complain ; they have a great deal to do in the fields and attending to the cattle, and there is never any good yarn to be had. But if you want to see a well-arranged spinnery you should go and visit the wife of the stonemason ; there you will find something really worth seeing as regards cotton-spinning, but here there is nothing.'

" ' Is the mason's wife of whom you speak called Gertrude ?' asked the lieutenant. ' Ah ! it seems that you know her already,' replied Marelli. ' No, but the squire has persuaded me to go straight from your house to see her,' said the lieutenant. ' Ah, you see, then, that I have given you good advice,' said Marelli.

" The foundation of a good school is the same as the foundation of all human happiness, and it is nothing less than the true wisdom of life.

" Her room was so full when they entered that they could scarcely make their way in for spinning. Gertrude, who was not by any means expecting strangers when she opened the door, bade the children stand up and make room ; but the squire would not allow any of them to move from their places, and offered his hand to the pastor and to the lieutenant in turn, in order to guide them along the wall behind the children's backs, to their seats at the table. You can have no idea how delighted these gentlemen were with this room. What they had seen at the farmer's seemed to them nothing at all in comparison. This was natural enough. When a rich man's estate is well ordered and in a prosperous condition, we are not much impressed ; we simply think that other people could not do the same for lack of money. On the other hand, when we find prosperity and well-being in a poor cottage, it proves incontestably that it would be well with everybody, if their affairs were well ordered and methodical, and if every-body had been well brought up. The sight makes a great, even an astounding impression on the mind. Now these gentlemen had a whole room full of such poor children before their eyes, in all the enjoyment of domestic bliss.

" For a few moments it seemed to the squire as if he actually saw, in a vision before him, a living picture of the first-born of those future generations for whom he was planning an improved education. The lieutenant's falcon eyes flashed like lightning round the room, passing from child to child, from hand to hand, from work to work, from eye to eye ; and the more he saw, the more his heart swelled with the thought that here, in Gertrude's room, was the school they had been looking for, and that she had already performed and accomplished what they were aspiring to do. For some time there was a deathlike stillness in the room, for the visitors could do nothing but gaze and gaze in speechless silence. During this silent period the lieutenant showed various signs of respect for Gertrude, which seemed to border almost on reverence, and these, combined with the stillness in the room, made her heart beat fast. But the children continued to spin away happily, and shot merry glances at each other, for they saw that the gentlemen were there on their account, and were regarding their work.

" The first question which the lieutenant asked was : ' Are these all your children, Frau Gertrude ?' ' No, they are not all mine,' said Gertrude, and, pointing from one wheel to another, she indicated which were Rudi's and which were hers. ' Just think, lieutenant,' said the pastor, ' only four weeks ago none of Rudi's children could spin a thread.' The lieutenant gazed at the pastor and at Frau Gertrude. ' Is it possible ?' he said. ' It is quite true,' answered Gertrude. ' A child ought to be able to learn to spin well in a few weeks ; I have known some who have learnt in a few days.' ' It is not that, but something quite different, which surprises me most in this room,' said the squire. ' These children look so different now from what they did three or four weeks ago when Frau Gertrude first took them in, that in good truth I should not have recognized them as the same. At that time their countenances expressed the most utter misery and all the horrors of a living death, but now all that has been wiped out, and no traces of their former wretchedness are to be seen.' ' But what does she do to the children, then ?' asked the lieutenant in French. ' God only knows,' said the squire. Then the pastor went on : ' When you spend the whole day with her, you hear no sound and see no sign of anything extraordinary ; you feel sure that any other woman could do exactly the same, and, truly, it would never occur to the most ordinary woman in the village that Frau Gertrude was doing or could do anything that she could not do.' 'You could say nothing which would exalt her more in my eyes,' said the lieutenant. 'Art is most perfect when its presence is entirely unsuspected, and the highest and most sublime things are so simple that children and young people always imagine they can do something much better.'

" While the gentlemen were talking French with one another, the children began to laugh and to exchange glances, and Heirli and the child who sat opposite to him started to screw their mouths up, and mumble 'French! French!' to one another. But Gertrude had only to give a sign, and everything was immediately quiet again. As the lieutenant noticed books lying beside all the spinning-wheels, he asked Gertrude what they did with them. She looked at him, and said : 'Why, they learn out of them !' 'But surely not while they are spinning ?' 'Yes, certainly,' said Gertrude. 'I should like to see that,' said the lieutenant, and the squire also put in a word. 'Yes, you must show us that, Gertrude.' 'Children, take your books in your hands and learn your lessons,' she said. 'Aloud, as usual ?' asked the children. 'Yes, aloud as usual, but correctly too,' said Gertrude. Then the children opened their books, and each one turned to the page marked, and began to learn the lesson which he had been given to learn that day, but the wheels went on as before though the children's eyes were all glued to their books.

" The lieutenant was never tired of seeing all these things, and he begged Gertrude to show them all that the children did and all that she taught them. She tried to excuse herself, saying that it was nothing at all, and that the gentlemen must know a thousand times better than she did what to do ; but when the squire also begged her to do as she was requested, she at once told the children to close their books, and began to go over a passage with them which was to be learnt by heart. This time it was a portion of the song which begins :

" ' Of the warm sun, so soft and mild,
　　How fair, how lovely, are the rays !
　They cheer our eyes, refresh our hearts,
　　And bring us comfort all our days.' "

" The third verse, which they were to learn now, ran as follows :

" ' Gone is the sun, as all the pride
　　And splendour of this world must go ;
　The Lord of Heaven just speaks one word,
　　And straight the mighty are brought low.' "

" Slowly and clearly she repeated one line of the verse after another, and the children said it just as clearly and slowly after her.  She continued to repeat it until at last one said : ' I can say it now.'  Then she made him say the verse alone, and, as it was perfectly correct, she told him to recite it to the others, while they repeated it after him until they all knew it.  Then she also sang with them the first three verses of this song, for they had already learnt the first two.  After all this she showed the gentlemen how she taught the children arithmetic, and that was also the simplest and most practical way that one can imagine ; but I will say more about this another time.

## School Organization.

" On the following morning, then, the school began.  I should not, however, like to advise any other school-master to do what this one did, first to make an announcement on the Sunday which everyone considered presumptuous, and then to allow his school on the Monday to be organized by a peasant woman.  Nevertheless, if one is a Glüphi one may do so, and no harm will come of it—but I mean a real Glüphi and not one in imagination. He made Gertrude arrange the children in the same order as if she had had them in her own home.  When they crowded together she separated them, according to their ages or their work, and placed her own children and those of Rudi, who were already accustomed to her methods, all in different parts of the room amongst the others. She put the little ones who did not yet know their alphabet in front and nearest to the table. Behind these she put those who were learning to spell, then those who could nearly read, and in the back row those who could read quite well. For the first row she put, this morning, only three letters on the blackboard, and made one of these children say them over. When he could say it quite correctly, the others had to repeat it after him; then she changed the order of the letters, and wrote them now as capitals, now as small letters, on the board, and left them there the whole morning before their eyes. She used this method of transposing the letters also with those who were learning to spell, and those who could nearly read had to spell with them. But the latter and all those who could read properly had to keep their books open on their spinning-wheels in front of them, and had to repeat, in a low tone, whatever was read aloud to them by one of their number. And not one of them could be certain that she would not suddenly call upon him to go on.

" She had taken a woman called Margaret with her to manage the handwork, and it was arranged that she should come to school every day to look after this, for it was impossible for Gertrude to do so. Margaret was a woman whose equal it would be hard to find. As soon as any child's hand or wheel stopped working she was at his side, and she did not leave him till hand and wheel were again in motion. Most of the children took home with them that evening some of the work they had done, and their mothers could hardly believe that they had really done it alone and unaided. Several of the children, however, answered their remarks by saying : ' Yes, but there is a difference in the way Margaret shows us how to do things. You could not do it as well.' They were just as ready to sing the praises of the lieutenant, for he conducted the school in the afternoon, and Gertrude sat and looked on, just as he did in the morning while she was teaching. Things went on so well that she said to him :

' If I had known that it would not take me more than
two hours a day to help you in managing your school, I
should not have been so unwilling when you asked me to
do so last Thursday.' He also was very glad to find that
things went so well. That evening he gave all the children
over seven years of age a sheet of paper and a few pens
to take home with them, and each child found his name
beautifully written in printed characters on his sheet of
paper. They were never tired of gazing at them, and
one after the other came to ask him how they were made.
He then showed them, and for quite a quarter of an hour
he wrote out big capital letters resembling printed ones.
They thought it all so beautiful that they would have
been quite willing for him to have gone on writing till
the next day, and they asked wonderingly if they were
to learn to write like that. His reply was : ' The more
you try to learn to write beautifully, the more pleased I
shall be.' Just as they were leaving he called out to them
to take care of their paper, and to stick the points of their
pens into rotten apples, for that was the best way of
preserving them. Several children answered : ' Yes, if
we only had some rotten apples left, but winter is over
now !' He laughed at this, and said to them : ' If you
have none, perhaps I shall be able to get some for you.
I think the pastor's wife has more rotten apples than she
cares about.' But others said : ' No, no, no ! We will
bring some ; we still have some left.' "

## "ENQUIRIES CONCERNING THE COURSE OF NATURE IN THE DEVELOPMENT OF THE HUMAN RACE"

PESTALOZZI himself tells us that he had spent three years
over this book when it appeared in 1797. The plan was,
however, much older. In 1781-1783 he was busy writing
*The Evening Hours of a Hermit*, the first part of *Leonard
and Gertrude*, the commentary thereon (*Christopher and
Elizabeth*), and *Legislation on Child-Murder*. All this

literary work concerned the condition of the labouring classes, and he wrote in 1793 to the Austrian Minister, Karl von Zinzendorf : " My work on the education of the children of the poor and on the treatment of criminals is carrying me so far that I tremble before what is involved. The effects of our social organization on the poorer classes, and its complete opposition to native human forces, must be put into a much clearer light than it is at present, if we are ever to approach perfection in these matters, and especially in respect of legislation upon them ; nevertheless, in spite of much uncertainty, I will try to put together various scattered ideas which seem to me to throw light on the subject."

Two years later (1785), when the third part of *Leonard and Gertrude* had already appeared, he wrote again to the same Zinzendorf : " Your approval encourages me greatly to proceed to the fourth part of my book—the more so as this part will bring me to my plan of setting out more clearly than has yet been done, the general theory of the direction in which mankind is moving, in the shape of a study of the characteristic impulses of our nature, and the actual history of those things which have so far contributed to man's happiness or misery." Here we have the fundamental idea of the book.

Nevertheless, it was ten years later that he seriously took up the task. In the meantime he had been busy revising *Leonard and Gertrude*, and writing political pamphlets, the most important of which (*Ja oder Nein*), a discussion of the political principles of the French Revolution, remained in manuscript for nearly a century. It was Fichte who persuaded him to put that manuscript in his desk until he had given literary form to his fundamental principles.

His book was a failure from the publisher's standpoint, but Pestalozzi always regarded it as one of his most important writings. It represented his fundamental point of view, the justice and soundness of which he maintained to the end. It permeates all his educational writings ; indeed, without a knowledge of his general standpoint it is often impossible to understand him.

The book is so completely Pestalozzi's own that it is not very useful to probe into its sources. Rousseau's influence is obvious. We know, of course, that Pestalozzi had read both the *Emile* and Rousseau's social studies, and had been much impressed by them. Fichte also probably discussed social problems with him. The German philosopher, not yet attained to distinction, had married a friend of Pestalozzi's wife. He was lecturing in Zurich during the winter session 1793-94, and often visited Pestalozzi, who was then living in the neighbourhood (Richtersweil). Their conversations were mainly on political, social, and educational questions. They were thinking and writing about the same things. Fichte was defending the French Revolution, and pleading for freedom of thought: Pestalozzi had written his *Ja oder Nein*.

A mysterious third person also contributed actively to these discussions. Of his identity, however, nothing certain is known. The book is dedicated to some *Hochgeborenen*, who has often discussed political and social questions with the author. Hunziker thinks the evidence points to Professor Fellenberg, the father of Daniel Fellenberg, whose school at Hofwyl gained world-wide fame. Fellenberg was then a magistrate, and a neighbour of Pestalozzi, and we know that they were on terms of intimacy. Seyffarth, however, suggests von Tscharner, who by common consent is the man on whom the Squire of Bonnal was modelled.

As it is not possible to give the whole text of the book, a brief analysis of certain parts will show its general structure, and place the translated extracts in their proper setting.

I.

INTRODUCTORY—THE PROBLEM ANALYZED.

The psychological development of the individual takes the same course as that of the race. This is the fundamental position from which he proceeds to ask:

" What am I, and what is man ?

" What have I done, and what is man doing ?

" What has my actual life made of me, what is man's life making of him ?

" What fundamental principles actually determine my actions and my way of looking at things ?

" What fundamental principles actually determine the actions and the point of view of the race ?"

To answer these questions, Pestalozzi proposes to appeal to experience, and to experience alone. " I can and must consider nothing but the truth as I find it in my own life," a procedure which he thinks will bring him into close touch with the characteristic experiences of a large proportion of mankind. Such, then, is his problem, and his method is in the main psychological. Reflection on these lines suggests the following as an outline scheme of the course of social development :

" Man's helplessness in the state of Nature provokes forethought, knowledge.

" Forethought leads him to seek to gain advantage over others.

" Advantage over others leads to ownership.

" Possession of property leads to society.

" Society leads to landed property, power, honour.

" Honour and power lead to subjection, control.

" Subjection and control lead to class divisions— kings, nobles, servants.

" Hence man arrives at legal rights.

" Legal rights give the freedom of the citizen.

" Want of them brings tyranny and slavery.

" But there is in man a kindly disposition which ennobles all these things that attach to social life, without which, indeed, all the advantages to be gained from it would be worth nothing.

" This kindly disposition is in its origin sensory—it belongs to my primitive animal nature ; yet I also recognize within me the power to ennoble and exalt it to the level of love.

" But this love is endangered through my native selfishness ; and if it goes, then indeed I am lost. I look, therefore, beyond the limits of knowledge to the very sources of my life, to religion, and try with its help to fight against my natural weakness."

3. He then proceeds to examine each of these steps in the " natural history " of man—to trace its origin, its crystallization, and its subsequent transformation.

4. After the examination of this series of sections, as it were, across the course of man's progress, he gives. a full-length picture of his development, beginning with his primitive condition and ending with the present : " Primitive man leaves his cave with a timid rather than a savage step. He finds a stone that is too heavy, a branch that is too high for him ; he feels, if only another man were there, he might lift that stone, reach that branch ; he sees another man near . . . he approaches his brother, and in his eye a new look beams ; it is the thought that they can help each other . . . their hands are joined, they lift the stone, they reach the branch . . . they see what they can do together. They enjoy this new knowledge ; it brings new power ; the bonds between them are multiplied, and their voice breaks into language. . . . It was language which made men subject to laws of their own making."

Thus, in distinct opposition to Rousseau, he makes the step from primitive to social man one of necessity. They are not opposite conditions, but the one is a modification of the other. And, as the origin of power lies in the natural inequalities of men, the misuse of power in primitive Nature is transplanted from the very beginning to the social stage. " Not power, but the man who wields it, is guilty of the degradation of the race." " Enthralled by a power which knows no law against itself, man sinks back into all the helplessness and obtuseness of his natural corruption ; and the general spread of Sansculottism leads to the break up of social bonds."

He passes now to the chief argument of his book :

" How is it that my fellow-men for the most part pass their lives in such misery, without any rights of their own, and in utter degradation, whilst here and there individuals rise to a noteworthy level of comfort and of morality ?   I must find an answer to this question, or life as I know it will remain for me an insoluble enigma.

" On reflection I soon found that men are the creatures of circumstances, but at the same time I felt that, after all, men make their own circumstances ; they have within them the power to bend circumstance in large measure to their will.   In so far as man uses this power, he takes a share in determining, not only himself, but also the things which influence him.   I tried then to come to grips with this mixture of capricious external control and individual freedom which seems to be characteristic of life, and asked myself, *What am I, then, in reality ?   How comes man to be what he actually is ?*   Is it of his own free will that a boy goes early in the morning to his work, and stops there all day long till the sun goes down and his limbs ache ?   If the peasant had what he wished, would he, day and year through, freeze and sweat alternately in the fields and the woods as he does ?   The merchant and the artisan, would they be tied to the desk or the bench all day long if they had not been driven to it from their youth upward ? I think not.   If they were really free to do as they would, they would surely follow restful and joyful occupation ; they would trouble about nobody but themselves ; they would live their lives through without care, without suffering, and without effort.   Thus man is what he is because he is driven to it.   He thinks, feels, and acts, differently from what he would if he were free.   Nevertheless, if the compelling forces were removed, and men were left free, then all the bonds that hold men together would be burst, and nameless misery and confusion would be the result.

" Must I not, then, give up all claims to my rights to the end that order may be preserved, although I do not know whether this order is at bottom a good or an evil thing ?   But I do not wish to know whether the ordering of the world is good or evil.   I cannot convince myself that the freedom which my soul desires would be good for me or my fellow-men, inasmuch as I could no longer win the love of my wife, the respect of my son, the confidence of my friend, the blessings of the poor, nor the gratitude of my country.

" Can I, then, long for primitive freedom ? Surely not. I could not bear the consequences of it if it were granted to me. Yet I cannot escape the measure of sensuousness in my nature. . . . I cannot be what I am, and share my property gladly and willingly with a man who did not help me to gather it. Yet I must do this and the like, as peasant, citizen, or artisan. And when I ask, Why am I a citizen, or a handicraftsman, or a peasant, instead of being just a man ? then I find that in all these relationships there are advantages that I cannot dispense with, and my primitive nature is not inclined to let them go for all the freedom it could get.

" Thus my social bondage is kept up by the will of my primitive nature. Education and experience confirm this attitude. Without any thought of what I might make out of myself, or of what my fellow-men might make of me, Nature places me in the world to make the best of an instinctive existence without the help of anybody. In this simple situation my primitive instincts set up primitive feeling, thinking, and doing.

" So soon, however, as I desire to make more of myself than Nature has made of my race, I must rise to the control of her. She cannot do that for me. Her might cannot compel me to become a good shoemaker or a good tailor. If she could, I should not be a man. I should want the true foundation of manhood. . . . There are ideals to be striven for, on the attainment of which man's happiness rests. There are such things as truth and right, which man for the most part has not sought. He may find them when he ceases to be actuated by primitive natural motives and to trust in his physical strength. When he seeks truth, he finds it ; when he demands righteousness, it is already his.

" In spite of this the unscrupulous struggle goes on. Treachery and faithlessness abound in every rank and in every office—amongst rulers and people, officials and merchants, scholars and clergy. It must be that truth and right are differently conceived from different points of view. Man looks upon the world in three different ways, and builds up for himself as many different ideas of the truth. There is the truth as primitive man views it —that is, the man who lives entirely for himself. There is the truth as social man views it—that is, the man who is bound by common agreements to his fellow-men. And there is the truth as the moral man sees it—that is, the man who sees things from the standpoint of his own inner worth, apart altogether from his primitive needs and his social obligations. Similarly, there are three systems of law—for the primitive, the social, and the moral man :

" (1) The law of the primitive man, in accordance with which his demands are regulated by the direct and simple needs of his animal nature.

" (2) The law of the social man, in accordance with which his demands are regulated by the recognition of his agreements with others.

" (3) The law of the moral man, in accordance with which all things are regarded from the point of view of their effect upon his own inner worth.

" And thus, according as my ideas of truth and right issue from my natural instincts, or my social demands, or my moral strength, I am in myself of a threefold nature— animal, social, or moral ; and this threefold difference in myself accounts for the fact that some of my demands are grounded on the law of the natural man, others on that of the social man, and others on that of the moral man."

Pestalozzi now proceeds to a closer examination of the characteristics of these three stages in man's development.

" What am I—i.e., what is the primitive man's point of view—as natural man ?

" What am I as a member of a social organization ?

" What am I as a moral personality ?"

## II.

### MAN IN HIS PRIMITIVE CONDITION.

" In this condition, before his deterioration has begun, man is a simple child of his instincts. He gives himself up absolutely to their innocent enjoyment. He loves the gazelle and the marmot, his wife and his child, his dog and his horse. He knows not God, he knows not sin. Sunlight, forest, earth, are all dear to him as God made them. Land broken by the plough is his curse. He spends his time in sleep, in sensory pleasures. . . . He takes the stranger into his gate and feeds him, after which he asks him whence he came. . . . He exchanges his cow for a few glass beads, and he will not sell the pipe he is smoking for a whole year's income. So life passes on as long as pleasures come without effort, and security without watchfulness.

"But we call him a primitive man long after he has found it necessary to put forth effort. He practises assiduously the use of his death-carrying weapons. He thinks more of his bow than of his wife and child—but he is still a natural man.

"He kills those who stand in his way; those who yield to him must do him service. Still he is a natural man.

"The world about him trembles at his powers; his will is his neighbour's law·. . . he drives his wife and his child from his cave. . . . Still we call this brutality that of the primitive man.

"He no longer reveres the earth and the rock as God made them; the earth broken by the plough is no longer accursed. He takes all the land he can get, and what he cannot use he allows others who pay for the privilege, to till.

"But now we do not call him ' primitive man.' When the ox is at the plough, and man rises with the sun in order to earn his rent, we say that he has entered society. When his relations to others become highly complicated and troublesome, we cease to think of him as primitive man. . . .

"But we divide the primitive stage into two periods—that of the unspoiled and that of the spoiled natural man. So long as he is an innocent child of his instincts, finding satisfaction without effort or forethought, we call him an unspoiled natural man. But when he has to struggle to achieve his pleasures, when his harmlessness and his primitive kindliness disappear, we call him a ' natural man spoiled.'

"But we extend the idea of native innocence too widely. His corruption begins earlier than we are wont to admit. We call him a ' child of Nature ' still, although the range of his curiosity is already determined by considerations which are only proper to the man who belongs to a community. Through all the stages of his passage from independent innocence to the complete subordination of his instincts to the recognized laws of society—yea, right up to the point when kings, laws, force, and calling, tear mistrust up by the roots, even when he is altogether under the social yoke—we are apt to regard him as if he were still in the state of Nature.

"What, then, constitutes his natural innocence, and when does it cease to be ? It belongs to the comfortable time when his wishes were easily satisfied—without painful effort, and without being in any way dependent on doubtful circumstances or doubtful wills. And is such a moment conceivable ? Has man ever lived in such complete ignorance of misfortune, and in such perfect independence ?

" The question means: Is there a moment in which childhood is completely pure, in which the infant knows naught of misfortune, of pain, of hunger, of suffering, of care, of mistrust, of dependence, or of uncertainty ?

" Certainly there is such a moment: it is that moment in which the child comes into the world. But no sooner is it there than it is passed. It is gone at his first cry. From that time onwards the child passes farther and farther away from this condition ; every unsatisfied need, every unfulfilled wish, every painful smart, is a step in this direction. In proportion to the growth of his experience he moves away from the innocence of his birth condition.

"As to the race we can only guess; we do not know of such a period of innocence. It lasted to the point at which he first knew of evil; his first wrong action, his first deception, began his degradation. Errors and deceit have continued to carry him farther and farther away from his primitive innocence. His corruption began when his instincts and kindly dispositions proved insufficient to guide his judgment and to give him all the help he needed. I have the consciousness within me of the reality of the time when instinct and kindly feeling sufficed. I can imagine myself once again in possession of these in their purity, just as I could imagine myself possessed once more of an arm or a leg which I had lost. I can thus imagine what I was like before my corruption began.

"Such a condition presents itself to me in two ways—what I was like before the conception of evil arose in my mind, and what I might be like if I could once again lose the impression of evil. If with this last I can combine the strength to reach after the noblest and best which I know, and which I ought to seek, then my picture of innocence represents the perfection for which I strive. This is the basis of my moral self. It could, however, never be the basis of a social law. . . .

"Without the consciousness of evil, neither the idea of law nor the feeling of law can enter my mind without causing suffering. Thus every idea of law is a social idea, and the feeling of law is a social feeling, and thus the idea of natural rights, strictly interpreted, is an illusion. But we are accustomed to call those ideas of social law which belong to times in close proximity to those of the primitive condition of man in its wider interpretation, ' natural rights.'

"But the conception of natural rights comes from a feeling that the institutions and arrangements of socially organized life ought to rest on principles which harmonize with man's unspoiled primitive nature. We wish, that is to say, that our idea of right and duty should rest on grounds that do not controvert the noblest and best that we are in a position to know. This will in us is the source of what we call ' natural rights.'

" But the so-called ' natural rights ' are not the source of this will. There is no trace of them in the primitive man's motive to self-maintenance. The idea comes about in this way : stirred by the strongest of all motives, primitive man opposes everything which he thinks will endanger his well-being—thus he learns to know the dangers that surround him ; experience teaches him that other men in the social organization are capable of behaving towards him in a way which is repugnant to his own primitive good-nature, of which some traces still remain. So he conceives the idea that it would be a good thing if nobody had such behaviour to fear.

" When the primitive man sees the body of the slain at his door, he cannot help thinking that it might have been himself, and it occurs to him how good it would be if men did not kill each other. This thought in combination with his primitive good-nature brings him into the state of mind in which man, from purely selfish motives, conceived the social law, ' Thou shalt not kill.' But he gives it up whenever he feels strongly that his own safety is endangered.

" This commandment and all others that arise from so-called ' natural rights ' is surely not the result of any primitive feeling of any right whatever, other than the fundamental one of self-preservation. A motive of this kind is purely individual, however ; without social experience it is as free from any feeling of participation as it is from any feeling of rights or wrongs. It becomes participatory in its nature in so far as social experiences, through a combination of our selfishness and our kindliness, make it so. The feeling of natural rights thus, obviously, arises from a sense of danger ; uneasiness of this sort leads us to feel the want of law in the world and at the same time it dawns upon us that we can make law ourselves if we will.

" This is also true of the social contract. At first we only realize that there is no such contract in Nature, but that if we wished we might introduce one. The feeling of wrongful suffering is the ground on which the idea of law unfolds in men's minds. Therefore the individual character of this feeling is of the first importance ; his conception of truth and law is entirely a result of the purity of this feeling.

" If the impression of wrongful suffering is united with kindliness and with an effort towards perfection, pure ideas of truth and law are engendered in me. I can do nothing else but hold out a friendly hand to my fellows. But if this is not the case, the slightest sense of wrong drives me to the worst horrors of which my nature is capable. Primitive man and social man allows himself any wrong to protect himself against wrong. So the representative of society, the government itself, does the same thing, when it is afraid of wrong being done against itself.

" Social training as such does not protect me from the consequences of my primitive selfishness. Only as a moral being can I actually prefer to suffer wrong than do wrong myself.

## III.

### What am I as a Member of a Social Order ?

" The social condition of man is in its essence that of the primitive man with certain restrictions placed upon him. Man does not, however, accept such limitations until he is forced, and until his primitive simplicity and good-nature are much corrupted. His object in making the change is to soften the consequences of his corruption, and to enable him to satisfy the needs of his primitive nature more easily and completely than he could in his state of freedom. He uses the same means to that end— namely, his primitive animal strength.

"But this primitive source of power has been already weakened by his corruption, nor does the social organization restore it.  On the contrary, it destroys the harmless contentment and simple rules of conduct of the primitive condition; even while it multiplies our pleasures, it increases our burdens, and emphasizes the difference between man and man to the point of bitterness.  In fine, man does not get what he hoped for from his new position.

"Simple enjoyment is the lot of primitive man; hoping and waiting are the lot of man in society.  This is inevitable, for society rests upon things that are not really there—that is, upon symbols.  Property, earnings, vocation, public authority, laws, are all artifices designed to make up for want of freedom.  Property is the symbol of my native capacity to maintain myself; authority symbolizes my primitive capacity to protect myself. What its talons are to the eagle so is the needle to the tailor, the pen to the writer, the scissors to the draper, his cattle to the farmer, his land to the nobleman, and his throne to the king.

"What a difference, however, between primitive man living at his ease among his roots, and the modern man who is driving a half per cent. bargain with the moneylender, or quarrelling with his agent about an additional expenditure of a hundred pounds a year among a hundred labourers. . . .  Primitive man knew not what he was losing when he took the step.  He was seeking primitive pleasures, and he lost infinitely in this regard.  The discomfort of the life he left is the very basis of the life into which he stumbled.  He wished to restore the charm of his old life.  To that end one man becomes a tailor, another a student, another drives a team across the mountains, another is a woodman, and another becomes a barber; one man seeks the old charm by using his head, another by his emotional life. . . .  These differences are the countless sources of discomfort.  The student has an ungainly stoop, the smith is stronger in his arms than in his legs, the tailor is bow-legged, and the peasant walks with the grace of an ox. Whether he will or no, man is driven into occupations which make such disproportionate demands upon his various powers.

" This tendency goes so far that governments are preparing a census of their subjects from the point of view of their special faculties—how many have specially good ears, how many are talented speakers, writers, wind-bags ! It does not matter that these fractional specimens of humanity are lame in all other respects—an attitude which has a pernicious effect upon man's powers in their entirety.

" This sort of one-sidedness produces the peculiar feelings of *esprit de corps* in every rank—that of patricians, noblemen, and statesmen, and that of each special type of citizen arrogance with which men protect their primitive standing in the social organization. . . . The greater their power, the stronger is the impulse of their native selfishness to assert their power with violence. The evil increases in proportion to the freedom which is given to man's primitive powers. It is only their limited physical strength that prevents men from becoming barbarians, and their limited intellectual powers that prevent them from becoming tyrants.

" Obviously, society weakens man's primitive good-nature. . . . The social condition of man is a mere continuation of the war of each against all, and all against each, that begins with the corruption of the primitive state. Moreover, the war is waged at far greater cost of human suffering. Social man as such stands upon the blood of his instincts, and on the grave of his good-nature, as a murderer on the blood of his victims ; whoever he was, the victim no longer counts, and the murderer counts how much money there is in his purse. The typical social man hates the smallest trace of primitive good-will in his institutions. All his efforts are directed to put such influences entirely out of count, and when he accepts the principle that good-will is as mischievous in public affairs as the forcible control of the people is right in the state, then he is completely in line. The rule is based on the inevitable ruin which the social organization brings upon our primitive nature.

" Unhappily, it is as much the popular view as it is that of the government. It is only with great reservations that we can affirm : ' Confidence in the government must exist among the people—without it no government can exist ' ; much less can we say : ' The government must itself trust the people, otherwise it cannot stand.' It is certainly not necessary, in a well-organized state, that the people should have confidence in the personnel of the government ; but if the object of the social order is to be achieved, it is necessary that the people should have confidence in the law which stands, or should stand, between him and the administrator.

" But the selfishness of men in authority leads them to think always of making the most of their positions. . . . At present it is as if a father had left his property to his eldest son, with the pious hope that he would provide adequately for the wants of his portionless brothers and sisters. The governmental administration stands to the people in the same relation as the eldest son to the rest of that family. The people have no rights at law.

" When a people is without rights, it is dangerous even to put the matter frankly forward ; but if it has rights and legal forms, then we may with advantage consider the position. In general, law promotes man's betterment, as its absence degrades him. Moral depravity deepens in proportion to the absence of law. There can in such circumstances be no real confidence on either side. Those in power know this well, and laugh at the idea of having confidence in the people. . . .

" Social man does not know when he is acting selfishly. He always assigns lofty motives to his actions. Authority is similarly unable to recognize the primitive motives which prompt its activity. It says it does not hate popular rights, but their ignorant misuse, and even this is not for its own sake, but for the sake of the public welfare. It says that everybody should have all the rights he desires if only it were feasible, but it would be fatal to yield weakly to popular clamour or to allow the feeling of the need of citizen independence, and even the appearance of legal security, to spread at all widely."

Then follows a discussion of " social " developments in France under Louis XVI. and his successors.

" Lawless Authority believes that she herself is the law, that law and justice spring from her, as eggs come from the hen.

" ' Social ' law regards truth and loyalty as a mutual duty of all men in the group. In France, Authority said that all owed loyalty to herself, but she owed it to none. . . .

" Social law regards the independence of the state as resting on the independence of the citizens, and the wealth of the state on the secure well-being of its individual members. But lawless authority founds the independence of the state on the facile obedience of a people without any rights, and the national wealth on the ease with which it can dip into the pockets of the citizens. . . .

" Our primitive nature when possessed of enormous social power cannot fail to misunderstand its true relation to other men. . . . Man in whom his primitive feelings have full play is unfitted to rule men in a socially just way. He can only do that when the law sets definite limits to his power. . . .

" Man enters the social relation either because he is compelled by his animal helplessness, or voluntarily, because of his overwhelming power. In the first case he is timid and docile ; in the other, cold, arrogant, lustful of power, and impatient of all opposition. In either case he is fundamentally the same as he was when the corruption of his primitive nature began.

" His social habits cannot crush the dispositions that belong to his primitive nature. Even where there are kings and soldiers, vocations and laws, where instinct seems entirely gone, men still love their domestic animals, their pets, and their children. To put thought aside and to sink into dreams is the great charm of life. What is new and what is brilliant is loved best. . . . In every land you will find men who will not give up a pipe of tobacco for a year's income.

" Not even the art of kings can give a different turn to life's essential character. Man in society will always be changed by its advantages and disadvantages, just as the advantages and disadvantages of Nature change him. Wealth makes him careless, just as does the enjoyment of Nature's bounty ; the fundamentals of human nature are not changed in the social order. Man as such is only an animal, and as animals men are always the same. Even the independence which he claims in his group is in keeping with the liveliness of his primitive feelings.

"Social law certainly separates the demands of my primitive nature from those of my social obligations ; but my nature does not separate them, and, as social law cannot bind my nature, it follows that my primitive nature swallows up my social obligations, and finally attaches the notion of citizen independence to the selfish feelings that belong to our particular position. Our hearts are hardened against all real social truth and justice, and amidst the maddest demands for dissolute social pleasures we fling away the basis of citizen law—the individual independence of the citizen—as we should a worthless tool. It is sold for any sensory pleasure. The poor man does it for bread, the rich man for some less worthy toy. . . .

" Primitive natural freedom and social law are ever at war. The king and the revolutionary, the noble and the Jew, the patrician and the free man, all struggle for the monopoly of this freedom against all others.

" Social law and citizen independence depend, therefore, upon so arranging the vocational training that it exercises a repressive influence on our primitive nature ; but this, of course, means influencing my primitive feelings in favour of the social order, a result which can only be achieved through deception. Man must not suspect that his primitive nature is being weakened ; he must think you are giving him that which in truth you are only leaving behind ; he must not know what you are taking away, nor

what you make him suffer ; you must make him wish for
that towards which you are leading him. . . . Effort,
order, the steady exercise of a calling, must become to
him what his instincts once were. . . .

"Only by such mutilation can man become a citizen.
It is not easy . . . and it is often done at the cost of introducing a poison into his nature which destroys his
humanity. If it is wisely completed before the man knows
right from left, then his primitive nature will build upon
that foundation. . . . The man enters the citizen yoke
without having known the charm of his primitive condition. He enjoys its advantages and accepts its limitations without question. His understanding is trained,
and he finds it a surer guide than instinct. Each work of
his hands gives him pleasure—the more difficult it seemed,
the greater the triumph ; he falls in love and shares his
burdens with others ; the repose of his old age is assured ;
his will operates beyond the grave. He encloses his property by locks and keys, and the world cannot gainsay him.

"But he was deceived ; he was mutilated. Is that right
or necessary ? He could not live as a social man without
it. There only remains the question whether the best
possible social conditions will always be satisfactory to
man ? When I am everything in my rank and calling
that I can be, when my position is assured at law . . .
when I am a citizen in the fullest sense of the word, and
if that word of my forefathers, ' Freedom,' ' Freedom,'
should ring again from the mouths of happy, entire,
and righteous men, should I be satisfied with social order
in perfection ? I think not. My dream has vanished ;
social law and the social state does not bring satisfaction.
. . . I live as a primitive man entirely dissatisfied with
the social position ; the enjoyment of law is for me only
a sham. Only the full free play of instincts is really
right, and that I do not enjoy.

" . . . The gaps in my nature which my social condition has inflicted must be filled up. The highest glory
of my primitive existence, the purity of my instincts, and
the good-nature resting thereon, must go in favour of

the highest worth of my nature—free human will and the moral power that goes with it. Man must gather experience amongst the ruins of his primitive instincts, which shall convince him of the errors and worthlessness of his animal nature, and lead him to the recognition of moral worth. In such circumstances there arises within him a new need, whose satisfaction leads him to the recognition of the duty of getting rid of the corruption of his primitive nature, and of breaking up the rigidity of his social outlook. . . .

## IV.

### What am I as a Moral Being?

" There is within me an inner force which enables me to look at the things of the world independently of my primitive animal desires and of my social obligations, and to regard them solely from the point of view as to how far they contribute to my spiritual advancement ; I can accept or reject them just as they satisfy or otherwise this point of view.

" This force is the very centre of my being ; it is entirely independent of all other forces, nor is it in any way the product of any of my other natural abilities. *It is because I am, and I am because it is.* It arises from the feeling that when I do what I ought to do, and when I impose my own will as law upon myself, I am putting the completing touch to my own character.

" My primitive animal nature knows nothing of this force. As a purely primitive creature I can do nothing myself against my own animal instincts, and as such I am quite incapable of imagining that I can improve myself by any means which would injuriously affect my animal comforts and my animal behaviour.

" As a social creature man is just as powerless. The social ruin of a nation is the most terrible thing one has to strive against, just as the animal ruin of one's individuality is the most terrible thing one has to fight against in one's own nature.

" Man as a social animal is in just as little need of morality as he himself, in his animal nature, is capable of it. We can in a social condition live quite a good life amongst other people without any morality whatever. In the same way we can comply with each other's wishes, and deal righteously and fairly with each other, without obeying any moral code.

" Morality is quite an individual thing, and cannot be shared by any two people. No man can feel for me that I am. No man can feel for me that I am moral. We may live in social relationships with other people without any belief in their morality, but in the midst of this unbelief I feel a need, and I am inspired by the elevating thought that it lies in my own power to make of myself something nobler than the purely animal and social creature which is all that Nature and sex can produce.

" Sensual enjoyment, social law, and morality, seem to bear the same relationship to one another as do childhood, adolescence, and manhood.

" It is as a child that I approach most nearly to the state of innocence of the lower animals, but it is then, also, that I am most inspired by animal impulses. In this condition one's aims and desires are quite simple ; sensual enjoyment is everything to one. But I suffer from my mistaken desires and the pain which they bring. I must therefore strive after such strength as will enable me to gain the mastery over both evils—my lustful desires and my pain. And in the middle classes it is during the period between my childish longings and the enjoyments of my rights of manhood—i.e., during the period of my apprenticeship—that I chiefly require this strength. For in this position I lose all the delights of childish days without in any way enjoying the freedom and the rights of manhood. The man to whom my father confides me forces me, by his right as master, to renounce the rights of my nature for an object for which, in reality, my egotism cares less than for the actual moment. In such a position I possess no rights. I am now the creature of a demoralizing compact, and I must look at everything from the point of view of how it affects my master's interests. The hope of future enjoyment from something which he may or may not make out of me—this hope must at this period be my sole compensation for the freedom which I miss so much. But this visionary hope cannot possibly satisfy my primitive nature ; therefore every apprentice strives with all his might to free himself from a position which carries him, as it were, to his fate, rather than to the attainment of his own aims. But the happiness and security of my future life depend entirely on the truth and good faith of the two parties to this agreement, and on this account I must stoically renounce all my desires for freedom, and strictly accept the restrictions imposed upon me during my years of apprenticeship. Meanwhile this time passes away ; the period of my demoralization, like that of purely sensual enjoyment, comes to an end. Now, as my own master, I regard everything from the standpoint of its influence on me and on my life's purpose. Freedom, independence, and personal rights, belong exclusively to this period. The two previous ways of regarding the world seem to have been due to my ignorance, my weakness, and a certain want of self-sufficiency and of independent rights ; they do not represent either truth or justice. Nevertheless, it was only through these illusions, through that unjust yoke, that I was able to arrive at my present mastery of truth and right. But for the illusions of my childhood and the absence of all rights during my years of apprenticeship, I should not have been stimulated to the strong and steadfast effort which is necessary if man is to rise to an independence based on law and on justice.

" In order to arrive at these two primary forces in my social and moral education, I must regard my earlier illusions as true and rightful, for otherwise I should now be living in a confused and uneducated state, neither child, apprentice, nor master ; and I should die in this condition, like a fruit whose tender blossom has been injured by the wind. But although I have been forcibly preserved from such misfortune by circumstances and by my illusions, the impressions due to those early illusions and to those adolescent restrictions will always remain with me, and my present position of mastery can never be independent of them—that is to say, my present truth is not absolute.

" All that is true of the threefold relationship of the child, the apprentice, and the man, is also true of the relationship between my social and moral nature. In my primitive state I saw everything from the point of view of simple sensuous enjoyment ; here, too, I suffered from erring desires and the pain which they brought, and I strove for strength to enable me to gain a mastery over them. I found it in a middle condition halfway between my primitive and my moral existence—*i.e.*, in the social condition. Once more I lost in this, all the delights of my primitive freedom, and at the same time I enjoyed but little of the complete and independent strength of which my moral nature is capable.

" As a social being I am a creature of the compact. The state in which my fate is cast, compels me to renounce my personal rights for an object about which I care less than for the pleasures of the moment. But my whole happiness depends on the good faith of myself towards the state, and of the state towards me, and I am compelled, therefore, to be loyal to the restrictions which have been placed about me. Just as in the period of apprenticeship I feel illusory desires, the attainment of which might or might not be a compensation for my losses, so now I long to be free from a position which fixes my destiny rather than helps me to pursue my own ends.

" But I am as little fit to be free as the apprentice himself until my suffering has brought me to a higher standpoint from which I see the world in relation to my own inner worth. If I had cast aside the social yoke and the sensory pleasures of my primitive nature as both illusory and wrong before experience had led me to the moral point of view, I should have lived without education, without clear purpose—neither citizen nor primitive man, neither happy nor moral, content with neither sensory pleasures nor prudent action. But although circumstances kept me from this fate, I can never get rid of the illusory impressiveness of the earlier period. I can never attain to absolute morality in which there is no trace of my lower nature and no trace of the merely legal point of view.

" Such absolute morality would lead me to neglect altogether the demands of my primitive nature, and of my particular social obligations, through which I attained to such morality as I am capable of. It would lead me to believe myself nearer to my lost innocence than I can be in the corruption of the social order ; in the midst of the sufferings and restrictions of my primitive corruption I should dream of knowing no evil, and take no thought for my life's needs. ' Take no thought for the morrow, neither what ye shall eat nor what ye shall drink.' ' Sell that thou hast and give it to the poor.' ' Who is my mother, and who are my brethren ?' ' Unless ye become as little children.' ' The foxes have holes, and the birds of the air have nests.' Such would be its behests. The ties of property, blood, and law, would all vanish.

" . . . Such a morality is not the lot of mortal man ; he lost it at his first infancy. He can see it at both ends, so to speak, of his existence, but he leaves it in the middle, driven hither and thither by the storms of his own guilt. But just as men leave their sheltering-places after a storm, and bend their energies to clearing up the mischief that is wrought, so, when they see their buried selves in the midst of this sinful life, men set to work to free themselves from the consequences of their corruption. They build upon the ruins of their old selves a new and better life.

" We really know nothing of our moral nature beyond what this work of rescue teaches us. In our dead selves morality takes its rise, but it is clouded with shadows which conceal its origin to the very end. It has therefore nothing to do with the morality of the philosopher. Shut up in his own circle, man knows only the actual objects which appear to him as right and wrong from the stand-

point of his native instincts. The rightness or otherwise
of these ideas cannot be the basis of my morality. On
the contrary, conduct is moral which is based on an effort
to be free from the illusions of my animal nature to such
a degree as would not have been possible without a will
standing out against my lower impulses.

" My morality is nothing more than the way in which
I relate my pure will to do right to the full measure of my
knowledge and my responsibilities—the way in which I, as
father, son, ruler, subject, man, or slave, in all sincerity
take pains to carry out my duties, not so much to my
own satisfaction and advantage, as to the satisfaction
and advantage of those to whom I owe, not only nourishment and protection, but obedience, loyalty, and gratitude. The more closely Nature attaches my instinctive
existence to a moral object, the more points from which
I am touched by my animal weal and woe, the more
stimuli I find, the more impulses I feel towards morality.
The farther Nature removes my instinctive nature from a
moral object, the less such stimuli move me to morality.

" Thus social duties favour my morality in proportion
as they concern objects which are in close natural relation
to me ; and, conversely, they are favourable to immorality
as the motives underlying them are remote from such
relations.

" Only those motives to duty are purely moral which
are entirely my own. Every motive which I share with
others is not so. It has, on the contrary, an immoral
tendency, because it induces inattention to the deceptive
character of my animal nature and the mischievous
hardness of my social outlook. The larger the number
with whom I divide my duty, the greater the danger. . . .
Everything which I do as a member of a body, a community, a corporation, or a party, unmans me more or
less. The larger the body which prescribes my duty, the
greater the danger. . . .

" The social order arises from the necessity of a mutual
sharing of duties ; it is in essence a series of ideas which
alternately unite and divide my selfish and my altruistic

feelings. When it brings them together, the effect is ennobling ; when it separates them, then it is demoralizing. The social order is therefore a means of moral elevation according as its rights and duties concern objects naturally near to our individuality, and *vice versa*. . . . Morality in the social order depends on whether the laws and customs hold fast to this principle to which Nature herself points.

" The natural nearness of moral objects, and the unity of my egoistic and altruistic feelings, do not, however, make me of themselves moral ; that I can only become through my own power. The union of these feelings prepares the ground in which morality—that is, the dominance of purified and lofty good-nature over my selfishness—becomes possible.

" Religion is the highest product of such a situation ; but the external religious organization, or any other state contrivance for equilibrating selfishness and altruism, cannot make social man as such moral. . . .

" This comes only when I of my own free will give up the principle of the harmony of my primitive nature, and subject myself and all my primitive selfishness to the freedom of my will and its purified benevolence. Until this happens I am the victim of the alternating dominance of selfish and altruistic points of view.

" Thus household and citizen duties, in so far as they rest on a basis of primitive selfishness, are not moral duties. They may, indeed, be opposed to my morality, and stand in the way of my moral development. This is always the case when they nourish my selfishness at the expense of my free good-will.

" The social will puts a complete stop to the harmony of my primitive nature. This legal system on which it rests is purely selfish, mistrustful, and armed with force ; it produces a condition of mind entirely opposed to morality.

" For this reason the mediating art of wise legislation is necessary even in the social order—an art that sees beyond the restrictions of primitive human motives, and works towards the elevation of human nature, in order to prevent its complete subordination to primitive instincts and indolence, in order to prevent men from going under altogether.

"The more the legislation tightens the bonds of blood and encourages the kindly feelings of natural kinship, the more difficult it makes it for might to assert itself over right ; the more the prevailing ideas and the moderation of official needs make a government modest in its demands, so much the more favourable will the disposition of the citizens be to their inner elevation. On the other hand, when the state is all-powerful, when the citizen feels that he is in the world for the state's sake, and not for his own, and that he is powerless against its demands, the less likely is the social order to favour his moral improvement.

" National morality is, therefore, always dependent on legislative wisdom in subordinating might to right, and selfishness to kindly good feeling. When legislation loses sight of these things, when it allows might and greed to play their unequal part among the people, when it leaves confidence and good-will a prey to privileged self-seeking, then the seeds of national degeneration are sown.

" The performance of the duty which judgment or principle lays upon me does not touch my morality in the same way as that which comes from the emotional effect of objects which stand in intimate relationship to me. What I as democrat, or aristocrat, or as a devotee of some principle or other, regard as my duty does not advance my moral worth in the same degree as that which results from the primitively near moral objects. Even the idea of filial duty does not favour moral growth in the same way as the laughter and tears of my son ; so sharing in national calamities and pleasures favours morality more than the contemplation of patriotic duty. The purest principles of legislation do not preserve us from social hardening unless they are supported by actual sensory participation in social triumphs and social woes.

" Social duties favour morality in proportion as their motives are not due merely to law or to the force of social circumstances, in proportion as they are not merely due to my official position in the state, but are a simple consequence of my manhood.

" The tendency to subordinate the interests of the individual to the interests of an impersonal state deprives the social order of its moral effectiveness."

After this discussion Pestalozzi formulates his general outlook in life:

" I see my nature in a threefold aspect—(1) as a product of Nature ; (2) as a product of the social order ; (3) as a product of my own work. It is only as my own creation that I can attain to inner harmony.

" As a product of Nature, I am a product of necessity—the same animal organism which for thousands of years has never been able to suppress its slightest inclination.

" As a product of the social order, I am like a drop of water which falls into a stream on the side of the Alps.

" As my own work, I busy myself within myself—a work for all time. No wave can tear me from my rock ; time cannot destroy the traces of the work which, as a moral personality, I have completed. . . .

" Should you remain on this middle point between your animal and your moral life, then do not be surprised that you are just a tailor, a cobbler, or a prince, and not a man. Do not be surprised that your life is a struggle without a victory, and that you are not even what Nature alone made of you, but much less—a citizen, and only half a man."

Proceeding to draw together the threads of his argument, he says:

" This threefold way of looking at things explains all the contradictions in our nature. They are, in fact, nothing but the fluctuating dominance of the primitive or the moral side of my nature.

" The social man as such lives in the midst of this

fluctuation, and the persistence with which men destroy the happiness and the repose of their race rests entirely on the instinctive inclination to think themselves perfected prematurely, and to remain at the social level to which they have reached.

" Man must, however, either sink below this level or rise above it. As the product of the social order he must be below what Nature made of him, or rise higher than his social self. . . . This work of rescue must be his own doing entirely. But since this is simply his inner conviction concerning his own true nature, it is clear that he can only accomplish the rescue through a sense of his dangerous helplessness in face of the corruption of his animal nature in the social organization—the sense, in fact, upon which religion is based."

His next step is to examine those products of social life with which he began, but this time from the threefold point of view—thus :

" Property, of which as a primitive, unspoiled man I knew nothing, and upon which the social order is built, receives recognition from the morally enlightened ; but he regards it as a means of ennobling his own nature and bringing happiness to others, even to the point of endangering what belongs to him. The morally enlightened man will never seek the possession of power, nor will the primitive man in his purity ; it is the breath of the social man's being. The merchant who regards his workmen as instruments for his own enrichment is a social product ; he has sunk below the level of primitive man. If the law compels him to regard them as independent persons to whom he must give a proper equivalent for their work, he is still a social product, obedient to social laws. If he does these things of his own free will, without external compulsion, he is a moral person.

" Of religion the primitive man knows nothing ; he offers no sacrifices and makes no prayers. As a product of his corrupted instincts, his religion is a false superstition. As the work of society—i.e., of the state—it is an illusion ; only as my own work is my religion true.

State-made religion is the handmaid of the circumstance which produced it."[1]

A brief restatement of the answers to his three great questions is followed by a paragraph of touching personal importance :

" Thousands pass away, as Nature gave them birth, in the corruption of sensual gratification, and they seek no more.

" Tens of thousands are overwhelmed by the burdens of craft and trade, by the weight of the hammer, the measuring-rod, the crown, and they seek no more.

" But I know a man who did seek more ; the joy of simplicity dwelt in his heart, and he had faith in mankind such as few men have ; his soul was made for friendship, love was his element, and fidelity his strongest tie.

" But he was not made by this world nor for it, and wherever he was placed in it he was found unfit.

" And the world that found him thus, asked not whether it was his fault or the fault of another ; but it bruised him with an iron hammer, as the bricklayers break up an old brick to fill up crevices.

" But though bruised, he yet trusted in mankind more than in himself, and he proposed to himself a great purpose, to attain which he suffered great agonies, and learned lessons such as few mortals had learnt before him.

" He could not, nor would he, become generally useful ; but for his purpose he was more useful than most men are for theirs, and he expected justice at the hands of mankind, whom he still loved with an innocent love. But he found none. Those who made themselves his judges, without further examination, confirmed the former sentence that he was absolutely useless.

" This was the grain of sand which decided the doubtful balance of his wretched destinies.

" He is no more ; thou wouldst know him no more. All that remains of him are the decayed remnants of his destroyed existence.

---

[1] These are only very imperfect and incomplete selections from these concluding discussions.

" He fell as the fruit that falls before it is ripe, whose blossom has been nipped by the northern gale or whose core is eaten out by the gnawing worm.

" Stranger that passest by, refuse not a tear of sympathy. Even in falling the fruit turned itself towards the stem, on the branches of which it lingered through the summer, and it whispered to the tree: ' Verily, in my death will I nourish thy roots.'

" Stranger that passest by, spare the perishing fruit, and allow the dust of its corruption to nourish the roots of the tree, on whose branches it lived, sickened, and died."

# III —"VIEWS AND EXPERIENCES"

[*The six letters following are, according to Hunziker, part of a scheme for a methodical revision of* How Gertrude Teaches her Children. *The project was begun in 1805, during the first year at Yverdun. He was living quietly with Krüsi at the time, and readers of the letters will find in them an atmosphere of repose, a systematic ordering of his thought, which is too rare in his writings. As he says in the* Address of 1818, Festina lente *had never been his guide in life. If ever it were, it was surely here.*

*The letters are remarkable for their clearness of expression, and for the admirable child psychology they contain, particularly in Letters V., VI., and VII. The reader will notice, too, how Pestalozzi excels in the concrete rather than in the philosophical analysis of his ideals. Compare, for example, Letters III. and IV.*

*The letters are preceded by a long introduction, at the close of which he expresses a wish for the establishment of an institution for the education of poor children, which should serve also as a centre of investigation and propaganda for the method. Of this need he speaks at greater length in appendices, from the third of which a long extract is translated. It relates to the need for special training for schoolmasters.*]

## THIRD LETTER

### PESTALOZZI DEFINES HIS IDEAL MAN

1. In order to determine from experience what is essential to a good education, you must observe men in all the realities of life, and look for the man who in the midst of

155

its labours and sufferings stands out among his fellow-
men as one who is all that he should be. If, however,
you should hear someone say of one who is present, " I
could wish all men were like him," you must remember
that his presence influences the minds of those who testify
of him. But if you hear it said at his tomb, in the midst
of those who are shedding bitter tears for him—children,
old men, and poor folk—then you may take it as true.

2. Of course, thousands will say at this point : " We
have never heard any man spoken of in that way. Men
do not speak like that, even of the few who may deserve
it." To this I answer : " Does no man die for whom the
poor weep ? Does no man die of whom the old man
who knew him, the widow who loved him, the orphan
who honoured him, and the neighbour who lived with
him, say with tears at his graveside : ' Would that I had
another like him ! If only all men were as he was !' "

3. You say : " The best and noblest men often die misunderstood and misrepresented." True, but this only
makes their friends sorry for those who err.

Let us, however, pass by those who suffer in this way,
for it is not they whom I have in mind. Men who live
nobly and yet die under a cloud of calumny have not
lived an ordinary life. They have experienced heights of
exaltation and depths of suffering beyond the common
lot. They are not typical, and I must pass them by.

4. Other men live and die who, without suffering as
these have suffered, carry this testimony with them to the
grave : " They were a pattern to all their fellows."

But you will not find them in the bustle of the world ;
you must seek them rather in quiet, peaceful cottages.
Not that men who live in turmoil, and even men who
occupy the world's high places, have never been so spoken
of ; but the vastness of the concourse dulls in death the
purity of their lives and the sense of the reality of their
human connections, even as it did during their lives.

It is true that in the lowly cottage there is rarely found
a man of whom the people who knew him bear this testimony ; but if you seek him there, and if your own dis-

position is such that you can recognize him when you see him, you will not search in vain. In more places than you would ever have imagined you will hear the words uttered : " That was a man, a woman, such as all others should be !"

5. Trust this saying ; it will not lead you astray ; it will guide you to the course which you should adopt for your child if you wish that he should win a like honour. But do not stop here. Go to the oldest and most reliable man among those who have spoken, and ask him what it really is that the people praise so highly.

6. Of a certainty he will answer : " He was a man upon whose judgment, kindness, and sense of duty, one could implicitly rely." Of a certainty he will answer : " This man showed in all his judgments, in all his counsels, in all his undertakings, a sound and practised intelligence, a steadfast, powerful, kindly heart, capable of the utmost exaltation and exertion, and a patient adroitness in action which in all cases insured success."

7. The one-sided man who has excelled only in one particular quality does not win the same complete admiration from men of common-sense. No ; these words will not be said of a man who, though highly cultured and sagacious beyond measure, was a slave to selfishness, whose love and sympathy were not affected by the sufferings of his fellow-men. Acquaintances and neighbours will never say these words of a man who, though he had the heart of an angel and the greatest capacity for self-sacrifice on behalf of the sufferings of his fellow-men, nevertheless showed want of tact in the way he offered his help. Just as little will you hear it said of a man who, in the exercise of his vocation, was a model of skill, of trustworthiness, and diligence, but who failed to attend faithfully and diligently to the other calls of life, or who, being of a grasping, unfriendly, and selfish nature, only laid up treasures to himself.

8. Unspoiled human nature will instinctively apply these words only to the man in whom insight, tactful efficiency, and purity of motive, are united ; to the man

who has acquired all the principles and all the powers which are characteristically human, who practises them consistently in all the relations of his life.

What, then, of the man whose character does not exhibit this harmonious blend, but yet stands out pre-eminent among his neighbours in some particular capacity for good, and leads a meritorious but a one-sided life ? Of him men will say : " He had a clever head," " He had a kind heart," " He was distinguished in his calling "; but they will not say : " All men should be as he was."

9. If you actually come across a case of the kind, do not content yourself with the knowledge of what the man was like. Go deeper into the matter. How did he become what he was ? The old man who spent his youth with him will, in a hundred cases to one, answer : " Father and mother, domestic surroundings and circumstances, awakened and fostered in him in various ways his capacities for, and inclinations towards, the good which was so marked in him. His social circle and his fatherland offered a wider sphere for putting this good into practice. At the same time, a pious belief in God lifted him out of himself, above his domestic circumstances, above the world and its selfishness, and made him capable of the sacrifice for the sake of truth and justice which won all men's hearts."

10. If you had heard him speak ! If he could rise from his grave, and if, in the humility which was the prime force of his life, you could hear him thank God for His guidance, as he thanked Him in his life, he would tell you that the characteristic feature of his education was that it did not aim solely or predominantly at producing intellectual attainments, or at establishing moral qualities, or at preparing for his future calling, but that it was carefully and consistently conducted with respect to all these. He would tell you the circumstances which roused his heart to nobler efforts and lightened the work of his mind and his hand in the struggle towards life's final goal. He will tell you how his efforts reacted upon him through the all-round care which had been spent upon his educa-

tion ; how his activity and effort were reflected in this harmony ; how in this way they had become a source of blessing to him, and were constantly prompting him to thankfulness and love towards God and man ; how this thankfulness and love continually increased the happiness of his life, and made it daily easier for him to do his duty, and by doing his duty to become—what he ought.

## FOURTH LETTER

### WHAT IS TO BE TAKEN FOR GRANTED

1. FRIEND, the judgment of sound common-sense uttered at the graveside of the man of high character is based on the supreme consciousness that man is to be regarded in his independent entirety, and only in so far as he maintains a right standard all round is his worth unassailable. The feelings which prompt an upright man to bear such testimony to one who has just completed a noble life are expressed more philosophically as follows : " Unless education is to make a man worse than he would have been without it, it must regard and treat him as a responsible person, and train him so that all the essential elements and forces of his nature are harmoniously called into activity, and made simultaneously efficient for everything that he is and does."

2. Every philosophical investigator of human nature is ultimately compelled to admit that the sole aim of education is the harmonious development of the faculties and dispositions which, under God's grace, make up personality. Such an investigator would realize that a man is not what he ought to be until those to whom he owes his life, and those who in their turn owe him their life, testify of him, as also do those who are bound to him by less intimate ties—his neighbours, his fellow-citizens, especially the destitute and oppressed among them—that " He was a man whose intelligence, good-will, and professional skill, could always be relied on. His judgment

showed sound discernment ; his counsels, his promises, and his help, revealed a strong character capable of the utmost exertion and unwavering perseverance.  Whenever his sympathy was gained, he showed an incorruptible sense of proportion, unfailing charity, and a lofty mind that shrank from no reasonable sacrifice.  A disciplined intelligence, lofty ideals, and trained capacity for work, distinguished everything he did.  The result was always satisfactory both to himself and to all concerned.  He was therefore recognized as an example for all.  As such he was appreciated and beloved."

3.  The man, however, be he a philosopher or an ordinary individual, who looks upon conduct as the fruit ripening upon the tree, whose aim it is to bring the inner life of his child to perfection ; the man who desires to make of his child that which by the provisions of Nature it can and ought to become, must first of all ask himself : " What is there firstly in the child himself, and secondly in the environment and conditions which are forced upon him, which Nature herself employs in the education of mankind, from which we may learn the principles of education ?"

4.  The answer to the second question depends on the answer to the first.  Looking at them both for the moment, it is clear that the native dispositions to feeling, thinking, and doing, and the stimulus thereto which comes from without, are all that Nature needs, to form a human being.  Here, too, she indicates the fundamental principles which should guide our efforts to educate.

5.  All that men have done, all progress in civilization, is an outcome of feeling, of action, and of the stimuli to both, and the life of man and of the race in general is nothing more than a perpetual manifestation of these factors and of their mutual interaction.  From further consideration of these factors it is clear that whatever is good, whatever is holy and ennobling, whatever tends to promote harmonious perfection in man, springs from a central force which regulates, guides, inspires, and sets

limits to, these things in accordance with a lofty ideal of man's inner sanctity.

6. Amongst human emotions, it is the feeling of love in the child which clearly expresses this ideal. Love therefore is the central force to which all other emotions must be in due subordination if harmony with the ideal is to be preserved. Again, in the same way, intellectual activity, inasmuch as it springs up side by side with love, is the central force which clearly expresses the ideal in human action. All man's other activities must be guided and inspired by it if we would achieve complete and harmonious development of our native dispositions, and thus unquestionably ennoble the whole nature. This love, then, and this intellectual activity in the child constitute the common, positive, and unalterable starting-point from which the development of all natural aptitudes must begin.

7. It is not possible to think of making a human child what he ought to be by any other means than solicitude for the development in him of love and of all-round intellectual activity, finally bringing the two into harmony.

Man, as a being capable of raising himself, whose duty it is to raise himself above the charms of the sensuous life, finds no other means of accomplishing his destiny than this union of love and action.

He is constitutionally perfectly adapted to the achievement of his lofty destiny and to the performance of his duty, because his manhood disposes him towards these high aims, coming as they do from love, based as they are on activity, and allied as they are with freedom.

## FIFTH LETTER

### EDUCATIONAL ASPECTS OF FAMILY LIFE

1. CORRESPONDING to this inner disposition to love and to activity, we find in the child's environment a Divine organization of stimuli and forces which animate his

inborn capacity for self-development through love and activity.

2. And just as everything which is holy and elevating in our emotions and in our acts springs from love and from the higher activity of our spiritual nature, so everything that is holy, inspiring, and helpful, in environment and circumstance is to be found in the child's parents and his relations to them.  This central force is, however, actively connected with the wider environment of the child, making his influence nobler and higher than it could have been otherwise.

Everything which tends to make the body and the soul of the child thrive has its outer source in the care of the parents.  Its inner source is in the child himself, the latter being inseparable from, and dependent, on the former.

3. Those, therefore, who undertake to replace the possible lack of parents must do so in the parental spirit, and try to resemble what they really are not.

If the child does not enjoy parental care, the conception of parenthood must still find a place in his education ; and if we are right in regarding it as the chief factor in the elevation of mankind, it must be introduced into the educational system by the help of the Church or the State.  Otherwise, in spite of schools, in spite of all the help in the matter of food and clothes, the orphan still lacks the fundamental " outer " source of true education.

4. But if the child enjoys all that parenthood implies, even at the hands of strangers, he receives an impression of love, and he loves in return.  He is grateful and trustful, and the higher elements of his nature are stimulated into activity.  It is therefore possible to replace the loss of actual parents—at least, to a certain extent.

It is the sacred side of parental solicitude that makes environmental influences themselves of spiritual value, contributing thereby to the higher intellectual and emotional life.

5. Every piece of bread which the child eats has, if his mother gives it to him, quite a different effect upon him than it would have had if he had found it in the street or

received it from a stranger. The stocking which his mother knits before his eyes has also a deeper significance in his education than one which he buys at the shop or puts on without knowing where it came from. The pleasures which come from maternal love give the sense of an imperishable, higher, inner life. The stimulus arouses the whole being of the child to reciprocal love, to thankfulness, trust, and to all the inner and outer activity connected with those feelings.

6. Family life must therefore be regarded as the sole external situation that God has provided for the education of man.

In the actions and reactions of family life man's native dispositions are developed.

The bond of family life is a bond of love. It is the means given by God for awakening the capacity for love in the individual. In its purest form it is the most sublime factor imaginable in the education of our race.

7. Where love and the capacity for love are present in the domestic circle, one might say beforehand that no form of education can fail to succeed. The child must become good. One might well-nigh affirm that, whenever a child does not seem to be kind, vigorous, and active, it is because his capacity for love has not found that succour and guidance at home which it should.

8. A child who is cared for daily and hourly with all the charm that love brings lives in the midst of increasing promptings to affection. But whilst he is being thus affectionately guided he grows more independent and more able to take care of himself, and at the same time he begins spontaneously to minister to the needs of his parents. Thus the love which has been awakened in him excites serviceable activity. His own love finds expression in every circumstance. Work and love, obedience and effort, thankfulness and industry, all blend together in family life, and by their mutual interaction attain sincerity and vigour.

He who shuns no effort for the object of his affection, through the inner and outer activity which he and his love invoke, establishes an intellectual vigour which is in harmony with it.   Love helps us to put mind and heart into all that we do, and in this way to achieve and acquire those things which insight and love suggest as worthy objects of our effort.

9. The success of such an education is based entirely upon the assumption that the child's parents exist, and that they impersonate the sacredness of love and the higher human activity which springs from it.   It presupposes a father and mother who are able to distinguish clearly their position towards the child from their position towards the rest of the world, and to raise the former to a position above everything else.   It presupposes parents to whom the world is nothing in comparison with their child.   It presupposes men—be they kings or cottagers—who set at naught all the claims of the world if they stand in the way of the rightful claims of their child—men who realize fully the truth of the sublime words: "If I could gain the whole world at the expense of my child, what compensation would that be?"

10. It presupposes parents who will so far control their child's surroundings that all improper influences are excluded, and who, on the other hand, will seek out and make full use of all the stimuli to love and activity which the particular conditions offer, whatever trouble, patience, and self-sacrifice, this may involve.

11. We need parents who have the will and the capacity to be to their children what they ought to be.   It is of no avail to be solicitous about the improvement of our race if we do not seek the first principles here.   It is only here that we shall find them.

12. The book of the depths of human nature is only revealed on their child's behalf to those who enjoy the parental feelings in their fullest purity.

The sacred expression of the purer and nobler emotions and capacities imprinted in that book by the flaming pencil of the Creator, is the fixed, unchangeable expression of the emotions, which are peculiar to parenthood and its circumstances, and of the capacities which are awakened and formed by parenthood and its relationships. It is the life and soul of parenthood to see the delight which shines in the eye of children when their hearts overflow with love. It is the desire and delight of their life, and the source of a deep satisfaction, to see the peaceful expression of the child lying in their arms, filled with a confidence the meaning of which he does not yet understand. They are delighted when they recognize gratitude and dumb dependence in the eyes of the child, and when he shows in a thousand ways that nobody and nothing in the world can give him the pleasure which father and mother awaken.

13. Their most sacred feelings are touched when they see their innocent child doing gladly and willingly, as if he could not help it, just what they would wish him to do, and in the same way avoiding what they would wish him to avoid.

How deeply they are stirred when they see signs of the Divine in their child—his delight in love, his blissful thankfulness, his peaceful confidence, the innocence and purity of his mind as it has developed in obedient dependence! The life and welfare of the child viewed in this spiritual way is more to them than their own bodies. Inspired with such feelings, parents feel an irresistible impulse always to be all to their child that they should be, and resolutely to do everything necessary to preserve in its purity the Divine element in their child, and to make him grow and prosper in the fullest sense.

14. The Divine element in the child springs from the depths of his being. It is straightway surrounded by the impurities of the world. Like the most delicate plant in the world, it requires warmth, nourishment, protective and indulgent patience, all of which it finds in the protection and love of parents. Under such influences the innocent child grows and matures to the full expression of love and power, and stands before his parents as the loving and active reflection of themselves; then, when your child feels, wishes, and acts as you, the child of God, feel, wish, and act, father and mother, how great is then your power!

15. It is a Divine power to be able to develop in your child everything which is noble and good, and to bring him to maturity by the sacred virtues of patience and care. To guide wisely and to keep within limits our sensory nature, which, although an essential element in our development, may easily become overpowerful and destructive, also requires the best that is in us. With such power you may achieve the highest object of an ideal education; you will be able to maintain your child's innocence without losing his love or undermining his childlike frankness. The more firmly your love resists his tendency to error and corruption, the more will you win what is most sacred in his confidence, and knit his heart more closely to yourself.

By your action, when the struggle of his sensuous nature with his better self began, you have already awakened in him a sense that your firmness and your tenderness have one and the same aim, and he himself is roused to resist and to unite his powers with yours for his own improvement.

16. An education based upon an ideal family life, upon the power of the father and mother, steadily pursuing its beautiful course, without swerving to the right or to the left, victoriously overcoming every obstacle in the narrow but only way which leads their child to the higher life—I find myself in a world where such parents are hardly to be found.

17. The world, abandoned as it is to sensual and selfish living, lays hold of men with oppressive power, and wages constant war against their higher nature and against a life of truth and love. Fathers and mothers are also of this world. There are in them, in the limitations and the luxuries of their circumstances, in the formal insincerities of civic life and in the false refinement which threaten more and more the real ennoblement of human nature—there are in all these things so many forces that confuse the mind, destroy the affections, stifle energy, and desecrate emotion, so many things which are in direct opposition to the higher nature upon which the

true education of the child depends, that one must not be surprised when men go astray in this matter. Indeed, one should rather wonder that the race has not quite gone under, but has continued to strive after inner improvement, and still recognizes love and activity in love as the only means of its advancement.

18. This striving and this recognition of the only true basis of the education of our race cannot be lost. Nature herself would first have to be destroyed. The best men, whether they occupy thrones or live in cottages, will always, and under all circumstances, recognize their own parental feelings as their noblest and greatest. It is with such feelings that whatever is good in education will always be associated, however the corruption of the world may limit or degrade it. Such corruption, of course, would prevent the general enjoyment of this blessing, and would limit, confuse, and misdirect individual efforts to attain it in the home life.

## SIXTH LETTER

### EDUCATIONAL VALUE OF OTHER SOCIAL RELATIONSHIPS

1. NEXT to the parents and the relations which exist between them and the child, his relations with other human beings constitute the most important and admirable factors which have been given for the development of his affections and his activity.

His relations with men are far-reaching and many-sided from the cradle upwards, and the points of contact increase daily. He is at once the child of his parents, and brother to his brothers and sisters. He is related to those who are related to him ; he is their neighbours' child to those who are neighbours of his parents ; he is a member of the town or village community in which his parents live.

2. The child, however, is not conscious of these relations until long after they have begun to influence him. These relations impress him differently at different stages of his development. At first he is only conscious of those persons around him who satisfy his wants. This is a law of Nature. The needs of the infant and the nature of his surroundings render this point of view imperative. His helplessness demands assistance from every side. Someone must come and give it to him. Father and mother, and whoever else goes to his cradle, only go to minister to him. Whoever goes near him occupies himself with him, waits upon him, helps and amuses him.

Thus, at this period the child learns to recognize those about him as people to gladden, help and wait upon him. He knows no other connection with the human race but this.

3. However, this limited childish view cannot last. The causes themselves are transitory, and he must learn to know men and the relations in which he stands to them from other points of view. He must consider them seriously ; he must learn to know what he is to hope, expect, and fear, at their hands.

Nature is never one-sided ; she never places restrictions in the way of truth. She quietens the helpless child like a good mother by his first notion of his relations to others ; then she works like a wise father to fashion and strengthen him, by broadening this idea that he may make good use of it. Gradually the child learns to distinguish men apart from the relations which characterized them in his infantile helplessness.

4. If, so far, he has only recognized James and John as persons who waited upon him, helped him, and played with him, he now gradually begins to distinguish James as his father's brother and John as the latter's servant. He begins to distinguish between the old lady whom mother and father honour as grandmother, and the old neighbour who comes to them for help and comfort. He begins to distinguish between the men whom his parents greet with smiles, and people at the sight of whom they frown and step aside. The existence and actions of men

thus appear to him more and more to disassociate themselves from the attention and services which were showered upon him from every side. He sees now that even his mother is not in the world solely for his sake, and that she is often prevented from attending to him. The more he sees people, the more he notices that their relations to him are unfamiliar, and the more he sees them in such relations, the more unfamiliar do they themselves appear. The circle of those who are not strange to him becomes daily smaller in proportion to those who are. As in the beginning he saw everybody around him occupied in helping and amusing him, he now sees all human beings much oftener occupied with other things. He sees men who have no desire to pay any attention to him, and others who from their own infirmities cannot attend to him—who, on the contrary, accept help and offers of assistance from him when he can give it to them ; in short, he soon realizes what a scramble life really is.

He himself now gradually ceases to require the attention without which he formerly could not exist, much less be happy. What formerly had to be brought to him he can now get for himself. He likes being able to help himself. He sees everybody doing their utmost to help themselves. His newly-awakened understanding forcibly incites him to self-help. As his power grows, his first idea of men's relations to him die away. At the same time he receives powerful and appropriate stimuli towards affection and activity in love, which gave him so much pleasure in the innocence of his early years.

5. His parents need no longer smile upon him or carry him about in order to kindle in his eyes and on his cheeks the expression of love. It lights up his face when he takes his younger sister in his arms and smiles at her as his mother used to smile at him. The child to whom formerly his parents were everything is now becoming a child who is something to his parents, and who daily becomes more to them as he renders affectionate service.

As he finds ever-widening scope for his affectionate activity, self-reliance gradually matures. He becomes consciously independent of father and mother in his inner and outer life. His principles grow clearer, and his sphere of action is constantly growing larger.

6. When he has realized the charm of such power and of such affection, it grows in two ways : Firstly, through his native human sympathies, and, secondly, through the outward relations of civic life. By these means he rises from the innocent irresponsibilities of infancy to the highest and most complex position which the turmoil of life can offer. In his extended responsibilities he is actuated by the same love which in his infancy he manifested in the narrower sphere of domestic life. The purity of the powers which were developed by his early training leads him to assume the character of brother or sister in the larger family whose father is God, with the same loftiness of mind and the same humanity he showed as the child at home.

7. The one desire of his heart and mind is to share in everything that is good and noble in this great family of God. This is his one aim and his one joy. His early home training has fitted him for the conception of the Fatherhood of God. His idea of human parenthood is also widened. Now, as the brother of all men and as father of the poor, his new position constantly renews his affections and increases his power of action. It is a new aid to his own further development.


## SEVENTH LETTER

### EDUCATIONAL VALUE OF INTERCOURSE WITH NATURE

1. NEXT must be added the whole realm of Nature, everything animate and inanimate, everything which appeals to the child's senses, as the third great factor in the process we are describing.

2. Just as the human race at first appears to the child to exist for the sole purpose of serving and helping him,

so everything else in his environment at first only affects him in so far as it bears upon the satisfaction of his wants. Gradually he rises from this limited initial point of view to one which is independent of his needs and his desires. All the objects in the world must appear to him in a light which is in agreement with their own nature and with their conduct under other and unfamiliar conditions. Bread as stilling his hunger, water as quenching his thirst, the pear, the grape, the cherry, as merely pleasing his palate—all have a great interest for the child before it occurs to him that bread must be prepared from vegetable products, that water belongs to the fluids of the earth, and pears, cherries, and grapes, are really the seed-vessels of trees and shrubs. His good mother wraps him up in linen before she shows him the growing hemp and flax ; his shoes are familiar to him before he knows that they come from the skin of an animal. He sleeps under the woollen coverlet before he realizes that it is made of wool which is shorn from the back of the sheep.

3. This state, however, like the former, does not and cannot last long. As it was with men, so other objects soon have a significance beyond that of merely satisfying his wants and furnishing enjoyment.

He now sees wool, having nothing to do with his coverlet, on the back of the sheep ; he sees flax, corn, and leather, which have no connection with the shirt he wears, the bread he eats, or the shoe in which he walks, or even with his mother who brought these things to his notice. In this way the world discloses ever-broadening phases. All objects show themselves more in their true nature and in less familiar aspects.

4. He now drops from his mother's arms, in which his helplessness had found the necessary protection, into the unfathomable sea of the world, where his mother has no control. Here he is affected by a thousand new objects, in which his interest ever grows. The sheep, the cock, the dove, and every living object, now gladden the child. His confidence in the life that surrounds him increases, he is happy in this growing confidence, and when he

places some beloved and trusted pet upon his mother's lap he is filled with joy.   He puts a titbit from his supper for the dove to peck at, he searches in the meadow for weeds and leaves which the sheep likes to eat.   The loving-hearted boy has hardly outgrown his infancy when his greatest delight is to go with father and the stable-boy to the stable or to the meadow, to the cows or to the horses.   When the fields are being ploughed or the cattle watered and fed, the child always wants to be there, and would like to help.

5. But the kindly mystery that shrouds these first impressions, and by reason of which the child pictures the world as full of happy beings, gradually melts away.   The child sees that the sheep cowers and trembles when the warm wool is shorn from his back, that the ox is at the plough under compulsion.   It exerts itself because his father holds it with a firm hand ; his strength compels the ox to do what he wants.   He sees his mother take away the calf from the cow that she may have more milk for her household.

He sees the beautiful rose carrying thorns, he sees the waste ground covered with thistles and useless growth, he sees his father coming home from the field tired and bathed in perspiration, he sees that the field does not yield what is wanted without exhausting effort.

6. Experience teaches him still more.   She shows him creatures who, instead of being a source of joy to their fellows, threaten them with death and destruction, and occasion great misery.   He sees his beloved pigeon seized by a hawk and carried away to die ; he sees the cruel cat playing with the mouse in its death-agony ; he sees the pigeon-cote broken into by martens, and the poultry-shed by foxes ; he sees his faithful and apparently innocent dog chasing the poor hare and the graceful roe to its death ; he sees him driving the sheep and the calf to the slaughter-house, and terrifying them by his bark and his bite ; he sees the dog tracking out the poor bird in its nest, and driving it away from its brood for the gun and the snare of the hunter.

7. This experience, however, does not kill the affection of the child who has enjoyed maternal love and human sympathy. On the contrary, the cruel power which the stronger creature exercises over the weaker always awakens in him an unspoken but strong feeling that man must not be like these animals. He must not take advantage of the weakness of his fellow-men ; he must not behave with them as the sparrow-hawk behaves with the dove, the cat with the mouse, the dog with the hare, the sheep, and the bird. The affectionate child cries when he sees his pet dove or his pet lamb dead before his eyes : " Oh, my dove !" " Oh, my little lamb !" With tears in his eyes he clasps his father's hand, and his father takes measures to protect the dovecote against the hawk and the poultry-shed against the fox.

8. Such a child, in whose heart noble human feelings have been deeply planted by his parents, is of himself inclined to be good and gentle, and every impression of Nature, the sight of the great works of God, the sky, and the earth, tends to make him still more gentle. He cannot look upon the splendour of the setting and the rising sun, or that of the moon and the stars, without joy. The flowers and the tree laden with fruit delight him. The better a man is, the more softening and ennobling the influences of mother-love and human kindness which he has enjoyed, so much the more is his love and activity awakened by all the beauties and blessings of Nature.

9. But inanimate Nature does not always appear to men in beautiful, beneficent form. The river which waters his meadows overflows its banks at times ; it destroys his fields, washes away the cottages on its banks, and carries men and cattle to untimely ends. The fire, without which you could not cook, and which makes your sitting-room comfortable when the frost is on the ground —this beneficent fire ravages towns and villages. The water from heaven, without which neither grass nor corn, vines nor wood, could grow, sometimes falls in heavy hail-storms on the growing corn, destroys all hopes of harvest, and deprives the unfortunate family for a whole year of

the small provision for which the father had toiled with the sweat of his brow.

10. But even when Nature acts thus (and even more than when she is kinder), she awakens the child's disposition to love and action, if he has enjoyed the gentle and ennobling influence of a mother's care and the love of other children. Poverty loosens the tears of love. Even he who is usually apathetic is driven to love by poverty.

The rich child weeps when the poor about him are in want, even if his father is a hard man or if he himself is naturally selfish. He hurries away from the sight of misery to ask his mother for clothes for the naked and food for the hungry. Boys and young men, and even the tottering old man, hasten to help their neighbour when his house is burning ; and if they cannot save it, they bring gifts to help the sufferer to build another house.

But the greater the privation, the more brightly does the Divine flame burn in the bosom of the man who has been nurtured in love, and at such moments he is roused to mighty effort on his own behalf.

The man whose field has been destroyed by the floods works like a slave with his wife and children to make good the loss, and the poor widow who has been deprived of her treasured provision for a year by a dreadful storm wears herself out with her spinning so that her babe may not starve, and that the rest of her children may be fed and clothed as they would have been if the terrible hail had not destroyed her hard-won store.

Thus we see that inanimate Nature, not only in its beautiful and beneficent aspects, but even as a force of destruction, awakens love, and the activity engendered by love, in the hearts of those who were nurtured by motherly care and human sympathy, and are therefore receptive to the emotions of love.

11. It would take too long to follow up the subject of the impression made upon the child by its environment. I will therefore now retrace my steps, and, in order to throw more light upon what has been said, by describing the opposite picture, will turn my attention to the con-

sequences which ensue in those cases when the child has not received the first and most natural boon which is the true source of a happy and contented life.

12. Consider the child who lacks motherly care and human kindness, whose parents fail in their most sacred duty. Under the malign influence of the world, the mother neglects her child that she may be a popular figure and shine in fashionable circles in large towns or among the foolish women of some provincial or country town. The country's misfortune and the poverty of thousands are the opportunity of the usurer. Even the father drags away the mother from the infant that he may lose none of the intoxicating pleasures of the world ; and when he has effectually choked up the only true source of welfare for his babe, he runs round distractedly to find outside and inefficient sources of education. He would replace father and mother by teachers, whose chief fault is that they have not the sacred feelings of parenthood, nor have they the trained power of parents. Indeed, this power is hardly to be found ; its purity in a stranger is the rarest thing in the world. And failing this, if parents engage those who act only as substitutes for the real parents, then there is no longer any hope of the child being brought up in the atmosphere of love and in its resultant activity. The child is surrounded by unreality and vanity from his cradle upwards.

Even if the nurse does not pinch him in her rage, she stands by the window taking the air, heedless of the cries of her charge, chafing under the burden laid upon her. So the tutor, even if he is a conscientious man, has certainly not sufficient time in a house where he was only engaged so that everyone excepting himself might leave the children and live a worldly life.

13. The consequences of such conditions upon the training of the child are disastrous. Since the original foundations of his culture are wanting in his whole environment, the child finds no thread by which he can bring his higher and nobler feelings into his barren life. It is his parents' fault that he develops a loveless nature. His lovelessness

deepens every day, and he begins to regard his fellow-creatures as a source of alarm and annoyance. Their insincerity, their underhand dealing, their trumpery display, their hypocrisy, make him hard and selfish. He has neither nobility nor gentleness in him. If his dove is seized by the hawk, and his lamb torn to pieces by the wolf, he does not take his father's hand and ask him to repair the dovecote and the poultry-shed, so that similar misfortunes may not happen again to their occupants. On the contrary, he begins to feel pleasure at the agony and suffering of his fellow-beings, and his delight in watching the dog, the fox, the hawk, and the marten, pursuing their prey, makes him indifferent to human life. He loses all sympathy for the weak struggling against the strong ; he begins to feel it is inevitable that the weak should be humbled and downtrodden.

With time these dark thoughts lead to a complete hardening of heart. If the poor man dies in the struggle, what cares the loveless man ? Why is the poor man such a worm ? Why can he offer no resistance to the man who walks over him ? And how can the hawk help his palate thirsting for blood ?

14. The whole world appears in a brutish guise to the child whose love has not been awakened by his parents. Such a child can never really love, though he may counterfeit it.

But it is the essence of love that is human ; only those who are not filled with its power venture to counterfeit it. This counterfeit leads to empty caresses. Wherever lovelessness has the semblance of Shame, she wraps herself in the mantle of this vanity. It is her peculiar garment. She seldom dares to appear in her own nakedness.

From the miserable woman, who closes the door upon her neighbours and repels the unhappy orphan children in her immediate environment, but showers her affections upon some pet, to the princess who at supper persuades her lord and master to offer his kingdom to her favourite, as the other woman would give her lapdog a titbit, the types of loveless caresses are many and diverse.

Among such people noble and worthy men are despised ; they are ridiculed by their inferiors. Wherever favourites creep in, love disappears. True love avoids the falseness of favourites, and hates their deception.

15. Neither animate nor inanimate Nature, neither heaven nor earth, will have an ennobling and refining influence on the child of the mother who, for the sake of her finery, forgets everything else, including her own child.

Heaven and earth awaken no more love in him than they do in his mother, who values that portion of the earth which she owns, not for the sake of the good it might do to others, but for the influence it actually has on the empty vanities of her life. To such people every aspect of Nature is distorted and corrupt.

16. If the pure and loving wife values the lamb that trustingly lays its head next to her child's on her lap, because she thinks of the wool with which by her industry she will clothe her child ; if she values her cow because she can nourish her dear ones every day with its milk ; if her husband cultivates the field in the sweat of his brow in order to provide the necessities of life for himself and his family, and with his produce help those who have neither cow nor sheep nor field ; if his strength is doubled by love, and he surpasses himself in the cultivation of the soil—none of these things bring satisfaction to the man and woman of the world. The glory of the field and of the vine awakens no joy in their hearts because the harvest will bring bread to the hungry, and refreshment to the weary, the child-bearing, and the dying. They rejoice only because the good harvest means that they may revel and glitter in the pomp of its produce.

17. The man is ever in danger of falling into this state who has not learned the promptings of love. His fellow-men will not teach him. Animate Nature is dead to him, and inanimate Nature has no power over him. God's world must be unsatisfying to such a man. He would like to have a world specially fitted up for himself and the companion of his fortunes, that they might juggle and struggle through life without let or hindrance.

But our world is not like that.   By the will of God, and in conformity with the characteristic of human nature, its well-being depends on other foundations than those which such a corrupt heart can grasp, suspect, or even believe.   For every prosperous man there are a thousand unfortunate.   It follows that they must have a thousand claims upon the one.   It is true the selfish heart is always too small for the claims of the thousand, however just these claims may be.   What a miserable world it is to the selfish man !   The sight of the most sublime and mag-n'ficent objects of Nature do not touch him.   If the sun could rise for him alone, and if he could ride in its chariot over the earth, destroying with the flames from its wheels all who would not worship him, then he would love the sun.   He would love the moon and the stars if he could shut them up in his tent, and, alone with them, how glorious his slumbers would be !

## EIGHTH LETTER

1. ALTHOUGH, speaking generally, men enjoy in more or less degree the blessings of maternal care, of human sympathy, and of intercourse with Nature, yet wrinkled foreheads and burdensome lives abound.

2. This is due to two causes : Children are too much stimulated by sensory pleasures, and their parents and friends are occupied more with those things than with deeds of love.   So even the external aspects of Nature have an unhappy influence upon them.

3. One might almost say that whoever would train a child in love must take him from his parents and his customary surroundings, and lead him to the innermost sanctuary of his being, there to find a genuine foundation for future love and power.

4. All good parents feel their own inadequacy and the inadequacy of their circumstances for a satisfactory education of their child.   They feel their own inferiority in everything which furthers the sure realization of their

aims.  They all feel that their tendencies and weaknesses are a hindrance to its realization.  They feel the evil influences of the environment which threaten to overpower the work of love.

This is necessarily so.  No mother who sincerely thinks of her child can fail to realize that the higher nature is endangered by man's corruption, and that all the stimuli of natural beauty can, for like reasons, have no formative effect.  The better the mother and the wiser the father, the more are they grieved and depressed at this corruption, and the more are they dissatisfied with their own power and their own effort against it.  The better and wiser they are, the more are they compelled to appeal for their child's sake to the feeling of a higher love and a higher power than their own.

5. The good which is in them raises them above the limits of all human good.  Only in God do they find satisfaction for all the good and all the power which they seek for their child.

## Belief in God is Essential.

6. The reality of their own love and their own power leads them to believe in God, and belief in God makes in its turn that love and that power purer and stronger.  The noblest mother believes in God with a purer and stronger faith through her child.  She sees that this faith makes her more to him than otherwise she could be.  Her efforts for her child increase as she separates herself from the world, and submits the success of her efforts to her God and Father, as she resigns herself to Him and directs her child above all things to this belief in God.  This belief is the bond of love and power which she seeks for her child, and by this belief her influence on the welfare of her child is increased.  As her love towards God is reflected in her child, and develops into assurance of His love and His power as he sees it in her, so his receptiveness for all good grows correspondingly.

7. The purer the glances which the mother casts round

the world, the more incontrovertibly will she realize how thousands of men are cared for who are too weak to look after themselves.  The purer her glance is, the more will she feel the presence and reality of the everlasting hand which guides her.

Each day man's destiny appears to her to depend more upon God, just as the fate of the child depends upon its mother.

8. The nobler she is, the more irresistibly is she impelled to place the welfare of the child in higher hands than her own ; the nobler she is, the more irresistibly is she impelled to desire for her child a guide, a Father who can never err or fail him in his need, whom the grave cannot snatch from him and the world cannot corrupt. She finds, in this devotion to God, the necessary supplement to the means at her own disposal and to those of the world for the child's guidance as planned by her unselfish mother-love.

9. By her faith in God these means themselves become holy, by this faith she finds herself more and more willing to utilize them more forcibly for her child, she finds in it a saving counter-weight to the weakness of her nature, and by it the world, with all its deception and misery, becomes a higher world in which, as she becomes freer, more grateful, and more loving, she receives more power to develop everything that is noble and good in the child.

And the child who by his mother's side unfolds his tendencies, his impressions and powers ; the child whom she sees praying to a Heavenly Father, who never deserts those who cling to Him and seek His love ; the child who sees his mother for the sake of her Heavenly Father loving and serving her fellow-men, sacrificing herself for them, and seeking and finding her only happiness in this patience, in this love, and in this self-sacrifice—such a child must fall on his knees and pray at his mother's side.

10. The innocence of his nature makes his attitude towards his Heavenly Father resemble that of his mother.

This first recognition of a supernatural union of human

nature with that of a loving, helping Divine Being must elevate all the child's feelings. He will love his father and mother more, he will be more grateful to them and have a firmer trust in them, if he believes in a God who is the Father of his father and of all other fathers, as well as of all other children.

He will of necessity love more purely every creature of his own species in whom he recognizes a child of his God and Father ; he will offer him his hand with nobler feelings and with higher motives.

All Nature will be holier to him than before, because it reveals the love and power of his God and Father.

He will find his God and Father in the shining sun, in the dripping cloud, in the growing corn, in the depth of the valley and in the height of the mountains ; he will prize more highly and employ more wisely the sun and the rain, and the fruits of the valley and of the mountains, than if he did not know God.

Like his mother, he will raise himself to such a height that even misfortune and suffering do not awaken resentment in his nature, but on the contrary he will profit by them, and by means of them his love, his trust, and his gratitude will be refined and upheld.

# APPENDIX III.

## OF SCHOOLMASTERS.

IF we examine the subject of national education, and consider first of all the institutions which are actually in existence for the education of the poor, such as schools, orphan asylums, industrial schools, etc., the ordinary schools are obviously the first, the most general, and the most far-reaching in their influence. Unquestionably, they may determine the failure or the success of a man's future life.

If the schoolmaster is a man with the spirit of love, of wisdom, of purity ; a man who is fitted for his calling,

and who enjoys the confidence of young and old ; a man
who esteems love, order, and self-control, as higher and
more desirable than actual knowledge and learning ; a
man who, with penetrating foresight, perceives what sort
of man or woman the child is likely to develop into, and
guides his school-days with that end in view, he will
become in the true sense of the word a father to the
village, he will in this way take the place of the best
father and the best mother, taking up the education of
the child when the parents can do no more.   Such a man
can and will improve the love of a whole village, and
train the powers and capacities, the mode of thought and
behaviour, of the youth in such a way as to maintain and
strengthen the holiest and best elements in the life and
thought of their forefathers conformable to the requirements of our times, thereby establishing the welfare of
the village for years to come.

If, on the other hand, the schoolmaster is a vain, selfish,
bumptious pedant and a dreamy bookworm, a presumptuous expounder of mysteries too deep to be explained, a
man ill-educated for his profession, who could earn his
bread in no other way but by vain mouthings, and who
prides himself upon the fact, despising the peasant at the
plough, although he is more exacting in the matter of
food, drink, and leisure, than the richest peasant, he is an
agent of evil rather than of good in the village, an agent
of grievous, far-reaching evil.   Even if the children learn
to speak and read and write in a satisfactory manner, and
give the latest answers to a thousand questions, the schoolmaster's influence is still undoubtedly injurious.   He is
incapable of taking the father's place and of linking his
own teaching to the early training of the good home, but
rather undermines and obscures by his life and action all
the good habits and principles which the child has already
acquired, and by his insincerity destroys the most sacred
ties of Nature.

The parents may be modest, skilful, and upright,
but the children become thoughtless, stupid, and arrogant, like their schoolmaster.   They become    feeble,

miserable, covetous creatures, such as he is, and the moral tone of the village is degraded for many years by his influence. Everything bad in the village finds fertile soil in the school, and yields thirty-, sixty-, or a hundred-fold increase. Such a choice of schoolmaster brings with it all the evils of idolatry. Nature, strong and jealous as the God of Israel, visits such errors on the part of the fathers unto the third and fourth generation of their children. . . .

However much wisdom and zeal are expended upon the choice of schoolmasters, examinations, and school organization, however much the scholars are stimulated by rewards and class places towards love of their school and of learning, if there is no one who, as schoolmaster, can, as far as is possible, take the place of the parents ; if there is no opportunity for encouraging and training a young man to do this ; if there is even no one in whose opinion it would be a good thing to encourage and train a young man to do this, the ideal of a suitable training for the children of the poor is not reached. On the contrary, all their undesirable qualities are nourished and forced like plants in a hothouse, as if their future success depended upon their speedy cultivation.

One thing is missing—namely, good schoolmasters ; and where these are lacking, the whole of educational activity is dust in the eyes of a man who cannot see what he needs. Consequently, he who is anxious that the poor should have the best type of schools must first of all secure an adequate supply of men who are able and fitted to train children with insight and love in the wisdom of life, and make them vigorous and disciplined members of the station in life to which they belong.

Such men do not fall from the clouds ; they do not come like snow or rain. No calling in life can be more important, but none is more difficult. Men of great intelligence and kindness of heart are only endowed by Nature with aptitudes for teaching, and in this, as in every other calling, these special aptitudes must be stimulated, developed, trained.

At present individuals spend infinitely more time in insuring that their sons have an adequate technical or professional training than princes or nations devote to the training of men for what is undoubtedly the most important and most difficult calling. So long as this is the case, popular education is inadequately provided for, and it is difficult to imagine that their schools can ever become what they should be—namely, instruments for supplying the advantages of home training, for helping the poor in their infirmities, and for remedying their deficiencies. A state which possessed such schools would ennoble human nature in every station of life. But where is the state which has them, or is making any attempt to possess them? We cannot conceal from ourselves the fact that no state has made any provision for this pressing need. We must, however, also admit that it is a difficult matter, and the initial step is precarious.

The training of good schoolmasters presupposes the existence of men of a different type from that which our teachers are striving to make of their scholars, and this different type appears at a first glance not to exist. They are lacking, however, only because those who are looking for them have neither the intelligence nor the character which is necessary for the search. There is nothing good on earth which does not lose the appearance of value when men speak slightingly of it and neglect it, but, in the words of Jesus Christ, " Those who seek shall find." No man has yet sought anything lofty and holy without inspiring others with his enthusiasm, and yet you say that it is impossible to find a man whose love for his country is so great that he is willing to share the heavy burdens of the poor ! Seek for him, and you will find him, but you yourself must be willing to help. Then you need have no fear that you will fail to find men in every station and condition of life who are filled with a like enthusiasm and love for human nature, men who are willing and fitted to become school-teachers of such a kind as the world has need. Inspire your country to join in the search, and teachers will not only be found, they will be supported, esteemed, beloved, and employed. When this is done, the apparently insurmountable difficulties of national education will all be overcome.

I must add one thing. This movement must not come from schoolmasters themselves. It must be quite independent of them, and must have its origin in the goodwill of the nation itself and in the general tendency of its aspirations. If this is not so, the number of men capable of being trained as teachers may be ample, but the nation is not interested in them ; they will be misjudged and solitary. The fact that they are more noble and disinterested than those who misjudge them only makes their position more difficult. Their work becomes ineffective, and they lose courage.

Where the opposite is the case, if men of influence and worth would seek out youths to be trained as teachers, and give them their support and assistance, they would revolutionize the world. Love would smooth away difficulties, the doings of teachers would be a matter of general interest, doubts would disappear. Faith in human nature would revive. Fathers and mothers would associate themselves with the teachers, and the sacred ties of human fellowship would be more firmly knit together. Children would become the joy of their parents, and parents the friends of their children. The poor would have the Gospel preached to them as they have not had it before. God would be honoured in heaven, and there would be peace upon earth.

# IV.—"ADDRESS TO MY HOUSE, 1818."

*[Pestalozzi was in the habit of addressing his school on all festival occasions. Some of these addresses have been preserved, and the one here translated is perhaps the most interesting. Its insistence upon the freedom of the human will, and the need for experimental schools and training colleges, are particularly noteworthy.]*

## POPULAR INDIFFERENCE TO EDUCATION.

**3.** I AM quite convinced that our part of the world is in such darkness concerning what has actually been accomplished in the investigation of education methods, and concerning the true cause of poverty, as neither the sunlight of truth nor the quiet moonlight of gentle love can pierce and light up. I know that what I have to say now will be variously misunderstood, but that cannot be helped, for the darkness of which I complain has become an element in which we live, move, and have our being. I only propose to speak of two things : popular education and the causes of poverty ; and I say again that these times of ruinous ostentation are not propitious to the cause I stand for—the sound treatment of these two problems— although, in spite of this darkness, there are many things we see more clearly and treat with more understanding. Generally speaking, we neglect what concerns man's higher nature. So true is this, that we have no idea of the extent of our present errors. The opinions, preconceptions, desires, and customs, which are current, affect the mental attitudes of rich and poor alike. To remove

them would mean a revolution of thought.    How can it
be brought about ?    Who will speak and who will listen ?
Indifference is too widespread.    We ourselves are affected.
We have lost much of our inspiration.    As for me, I am
dead to my time ; this world is mine no more.    I dream
dreams of education—of popular education, of education
of men, of the education of the poor—which are only
possible in a simpler world.    Yet I give myself up to my
dream ; I dream with the utmost enthusiasm.    The better
education of which I dream reminds me of a tree planted
by the riverside.    What is that tree ?    Where has it
sprung from, with its roots, trunk, branches, twigs, and
fruits ?    You plant a tiny seed in the ground ; in that
seed lies the whole nature of the tree.

### ANALOGY OF THE DEVELOPMENT OF THE TREE.

" God is its Father,
God its Creator ;
Mighty is God
In the seed of the tree.
The hand of man
Places it as God's seed
In the gentle earth ;
He places it as God's seed
In the land of God,
In the dear land of his God."

4. The seed is the spirit of the tree, which it produces
through its own power.    Watch how it unfolds out of
the mother earth.    Already before you can see it, before
it breaks through the earth, it has struck its roots.    As
the inner life of the seed unfolds, its external covering
disappears.    The seed decays when it germinates.    It
disappears as it develops.    Its life has passed over into
the roots.    It has become a root.    The power of the seed
has become the power of the root.    We have now the root
of the tree.    The tree to its outermost twig on which

hangs the fruit, has sprung from its roots. Its whole
being is nothing more than an unbroken extension of
elements, which were already in its roots. . . .

## ULTIMATE UNITY AMIDST DIVERSITY OF PARTS.

Observe all these parts of the tree. In spite of their
number, there is no confusion ; each is independent and
clearly marked off from the others. Each has developed
after its own laws, but has never lost its connection with
the tree as a whole ; it is this unity which enables the
tree to fulfil its destiny. The growth of the tree is like
that of man. Even before the child is born, the germs
of future capacity are all there. Man's powers continue
to develop through his whole life, just as is the case with
the tree. His capacities are distinct from, and independent
of, one another. But just as the separate parts of a tree
through the unseen spirit of its organic life work together
in divinely ordered unity to fulfil the common function,
the production of fruit, so it is with man. His inner
spirit, moved by Divine love, brings unity into his life.
His varied powers work together to a common end—
manhood, the inner nature of which is not dependent
upon the body. Men who have sprung from God were
made in God's image to become perfect as their Father
in heaven is perfect. It is the soul which is effective
in this case ; the body is useless. But man's soul is not
revealed in any one of his powers ; indeed, what we call
" capacity " does not reveal it at all ; it is neither in his
hand nor in his brain. The unifying centre of man's
nature, the power that is peculiar to and characteristic
of man, is his faith and his love. They bring into holy
union his powers of knowing and doing, of wisdom and
action ; they make him really human.

Man's capacity for faith and love is to him, from
the point of view of his education, just what the roots
are to the growth of the tree. By means of the root the
tree draws nourishment from the earth for all its parts.
Men must see that the roots of their own high nature

preserve a like power.  They can see how the root makes
the tree grow when the ground is soft and moist and the
sun is warm, until finally the tree stands perfect in its
kind, a sublime work of God, a noble example of His
creative activity in the world of plants.  But consider,
again, the tree as a whole : it would die if the root should
dry up in barren, stony ground ; and the same thing
would happen if it were placed in a swamp or in an over-
manured soil, its powers of absorption and assimilation
being overtaxed.

5. Such are the sources and conditions of the tree's
organic life and death.  Now look at yourself, and how
your powers have attained to life, and notice, too, what
it is that brings you with all your powers to decay and
death.  Ask yourself wherein you are like, and wherein
you are unlike, that tree and its organic nature.

### The Tree is unable to help itself—Man can.

6. Your powers, like those of the tree, are independent
of each other ; but just as the " soul " of the tree combines
its various powers in the common purpose of bringing
forth fruit, so is it with you.  Each of your powers has
its separate existence, each is controlled by its own laws,
yet all are united by an inner human spirit to the attainment of the common human aim.  As the organic spirit
which is in the root of the tree rapidly absorbs nourishment from the mother earth for all parts of the tree, or
is rapidly dried up or is poisoned at this same source, so
also has the human organism in its inmost parts a root
in which the spirit of its whole being dwells.  Through
it the forces of human life are absorbed from the body
itself, and from the environment.  From the same sources
and through the same agency come the influences which
wither and poison all that is truly human in us.  But
the human organism differs from inanimate objects ;
it differs, too, from animals and plants ; the human
organism is a sensory framework in which a Divine being
lives.  The true source of human life, of the good and

evil that is absorbed from his sensory self and his sensory environment, is not in any physical sense attached to his body ; it is superior to all physical bonds, it is free. It utilizes all the forces of physical growth which are in the body, as they are in a plant, with the skill of the gardener, who, when the soil about the tree is hard and dry, waters and moistens it, though, if he would, he might leave it unwatered, to its consequent destruction. Similarly, when the tree is in a swamp, the gardener drains the swamp and regulates the moisture, or leaves the tree to die, whichever he wishes. The tree is subject to the influences of inanimate Nature, against which its vital powers can offer no resistance, whereas the higher spirit which dwells in man is free to allow his sensory nature and sensory environment to bring about his ruin, or to work against and overcome them.

## Man's Will is Free.

7. Man's sensory nature, his hereditary tendencies, the appeals which his worldly environment make upon him, stand to his real nature, Divine as it is, in the same relation as the hard earth, the rocks, the stones, the burning sand, and the quagmire, stand to the roots of the tree which they dry up and poison. But the tree is at the mercy of these external influences, even though they threaten its existence, whilst the higher nature of man, which lends unity and singleness of purpose to his varied activities, is free. Through the voice of conscience all men hear God's message concerning what is good and what is evil. God is in them, and calls them through faith, love, truth, and right, to be at one with themselves, and so to be at one with God. They can hear this voice of God within them, and continue to be free. They can also shut out that voice ; they may close their ears. They can deny freedom to their own will, and become the slave of sensuous and worldly pleasures. They can cast love, truth, faith, and right, away. They can live like animals, and say to themselves and to all who approach them :

" This and this do not please me." They can live at strife
with themselves and with their race, and so come to
regard the things that are of Divine and human worth as
of less importance than physical prowess.

8. Let men examine themselves and find out how far
they are at peace with themselves and with their fellows.
Let them consider how they might have been friendly to
faith, to love, to truth, to light, at peace with God and
at peace with man, and how far circumstances have forced
them in opposition to these things.  Look at the men
around you, and at yourself more closely ; follow in your
minds the course of man's development.  He grows, he
is trained and educated.  Inner forces bring about his
growth.  His training comes from the chance circumstances
that arise in dealing with things about him ; his education
is dependent on the methods and purposes of his fellows.
Man's physical growth is God's business ; it follows
eternal law.  Man's training is casual and dependent on
the changing circumstances of his position.  His education is moral ; it is a product of the freedom of the human
will in so far as that can influence the unfolding of power
and capacity.

## Man a Threefold Product.

9. From the point of view of the mere growth of these
powers and capacities, man is the product of the eternal
laws which he embodies.  From the point of view of his
training he is a result of chance circumstances and relations which influence the freedom and purity of his powers.
From the standpoint of his education he is a product of
the influences which moral forces have upon their freedom
and purity.  The law which governs man's growth is
in itself eternal and God-given ; the influences which
train him are in themselves sensory and environmental.
Educative influences are in themselves contingent and
free.

10. The training and education of men must be regarded as influences contributing to the inner tendency

of our powers towards development. We can control the influence of circumstances, and bring it into line with the laws that govern the growth of human powers. Educational effort should be brought into like agreement ; both education and training can, however, be set in contradiction thereto. It is only when they agree with those laws that man is trained and educated in the proper sense of the words. When they are not so, man's nature is distorted just as plants become distorted through external forces which disturb the physical organization of their parts. When education and training are not in harmony with the laws that govern the development of human powers, and with the original purity of the human will which unites them in a common purpose, we have external forces operating against the laws of human nature as destructively as like external forces acting upon a plant or animal. In men, by God's grace, practical capacity and knowledge are independent of each other, but they are eternally united in the exercise of will, which, through the freedom which faith and love bring to it, directs the development of all our powers of knowing and doing to the complete unfolding of our inner humanity, and subordinates the bodily appetites, with God's help, to the claims of faith and love, of truth and right. But unless God is in his soul, bodily appetites come into the ascendant. They undermine our humanity and deprive us of the blessings of faith and love.

11. Man's will is free, and it is his business to seek God, or, rather, the hand of God which paternal watchfulness reveals to him. But man can reject the hand of God, and say to himself : " I will for my part follow my bodily appetites, and not live amongst men as their brother nor as the child of God." . . . But as it is true that God speaks to man through his conscience, and leaves no man ignorant, so it is also true that the circumstances of one man are much more favourable than those of another for the development of faith and love, and of the knowledge of truth and right. One finds the way thereto ready before his eyes ; the other finds the way to unbelief,

to lovelessness, and to inhumanity artfully prepared. This difference, which exists between men exists also between different times, and we must not forget that the days in which we live are made dangerous to our race by the attractiveness of the temptation which it offers. . . .

Life is less simple and straightforward than it used to be. We have lost the old spirit of sincerity, and we hardly believe that it is recoverable. We praise our fathers with our mouths, whilst we stand in our hearts far from them ; our conduct is as unlike theirs as that of the Antipodeans is unlike ours. We have transformed their knowledge of the necessary and their ignorance of the useless into wide knowledge of the useless and ignorance of the necessary. Instead of their healthy and active mother-wit, we have the verbal forms of thought without the content—verbal expressions which suck the blood from good sense, as a marten does that of a dove when it gets hold of her neck. We know our neighbours, our poor relations, our fellow-citizens, no longer. Instead of that we read the newspapers, know the family history of kings, anecdotes of the court, of the theatre, of the metropolis, and change our political and religious opinions daily as we change our clothes ; we change from unbelief to the faith of a St. Francis, and back again to unbelief, just as we change our fashions. Our fathers trained their thought powers simply and powerfully ; few of them bothered about inquiries into higher and more difficult truths. We, on the other hand, do little to become equal to such a task through the training of thought powers ; but we learn to talk a great deal of lofty metaphysical stuff ; we scan the popular newspapers for results of the deepest investigations ; everybody is talking about them. Amongst our fathers, every good man tried at least to know one thing well—namely, his calling. This was a point of honour. Now men in high position are there by right of birth ; many are ashamed of their father's calling or position ; instead of mastering that, they criticize the work of other people, and manage their own business badly. The whole spirit that made citizenship strong has disappeared from our midst. We no longer even ask what we are, but what we have and what we know; we try to show off these things as if they were for sale....

13. All this cloud of artifice must be cleared away by educational reform, which is the same thing as looking after the poor. But what is the true type of education? It is like the art of the gardener under whose care a thousand trees blossom and grow. He contributes nothing to their actual growth; the principle of growth lies in the trees themselves. He plants and waters, but God gives the increase. It is not the gardener who opens the roots of the trees that they may draw food from the earth; it is not he who divides the pith from the wood and the wood from the bark, and thus helps forward the development of the separate parts, from the root right up to the outermost twig, and holds them together in the eternal unity of their being, thereby producing the final object of their existence—namely, the fruit. Of all this he does nothing; he only waters the dry earth that the roots may not strike it as a stone. He only drains away the standing water that the tree may not suffer. He only watches that no external force should injure the roots, the trunk, or the branches, of the tree, or disturb the order of Nature in which the several parts combine to insure the success of the tree. So with the educator: he imparts no single power to men. He gives neither life nor breath. He only watches lest any external force should injure or disturb. He takes care that development runs its course in accordance with its own laws. But he must recognize fully the peculiar constitution of man's mind, adapted as it is to unite man's various powers in the interest of his final mission. He knows that sound methods of popular education must agree with the eternal laws according to which these powers unfold, and that these methods must be sought in that which strengthens and purifies the moral and religious bonds of our powers. The moral, the intellectual, and practical powers of our nature must, as it were, spring out of themselves for themselves. Faith must have its source in faith, and not in the knowledge

of that which is believed. Thought must be produced through thought, and not through the knowledge of what is thought or of the laws of thought. Love, again, must develop from love, and not from talk about what is worthy to be loved and love itself. And, likewise, practical power must come from doing, and not from the thousand-fold talk about doing ; but human influence upon what we know and what we can do must be subordinate to the higher laws of our will. . . .

Amidst the ups and downs of my experience, I soon found that the problem of education is in essentials the same whatever the social position of the children, and that it does not consist in communicating special know-ledge or special dexterities, but in developing the funda-mental human powers (*which are, of course, the same for rich and poor*). Already in *Leonard and Gertrude*, I spoke of the need of more care for the education of the will—the centre point, as it were, of human capacity, and the source of his welfare. I tried to make people see that the home was the starting-point for all measures in this direction.

## The Progress of Pestalozzi's Work.

In my later years, and especially here in Yverdun, my friends and I have striven to reduce the training of individual power to psychological method, for this seemed to us the pedagogical problem of primary impor-tance, and we have given much time and energy to research in this direction. Nevertheless we recognize how much we are in arrear of the results we hoped to attain. Many others also have shared in our work . . . borrowing from it and extending it each in their own way. . . . May God's blessing rest on all those who see further in these beloved views of mine than I do myself! My honour becomes their honour, and I am grateful to them for helpful work in forwarding the cause.[1]    Never-

---

[1] Pestalozzi is thinking especially of his former colleague Niederer, who at times "philosophized" his master's ideas beyond recognition.

theless I should like to keep as my own what really belongs to me, that its spirit may not be lost in the improving process which another may apply to it. I would have it play its part along with the God-given powers of others in working towards the great end which will survive when all that is merely human in our efforts shall have disappeared for ever. . . . Yes, in gratitude to God for His not-always-understood gifts, I will continue to stand for the independence of what is true and right in my message. In spite of the wreckage of my home, I have not been entirely unsuccessful in my weak efforts. I venture to say that before this century closes it will see our work taken up by men who will express their indebtedness to it. I believe in its lasting qualities as strongly as ever. I have ceased to trouble about hindrances and doubts. I suffered much in this way, but I have been happier latterly. I have even ceased to trouble lest I should be a grey-headed old man before I could put a practical hand to the problem of popular education. I feel now that, had the opportunity arisen, I could not expect to have influenced the course of national education, or to have helped to raise the actual conditions and way of life of the people. I had not realized the moral destruction in the midst of which the poor live as convincingly as they must be realized if the causes of poverty, which are not in the poor themselves, are to be stopped—causes which so completely overwhelm all capacity for self-help that the poor man must go under. He is in no better case than the tiny hut which is overwhelmed by an avalanche from the mountain-tops, or is caught, undermined, and washed away, by a forest torrent. . . . I had not clearly grasped such means of helping the poor as lie in the poor themselves ; I did not feel it with the force and conviction that are necessary if the poor are to be awakened to a sense of the greatest and holiest of all means of helping them ; I could not then make that appear as the most powerful national instrument of their salvation. . . .

Circumstances have compelled me to look more deeply

into the process of development of human power and into the bases of sound popular education. Ripe ideas about the value of elementary education are absotutely necessary if we are to attain decided and satisfactory ideas about popular education and the intimately associated question of the education of the poor. Such ideas demand on the one side the development of each individual power in accordance with the laws of its own nature, and the absolute recognition of the freedom of the will as the centre of the system of human capacities. They demand the recognition of the duty of educating the will through faith and love to self-sacrificing devotion to the cause of truth and right—for the truth of God and the cause of men. Reason also lays it down that systematic knowledge must proceed from trained capacity, and not *vice versa*. The same principle holds good in physical education—first train general capacity, and then specific dexterities. This is God's order, and no timely educational process can neglect it. . . . Otherwise you get an appearance of culture without the reality such as we mourn in our day.

## A Science of Education.

15. I thank God, therefore, that I have not been able to work continuously at the problem of popular education, before I have definitely come to the conclusion that education must be raised to the level of a science which must spring from, and be based upon, the deepest possible knowledge of human nature. I am, of course, grossly ignorant of this science. I have little more than a presentiment of it in my mind, but so lively has this presentiment become that my mind is full of it, as if it were already an established fact. But it is not my idea only. The whole circumstances of the time have made it a world-need. The world will recognize it. It will not refuse to welcome the mite which I—old man as I am—at this time of rejoicing, wish to lay upon the altar of humanity ; nor will you, my friends and brothers whom

I have gathered around me to beg your co-operation in what I still think I may do for the working out of sounder and more systematic principles and methods of popular education—for which cause I have decided to make sure provision after my death.

## FUTILE PHILANTHROPY.

But while I am speaking about what I myself would like to do for popular education, and for the betterment of the poor, I see around me much philanthropic activity. It does not please me, but I must take it into account, and not underestimate its value. Pity for the poor is common to all who are not blindly selfish, and in old times great things were quietly done by wealthy men on their behalf, relatively much more than is possible nowadays. The luxury of modern life creates thousands of suffering poor, where under simpler conditions there were not hundreds ; moreover, the assistance given to the poor in those days was animated more than now by sacred respect for the relations in which men stood to one another, relations which no longer hold in the estrangements of our social life. Poor dependents, poor neighbours, poor relations, poor servants, poor godchildren, do not appeal to us so directly as they formerly did. . . . The inequalities of position, which in the old times, through the noble free-handedness of neighbours, were helpful to the poor, now bring him to destruction. Any association of the poor with the luxuries of the rich makes them unworthy poor to whom our hearts are always closed. Thus, after making them unworthy, we excuse our inattention to them on the grounds of their unworthiness. We poison them with the sources of our own ruin, and then are shy of going near them. They fall out of notice through the contrast of their wretchedness with the glitter and parade of our own life. But, in spite of this, much is being done to help the real needs of the poor. Human selfishness, however much it increases, however unintelligent and unfeeling are its growing modes of expression, even in the worst times, never entirely fails to provide measures for the assistance of the poor; and in the dreadful days, when the insufficiency of temporary assistance is most striking, charitable impulses well up in places where one would least expect to find them. But impulses of this kind cannot really help poverty, until we are more generally convinced that there are hidden in men—therefore also in poor men—powers which, for him who knows how to use them, are inexhaustible treasures.

It is now extremely urgent that men should be convinced of the truth of these statements, and, if God will, this present generation which is given up to the pursuit of gold, of pleasure, and of fame, will gradually realize that a poor child well cared for is of more value than a fat sheep, and that to raise villages from poverty and misery to a happy, self-respecting standard of life is more honourable than to possess ballrooms; that to awaken, in degraded manhood, gratitude and a desire for service brings more pleasure than stables filled with horses and numbers of footmen and lackeys. . . .

## WHAT WEALTHY MEN MIGHT DO FOR POOR.

16. But I go into greater detail.

The better a private establishment is kept up as regards business efficiency, educative influence, and even comfort, the easier it is for the owner to receive a poor man into his house, to find him work of some kind, and in this way to make him independent, skilled, and employable. Upon further examination, one realizes what great opportunities for humanity and for education lie in the hands of the wealthier classes, if they realized the position. They might rescue thousands of young men and women from the overstocked agricultural market in which they were not pre-eminently successful, and enlist them in the service of humanity and the state. Assuredly the advantages would not be only on the side of the poor ; we do not know what benefits rich and proud families might gain if their children came into closer contact with the robust, unpretentious children of the working classes. . . . In possession of the soil, and thus driven to agriculture, the most primitive and simple instrument for human culture, the larger landed proprietor can make use of the work of poor children throughout the year to his own profit. It would cost him nothing to educate a few children, in addition to the oxen he is rearing for the plough, so that they may stay in his service about the same length of time as an ox is fit for work ; and if at the same time he makes them men of independent minds, what pleasure they would give him ! if he would introduce even a small element of humanity into his relations with them, his people would be happy in his service. Without trouble or expense, and even to his own advantage, he can make the stupid and helpless farm-labourer into a proficient workman, and so raise the standard of agricultural work in the country. Every large landed proprietor who does not prefer to spend the greater part of his time at court, or in the woods, or in the more or less harmless amusements which are possible on his estate, can, in the way I have described, render great service to the state, and open out new avenues for general national culture, by gradually making it possible for the most helpless of his labourers to become independent owners of small pieces of land. In this way the land would be levelled and become more profitable, and the position and welfare of the people would be improved.

Almost every head of an important branch of industry has some such opportunity of helping the poor, and of co-operating with them in their amelioration. All employés know that good manual work is a source of wealth, and employers are in a position to promote the training, welfare, and education of the poor, if they can in the first place enable the children of their workpeople to get a sound training in the special knowledge and practical skill which is essential to that particular industry, and, secondly, encourage them in their early years to put by their pence, and thus foster the idea of saving towards a small competence of their own. It is impossible to estimate the amount that can be done to promote the integrity and morality of the poor by the respect for ownership and the spirit of thrift. What individuals can do in this way might be done on a larger scale if schools for poor children were established in which, not only some isolated branch of technical work would be taught, but also the fundamental, intellectual, and physical capacities could be trained, and the children would receive a good all-round education and reach a high degree of proficiency. The poor town youth who was enabled in this way to earn his own living would acquire those feelings of integrity and morality which are so intimately related to pecuniary independence ; moreover, the towns would no longer have to rely upon foreign workers and foreign manufacturers, and expenditure could be reduced all round.

## Rural Education.

17. The highest development of popular education and culture may, however, be reached in those districts where the poverty of the soil or scarcity of population makes it desirable to unite agricultural science with one or other town industry. This idea has always seemed to me to be the real basis of all popular education and culture. If it were scientifically organized, I believe it would be possible to achieve the best results for the population and prosperity of rural districts. I myself, more than forty years ago, conducted an institution for poor children at Neuhof, which aimed at combining agriculture with another local industry. My experience led to failure, but even so I am more than ever certain of the soundness of my idea. Neuhof is inexpressibly dear to me, both on account of my experiment and on account of the long period of distress into which it plunged me. I have held the place for forty years, although it has always meant pecuniary loss. It costs me twice as much as it is worth, but the thought, " You can still erect an institution for poor children there," prevents me from selling it. I still

hold to my youthful ideas, and although my views as to what is essential for the welfare of the poor are altered, I am filled with a kind of irrepressible longing to lose no time in carrying out some of my former aims on the old spot. But as this would be the last undertaking of my life, the preliminary steps must be carefully thought out before I make any public announcement. *Festina lente* is a precept which I have never followed, but its neglect has cost me many tears and sacrifices, and now, when I stand on the borders of the grave, I do not wish to wreck this, my last and most important enterprise, by committing the same mistake.

In the meantime, considering how easily and how cheaply poor children can be brought up on every farm, I can do something of this kind before waiting to set on foot those larger schemes, and I am desirous that in these times of national need and danger every possible step should be taken for the rescue of the poor. We should try to combine the few industries our nation possesses with the most scientific knowledge of agriculture in districts where natural resources are favourable, and we should in addition encourage a comprehensive knowledge of domestic thrift. Every method for relieving the distress of the nation by the advancement of culture is important to my plans.

18. But the various methods of poor relief in vogue are not really helpful to the nation or to the poor. In many cases they resemble the action of a man who throws a pair of shoe-buckles to the beggar who stands before his window without shoes or stockings, and asks for alms. Even under the most favourable circumstances they can have no effect upon the sources of our national corruption. . . .

### Spirit of Poor Relief.

19. If we examine more closely the customary methods of poor relief, we see how they are all wanting in the spirit of educational missionary effort—namely, that of divinely inspired parental love, the ennobling stimulus of the

childlike spirit, the purity of brotherly love and sisterly devotion which are not found outside the family circle ; they none of them offer the certain and continuous inter-action of the sensory stimuli to faith and love with the equally powerful stimuli to intellectual and practical activity which freely and convincingly affect all human beings.  They all lack the holy and elevating influence of family life.  On the one hand, by their very magnitude they are deprived of the intimacy of the home, which is only found in a narrow circle in humble circumstances ; and, on the other hand, they are an expression of the power of the public, or at any rate of external authority, rather than of the happy good feeling of the domestic hearth.  Who can doubt that such institutions, by their environment, and more particularly by the varied in-fluence of directors, managers, house-keepers, etc., are exposed to situations in which parental sympathy would almost be out of place ?  In the present condition of national ignorance, of moral, intellectual, and domestic decadence, of distress increasing in certain districts so seriously as to become a menace to the state—such institutions are absolutely essential.  God grant that our hearts may always be inclined to minister to the physical and spiritual wants of the poor, in spite of the fact that our theories may be unscientific ; but at the same time let us not forget that institutions which may be efficient for the organization of fire-brigades, and for repairing the devastations of floods, are not therefore good educational organizations.  Advisory precautions against the outbreak of fire and flood can be introduced into the rubric of national Boards, but the appliances for the relief of actual distress cannot come under that category.

## HOME IS THE STARTING-PLACE OF EDUCATION.

20. The only genuine basis for popular education, national culture, and poor relief, is parental sympathy, which by its innocence, sincerity, and power, awakens the confidence of love in the hearts of the children.  Thus

all their physical and spiritual capacities are combined towards loving and active obedience. It is in the sanctity of the home, where Nature herself makes full provision for harmony and direction in the development of human capacities, that we must seek the starting-point of our science of education. Only then can it become a national force and unite the external expression of human knowledge, power, and action, with the inner, eternal, Divine essence of our nature.

21. If the proposition *Inventis facile est addire* is true, much truer is it that the benefits which human ingenuity can give our race are easily linked on to the inner Divine element of our nature, but the reverse process, which makes this Divine element proceed from the man's paltry ingenuity, is the result of our modern misconceptions of life.

The living-room of the poor—I am not referring to those who are so degraded as to have no home life—is the centre of unity for all the Divine elements which belong to the formative powers of human nature. There, where God has provided wealth of power, it is easy for man to add his mite of service ; but when, neglecting this consecrated spot, neglecting all the ties of home life, I might almost say neglecting God Himself, he casts his small contribution outside the unifying circle of faith and love into the mire of the world, or places it as a sacrifice upon the altar of selfishness, his attempts at education are of little avail. They illustrate the truth of the text, " He that hath not, from him shall be taken even that which he hath," and present neglect of home life and its blessings has surely left us in the clouds. It is not only in the outer forms of modern life, with its fashions and ambitions in place of the pure joys and educative influence of the home, that we have come to grief. We have lost the religious faith of our fathers and the benefits which sprang from it.

Religion, which was the salvation of the quiet family circle, has in our days been robbed of all its spiritual character ; it has become nothing better than an arrogant tendency to argue and dispute about Divine things, though there are not wanting signs of improvement.

22. One great evil of modern times which is a serious obstacle to progress is the fact that parents have lost the conviction that they themselves can do anything in the education of their children. This loss of self-confidence on the part of the parents explains the superficiality of our methods.

## THE SEVEN EDUCATIONAL NEEDS.

### 1. *Parental Interest.*

23. The first object of national education should therefore be to restore this feeling, and to make parents realize that they are actually capable of training their children. Our fathers and mothers must, before everything else, be brought back to the conviction that the education of their children is primarily their concern rather than that of the tutors and nurses, and in this respect it is imperative that public opinion should return to the old-fashioned idea that every child who has lost his parents is still an unfortunate orphan, even though his guardian is in a position to employ the best educator in the world as his tutor. It is even more imperative that parents should realize the delight that comes from taking a personal interest in the education of their children, so that they may be loath to deprive themselves of it. It is imperative that they should realize what they miss through neglecting to interest themselves in their children's education. It is imperative that the present generation should learn that this loss of parental influence in education means not only that the most solid and satisfying side of life is no longer theirs, but also that the most sacred thing in the Christian home life is gone. Fathers and mothers must learn to reorganize their households, and find out what God has appointed them to be towards their children. They must realize the great possibilities of human nature, and mothers must regard their love for their child and their untiring devotion to his needs, not only as a primitive instinct which they share with the beasts of the field, but as a Divine power

through which they foster in the child the Divine unity of all the dispositions and impulses of human nature, maintaining that unity as a fixed principle throughout the period of the child's education. The father must look on the force which comes from his love as a God-given means for training his child to trustful obedience, and later to activity in all good work. Fathers and mothers in every rank of life must learn once more that God has given them in great measure the faculty of educating, and this faculty is intimately bound up with their faith in Him. They may see it always in their impulse to live for their children. We dare not conceal from ourselves the fact that it is the connection between the inner and the outer ; it is the dominance of the inner over the outer which enables us to find the true way of promoting a genuine national culture, and of wrestling successfully with our national evils.

[*Pestalozzi proceeds to describe the seven cardinal necessities for educational reform.*]

## 2. *A Book for the People.*

24. All those who are interested in education should make it their first care to compile a book for the people which would give parents of all ranks some idea of what might be done by them in training their children. It should be a book for mothers and for the home, and would in the first place aim at rousing men from their apathy concerning education. The task would be a Herculean one ; to produce it we should have to make use of all that is best in human nature, with its powers of comradeship, its insight, and its practical skill. It should describe the pleasures of educational effort so vividly as to attract parents towards it. It should unfold simply and convincingly the manifold opportunities which offer themselves to parents in leading their children to make use of their senses, as well as in the elevation of their emotional life. It would show them, too, how they might use the environment of the child, and employ systematic exercises in sensory apprehension to form, as it were,

as a basis for the complete and more scientific studies of later life.  In a like way it would lead parents to see how the thought powers and the practical powers of the children could be exercised and developed.  In a word, the book would seek to show how the will, the knowledge, and the capacity, of the race could be " naturally " helped on by simple means available in the poorest home.[1]

25. It is, however, impossible to produce such a book so long as the attempts to do so are not based upon a comprehensive and uninterrupted investigation of the ways and means employed by Nature herself in the unfolding of our separate powers and of those higher laws by which she brings those separate powers into relation with the sum-total of all our faculties.  Our efforts to establish a sound national culture must therefore have as their foundation a careful investigation of the procedure of Nature in the development of the human race. This, then, is our second need.

### 3. The Organization of Instruction in Particular Branches of Knowledge.

26. There is, thirdly, another not less important object— namely, that instruction in every branch of knowledge must be considered in relation to the fundamental faculties of human nature, and we must find out whether the devices and exercises in that particular study are in harmony with the natural, development of those powers.  We must also ascertain, in regard to every subject, what parts of it can be properly acquired by children—firstly through simple sensory activity, secondly through memory, and thirdly through imagination—and how such constituent parts can themselves be utilized on the one hand as a means of developing and exercising the fundamental natural faculties, and on the other hand simply as materials for acquiring knowledge of the subject, such as may be used later on when age and capacity permit,

---

[1] With this ambition of Pestalozzi's the student will compare Basedow's *Elementary Work.*

just as a man might bring wood, stone, mortar, and sand, to a plot of land some time before he intends to erect the building for which he has gathered them.

### 4. *Use of Results already achieved in Number, Form, and Language.*

27. It is also equally important, in organizing a national system of culture, that we should contrive to make use of our experimental results in language, number, and form, as the pure elements of thought. Their practical application must be brought into harmony with the elementary exercises by which the social faculties of faith and love, as well as the practical capacities, are developed. . . .

### 5. *Organization of Physical Education.*

28. Next we need to organize physical education on these intellectual bases, starting with the training of hand and eye, and leading up to specific vocational training.

### 6. *Experimental Schools.*

29. It is, however, impossible that these measures can have a real influence upon national culture unless ways are found by which everyone can acquire the knowledge and skill which we have been discussing. It is therefore imperative that we should aim at establishing intimate relations between the education of the school and the home. Only in this way can knowledge and skill become the possession of the people, and at the same time be beneficial. Trial schools (*Probe Schulen*) must therefore be established in which the children may obtain such a mastery of the elements of intellectual and practical education that each of them, on leaving school, would be able in his turn to train his brothers and sisters. In this way the higher aim would gradually be achieved of enabling parents, not only to undertake the intellectual and moral training of their children at home, but also to provide for the development of their physical and practical capacities.

### 7. *Trained Teachers also wanted.*

30. In order, however, to make the establishment of such schools feasible, we must first of all insure a constant supply of reliable men and women who might control them. It is essential, if we are really to arrive at a psychologically sound national culture, to seek out a large number of poor young men and women of undoubted talent, assured morality, and proven skill, and to educate them with the greatest care for this special purpose. They must themselves have enjoyed—as far as is possible at the present time—a systematic training in the whole range of human faculties and dexterities in so far as they can be applied and put into practice in the homes of the people. . . .

42. To speak frankly, if I were in a position to put on a sound basis the promotion of those measures which, in my opinion, are essential for a sound national education, I would first of all do everything in my power to create and maintain a high standard in the homes of the people.

43. To that end I would set on one side the sum of £50,000, the yearly interest from which should only be used for the following purposes :

(1) The more extensive investigation of, and research into, the principles and practice of education, whereby the process might be still more simplified and made more applicable in the home.

(2) The education of " elementary " teachers (both men and women) in this spirit and for this purpose.

(3) The erection of one or more schools as " testing stations " in which the children shall be trained in the " elementary " method.

(4) The continuous working out of methods of home instruction and home education.

[*Pestalozzi concludes this long address by discussing further the conditions he would lay down, and by appealing for the sympathy and help of his staff.*]

# V.—LETTERS TO GREAVES

[MR. J. P. GREAVES, *an Englishman, had been a student of the Pestalozzian method in Yverdun in 1817-18. He had impressed Pestalozzi so favourably that the following, amongst other important letters, were addressed to him in the winter of 1818-19. They were translated and published in 1827. Who the translator was is not certain. The evidence points to Biber, who was in England at the time. That the translation is not a faithful one is admitted, whosoever did the work. The translator had obtained permission " to make any alterations that might become necessary from the circumstances under which the letters had originally been written," and he " availed himself freely " of the privilege.*

*Although a close student of Pestalozzi would detect passages that have been polished almost out of recognition, the letters nevertheless represent the Pestalozzi spirit admirably. It is matter of surprise that they should never have been reprinted. The letters and passages which are omitted either deal with subjects already treated sufficiently elsewhere, or are repetitions within the letters themselves. A few verbal changes have been made in the text.*]

## LETTER XI

### EARLY INFANCY

... I KNOW not if philosophers would think it worth their while, but I feel confident that a mother would not decline to follow us in the consideration of the state in which the infant remains for some time after his birth.

## Helplessness of Infancy.

This state, in the first place, strikes us as a state of utter helplessness. The first impression seems to be that of pain, or, at least, of a sensation of uneasiness. There is not yet the slightest circumstance that might remind us of any other faculties, except those of the animal nature of man ; and even these are on the very lowest stage of development.

## A Fundamental Difference between the Animal and the Human.

Still, there is in this animal nature an instinct which acts with greater security, and which increases in strength as the functions of animal life are repeated day for day : this animal instinct has been known to make the most rapid progress, and to arrive very early at the highest point of strength and intensity, even when little or no attention has been paid to protect the infant from surrounding dangers, or to strengthen it by more than ordinary nourishment and care. It is a well-known fact that among savage nations the animal powers of children are capable of great exertions, and of rapid development, which proves sufficiently that this part of human nature is altogether parallel with the instinct in the rest of the animal creation.

## Animal and Human Infant compared.

So striking is this similarity that we frequently find every attempt to discover any trace of another faculty treated with ridicule. Indeed, while we are assiduous in our attention to that part of human nature in the earliest stage of life, which would require but little of our care, we are but too apt to overlook and to neglect that which in its first appearance is certainly very weak, but which is by its very weakness entitled to our care and support, and which may well inspire in us an interest in its development that would amply reward us for our labours.

For, striking as this similarity may be, we can never be justified in overlooking the distinction that exists between the infant, even in the first era of life, and the animal, which apparently may have made a more rapid progress, and may be far superior in the qualifications which constitute a sound and comfortable state of animal existence.

The animal will for ever remain on that point of bodily strength and sagacity to which its instinct has conducted it so rapidly. For the whole duration of its life, its enjoyments and exertions, and, if we may say so, its attainments, will remain stationary. It may through old age, or through unfavourable circumstances, be thrown back ; but it will never advance beyond that line of physical perfection which is attendant on its full growth. A new faculty, or an additional use of the former ones, is an event unheard of in the natural history of the animal creation.

*It is not the same with man.*

## Instinct and Germ of Morality.

In him there is something which will not fail, in due time, to make itself manifest in a series of facts altogether independent of animal life. While the animal is for ever actuated by that instinct to which it owes its preservation and all its powers and enjoyments, a something will assert its right in man to hold the empire over all his powers ; to control the lower part of his nature, and to lead him to those exertions which will secure for him a place in the scale of moral being.

The animal is destined by the Creator to follow the instinct of its nature. Man is destined to follow a higher principle. *His* animal nature must no longer be permitted to rule him, as soon as his spiritual nature has commenced to unfold.

It will be the object of my next letter to point out to the mother the epoch at which she may expect the first tokens of a spiritual nature in her infant.

## LETTER XII

### MATERNAL LOVE—A WARNING

WE have seen that the animal instinct is always intent on instantaneous gratification, without ever adverting to the comfort or interest of others.

As long as no other faculty is awake, this instinct, and its exclusive dominion over the child, cannot properly be considered as faulty ; there is not yet any consciousness in it : if it be selfish in appearance, it is not wilfully so ; and the Creator Himself seems to have ordained that it should be so strong, and, indeed, exclusively prevailing, while consciousness and other faculties could not yet contribute to secure even the first condition of animal life—self-preservation.

But if, after the first indication of a higher principle, this instinct be still allowed to act, unchecked and uncontrolled as before, then it will commence to be at war with conscience, and every step in which it is indulged will carry the child further in selfishness, at the expense of his better and more amiable nature.

### BALANCE BETWEEN OVER-INDULGENCE AND NEGLECT.

I wish this to be clearly understood ; and I shall perhaps better succeed in explaining the rules which I conceive to flow from it for the use of the mother, than in dwelling longer on the abstract position. In the first place, let the mother adhere steadfastly to the good old rule, to be regular in her attention to the infant ; to pursue as much as possible the same course ; never to neglect the wants of her child when they are real, and never to indulge them when they are imaginary, or because they are expressed with importunity. The earlier and the more constant her adherence to this practice, the greater and the more lasting will be the real benefit obtained for her child.

The expediency and the advantages of such a plan will soon be perceived, if it is constantly practised. The first advantage will be on the part of the mother. She will be subject to fewer interruptions ; she will be less tempted to give way to ill-humour ; though her patience may be tried, yet her temper will not be ruffled : she will upon all occasions derive real satisfaction from her intercourse with her child ; and her duties will not more often remind her, than her enjoyments, that she is a mother.

But the advantage will be still greater on the part of the child.

Every mother will be able to speak from experience either of the benefit which her children derived from such a treatment, or of the unfavourable consequences of a contrary proceeding. In the first instance, their wants will have been few and easily satisfied ; and there is not a more infallible criterion of perfect good health. But if, on the contrary, that rule has been neglected ; if, from a wish to avoid anything like severity, a mother has been tempted to give way to unlimited indulgence, it will but too soon appear that her treatment, however well meant, has been injudicious. It will be a source of constant uneasiness to her, without giving satisfaction to her child ; she will have sacrificed her own rest without securing the happiness of her child. . . .

We are not all born to be philosophers ; but we aspire all to a sound state both of mind and body, and of this the leading feature is—to desire little, and to be satisfied with even less.

## LETTER XIV

### CHILD'S RESPONSE TO MOTHER'S LOVE

FROM the reasons stated in my last letter, I think it right to assume that maternal love is the most powerful agent, and that affection is the primitive motive in early education.

### AUTHORITY *v*. AFFECTION.

In the first exercise of her authority, the mother will therefore do well to be cautious, that every step may be justified by her conscience and by experience ; she will do well to think of her responsibility and of the important consequences of her measures for the future welfare of her child ; she will find that the only correct view of the nature of her own authority is to look upon it as a duty rather than as a prerogative, and never to consider it as absolute. If the infant remains quiet, if it is not impatient or troublesome, it will be for the sake of the mother.

I would wish every mother to pay attention to the difference between a course of action adopted in compliance with authority and conduct pursued for the sake of another.

The first proceeds from reasoning ; the second flows from affection. The first may be abandoned when the immediate cause may have ceased to exist ; the latter will be permanent, as it did not depend upon circumstances or accidental considerations, but is founded in a moral and constant principle.

In the case now before us, if the infant does not disappoint the hope of the mother, it will be a proof, first of affection, and secondly of confidence.

### AFFECTION WINS AFFECTION AND CONFIDENCE.

Of affection—for the earliest and the most innocent wish to please is that of the infant wishing to please the mother. If it be questioned whether that wish can at all exist in one so little advanced in development, I would again, as I would do upon almost all occasions, appeal to the experience of mothers.

It is a proof, also, of confidence. Whenever an infant has been neglected, when the necessary attention has not been paid to its wants, and when, instead of the smile of kindness, it has been treated with the frown of severity, it will be difficult to restore it to that quiet and

amiable disposition in which it will wait for the gratification of its desires without impatience, and enjoy it without
greediness.

If affection and confidence have once gained ground in
the heart, it will be the first duty of the mother to do
everything in her power to encourage, to strengthen, and
to elevate, this principle.

She must encourage it, or the yet tender emotion will
subside, and the strings which are no longer attuned to
sympathy will cease to vibrate, and sink into silence.
But affection has never yet been encouraged except by
affection, and confidence has never been gained except
by confidence : the tone of her own mind must raise that
of her child.

### Maternal Constancy.

For she must be intent also upon strengthening that
principle.  Now, there is one means only for strengthening
any energy, and that means is practice.  The same effort,
constantly repeated, will become less and less difficult,
and every power, mental or physical, will go through a
certain exercise with more assurance and success the
more it grows familiar with it by custom.  There cannot,
therefore, be a safer course for the mother to pursue than
to be careful that her proceedings may, without inter-
ruption or dissonance, be calculated to excite the affection
and secure the confidence of her child.  She must not
give way to ill-humour or tedium, not for one moment ;
for it is difficult to say how the child may be affected by
the most trifling circumstance.  It cannot examine the
motives, nor can it anticipate the consequences, of an
action : with little more than a general impression of the
past, it is entirely unconscious of the future ; and thus the
present bears upon the infant mind with the full weight of
pain, or soothes it with the undiminished charm of pleasing
emotions.  If the mother consider this well, she may spare
her child the feeling of much pain, which, though not
remembered as occasioned by special occurrences, may yet
leave a cloud as it were upon the mind, and gradually

weaken that feeling which it is her interest, as well as her duty, to keep awake.

But it is not enough for her to encourage and strengthen, she must also elevate that same feeling.

She must not rest satisfied with the success which the benevolence of her own intentions, which the disposition and temper of her child, may have facilitated : she must recollect that education is not a uniform and mechanical process, but a work of gradual and progressive improvement.  Her present success must not betray her into security or indolence ; and the difficulties which she may chance to meet with must not damp her zeal or stop her endeavours.  She must bear in mind the ultimate ends of education ; she must always be ready to take her share in the work which as a mother she stands pledged to forward—the elevation of the moral nature of man.


## LETTER XVI

### MOTHER AND MORAL DEVELOPMENT OF CHILD

IF the mother has once accustomed herself to take the view to which I alluded in my last, of the affection and the confidence of her infant, the whole of her duties will appear to her in a new light.


#### EDUCATION A SACRED OBLIGATION OF THE MOTHER.

She will then look upon education, not as a task which to her is invariably connected with much labour and difficulty, but as a work of which the facility, and in a great measure the success also, is dependent on herself. She will look upon her own efforts in behalf of her child, not as a matter of indifference, or at least of convenience, but as a most sacred and most weighty obligation.  She will be convinced that education does not consist in a series of admonitions and corrections, of rewards and punishments, of injunctions and directions, strung together without unity of purpose or dignity of execution ; but that it ought to present an unbroken chain of measures, originating in the same principle—in a knowledge of the constant laws of our nature ; practised in the same spirit— a spirit of benevolence and firmness ; and leading to the same end—the elevation of man to the true dignity of a spiritual being.

But will the mother be able to spiritualize the unfolding faculties, the rising emotions, of her infant ?   Will she be able to overcome those obstacles which the preponderance of the animal nature will throw in her way ? . . .

## Mother's Self-Denial leads to Like in Child.

Her best and almost infallible criterion will be whether she really succeeds in accustoming her child to the practice of self-denial.

Of all the moral habits which may be formed by a judicious education, that of self-denial is the most difficult to acquire, and the most beneficial when adopted. . . .

The greatest difficulty which the mother will find in her early attempts to form that habit in her infant does not rest with the importunity of the infant, but with her own weakness.

If she is not herself able to resign her own comfort and her own fond desires to her maternal love, she must not think of obtaining such a result in the infant for her own sake.   It is impossible to inspire others with a moral feeling if she is not herself pervaded with it.   To endear any virtue to another, she must herself look upon her own duty with pleasure.   If she has known Virtue only as the awe-inspiring goddess—

> " With gait and garb austere,
> And threatening brow severe "

—she will never obtain that mastery over the heart, which is not yielded up to authority, but bestowed as the free gift of affection.

But if the mother has in the discipline of early years,

or in the experience of life, herself gone through a school of self-denial ; if she has nourished in her own heart the principle of active benevolence, if she knows resignation, not by name only, but from practice ; then her eloquence, her look of maternal love, her example, will be persuasive, and the infant will in a future day bless her memory, and honour it by a virtuous life.

# LETTER XX

## EARLY INTELLECTUAL AND MORAL ACTIVITIES

### Child's Increasing Independence.

. . . In the progress of time the child not only is daily exercising and strengthening its physical faculties, but it begins also to feel intellectually and morally independent.

### Curiosity.

From observation and memory there is only one step to reflection. Though imperfect, yet this operation is frequently found among the early exercises of the infant mind. The powerful stimulus of inquisitiveness prompts to exertions, which if successful or encouraged by others will lead to a habit of thoughtfulness.

If we inquire into the cause of the habit of thoughtlessness, which is so frequently complained of, we shall find that there has been a want of judicious encouragement of the first attempts at thought.

### The Child's Questions.

Children are troublesome ; their questions are of little consequence ; they are constantly asking about what they do not understand ; they must not have their will ; they must learn to be silent.

This reasoning is frequently adopted, and in consequence means are found to deter children from the provoking practice of their inquisitiveness.

I am certainly of opinion that they should not be indulged in a habit of asking idle questions. Many of their questions certainly betray nothing more than a childish curiosity. But it would be astonishing if it were otherwise ; and the more judicious should be the answers which they receive.

You are acquainted with my opinion, that, as soon as the infant has reached a certain age, every object that surrounds him might be made instrumental to the excitement of thought. You are aware of the principles which I have laid down, and the exercises which I have pointed out to mothers.[1] You have frequently expressed your astonishment at the success with which mothers who followed my plan, or who had formed a similar one of their own, were constantly employed in awakening, in very young children, the dormant faculties of thought. The keenness with which they followed what was laid before them, the regularity with which they went through their little exercises, has given you the conviction that upon a similar plan it would be easy, not only for a mother to educate a few, but for a teacher also to manage a large number of very young children. But I have not now to do with the means which may be best appropriated to the purpose of developing thought. I merely want to point to the fact that thought will spring up in the infant mind ; and that, though neglected, or even misdirected, yet a restless intellectual activity must sooner or later enable the child, in more than one respect, to grow *intellectually independent* of others.

### Child takes up Attitudes towards Persons.

But the most important step is that which concerns the affections of the heart.

The infant very soon commences to show by signs, and by its whole conduct, that it is pleased with some person,

[1] The best practical illustration, in English, of these details, will be found in the several numbers of the publication *Hints to Parents : In the Spirit of Pestalozzi's Method* (1827).

and that it entertains a dislike, or rather that it is in fear, of others.

In this respect habit and circumstances may do much, but I think it will be generally observed that an infant will be easily accustomed to the sight and the attentions of those whom it sees frequently and in friendly relation to the mother.

Impressions of this kind are not lost upon children. The friends of the mother soon become those of the infant. An atmosphere of kindness is the most kindred to its own nature. It is unconsciously accustomed to that atmosphere, and from the undisturbed smile, and the clear and cheerful glance of the eye, it is evident that it enjoys it.

The infant, then, learns to love those whom the mother considers with affection. It learns to confide in those to whom the mother shows confidence.

Thus it will go on for some time. But the more the child observes, the more distinct are the impressions produced by the conduct of others.

It will therefore become possible even for a stranger, and one who is a stranger also to the mother, by a certain mode of conduct to gain the affection and the confidence of a child. To obtain them, the first requisite is constancy in the general conduct. It would appear scarcely credible, but it is strictly true, that children are not blind to, and that some children resent, the slightest deviation, for instance, from truth.

In like manner, bad temper, once indulged, may go a great way to alienate the affection of the child, which can never be gained a second time by flatteries. This fact is certainly astonishing ; and it may also be quoted as evidence for the statement that there is in the infant a pure sense of the true and the right, which struggles against the constant temptation, arising from the weakness of human nature, to falsehood and depravity.

The child, then, begins to judge for himself, not of things only, but also of men ; he acquires an idea of character ; he grows more and more *morally independent*.

## LETTER XXI

### EDUCATION AND LIFE

CHILD'S RIGHT TO THE DEVELOPMENT OF ALL HIS
FACULTIES.

. . . WE must bear in mind that the ultimate end of
education is, not a perfection in the accomplishments of
the school, but fitness for life ; not the acquirement of
habits of blind obedience and of prescribed diligence, but
a preparation for independent action. We must bear in
mind that, whatever class of society a pupil may belong
to, whatever calling he may be intended for, there are
certain faculties in human nature common to all, which
constitute the stock of the fundamental energies of man.
We have no right to withhold from anyone the opportunities of developing all their faculties. It may be
judicious to treat some of them with marked attention,
and to give up the idea of bringing others to high perfection. The diversity of talent and inclination, of plans
and pursuits, is a sufficient proof for the necessity of such
a distinction. But I repeat that we have no right to
shut out the child from the development of those faculties
also, which we may not for the present conceive to be
very essential for his future calling or station in life.

Who is not acquainted with the vicissitudes of human
fortune, which have frequently rendered an attainment
valuable that was little esteemed before, or led to regret
the want of application to an exercise that had been treated
with contempt ? Who has not at some time or other
experienced the delight of being able to benefit others by
his advice or assistance, under circumstances when, but
for his interference, they must have been deprived of that
benefit ? And who, even if in practice he is a stranger
to it, would not at least in theory acknowledge that the
greatest satisfaction that man can obtain is a consciousness that he is pre-eminently qualified to render himself
useful ?

But even if all this were not deserving of attention, if the sufficiency of ordinary acquirements for the great majority were vindicated on grounds, perhaps, of partial experience, and of inference from well-known facts, I would still maintain that our systems of education have for the most part been labouring under this inconvenience, that they did not assign the due proportion to the different exercises proposed by them.

The only correct idea of this subject is to be derived from the examination of human nature with all its faculties. . . .

Thus education, instead of merely considering what is to be imparted to children, ought to consider first what they may be said already to possess, if not as a developed, at least as an innate faculty capable of development. Or if, instead of speaking thus in the abstract, we will but recollect that it is to the great Author of life that man owes the possession, and is responsible for the use, of his innate faculties, education should not only decide what is to be made of a child, but rather inquire, What is a child qualified for? what is his destiny as a created and responsible being? what are his faculties as a rational and moral being? what are the means pointed out for their perfection, and the end held out as the highest object of their efforts, by the Almighty Father of all, both in creation and in the page of revelation?

To these questions the answer must be simple and comprehensive. It must combine all mankind; it must be applicable to all without distinction of zones or nations in which they may be born. It must acknowledge, in the first place, the rights of man in the fullest sense of the word. It must proceed to show that these rights, far from being confined to those exterior advantages which have from time to time been secured by a successful struggle of the people, embrace a much higher privilege, the nature of which is not yet generally understood or appreciated. They embrace the rightful claims of all classes to a general diffusion of useful knowledge, a careful development of the intellect, and judicious attention to all the faculties of man, physical, intellectual, and moral.

It is in vain to talk of liberty when man is unnerved, or his mind not stored with knowledge, or his judgment neglected, and, above all, when he is left unconscious of his rights and his duties as a moral being.

## LETTER XXII

### PHYSICAL EDUCATION—GYMNASTICS

IF, according to correct principles of education, all the faculties of man are to be developed, and all his slumbering energies called into play, the early attention of mothers must be directed to a subject which is generally considered to require neither much thought nor experience, and therefore is generally neglected. I mean the physical education of children. . . .

### GRADATION OF EXERCISES NECESSARY.

The revival of gymnastics is, in my opinion, the most important step that has been done in that direction. The great merit of the gymnastic art is not the facility with which certain exercises are performed, or the qualification which they may give for certain exertions that require much energy and dexterity ; though an attainment of that sort is by no means to be despised. But the greatest advantage resulting from a practice of those exercises is the natural progress which is observed in the arrangement of them, beginning with those which, while they are easy in themselves, yet lead as a preparatory practice to others which are more complicated and more difficult. There is not, perhaps, any art in which it may be so clearly shown that energies which appeared to be wanting may be produced, as it were, or at least may be developed, by no other means than practice alone. This might afford a most useful hint to all those who are engaged in teaching any object of instruction, and who meet with difficulties in bringing their pupils to that proficiency which they had expected. Let them recommence on a new plan, in which the exercises shall be differently arranged, and the subjects brought forward in a manner that will admit of the natural progress from the easier to the more difficult. When talent is wanting altogether, I know that it cannot be imparted by any system of education. But I have been taught by experience to consider the cases in which talents of any kind are absolutely wanting, but very few. And in most cases I have had the satisfaction to find that a faculty which had been quite given up, instead of being developed, had been obstructed rather in its agency by a variety of exercises which tended to perplex or to deter from further exertion.

And here I would attend to a prejudice which is common enough concerning the use of gymnastics : it is frequently said that they may be very good for those who are strong enough, but that those who are suffering from weakness of constitution would be altogether unequal to, and even endangered by, a practice of gymnastics.

## Remedial Gymnastics.

Now, I will venture to say that this rests merely upon a misunderstanding of the first principles of gymnastics ; the exercises not only vary in proportion to the strength of individuals, but exercises may be, and have been, devised for those also who were decidedly suffering. And I have consulted the authority of the first physicians, who declared that, in cases which had come under their personal observation, individuals affected with pulmonary complaints, if these had not already proceeded too far, had been materially relieved and benefited by a constant practice of the few and simple exercises which the system in such cases proposes.

And for this very reason, that exercises may be devised for every age and for every degree of bodily strength, however reduced, I consider it to be essential that mothers should make themselves acquainted with the principles of gymnastics, in order that, among the elementary and preparatory exercises, they may be able to select those which, according to circumstances, will be most likely to suit and benefit their children.

I do not mean to say that mothers should strictly adhere to those exercises only which they may find pointed out in a work on gymnastics ; they may, of course, vary them as they find desirable or advisable ; but I would recommend a mother much rather to consult one who has some experience in the management of gymnastics *with children*, before she decides upon altering the course proposed, or upon adopting other exercises of which she is unable to calculate the exact degree of strength which they may require, or the benefit that her children may derive from them.

### GYMNASTICS AND MORAL TRAINING.

If the physical advantage of gymnastics is great and incontrovertible, I would contend that the moral advantage resulting from them is as valuable. I would again appeal to your own observation. You have seen a number of schools in Germany and Switzerland of which gymnastics formed a leading feature[1]; and I recollect that, in our conversations on the subject, you made the remark, which exactly agrees with my own experience, that gymnastics, well conducted, essentially contribute to render children, not only cheerful and healthy, which, for moral education are two all-important points, but also to promote among them a certain spirit of union, and a brotherly feeling, which is most gratifying to the observer ; habits of industry, openness and frankness of character, personal courage, and a manly conduct in suffering pain, are also among the natural and constant consequences of an early and continued practice of exercises on the gymnastic system.

[1] Gymnastics were a leading feature of the schools of the Philanthropinists, *e.g.*, that of Salzmann.

## LETTER XXIII

### TRAINING OF EYE AND EAR—MUSIC IN EDUCATION

PHYSICAL education ought by no means to be confined to those exercises which now receive the denomination of " gymnastics." By means of them strength and dexterity will be acquired in the use of the limbs in general ; but particular exercises ought to be devised for the practice of all the senses.

This idea may at first appear a superfluous refinement or an unnecessary encumbrance of free development. We have acquired the full use of our senses, to be sure, without any special instruction of that sort ; but the question is not whether these exercises are indispensable, but whether, under many circumstances, they will not prove very useful.

### TRAINING IN SENSORY DISCRIMINATION.

How many are there of us whose eye would, without any assistance, judge correctly of a distance or of the proportion of the size of different objects ? How many are there who distinguish and recognize the nice shades of colours, without comparing the one with the other ; or whose ear will be alive to the slightest variation of sound ? Those who are able to do this with some degree of perfection will be found to derive their facility either from a certain innate talent or from constant and laborious practice. Now, it is evident that there is a certain superiority in these attainments, which natural talent gives without any exertion, and which instruction could never impart, though attended by the most diligent application. But if practice cannot do everything, at least it can do much ; and the earlier it is begun, the easier and the more perfect must be the success.

A regular system of exercises of this description is yet a desideratum. But it cannot be difficult for a mother to introduce a number of them, calculated to develop and perfect the eye and the ear, into the amusements of her children. For it is desirable that everything of that kind should be treated as an amusement, rather than as anything else. The greatest liberty must prevail, and the whole must be done with a certain cheerfulness, without which all these exercises, as gymnastics themselves, would become dull, pedantic, and ridiculous.

## EARLY TRAINING IN ÆSTHETICS.

It will be well to connect these exercises very early with others, tending to form the taste. It seems not to be sufficiently understood that good taste and good feelings are kindred to each other, and that they reciprocally confirm each other. Though the ancients have said that " to study those arts which are suited to a free-born mind soothes the character, and takes away the roughness of exterior manners," yet little has been done to give free access to those enjoyments or accomplishments to all, or even to the majority of the people. If it is not possible for them to give much of their attention to subordinate or ornamental pursuits, while so much of their time is taken up by providing for their first and necessary wants, still, this does not furnish a conclusive reason why they should be shut out altogether from every pursuit above the toil of their ordinary avocations.

Yet I know not a more gratifying scene than to see, as I have seen it among the poor, a mother spreading around her a spirit of silent but serene enjoyment, diffusing among her children a spring of better feelings, and setting the example of removing everything that might offend the taste—not, indeed, of a fastidious observer, but yet of one used to move in another sphere. It is difficult to describe by what means this can be effected. But I have seen it under circumstances which did not promise to render it even possible. Of one thing I am certain, that it is only through the true spirit of maternal love that it can be obtained. That feeling, of which I cannot too frequently repeat that it is capable of an elevation to the standard of the very best feelings of human nature, is intimately connected with a happy instinct that will lead to a path equally remote from listlessness and indolence, as it is from artificial refinement. Refinement and fastidiousness may do much, if upheld by constant watchfulness ; a nature, however, a truth, will be wanting ; and even the casual observer will be struck with a restraint incompatible with an atmosphere of sympathy.

## Music.

Now that I am on the topic, I will not let the opportunity pass by without speaking of one of the most effective aids of moral education. You are aware that I mean Music ; and you are not only acquainted with my sentiments on that subject, but you have also observed the very satisfactory results which we have obtained in our schools. The exertions of my excellent friend Nageli, who has with equal taste and judgment reduced the highest principles of his art to the simplest elements, have enabled us to bring our children to a proficiency which, on any other plan, must be the work of much time and labour.

## National Songs.

But it is not the proficiency which I would describe as a desirable accomplishment in education. It is the marked and most beneficial influence of music on the feelings, which I have always thought and always observed to be most efficient in preparing or attuning, as it were, the mind for the best of impressions. The exquisite harmony of a superior performance, the studied elegance of the execution, may indeed give satisfaction to a connoisseur ; but it is the simple and untaught grace of melody which speaks to the heart of every human being. Our own national melodies, which have since time immemorial been resounding in our native valleys, are fraught with reminiscences of the brightest page of our history, and of the most endearing scenes of domestic life. But the

effect of music in education is not only to keep alive a
national feeling: it goes much deeper ; if cultivated in
the right spirit, it strikes at the root of every bad or
narrow feeling : of every ungenerous or mean prosperity,
of every emotion unworthy of humanity.   In saying so
I might quote an authority which commands our attention on account of the elevated character and genius of
the man from whom it proceeds   It is well known that
there was not a more eloquent and warm advocate of the
moral virtues of music than the venerable Luther.   But
though his voice has made itself heard, and is still held in
the highest esteem among us, yet experience has spoken
still louder, and more unquestionably, to the truth of the
proposition which he was among the first to vindicate.
Experience has long since proved that a system proceeding upon the principle of sympathy would be imperfect, if it were to deny itself the assistance of that powerful
means of the culture of the heart.   Those schools, or
those families in which music has retained the cheerful
and chaste character which it is so important that it
should  preserve  have  invariably  displayed  scenes  of
moral feeling, and consequently of happiness, which leave
no doubt as to the intrinsic value of that art, which has
sunk into neglect, or degenerated into abuse, only in
the ages of barbarism or depravity.

I need not remind you of the importance of music in
engendering and assisting the highest feelings of which
man is capable.   It is almost universally acknowledged
that Luther has seen the truth, when he pointed out
music, devoid of studied pomp and vain ornament, in
its solemn and impressive simplicity, as one of the most
efficient means of elevating and purifying genuine feelings
of devotion.

We have frequently, in our conversations on this
subject, been at a loss how to account for the circumstance that in your own country, though that fact is as
generally  acknowledged,  yet  music  does  not  form  a
more prominent feature in general education.   It would
seem that the notion prevails, that it would require

more time and application than can conveniently be
bestowed upon it to make its influence extend also on the
education of the people.

Now, I would appeal, with the same confidence as I
would to yourself, to any traveller, whether he has not
been struck with the facility, as well as the success, with
which it is cultivated among us.   Indeed, there is scarcely
a village school throughout Switzerland, and perhaps
there is none throughout Germany or Prussia, in which
something is not done for an acquirement at least of the
elements of music on the new and more appropriate plan.

This is a fact which it cannot be difficult to examine,
and which it will be impossible to dispute ; and I will
conclude this letter by expressing the hope which we
have been entertaining together, that this fact will not
be overlooked in a country which has never been backward in suggesting or adopting improvement, when
founded on facts and confirmed by experience.


# LETTER XXIV

## DRAWING

In the branch of education of which I have been treating
in the two last letters, I conceive that to the elements
of music should be subjoined the elements of drawing.


### Imitative Powers of Children.

We all know from experience that among the first
manifestations of the faculties of a child is a desire and
an attempt at imitation.   This accounts for the acquirement of language, and for the first imperfect utterance of
sounds imitative of music, which is common to most
children when they have heard a tune with which they
were pleased.   The progress in both depends on the greater
or smaller portion of attention which children give to
the things that surround them, and on their quickness of

perception. In the very same way as this applies to the ear and the organs of speech, it applies also to the eye and the employment of the hand. Children who evince some curiosity in the objects brought before their eyes very soon begin to employ their ingenuity and skill in copying what they have seen. Most children will manage to construct something in imitation of a building, of any materials they can lay hold of.

## THEIR RELATION TO DRAWING.

This desire, which is natural to them, should not be neglected. It is, like all the faculties, capable of regular development. It is therefore well to furnish children with playthings which will facilitate these their first essays, and occasionally to assist them. No encouragement of that sort is lost upon them, and encouragement should never be withheld when it promotes innocent pleasure, and when it may lead to useful occupation. To relieve them from the monotonousness of their daily and hourly repeated trifles, and to introduce variety into their little amusements, acts as a stimulus to their ingenuity, and sharpens their observation, while it gains their interest.

As soon as they are able to make the essay, there is nothing so well calculated for this object as some elementary practice of drawing. You have seen the course of preparatory exercises by which some of my friends have so well succeeded in facilitating these pursuits for quite young children. It would be unreasonable to expect that they should begin by drawing any object before them as a whole. It is necessary to analyze for them the parts and elements of which it consists. Whenever this has been attempted, the progress has been astonishing, and equalled only by the delight with which the children followed this their favourite pursuit. . . .

The general advantages resulting from an early practice of drawing are evident to everyone. Those who are familiar with the art are known to look upon almost every object with eyes different, as it were, from a common observer. One who is in the habit of examining the structure of plants, and conversant with a system of botany, will discover a number of distinguishing characteristics of a flower, for instance, which remain wholly unnoticed by one unacquainted with that science. It is from this same reason that, even in common life, a person who is in the habit of drawing, especially from Nature, will easily perceive many circumstances which are commonly overlooked, and form a much more correct impression even of such objects as he does not stop to examine minutely, than one who has never been taught to look upon what he sees with an intention to reproduce a likeness of it. The attention to the exact shape of the whole, and the proportion of the parts, which is requisite for the taking of an adequate sketch, is converted into a habit, and becomes in many cases productive of much instruction and amusement.

### DRAWING FROM NATURE.

In order to attain this habit, it is very material, and almost indispensable, that children should not be confined to copying from another drawing, but from Nature. The impression which the object itself gives is so much more striking than its appearance in an imitation; it gives a child much more pleasure to be able to exercise his skill in attempting a likeness of what surrounds him, and of what he is interested in, than in labouring at a copy of what is but a copy itself, and has less of life or interest in its appearance.

It is likewise much easier to give an idea of the important subject of light and shade, and of the first principles of perspective, as far as they influence the representation of every object, by placing it immediately before the eye. The assistance which is given should by no means extend to a direction in the execution of every detail; but something should be left to the ingenuity, something also to patience and perseverance: an advantage that has been found out after some fruitless attempts is not easily forgotten ; it gives much satisfaction and encouragement to new efforts ; and the joy in the ultimate success derives a zest from previous disappointment.

## MODELLING.

Next to the exercises of drawing come those of modelling, in whatever materials may be most conveniently employed. This is frequently productive of even more amusement. Even where there is no distinguished mechanical talent, the pleasure of being able to do something at least is, with many, a sufficient excitement ; and both drawing and modelling, if taught on principles which are founded in Nature, will be of the greatest use when the pupils are to enter upon other branches of instruction.

## DRAWING AS A HELP IN OTHER SUBJECTS.

Of these I shall here only mention two—geometry and geography. The preparatory exercises by which we have introduced a course of geometry present an analysis of the various combinations under which the elements of form are brought together, and of which every figure or diagram consists. These elements are already familiar to the pupil who has been taught to consider an object with a view to decompose it into its original parts, and to draw them separately. The pupil, of course, will not be a stranger to the materials, of which he is now to be taught the combinations and proportions. It must be easier to understand the properties of a circle, for instance, or of a square, for one who has not only met with these figures occasionally, but who is already acquainted with the manner in which they are formed. Besides, the doctrine of geometrical solids, which cannot in any degree be satisfactorily taught without illustrative models, is much better understood, and much deeper impressed on the mind, when the pupils have some idea of the construction of the models, and when they are able to work out at least those which are less complicated.

In geography, the drawing of outline maps is an exercise

which ought not to be neglected in any school. It gives the most accurate idea of the proportional extent and the general position of the different countries; it conveys a more distinct notion than any description, and it leaves the most permanent impression on the memory.

## LETTER XXV

### THE EDUCATION OF MOTHERS

To the courses of exercises which I have recommended, I anticipate that an objection will be raised which it is necessary for me to meet before I proceed to speak of intellectual education.

Granting that these exercises may be, as the phrase is, useful in their way; granting, even, that it might be desirable to see some of the knowledge they are intended to convey diffused among all classes of society, yet where, it will be asked, and by what means, can they be expected to become general among any other than the higher classes? There you may expect to find mothers competent, if at all inclined, to undertake the superintendence of such exercises with their children. But, considering the present state of things, is it not absolutely chimerical to imagine that among the people mothers should be found who were qualified to do anything for their children in that direction?

To this objection I would answer, in the first place, that it is not always legitimate to argue from the present state of things to the future; and whenever, as in the case before us, the present state of things can be proved to be faulty, and at the same time capable of improvement, every friend of humanity will concur with me in saying that such an argument is inadmissible.

It is inadmissible; for experience speaks against it. The page of history, to a thinking observer, presents mankind labouring under the influence of a chain of prejudice, of which the links are successively broken.

The most interesting events in history are but the

consummation of things which had been deemed impossible. It is in vain to assign limits to the improvements of ingenuity ; *but it is still more so to circumscribe the exertions of benevolence.*

Such a conclusion, then, is inadmissible. And history speaks more directly to the point. The most consequential facts plead in favour of our wishes and our hopes. The most enlightened, the most active philanthropists, two thousand years ago, could not have foreseen the change that has taken place in the intellectual world : they could not have anticipated those facilities by which not only the research of a few is encouraged, but by which the practical results of that research are, with wonderful rapidity, communicated to thousands in the remotest countries of the globe. They could not have foreseen the glorious invention by which ignorance and superstition have been driven out of their stronghold, and knowledge and truth diffused in the most universal and the most effective channels. They could not have foreseen that a spirit of inquiry would be excited even among those who had formerly been doomed to blind belief and to passive obedience.

## THE SPREAD OF KNOWLEDGE.

Indeed, if there is one feature by which this present age bids fair to redeem its character, and to heal the wounds which it has inflicted on the suffering nations, it is this—that we see efforts being made in every direction, with a zeal and to an extent hitherto unparalleled, to assist the people in acquiring that portion of intellectual independency without which the true dignity of the human character cannot be maintained nor its duties adequately fulfilled. There is something so cheering in the prospect of seeing the number of those for whom it is destined extending with the range of knowledge itself, that there is scarcely a field left of which men of superior talent have not undertaken to cull the flowers and to store the fruits for those who have not time or faculty to toil at the elements or follow up the refinements of science ; and the still more material object of facilitating the first steps, of laying the foundation, of insuring slow but solid progress, and this in the manner best adapted to the nature of the human mind and to the development of its faculties— this object has been pursued with an interest and an ardour that even the results which I have seen in my own immediate neighbourhood are a sufficient pledge that the pursuit will not be abandoned, and that it is not now far from its ultimate success.

### Not enough without Maternal Love.

This prospect is cheering ; but, my dear friend, it is not upon this prospect that I have built the hopes of my life. It is not the diffusion of knowledge, whether it be grudgingly doled out in schools on the old plan, or more liberally supplied in establishments on a new principle, or submitted to the examination, and laid open for the improvement of the adults—it is not the diffusion of knowledge alone to which I look up for the welfare of this or of any generation. No : unless we succeed in giving a new impulse, and raising the tone of Domestic Education ; unless an atmosphere of sympathy, elevated by moral and religious feeling, be diffused there ; unless maternal love be rendered more instrumental in early education than any other agent ; unless mothers will consent to follow the call of their own better feelings more readily than those of pleasure or of thoughtless habit ; unless they will consent to be mothers and to act as mothers—unless such be the character of education, all our hopes and exertions can end only in disappointment.

### Home Life the True Centre of Education.

Those have indeed widely mistaken the meaning of all my plans, and of those of my friends, who suppose that in our labours for popular education we have not a higher end in view than the improvement of a system of instruction, or the perfection, as it were, of the gymnastics of the intellect. We have been busily engaged in reforming the schools, for we consider them as essential in the progress of education ; but we consider the fireside circle as far more essential. We have done all in our power to bring up children with a view to become teachers, and we have every reason to congratulate the schools that were benefited by this plan ; but we have thought it the most important feature and the first duty of our own schools, and of every school, to develop in the pupils confided to our care those feelings, and to store their minds with that knowledge, which, at a more advanced period of life, may enable them to give all their heart and the unwearied use of their powers to the diffusion of the true spirit which should prevail in a domestic circle. In short, whoever has the welfare of the rising generation at heart cannot do better than consider as his highest object the *Education of Mothers*.

## LETTER XXVI

### MOTHER AND CHILD'S EDUCATION

LET me repeat that we cannot expect any real improvement in education, improvement that shall be felt throughout an extensive sphere, and that shall continue to spread in the progress of time, increasing in vigour as it proceeds —we cannot expect any improvement of that character unless we begin by *educating mothers*.

It is their duty in the domestic circle to do what school instruction has not the means of accomplishing : to give to every individual child that degree of attention which in a school is absorbed in the management of the whole ; to let their heart speak in cases where the heart is the best judge ; to gain by affection what authority could never have commanded.

But it is their duty also to turn all the stock of their knowledge to account, and to let their children have the benefit of it.

I am aware that under the present circumstances many mothers would either declare themselves, or would be looked upon by others, as incompetent to attempt any such thing ; as so poor in knowledge, and so unpractised in communicating knowledge, that such an undertaking on their part would appear as vain and presumptuous.

Now, this is a fact which, as far as experience goes, I am bound to deny. I am not now speaking of those classes or individuals whose education has been, if not very diligently, at least in some measure attended to. I have now in view a mother whose education has from some circumstances or other been totally neglected. I will suppose one who is even ignorant of reading and writing, though in no country in which the schools are in a proper state you would meet with an individual deficient in this respect. I will add, a young and inexperienced mother.

Now, I will venture to say that this poor and wholly ignorant, this young and inexperienced mother is *not quite destitute* of the means of assisting even in the intellectual development of the child.

### She teaches him Names of Objects.

However small may be the stock of her experience, however moderate her own faculties, she must be aware that she is acquainted with an infinite number of facts —such, we will say, as they occur in common life—to which her infant is yet a stranger. She must be aware that it will be useful to the infant to become soon acquainted with some of them, such, for instance, as refer to things with which it is likely to come into contact. She must feel herself able to give her child the possession of a variety of names simply by bringing the objects themselves before the child, pronouncing the names and making the child repeat them. She must feel herself able to bring such objects before the child in a sort of natural order—the different parts, for instance, of a fruit. Let no one despise these things because they are little. There was a time when we were ignorant even of the least of them, and there are those to whom we have reason to be thankful for teaching us these little things.

### She talks to him about Home Surroundings.

But I do not mean to say that a mother should stop there. Even the mother of whom we are speaking, that wholly ignorant and inexperienced mother, is capable of going much farther, and of adding a variety of knowledge which is really useful. After she has exhausted the stock of objects which presented themselves first, after the child has acquired the names of them, and is able to distinguish their parts, it may probably occur to her that something more might still be said on every one of these objects. She will find herself able to describe them to the child with regard to form, size, colour, softness or hardness of the outside, sound when touched, and so on. She has now gained a material point; from the mere knowledge of the names of objects she has led the infant to a knowledge of their qualities and properties. Nothing can be more natural for her than to go on and compare different objects with regard to these qualities, and the greater or smaller degree in which they belong to the objects. If the former exercises were adapted to cultivate the memory, these are calculated to form the observation and judgment. She may still go much farther: she is able to tell her child the reasons of things and the causes of facts. She is able to inform him of the origin, and the duration, and the consequences, of a variety of objects. The occurrences of every day and of every hour will furnish her with materials for this sort of instruction. Its use is evident; it teaches the child to inquire after the causes, and accustoms him to think of the consequences, of things. I shall have an opportunity in another place to speak of moral and religious instruction; I will therefore only remark, in a few words, that this last-mentioned class of exercises, which may be varied and extended in an almost endless series, will give frequent occasion for the simplest illustration of truths belonging to that branch. It will make the child reflect on the consequences of actions; it will render the mind familiar with thought; and it will frequently lead him to recognize, in the objects before him, the effects of the infinite wisdom of that Being whom, long before, the piety of the mother, if genuine, must have led him to revere, and to love " with all his heart, and with all his soul, and with all his strength, and with all his mind.". . .

And I know not a motive which might render those efforts more interesting than the desire of a mother to do all in her power for the mental as well as for the physical and moral development of her children. However circumscribed her means, and however limited at first may be her success, still, there is something that will and must prompt her not to rest, that will stimulate her to new efforts, and that will at last crown them with fruits which are the more gratifying the more they were difficult to obtain.

Experience has shown that mothers, in that seemingly forlorn situation which I have described, have succeeded beyond their own expectation. I look upon this as a new proof of the fact that nothing is too difficult for maternal love, animated by a consciousness of its purity, and elevated by a confidence in the power of Him who has inspired the mother's heart with that feeling. I do indeed consider it as a free gift of the Creator, and I firmly believe that in the same measure as maternal love is ardent and indefatigable, in the same measure as it is inspired with energy and enhanced by faith—I firmly believe that in the same measure maternal love will be strengthened in its exertions, and supplied with means, even where it appears most destitute.

Though, as I have shown above, it is by no means so difficult to direct the attention of children to useful objects, yet nothing is more common than the complaint, " I can do nothing with children." If this comes from an individual who is not called upon by his peculiar situation to occupy himself with education, it is but fair to suppose that he will be able to make himself more useful in another direction than he could have done by a laborious and persevering application to a task for which he is neither predisposed by inclination nor fitted

by eminent talent. But those words should never come
from a mother. A mother *is* called upon to give her
attention to that subject. It is her duty to do so ; the
voice of conscience in her own breast will tell her that it
is ; and the consciousness of a duty never exists without the qualification to fulfil it ; nor has a duty ever
been undertaken with the spirit of courage, of confidence,
of love, that has not been ultimately crowned with
success.

## LETTER XXVII

### CHARACTER *V*. KNOWLEDGE IN THE EDUCATION OF WOMEN

IF ever an uneducated and totally unassisted mother has
it in her power to do so much for her child, how much
better qualified must she be, and how much more confidently may she look forward to the results of her
maternal exertions, if her faculties have been properly
developed, and her steps guided by the experience of
those who had engaged in that work before her !

#### IMPORTANCE OF EARLY EDUCATION.

The fact, therefore, which I stated in my last letter,
far from rendering my proposition questionable, goes
directly to confirm its validity and to illustrate its expediency. I therefore repeat it, and I would address it
in the strongest language to all those who, like myself,
are desirous of bringing about a change in our present
imper ect system of education. If you really wish to
embark with your facilities, your time, your talents, your
influence, in a cause likely to benefit a large portion of
your species; if you wish not to be busy in suggesting
palliatives, but in effecting a permanent cure of the evils
under which thousands have sunk, and hundreds of
thousands are still suffering ; if you wish not merely to
erect an edifice that may attract by its splendour and

commemorate your name for awhile, but which shall pass away like " the baseless fabric of a vision "; if, on the contrary, you prefer solid improvement to momentary effect, and the lasting benefit of many to the solitary gratification of striking results, let not your attention be diverted by the apparent wants, let it not be totally engrossed by the subordinate ones, but let it at once be directed to the great and general, though little known, source from which good or evil flows in quantity incalculable, and rapidity unparalleled—to the manner in which the earliest years of childhood are passed, and to the education of those to whose care they are, or ought to be, consigned.

### WANTED : A SCHOOL FOR FUTURE MOTHERS.

Of all institutions, the most useful is one in which the great business of education is not merely made a means subservient to the various purposes of ordinary life, but in which it is viewed as an object in itself deserving of the most serious attention, and to be brought to the highest perfection ; a school in which the pupils are taught to act as teachers, and educated to act as educators ; a school, above all, in which the *female character* is at an early age developed in that direction, which enables it to take so prominent a part in early education.

To effect this, it is necessary that the female character should be thoroughly understood and adequately appreciated. And on this subject nothing can give a more satisfactory illustration than the observation of a mother who is conscious of her duties and qualified to fulfil them. In such a mother, the moral dignity of her character, the suavity of her manners, and the firmness of her principles, will not more command our admiration than the happy mixture of judgment and feeling which constitutes the simple but unerring standard of her actions.

## Women's Education.

It is the great problem in female education to effect this happy union in the mind, which is equally far from imposing any restraint on the feelings as it is from warping or biassing the judgment. The marked preponderance of feeling which is manifested in the female character requires not only the most clear-sighted, but also the kindest attention, from those who wish to bring it into harmony with the development of the faculties of the intellect and the will.

It is a mere prejudice to suppose that the acquirement of knowledge and the cultivation of the intellect must either not be solid and comprehensive, or that they are apt to take away from the female character its simplicity and all that renders it truly amiable. Everything depends on the motive from which, and the spirit in which, knowledge is acquired. Let that motive be one that does honour to human nature, and let that spirit be the same which is concomitant to all the graces of the female character—" Not obvious, not obtrusive, but retired "—and there will be modesty to insure solidity of knowledge, and delicacy to guard against the misdirection of sentiment.

For an example, I might refer to one of the numerous instances, which are not the less striking because they are not extensively known, in which a mother has devoted much of her time and her best abilities to the acquirement of some branches of knowledge in which her education had been defective, but which she conceived to be valuable enough to be brought forward in the education of her own children. This has been the case with individuals highly accomplished in many respects, but still alive to every defect, and desirous of supplying it, if not for their own, at least for the benefit of their children.

And no mother has ever been known to have repented of any pains that she took to qualify herself for the most perfect education of those nearest and dearest to her heart. Even without anticipating the future accomplishment of

her wishes, by their progress in the path in which she has
undertaken to guide them, she is amply repaid by the
delight immediately arising from the task,

> " . . . To rear the tender thought,
> And teach the young idea how to shoot."

I have here supposed the most powerful motive, that
of maternal love ; but it will be the task of early education to supply motives, which even at a tender age may
excite an interest in mental exertion, and yet be allied
to the best feelings of human nature.


# LETTER XXVIII

## THINGS *V*. WORDS

### MEMORY *v*. UNDERSTANDING.

IF a mother is desirous of taking an active part in the
intellectual education of her children, I would first direct
her attention to the necessity of considering, not only
what sort of knowledge, but in what manner that knowledge should be communicated to the infant mind.  For
her purpose, the latter consideration is even more essential
than the former ; for, however excellent the information
may be which she wishes to impart, it will depend on the
mode of her doing it whether it will at all gain access to
the mind, or whether it will remain unprofitable, neither
suiting the faculties nor being apt to excite the interest
of the child.

In this respect a mother should be able perfectly to
distinguish between the mere action of the memory and
that of the other faculties of the mind.

To the want of this distinction I think we may safely
ascribe much of the waste of time, and the deceptive
exhibition of apparent knowledge, which is so frequent
in schools, both of a higher and of a lower character.  It
is a mere fallacy to conclude, or to pretend, that knowledge has been acquired from the circumstance that

terms have been committed to the memory, which, if rightly understood, convey the expression of knowledge. This condition, *if rightly understood*, which is the most material, is the most generally overlooked. No doubt a proceeding of this sort, when words are committed to the memory, without an adequate explanation being either given or required, is the most commodious system for the indolence or ignorance of those who practise upon it as a system of instruction. Add to which the powerful stimulus of vanity in the pupils—the hope of distinction and reward in some, the fear of exposure or punishment in others—and we shall have the principal motives before us owing to which this system, in spite of its wretchedness, has so long been patronized by those who do not think at all, and tolerated by those who do not sufficiently think for themselves.

What I have said just now of the exercise of the memory, exclusive of a well-regulated exercise of the understanding, applies more especially to the manner in which the dead languages have long been, and in some places still are, taught—a system of which, taking it all in all, with its abstruse and unintelligible rules and its compulsive discipline, it is difficult to say whether it is more absurd in an intellectual or more detestable in a moral point of view.

## THINGS RATHER THAN WORDS.

If such a system, enforcing the partial exercise of the memory, is so absurd in its application and so detrimental in its consequences, at a period when the intellect may be supposed to be able to make some progress, at least, without being so constantly and anxiously attended to, an exclusive cultivation of the memory must be still more misapplied at the tender age when the intellect is only just dawning, when the faculty of discerning is yet unformed, and unable to consign to the memory the notions of separate objects in their distinction from each other. For a mother to guard against an error of this kind, the first rule is, to teach always by *things* rather than by *words*. Let there be as few objects as possible named to the infant, unless you are prepared to show the objects themselves. If this is the case, the name will be committed to the memory, together with the recollection of the impression which the object produced on the senses. It is an old saying, and a very true one, that our attention is much more forcibly attracted, and more permanently fixed, by objects which have been brought before our eyes, than by others of which we have merely gathered some notion from hearsay and description, or from the mention of a name.

But if a mother is to teach by *things*, she must recollect, also, that to the formation of an idea more is requisite than the bringing the object before the senses. Its qualities must be explained ; its origin must be accounted for ; its parts must be described, and their relation to the whole ascertained ; its use, its effects or consequences, must be stated. All this must be done, at least, in a manner sufficiently clear and comprehensive to enable the child to distinguish the object from other objects, and to account for the distinction which is made.

It is natural that the degree of perfection with which the formation of ideas on this plan can be facilitated depends upon circumstances which are not always under the control of a mother ; but something of the kind should be attempted, and must be, wherever education is intended to take a higher character than mere mechanical training of the memory.

## PICTURES.

Of objects which cannot be brought before the child in reality, pictures should be introduced. All instruction founded on pictures will be found a favourite branch with children ; and if this curiosity is well directed, and judiciously satisfied, it will prove one of the most useful and instructive.

Whenever the knowledge of an abstract idea, which

will not, of course, admit of any representation of that kind, is to be communicated to the child, on the same principle an equivalent of that representation should be given by an illustration, through the medium of a fact, laid before the child. This is the original intention and the use of moral tales ; and this, too, agrees with the excellent old adage, " that the way by precept is long and laborious, that by example short and easy."

## LETTER XXIX

### THE CHILD HIS OWN EDUCATOR

THE second rule that I would give to a mother, respecting the early development of the infant mind, is this : Let the child not only be acted upon, but let him be an *agent* in intellectual education.

### SPONTANEOUS ACTIVITY OF CHILD.

I shall explain my meaning : Let the mother bear in mind that her child has not only the faculties of attention to, and retention of, certain ideas or facts, but also a faculty of reflection, independent of the thoughts of others. It is good to make a child read, and write, and learn, and repeat—but it is still better to make a child think. We may be able to turn to account the opinions of others, and we may find it valuable or advantageous to be acquainted with them ; we may profit by their light ; but we can render ourselves most useful to others, and we shall be entitled to the character of valuable members of society, by the efforts of our own mind ; by the result of our own investigations ; by those views, and their application, which we may call our intellectual property.

I am not now speaking of those leading ideas which are from time to time thrown out, and by which science is advanced or society benefited at large. I am speaking of that stock of intellectual property which everyone, even the most unpretending individual, and in the humblest walks of life, may acquire. I am speaking of that habit of reflection which guards against unthinking conduct under any circumstances, and which is always active to examine that which is brought before the mind ; that habit of reflection which excludes the self-sufficiency of ignorance or the levity of " a little learning "— which may lead an individual to the modest acknowledgment that he knows but little, and to the honest consciousness that he knows that little well. To engender this habit, nothing is so effective as an early development, in the infant mind, of thought — regular, self-active thought.

## MOTHER'S EMPIRICAL KNOWLEDGE BETTER GUIDE THAN PHILOSOPHY.

Let not the mother suffer herself to be detained from this task by the objections of those who deem the infant mind altogether incapable of any exertion of that kind. I will venture to say that those who propose that objection, though they may be the profoundest thinkers or the greatest theorists, will be found to have no *practical* knowledge whatsoever of the subject, nor any moral interest in the investigation of it. And I for one would trust more in the empirical knowledge of a mother, proceeding from exertions to which she was prompted by maternal feeling—in that empirical knowledge, even of an illiterate mother, I would trust more than in the theoretical speculations of the most ingenious philosophers. There are cases in which sound sense and a warm heart sees farther than a highly refined, cold and calculating head.

I would therefore call upon the mother to begin her task, in spite of any objections that may be raised. It will be enough if she is persuaded to *begin* ; she will then continue of herself ; she will derive such gratification from her task that she will never think of relaxing.

While she unfolds the treasures of the infant mind,

and awakens the world of hitherto slumbering thought, she will not envy the assurance of philosophers, who would have the human mind to be a " universal blank." Engaged in a task which calls into activity all the energies of her mind and all the affections of her heart, she will smile at their dictatorial speculations and their supercilious theories. Without troubling herself about the knotty question, whether there are any *innate ideas*, she will be content if she succeeds in developing the *innate faculties of the mind*.

If a mother asks for the designation of the subjects which might be profitably used as vehicles for the development of thought, I would answer her that any subject will do, if it be treated in a manner suitable to the faculties of the child. It is the great art in teaching never to be at a loss for the choice of an object for the illustration of a truth. There is not an object so trivial that in the hands of a skilful teacher might not become interesting, if not from its own nature, at least from the mode of treating it. To a child everything is new. The charm of novelty, it is true, soon wears off ; and if there is not the fastidiousness of matured years, there is at least the impatience of infancy to contend with. But then there is for the teacher the great advantage of a combination of simple elements which may diversify the subject without dividing the attention.

If I say that any subject will do for the purpose, I mean this to be understood literally. Not only is there not one of the little incidents in the life of a child—in his amusements and recreations, in his relations to his parents and friends and playfellows—but there is actually nothing within the reach of the child's attention, whether it belong to Nature or to the employments and arts of life, that might not be made the object of a lesson, by which some useful knowledge might be imparted, and, which is still more important, by which the child might be familiarized with the habit of th'nking on what he sees, and speaking after he has thought.

METHOD THAT OF CONVERSATION AND QUESTIONS.

The mode of doing this is not by any means to talk much *to* a child, but to enter into conversation *with* a child ; not to address to him many words, however familiar or well chosen, but to bring him to express himself on the subject ; not to exhaust the subject, but to question the child about it, and to let him find out, and correct, the answers. It would be ridiculous to expect that the volatile spirits of an infant could be brought to follow any lengthy explanations. The attention of a child is deadened by long expositions, but roused by animated questions.

Let these questions be short, clear, and intelligible. Let them not merely lead the child to repeat, in the same or in varied terms, what he has heard just before. Let them excite him to observe what is before him, to recollect what he has learned, and to muster his little stock of knowledge for materials for an answer. Show him a certain quality in one thing, and let him find out the same in others. Tell him that the shape of a ball is called " round "; and if, accordingly, you bring him to point out other objects to which the same predicament belongs, you have employed him more usefully than by the most perfect discourse on rotundity. In the one instance he would have had to listen and to recollect ; in the other he has to observe and to think.

## LETTER XXX

### "WEARINESS IS THE CARDINAL SIN OF INSTRUCTION"

#### EXERTION MUST BE EXPECTED.

WHEN I recommend to a mother to avoid *wearying* a child by her instructions, I do not wish to encourage the notion that instruction should always take the character of an amusement, or even of a play. I am convinced that such a notion, where it is entertained and acted upon by a teacher, will for ever preclude solidity of knowledge, and, from a want of sufficient exertions on the part of the pupils, will lead to that very result which I wish to avoid by my principle of a constant employment of the thinking powers.

A child must very early in life be taught a lesson which frequently comes too late, and is then a most painful one —that exertion is indispensable for the attainment of knowledge. But a child should not be taught to look upon exertion as an unavoidable *evil*. The motive of *fear* should not be made a stimulus to exertion. It will destroy the interest, and will speedily create disgust.

### INTEREST SHOULD PROMOTE IT, NOT FEAR.

This *interest* in study is the first thing which a teacher, and, in the instances before us, which a mother, should endeavour to excite and keep alive. There are scarcely any circumstances in which a want of application in children does not proceed from a want of interest ; and there are, perhaps, none under which a want of interest does not originate in the mode of treating adopted by the teacher. I would go as far as to lay it down for a rule, that whenever children are inattentive, and apparently take no interest in a lesson, the teacher should always first look to himself for the reason. When a quantity of dry matter is before a .child, when a child is doomed to listen in silence to lengthy explanations, or to go through exercises which have nothing in themselves to relieve or attract the mind—this is a tax upon his spirits which a teacher should make it a point to abstain from imposing. In the same manner, if the child, from the imperfection of his reasoning powers or his unacquaintance with facts, is unable to enter into the sense, or to follow the chain of ideas in a lesson ; when he is made to hear, or to repeat, what to him is but " sound without sense "—this is perfectly absurd. And when to all this the fear of punishment is added—besides the tedium, which in itself is punishment enough—this becomes absolutely cruel.

PUNISHMENTS.

Of all tyrants, it is well known that little tyrants are the most cruel ; and of all little tyrants, the most cruel are *school tyrants.* Now, in all civilized countries cruelty of every description is forbidden, and even cruelty to animals is very properly punished, in some by the law of the land, and in all stigmatized by public opinion. How, then, comes CRUELTY TO CHILDREN to be so generally over-looked, or, rather, thought a matter of course ?

Some, forsooth, will tell us that their own measures are wonderfully humane—that their punishments are less severe—or that they have done away with corporal punishments. But it is not to the severity of them that I object—nor would I venture to assert, in an unqualified manner, that corporal punishments are inadmissible under any circumstances in education. But I do object to their application—I do object to the principle *that the children are punished when the master or the system is to blame.*

As long as this shall continue—as long as teachers will not take the trouble, or will not be found qualified, to inspire their pupils with a living interest in their studies—they must not complain of the want of attention, nor even of the aversion to instruction which some of them may manifest. Could we witness the indescribable tedium which must oppress the juvenile mind while the weary hours are slowly passing away, one by one, in an occupation which they can neither relish nor understand its use ; could we remember the same scenes which our own childhood has undergone, we would then no longer be surprised at the remissness of the school-boy " creeping like a snail, unwillingly, to school."

In saying this I do not mean to make myself the advocate of idleness, or of those irregularities which will now and then be met with even in the best-conducted schools. But I would suggest that the best means to prevent them from becoming general is to adopt a better mode of instruction, by which the children are less left to themselves, less thrown upon the unwelcome employment of passive listening, less harshly treated for little and excusable failings—but more roused by questions, animated by illustrations, interested and won by kindness.

## SYMPATHY BETWEEN TEACHER AND TAUGHT.

There is a most remarkable reciprocal action between the interest which the teacher takes and that which he communicates to his pupils. If he is not with his whole mind present at the subject; if he does not care whether it is understood or not, whether his manner is liked or not, he will never fail of alienating the affections of his pupils, and of rendering them indifferent to what he says. But real interest taken in the task of instruction—kind words and kinder feelings, the very expression of the features, and the glance of the eye—are never lost upon children.

## LETTER XXXI

### THE ELEMENTARY MEANS

You are aware of the nature of those exercises which were adopted at my suggestion, as calculated to employ the mind usefully, and to prepare it for further pursuits, by eliciting thought and forming the intellect.

I would call them preparatory exercises, in more than one respect. They embrace the elements of number, form, and language; and whatever ideas we may have to acquire in the course of our life, they are all introduced through the medium of one of these three departments.

## NUMBER AND FORM.

The relations and proportions of number and form constitute the natural measure of all those impressions which the mind receives from without. They are the measures, and comprehend the qualities, of the material world; form being the measure of space, and number the measure of time. Two or more objects, distinguished from each other as existing separately in space, presuppose an idea of their forms, or, in other words, of the exact space which they occupy ; distinguished from each other as existing at different times, they come under the denomination of number.

The reason why I would so early call the attention of children to the elements of number and form is, besides their general usefulness, that they admit of a most perspicuous treatment—a treatment, of course, far different from that in which they are but too often involved, and rendered utterly unpalatable to those who are by no means deficient in abilities.

The elements of number, or preparatory exercises of calculation, should always be taught by submitting to the eye of the child certain objects representing the units. A child can conceive the idea of two balls, two roses, two books ; but it cannot conceive the idea of " two " in the abstract. How would you make the child understand that two and two make four unless you show it to him first in reality ?  To begin by abstract notions is absurd and detrimental, instead of being conducive.  The result is, at best, that the child can do the thing by rote—without understanding it ; a fact which does not reflect on the child, but on the teacher, who knows not a higher character of instruction than mere mechanical training.

If the elements are thus clearly and intelligibly taught, it will always be easy to go on to more difficult parts, remembering always that the whole should be done by *questions*.  As soon as you have given to the child a knowledge of the names by which the numbers are distinguished, you may appeal to it to answer any question of simple addition, or subtraction, or multiplication, or division, performing the operation in reality by means of a certain number of objects, balls for instance, which will serve in the place of units.

## Higher Arithmetic.

It has been objected that children who had been used to a constant and palpable exemplification of the units, by which they were enabled to execute the solution of arithmetical questions, would never be able afterwards to follow the problems of calculation in the abstract, their balls, or other representatives, being taken from them.

Now, experience has shown that those very children, who had acquired the first elements in the concrete and familiar method described, had two great advantages over others. First, they were perfectly aware, not only what they were doing, but also of the reason why. They were acquainted with the principle on which the solution depended ; they were not merely following a formula by rote ; the state of the question changed, they were not puzzled, as those are who see only as far as their mechanical rule goes, and not farther. This, while it produced confidence and a feeling of safety, gave them also much delight— a difficulty overcome, with the consciousness of a . . . happy effort, always prompts to the undertaking of a new one.

## Mental Arithmetic.

The second advantage was that children well versed in those illustrative elementary exercises afterwards displayed great skill in *head calculation* (*calcul de tête*). Without repairing to their slate or paper, without making any memorandum of figures, they not only performed operations with large numbers, but they arranged and solved questions which at first might have appeared involved, even had the assistance of memoranda or working on paper been allowed.

Of the numerous travellers of your nation who did me the honour to visit my establishment, there was none, however little he might be disposed or qualified to enter into a consideration of the whole of my plan, who did not express his astonishment at the perfect ease, and the quickness, with which arithmetical problems, such as the visitors used to propose, were solved. I do not mention this, and I did not then feel any peculiar satisfaction, on account of the display with which it was connected, though the acknowledgment of strangers can by no means be indifferent to one who wishes to see his plan judged of by its results. But the reason why I felt much interested and gratified by the impression which that department of the school invariably produced was, that it singularly confirmed the fitness and utility of our elementary course. It went a great way, at least with me, to make me hold fast the principle that the infant mind should be acted upon by illustrations taken from reality, not by rules taken from abstraction ; that we ought to teach by *things* more than by *words*.

## GEOMETRY.

In the exercises concerning the elements of form, my friends have most successfully revived and extended what the ancients called the *analytical method*—the mode of eliciting facts by problems, instead of stating them in theories ; of elucidating the origin of them, instead of merely commenting on their existence ; of leading the mind to invent, instead of resting satisfied with the invention of others. So truly beneficial, so stimulating, is that employment to the mind, that we have learned fully to appreciate the principle of Plato, that whoever wished to study metaphysics with success ought to prepare himself by the study of geometry. It is not the acquaintance with certain qualities or proportions, of certain forms and figures (though, for many purposes, this is applicable in practical life, and conducive to the advancement of science), but it is the precision of reasoning, and the ingenuity of invention, which, springing as it does from a familiarity with those exercises, qualifies the intellect for exertion of every kind.

## LANGUAGE—MATERNAL AND FOREIGN.

In exercises of number and form, less abstraction is at first required than in similar ones in language. But I would insist on the necessity of a careful instruction in the maternal language. Of foreign tongues, or of the dead languages, I think that they ought to be studied, by all means, by those to whom a knowledge of them may become useful, or who are so circumstanced that they may indulge a predilection for them, if their taste or habits lead that way. But I know not of one single exception that I would make of the principle, that as early as possible a child should be led to contract an intimate acquaintance with, and make himself perfectly master of, his native tongue.

Charles the Fifth used to say that as many languages as a man possessed, so often was he man. How far this may be true I will not now inquire; but thus much I know to be a fact, that the mind is deprived of its first instrument or organ, as it were, that its functions are interrupted and its ideas confused, when there is a want of perfect acquaintance and mastery of at least *one* *language*. The friends of oppression, of darkness, of prejudice, cannot do better, nor have they at any time neglected the point, than to stifle the power and facility of free, manly, and well-practised speaking; nor can the friends of light and liberty do better, and it were desirable that they were more assiduous in the cause, than to procure to everyone, to the poorest as well as to the richest, a facility, if not of elegance, which would enable them to collect and clear up their vague ideas, and embody those which are distinct, and which would awaken a thousand new ones.

## LETTER XXXII

### AIM OF EDUCATION

#### EDUCATION AND GOD.

NEED I point out to you the motive from which I have said thus much on the early attention to be paid to physical and intellectual education? Need I remind you that I consider these branches merely as leading to an higher aim—to qualify the human being to the free and full use of all the faculties implanted by the Creator—

and to direct all these faculties towards the perfection
of the whole being of man, that he may be enabled to
act, in his peculiar station, as an instrument of that all-
wise and almighty Power that has called him into life.
This is the view which education should lead an individual
to take of his relation to his Maker—a view which will
at once give him humility to acknowledge the imperfection
of his attempts and the weakness of his power, and
inspire him with the courage of an unshaken confidence
in the Source of all that is good and true.

## EDUCATION AND SOCIAL EFFICIENCY.

In relation to society, man should be qualified by
education to be a useful member of it. In order to be
truly useful, it is necessary that he should be truly *independent*. Whether that independence may arise from his
circumstances, or whether it be acquired by the honourable
use of his talents, or whether it be owing to more laborious
exertion and frugal habits, it is clear that true independence must rise and fall with the dignity of his moral
character rather than with affluent circumstances, or
intellectual superiority, or indefatigable exertion. A
state of bondage or of self-merited poverty is not more
degrading than a state of dependence on considerations
which betray littleness of mind, or want of moral energy
or of honourable feeling. An individual whose actions
bear the stamp of independence of mind cannot but be
a useful as well as an esteemed member of society. He
fills up a certain place in society, belonging to himself and
to no other, because he has obtained it by merit and
secured it by character. His talents, his time, his opportunities, or his influence, are all given to a certain end.
And even in the humbler walks of life, it has always been
acknowledged that there were individuals who, by the
intelligent, the frank, the honourable character of their
demeanour, and by the meritorious tendency of their
exertions, deserved to be mentioned together with those
whose names were illustrated by the halo of noble birth
and by the still brighter glory of genius or merit. That

such instances are but exceptions, and that these exceptions are so few, is owing to the system of education which
generally prevails, and which is little calculated to promote independence of character.

## Education and Happiness—Conditions of Happiness.

Considering man as an individual, education should
contribute in giving him happiness.　The feeling of happiness does not arise from exterior circumstances ; it is a
state of mind, a consciousness of harmony both with the
inward and the outward world : it assigns their due limits
to the desires, and it proposes the highest aim to the
faculties of man.　For happy is he who can bring his
desires within the measure of his means, and who can
resign to every individual and selfish wish, without giving
up his content and repose—whose feeling of general
satisfaction is not dependent on individual gratification.
And happy again is he who, whenever self is out of the
question, and the higher perfection of his better nature,
or the best interests of his race, are at stake—happy is
he who then knows of no limits to his efforts, and who
can bring them to keep pace with his most sanguine
hopes !　The sphere of happiness is unbounded, it is extending as the views are enlarged ; it is elevated as the
feelings of the heart are raised, it " grows with their
growth, and strengthens with their strength."

In order to give the character described here to the
actions and to the life of an individual, I consider it as
necessary that all the faculties implanted in human
nature should be properly developed.　It is not that
*virtuosity* ought to be attained in any direction, or that a
degree of excellence ought to be anxiously aspired to,
which is the exclusive privilege of pre-eminent talent.
But there is a degree of development of all the faculties
which is far from the refinement of any ; and of such a
course the great advantage will be, to prepare the mind
for a more especial application to any line of studies con-
genial to its inclination or connected with certain pursuits.

With regard to the claim which every human being has to a judicious development of his faculties by those to whom the care of his infancy is confided—a claim of which the universality does not seem to be sufficiently acknowledged—allow me to make use of an illustration which was on one occasion proposed by one of my friends. Whenever we find a human being in a state of suffering, and near to the awful moment which is for ever to close the scene of his pains and his enjoyments in this world, we feel ourselves moved by a sympathy which reminds us that, however low his earthly condition, here too there is one of our race, subject to the same sensations of alternate joy and grief—born with the same faculties, with the same destination, and the same hopes for a life of immortality.    And as we give ourselves up to that idea, we would fain, if we could, alleviate his sufferings, and shed a ray of light on the darkness of his parting moments.    This is a feeling which will come home to the heart of everyone —even to the young and the thoughtless, and to those little used to the sight of woe.    Why, then, we would ask, do we look with a careless indifference on those who enter life ?  why do we feel so little interest in the feelings and in the condition of those who enter upon that varied scene, of which, if we would but stop to reflect, we might contribute to enhance the enjoyments and to diminish the sum of suffering, of discontent and wretchedness ?

And that education might do that is the conviction of all those who are competent to speak from experience. That it *ought* to do as much is the persuasion, and that it *may once* accomplish it is the constant endeavour, of all those who are truly interested in the welfare of mankind.

## LETTER XXXIII

### INDIVIDUAL AMBITION *V.* SOCIAL SYMPATHIES

In my last letter I described the end of education to be, to render man conscientiously active in the service of his Maker ; to render him useful, by rendering him independent with relation to society ; and, as an individual, to render him happy within himself.

To this end I conceive that the formation of the intellect, the attainment of useful knowledge and the development of all the faculties, may be made instrumental. But though they will be found highly serviceable as furnishing the means, they will not supply the spring of action. It would be preposterous, no doubt, to provide for the facilities of execution, without exciting the motives of a certain plan or line of conduct.

## AMBITION AS SPRING OF ACTION.

Of this fault, the process which frequently goes by the name of education, and which might more appropriately be denominated a mechanical training, is often guilty. The common motive by which such a system acts on those over whose indolence it has conquered is *fear ;* the very highest to which it can aspire, in those whose sensibility is excited, is *ambition.*

It is obvious that such a system can calculate only on the lower selfishness of man. To that least amiable or estimable part of the human character it is, and always has been, indebted for its best success. Upon the better feelings of man it turns a deaf ear.

How is it, then, that motives leading to a course of action which is looked upon as mean and despicable, or at best as doubtful, when it occurs in life—how is it that motives of that description are thought honourable in education ? Why should that bias be given to the mind in a school, which, to gain the respect or the affection of others, an individual must first of all strive to unlearn—a bias to which every candid mind is a stranger ?

I do not wish to speak harshly of ambition, or to reject it altogether as a motive. There is, to be sure, a noble ambition—dignified by its object, and distinguished by a deep and transcendent interest in that object. But if we consider the sort of ambition commonly proposed to the schoolboy—if we analyze " what stuff 'tis made of, whereof it is born "—we shall find that it has nothing to do with the interest taken in the object of study ; that such an interest frequently does not exist ; and that, owing to its being blended with that vilest and meanest of motives, with *fear*, it is by no means raised by the wish to give pleasure to those who propose it ; for a teacher who proceeds on a system in which fear and ambition are the principal agents must give up his claim to the esteem or affection of his pupils.

Motives like fear or inordinate ambition may stimulate to exertion, intellectual or physical, but they cannot warm the heart. There is not in them that life which makes the heart of youth to heave with the delight of knowledge—with the honest consciousness of talent—with the honourable wish for distinction—with the kindly glow of genuine feeling. Such motives are inadequate in their source and inefficient in their application, for they are nothing to the heart, and " out of the heart are the issues of life."

### Sympathy as Counter-Weight.

On these grounds it is that, in moral as well as the intellectual education, I have urged the supreme character of the motive of sympathy as the one that should early, and indeed principally, be employed in the management of children. On these grounds I have repeatedly urged the propriety of attending to that feeling, which I have no hesitation in declaring to be the first feeling of a higher nature that is alive in the child—the feeling, in the infant, of love and confidence in the mother. Upon this feeling I wish to ground the first foundation, and on a feeling analogous to it, and springing from it, I wish to guide the future steps of education. That in the infant that feeling exists there can be no doubt. We have for it the testimony of those who are most competent to judge, because best enabled to sympathize with it—of the mothers.

To the mothers, therefore, I would again and again address the request, to let themselves be governed by their maternal feelings, enlightened by thought, in guiding those rising impressions, in developing that tender germ, in the infant's heart. They will find that at first it is yet involved in the animal nature of the infant ; that it is an innate feeling, strong because not yet under the control of reason, and filling the whole mind because not yet opposed by the impulse of conflicting passions. That feeling, let them believe, has been implanted by the Creator. But together with it there exists in the infant that instinctive impulse of its animal nature, which is first made subservient to self-preservation, and directed towards the satisfaction of natural and necessary wants ; which is next bent on gratification ; which, unless it be checked in time, runs out into a thousand imaginary and artificial wants ; which would hurry us from enjoyment to enjoyment, and which would end in consummate selfishness.

To control and to break this selfish impulse, the best, the only, course is for the mother to strengthen daily that better impulse, which so soon gives her the pledge, by the first smile on the lips, the first glance of affection in the eye of the infant, that, though the powers of the intellect are yet slumbering, she may soon speak a language intelligible to the *heart*. She will be enabled, by affection and by firmness, to bring her child to give up those cravings which render it so unamiable, and to give them up for her, the mother's, sake. By what means she can make herself understood—how she can supply the want of words and of precepts—I shall not undertake to answer for her ; but let a mother answer, whether, conscious as she is of her own love for her child—a love enhanced by a feeling of duty, and enlightened by reflection—she will not, without either words or precepts, be able to find the way to the heart and the affection of her infant.

But if the mother has succeeded in this, let her not fancy that she has done everything. The time will come when the hitherto speechless emotions of the infant will find a language—when his eye will wander from the

mother to other individuals within the sphere that surrounds him—and when that sphere itself will be extended.
His affections must then no longer rest concentrated in
one object, and that object, though the dearest and kindest
of mortals, yet a mortal, and liable to those imperfections
which " our flesh is heir to." The affections of the child
are claimed by higher objects—and, indeed, by the highest.

## How Child is led to God through Maternal Love.

Maternal love is the first agent in education ; but
maternal love, though the purest of human feelings, is
human ; and salvation is not of the power of man, but of
the power of God. Let not the mother fancy that she
of her own power, and with her best intentions, can raise
the child's heart and mind beyond the sphere of earthly
and perishable things. It is not for her to presume
that her instructions or her example will benefit the
child, unless they be calculated to lead the child to that
faith, and to that love, from which alone salvation springs.

The love and confidence of the infant in the mother
is but the adumbration of a purer, of the purest and
highest feeling which can take up its above in a mortal
breast—of a feeling of love and faith, now no more confined to an individual, now no more mixed with " baser
matter," but rising superior to all other emotions, and
*elevating* man by teaching him *humility*—the feeling of
love and faith in his Creator and his Redeemer.

In this spirit let education be considered in all its
stages ; let the physical faculties be developed, but without forgetting that they form the lower series of human
nature ; let the intellect be enlightened, but let it be remembered that the first science which thought and knowledge should teach is modesty and moderation ; let the
discipline be regulated and the heart be formed, not by
coercion, but by sympathy—not by precept, but by
practice ; and, above all, let it be prepared for that
influence from above which alone can restore the image
of God in man.

# VI.—"THE SWANSONG"

[*WHAT commonly passes under this name is in reality two separate books. The first part—about two-thirds of the whole—is the most careful statement of Pestalozzi's educational doctrine that we have. The* Lenzburg Address *is a scientifically more perfect production, but it is very largely due to Pestalozzi's philosophical colleague, Niederer. In the* Swansong *we have the master himself, with all his peculiar weaknesses alongside his strength. It was written in the period between 1811 and 1813, and intended for publication under the title of* Education according to Nature. *Circumstances prevented its publication until 1826, when it was issued in connection with a review of his life's activities, intended as a message from " the sick Pestalozzi to the healthy public."*

*The translation which follows has been a good deal condensed, especially in the later sections, where Pestalozzi repeats many of his earlier statements in new contexts.*]

Examine everything, hold to that which is good ; and if you conceive anything better, let it in truth and love be a further contribution to that which I in truth and love have endeavoured to give you in these pages.

## EDUCATION MEANS THE DEVELOPMENT OF THE WHOLE MAN.

1. The problem of the Elementary Method, upon which, more or less conscious of its full magnitude, I have spent the greater part of my later life in endeavouring to solve, is nothing other than the problem of how to conform to the order of Nature in the cultivation of man's capacities and powers.

2. If we are to know what this involves, we must first find out what is meant by human nature. What is its intrinsic essence, and what are its distinguishing features ? Clearly, the capacities and powers which we share with other animals cannot be the essential things. On the contrary, must not these essentials be the aggregate of those capacities and powers in the possession of which men differ from other animals ? It is not my corruptible body nor my sensory appetites, but my moral and religious capacities, my intellectual capacities, and my practical capacities, which constitute the humanity in me.

It follows that the problem of the Elementary Method is the problem of following the order of Nature in the unfolding and developing of these specifically human powers of head, heart, and hand.

Conformity to Nature implies the constant subordination of our animal nature to higher and characteristically human claims (Divine as these are in their essential nature) —that is, in brief, the subordination of body to mind.

It follows, further, that every attempt to assist by artifice this developing process presupposes a lively and more or less clear sense of the course which Nature herself takes.

Now, this course is determined by eternal laws which are inherent in the constitution of each separate capacity, within which they are bound up with an inextinguishable force that favours development. When the occasion arises, this force drives us forward. What is felt to be within our reach, that we will ; it could not be otherwise, such is the strength of this latent disposition.

3. The feeling " I can " as a condition of progress is a law of our being, but the specific form of the law varies with the characteristics of each capacity to which it relates. In spite of this variety of form, their unity is never lost by reason of the unity from which they emanate —the unity of human nature. It is only when their harmony is maintained that they are in conformity with human nature. Conversely, only that which affects man as an indissoluble unit is educative in our sense of that word. It must reach his hand and his heart as well as

his head. No partial approach can be satisfactory. To consider any one capacity exclusively (head or heart or hand) is to undermine and destroy man's native equilibrium. It means unnatural methods of training, and produces partial human products. It is as wrong to think only of morality and religion as it is to have the intellect solely in mind.

4. Specialized development of one side of human nature is unnatural and false. It is as sounding brass and tinkling cymbal, a hollow unreality. Education worth the name necessarily strives after the perfection of man's powers in their completeness.

The unity of human faculties is a Divine and permanent gift to the race. Respect for that unity is an essential condition of successful education. "What God has joined let no man put asunder." Whoever disregards this principle in the practice of education, in any way whatever, makes but half-men of us, in whom no satisfaction can be sought or found.

5. Men whose development is thus specialized are a prey to self-deception. They do not know their own weaknesses and deficiencies.

They are severely handled by those who have been educated in a different way. Want of balance, whether it is due to excessive emotional or to excessive intellectual development, brings ultimate discomfiture.

Domestic and civic welfare depend, however, upon spiritual factors, without which the practical qualities which are wanted in domestic and civic life are dangerously illusory. They occasion every sort of discontent, and produce injured feelings, grievances, and variance of all kinds.

## DEVELOPMENT OF EACH OF OUR POWERS COMES FROM ITS SPECIFIC EXERCISE.

6. The equilibrium of the capacities, which is the keynote of our idea of an Elementary Method, demands the full development of all man's fundamental powers. The

natural process in each case takes place in accordance with unchanging law, opposition to which means artificial interference with Nature. The laws governing development differ for each capacity. Intellectual development takes a different course from that in which the emotional life is purified and made effective, and both differ, again, from the principles which govern the development of our physical powers.

7. In each case the evolution of capacity depends on exercise. Morality, love, and faith, develop only through putting these virtues into practice. Intellectual capacity only comes through thinking, and practical and professional power comes from using our senses and our limbs in a natural way.

8. The stimulus to exercise varies with the power in question. The eye is disposed to see, the ear to listen, the foot to walk, and the hand to grasp. Just in the same way the heart is disposed to believe and love, the intellect to think. Whatever capacity man has within him is associated with a disposition to activity ; the disposition tends to realize itself, and to develop through activity into trained capacity.

9. A fall will check a child's desire to walk ; his confidence is checked when the cat meets his blandishments with scratches, and when the puppy meets them with a snarl. Similarly, his desire to learn is cooled when his teacher adopts unattractive methods which confuse and stupefy him instead of rousing his interests.

### Nature v. Nurture in Development.

The course of Nature, when left to herself, in the development of human capacities is a slow progress from the prison-house of his sensuous nature. If it is to be raised to an effort to develop the human in man, two things must be taken for granted—viz., the help of intelligent love, the germ of which belongs to our idea of the family, in spite of its sensory limitations ; and the intelligent use of such skill as long experience has given to man.

10. We see, then, that the idea of the Elementary Method simply comes from the efforts of man to supplement the course of Nature in developing and cultivating our dispositions and capacities by such assistance as clear-sighted love, cultivated intelligence, and practical insight, can give.

Although the course of Nature in the development of man is laid down by God, nevertheless, when children are left entirely to themselves, only his primitive instincts are awakened, whereas it is man's object—it is the aim of the Elementary Method, it is the aim of the wise and god-fearing—to call the human and Divine elements into life.

11. Let us examine the question more closely from the standpoint of (A) morality, (B) intelligence, and (C) practical everyday life.

### A. NURTURE AS SOURCE OF MORALITY.

Let us ask ourselves, How do the bases of our moral life, faith and love, actually develop in the human race, and how do the first germs of our moral and religious dispositions become active ? How do they get nourishment and increase in strength under man's fostering care, and at the same time preserve their human characteristics as Nature herself designed them ? It all comes from the quiet and steady satisfaction of the child's physical requirements ; this is the natural condition under which the germs of the child's future morality are quickened into life. The instinctive watchfulness of maternal love secures this condition ; the neglect of it speedily disturbs the physical well-being of the infant.

12. It is therefore of the utmost importance for education that peaceful quiet and content should be secured to the infant, and that we should recognize this as the method of calling into life the still dormant feelings which distinguish man from other creatures. Every disturbance of the infant's vegetative life tends to quicken and strengthen his primitive sensuous nature, and to hinder the natural development of the dispositions and faculties which are peculiar to mankind.

13. The first and most potent means to this end is provided by Nature in the heart of the mother. Maternal power, maternal devotion, are universal. To be lacking in these qualities reveals an unnatural mother : it represents an abnormal degeneration of the mother's heart. Without the mother, the father's helpful presence and the quickening forces of family life are of little avail. It is the faithful mother who makes these things tell, and just as solicitude for the child's repose in early infancy is generally thought of only as a sign of the mother's devotion, so we think of it as necessary to the natural development of the child's moral forces. Human qualities only unfold in repose. Without repose love is no longer a source of truth and blessedness. Unrest itself springs from physical suffering or from unfulfilled desires, from improper needs or from worse selfishness. ' In all cases it generates lovelessness, mistrust, and all that springs therefrom.

14. Repose, then, is a first necessity of infant life ; babies must be protected from all sources of organic derangement. Such disturbance may come either from inattention to physical needs or from over-indulgence, which encourages uncontrolled selfishness.

When the mother frequently, but irregularly, neglects the crying infant, even letting him wait so long that his discomfort becomes real suffering, the canker of dissatisfaction, with all its evil consequences, is set up in the child. Such tardy attention is not the natural way of quickening love and confidence in the child. Instead, the mother is sowing the seeds of his future demoralization. Such infantile unrest generates a sense of outrage in the physical side of his nature ; tendencies to brute violence are awakened, and the start is given to that widespread spirit of immorality and irreligion which blackens and vilifies the Divine elements in man.

15. A neglected child, torn by its sufferings, throws itself like a hungry and thirsty animal upon its mother's breast, instead of seeking it in a gentle, human way, and finding pleasure in the moderate satisfaction of its wants.

When the tender hand and the smiling face of the mother are wanting, one misses, too, the smile and the charm which are so natural to healthy and happy infancy. We miss the first sign of awakening humanity in the restless child, and find instead every indication of dissatisfaction and mistrust. Feelings of love and trustfulness are not developed, and the whole course of the child's development is endangered.

16. Over-indulgence is no less disturbing. The rich fool of whatever rank who spoils her child establishes within him improper desires, and undermines his powers of satisfying his needs by his own efforts. He becomes a source of constantly increasing dissatisfaction, disappointment, and violence.

17. True motherly solicitude for the awakening humanity in her child confines its attention to the satisfaction of its essential wants. The intelligent and thoughtful mother follows the dictates of her love, instead of becoming subservient to the child's caprices and physical selfishness. Her solicitude for the child's repose does not incite his sensuous appetites, but simply satisfies his physical necessities. Although maternal care is instinctive, it should harmonize with what her intellect and her heart would tell her ; it is, in fact, a product of all three. It is only called into life by instinct, and is not, therefore, a sign of the subjection of her nobler dispositions to organic demands. Organic dispositions simply co-operate in an effort to achieve what her intellect and her heart desire.

18. Thus the mother's influence is the natural way of arousing the beginnings of love and faith. At the same time it prepares the ground for the impressions, fraught with happiness, which father and brothers and sisters make upon him. The feelings of love and truthfulness are extended to the whole circle of domestic life. The child's sensory attachment to, and confidence in, his mother rises to the level of true human love and human faith. It reaches first to the father, brothers, and sisters, but the circle is constantly extended. Whom the mother

loves, the child loves also ; whom the mother trusts, he trusts.    Even when the mother says of some stranger, whom he sees for the first time, " He loves you : you must trust him ; he is a good man : give him your hand," the child smiles and gladly proffers the hand of innocence. Again, if the mother says to him, " You have a grand-father in distant lands who loves you," the child believes her.    He likes to speak to his mother of the grandfather, believes in his love and hopes for his inheritance.    Just in the same way, when the mother says, " I have a Father in heaven from whom all the good things come that you and I possess," the child believes his mother's words and trusts in this Heavenly Father.    And when she, as a Christian, prays to Him, when she reads the message of God's love in the Bible, and is quickened by its spirit, the child likes to pray with her ; he also believes in the word of Him whose spirit he has already learned to recog-nize in his mother's own doings.    In this way the child's simple love for his mother is naturally extended to the love of his fellows, and from this to the ideal faith and love of the true Christian.

This is the process by which the Elementary Method as we conceive it attempts to develop the moral and religious life of the child from its cradle onwards.

### B. Nature *v.* Nurture in the Development of Intellectual Power.

19. I pass to the next question.

How does man's intellectual life begin ?    What are the starting-points of his powers of thought, of investiga-tion and judgment, when Nature has its way ?

We find that our powers of thought begin in the im-pressions which objects make upon us.    Sensory contact with objects awakens their inherent readiness to develop of themselves.

20. Quickened by the impulse to development which it has awakened, this experience leads first of all to the consciousness of the impression which objects have made

upon us, and subsequently to their recognition. Then we feel the need of giving expression to the impressions which these experiences have made upon us. At first this takes the form of gesture and imitation, and then we are brought face to face with the more characteristically human need of language, the development of which renders gesture and imitation superfluous.

## Nature in the Development of Language.

21. The power of speech, which is essential to the development of the powers of thought, is a human device for making the knowledge gained by experience, of universal service. From the beginning, it develops only in close connection with the growth and extension of human knowledge ; this always takes precedence. The natural use of speech is concerned only with the things we have learned and the way we have learned them. What we have learned superficially we speak of in a superficial way. What we have learned wrongly we talk of incorrectly.

22. The natural way of acquiring the mother tongue and all other languages is associated with the acquisition of knowledge through experience, and the process of learning must follow the natural order in which the impressions of experience pass over into knowledge. If we apply this point of view to the question of the mother tongue, we find that as everything distinctively human only differentiates itself slowly from the lower elements of our nature from which it evolves, so also do our linguistic powers develop by slow degrees. The infant cannot speak until its organs of speech are formed. Moreover, it knows nothing at first, and cannot therefore desire to speak. Its desires and its capacity develop in proportion to the knowledge which it gradually acquires through experience. This is Nature's only way of teaching the infant how to speak, and all artificial aid must be directed along the same slow course, seeking to further it by making use of stimuli which the objects in the environment. and the various sounds and tones of the human voice afford.

*Nurture in the Development of Language.*

In order to teach the child to speak, the mother must work in line with his nature, and utilize all the stimuli to which ear, eye, and hand, are sensitive. When he is conscious of seeing, hearing, feeling, smelling, and tasting, he wants expressions for these impressions—*i.e.*, the desire to learn to speak of them and the power to do so grows in him. The mother must also employ the stimulus of sounds for this purpose. If she is anxious to teach the child to talk in a short time, she must repeat sounds now loudly, now softly, now singing, now laughing, and so on, with ever lively variety.

Her aim should be to make him want to imitate her. In the same way she must see that the impressions of the objects whose names she wants the child to remember accompany the words. She must bring these objects to his notice in their most important bearings and in the most diverse and entertaining relations, and must keep them there. She must only advance in the exercise of expression to the point at which impressions have been matured in the child. Skill, or rather the constant devotion of an intelligent mother, can hasten and enliven the slowness of this natural method of acquiring language, and it is the duty of the Elementary Method to find out how this hastening and enlivening may take place, with a view to providing the mother with precise and suitably ordered exercises. If this is done, the mother's heart will assuredly be found ready to make full use of them.

23. Nature's order in the acquisition of any other language is not so slow. (1) The child's organs of speech are fully developed in such circumstances. There are only a few new sounds to be mastered. In other respects his organs are quite efficient. (2) A child who is beginning another language has somehow through experience acquired a large variety of information which he expresses in his mother tongue with the utmost precision. Consequently the acquisition of each new language entails nothing but learning to exchange the familiar and mean-

ingful sounds of his own tongue for sounds with which he is unfamiliar. How to simplify this exchange by making use of mechanical methods, and by the preparation of exercises arranged in a psychological order, designed to elucidate ideas, the verbal equivalents for which have been already learned by these simple mechanical devices, is one of the most important problems awaiting solution at our hands.

Everybody feels the need of a psychological basis for the rudiments of language teaching, and I believe that in the continuous attempts which I have made during the last fifty years to simplify education in its initial stages I have arrived at some natural and effective methods of achieving this object.

### Higher Intellectual Training—

24. But, in order not to lose the thread of the exposition of my ideas concerning the Elementary Method, I will return to the argument that intellectual education, which always starts in experience, must be helped first of all by a natural system of language teaching. This help, if it is to serve in elucidating knowledge, must also be based on direct experience. Intellectual training, however, demands, by reason of its nature, treatment which will carry us still farther. We must provide assistance in the development of its powers of grouping, separating, and comparing objects which have been clearly apprehended by the senses. In this way we shall help the mind to rise to the power of correct judgment concerning the objects themselves and their properties— that is to say, to actual thought powers.

25. Intellectual training, and the race culture which depends upon it, demand continual search after devices designed to help forward the natural development of our powers of thought, of investigation, and of judgment, to the conscious possession of which mankind attained thousands of years ago. These devices, both in their nature and in their scope, are dependent on our power

of grouping, separating, and comparing, on our own
initiative, the objects which have been clearly apprehended
by our senses—in other words, on our power of logical
investigation and on the possibility of our rising in this
way to the level of the trained judgment.

### given by Number, Form, and Language Teaching.

26. These devices whereby it is hoped our capacity for
thought will be realized in the man of cultivated judgment
demand inquiry.   The problem of their nature and their
perfection constitutes another important concern of the
theory of the Elementary Method.   And since the logical
investigation of objects which have been clearly apprehended in experience manifestly finds its first natural
stimulus in the use we make of our acquired powers of
numbering and measuring, it follows that the best method
of achieving power in that regard will be found in simplified exercises in number and form.   We see, too, why
the theory of the Elementary Method regards simple
psychological treatment of number and form, together
with a similar treatment of language, as the most general
and the most effective means for the education of our
thought capacities, which is at the same time in conformity with Nature.

27. At Burgdorf our first experimental attempts to
apply these principles of simplified number and form
teaching met with strikingly uniform success.   It is, however, still more remarkable how later successes (in spite of
the narrowness of our tentative Burgdorf procedure and
of the apathy of later days) made it possible for my
school to live until now.   (It had been so long in a state
of decay ; for many years it was struggling against open
rebellion, and in the end it was brought to the very verge
of destruction.)   Even now, although our external
resources have sunk almost to zero, we have erected an
institution for men and women teachers.   This evidence
of vitality makes me still hopeful of the future.

## C. Nature v. Nurture in Development of Practical Capacity.

### 1. *Intellectual and Moral Factors.*

28. Thirdly, in answer to the question, " How does practical capacity begin to unfold ?" (the power, that is to say, of giving expression to the products of the intellect and of putting into action the impulses of the heart, the power which makes it possible to fulfil the duties of domestic and civic life), we see at once that it rests on a foundation of twofold character, an inner and an outer, an intellectual and a physical. It is also obvious that the secret of the training of practical and professional capacity lies in training intellectual capacity, in cultivating the power of thought and judgment, which in its turn depends upon methodical training in the use of the senses. We must admit that he who has had a good—that is, a natural—and liberal grounding in arithmetic, in mensuration, and in the drawing which they involve, has within him the requisite bases of practical capacity and technical skill. It only remains for him to cultivate systematically within the limits of his theoretical acquirements the external use of his senses and limbs, giving special attention to the particular dexterities required for the craft which he wishes to learn. Just as simplified exercises in number and form must, from their nature, be regarded as the special intellectual gymnastic of practical capacity, so, again, the mechanical exercise of the senses and of the limbs, which is necessary in training external technique, must be recognized as the physical gymnastic of practical capacity.

29. The Elementary training of practical capacity (of which vocational capacity must be regarded as a particular application suited to individual position and circumstances) thus rests upon two foundations, and the natural methods of training it consist in the stimulation and training of two fundamentally different capacities, the intellectual and the physical. Such methods are, however, only truly educational when they are at the same time part and parcel of the general training of the three sides of human culture.

## 2. *Physical Factors.*

30. I have already dealt with the moral and intellectual elements in practical training; it remains to deal with the physical side. As the disposition to develop is the chief source of power in the development of our moral and intellectual capacities, so the necessary stimulus to the natural training of practical capacity on its physical side is to be found in a like disposition which is also characteristic of our senses and of our limbs. Naturally disposed to activity, the oncoming of intellectual and physical stimuli makes the realization of that disposition a practical certainty. The teacher's art has really little to do with this disposition. The physical impulse to put senses and limbs to use belongs to our primitive nature. The teacher's aim will be to make this primitive impulse conform to the moral and intellectual principles which guide him, in which he is assisted and encouraged by environmental forces and by the influences of home life.

The wise and careful use of the educational resources of domestic life is just as important in physical advancement as in moral and intellectual. These resources vary with the position and circumstances of the home, but, though available resources differ greatly, the use we make of them—physical, moral, and intellectual—is subjected to unchangeable laws, and is therefore itself unchanging. To illustrate from our methods of art education : we teach the child first to recognize the accuracy of each artistic form ; then he learns to reproduce it. After practising in this way, he tries to gain facility and delicacy in representing other forms, and when he can do this he is ready for freedom and independence in his work.

That is Nature's typical procedure in the practical education of our race. In her hands the child practises a graded series of exercises designed to bring him up to a certain standard of correctness (of form), of power (in reproducing), and of delicacy (in representing), and the results of these several exercises harmonize and blend among themselves to give him the technique without which a man's craft can never be ennobling in its influence upon him, nor will he in all sincerity seek perfection in it.

31. The natural order of development of the mechanical[1] bases of practical capacity agrees perfectly with Nature's order in the development of its inner, intellectual bases, and thus fixes for us the natural way of coming into harmony with the fundamental methods employed in training mind and heart. The education of all three sides of our nature proceeds on common lines in equal measure, as is necessary if the unity of our nature and the equilibrium of its powers are to be recognized from the outset.

## Equilibrium and Harmony of our Powers.

32. I will now look more closely into that important witness to the unity of man's nature—namely, the equilibrium of his moral, intellectual, and physical capacities, or, in other words, the equilibrium of the capacities of heart, head, and hand. Although the effect of dominance in one direction is accomplished at the expense of all the good that comes from their proper co-ordination (and from that alone), it is nevertheless the fact that undue emotional and religious development of a superficial kind, along with weakness and confusion on the intellectual and practical side, may be associated in a loving soul with an earnest seeking after Divine and human sources of strength. But when a man's balance of mind has been lost in this way, in spite of his well-meant efforts to make up for intellectual deficiencies, and in spite of a weak and superficial search after knowledge of the truth, he only sinks still more into dreamy speculation, and becomes almost incapable of recognizing truth and justice and of fulfilling the duties which depend upon such recognition.

However honest his heart may have been, the violence

---

[1] If the student will read "habit" for "mechanical," he will have a clearer idea of Pestalozzi's meaning.

of his efforts to attain what he must misunderstand, and even despise, because of the paltriness and deceit associated with the circumstances of its attainment, must weaken the Divine purity of his own love, and leave him deplorably divided against himself, and, from man's point of view, incurably impotent. Yet he is not beyond the power of God. He who seeks His aid, and, under His direction, that of man also, is not beyond the power of restoration. He can never lose recuperative capacity to the same extent as those who, in spite of their shortcomings in essential matters, lack the holy impulse to seek new strength in their faith in God and in their love for their fellow-men. The low pleasure we take in the external results of special capacity, intellectual or practical or vocational, tends to prevent our feeling the absence of love and faith in ourselves ; and, not realizing the want, there is no effort to make up, and so to restore, the balance of our nature. This takes place in such a way that its reparation, from a human point of view, is almost impossible. It leads in extreme cases to a condition of callousness which is inconceivable in the futile blunderings of the most unintelligent love or the most inactive faith.

33. Piety, faith, and love, with all their weakness and all their error, make for restful adjustment. Intellectual, practical, or professional power without faith and love is an inexhaustible source of unrest, which vitally affects the natural development of human capacity.


## Esprit de Corps.

34. However, it is certain that the callousness which completely paralyzes sincere effort to improve (that callousness to which pride in our intellectual and physical capacities leads so easily and in such divers ways) is not engendered so readily in pious and loving natures or in those who are intellectually or physically weak. But this only holds good of individuals as such. As soon as men are associated in groups they lose that sense of individual weakness which is the essential foundation

of true love and faith, and so necessary to sincere effort towards improvement. *En masse* their lower instincts lead them to feel individually and socially stronger than they really are. The sense of individual weakness in conflict with the stirring sense of their power and their rights as a body produces in them a tendency to hypocritical self-deception. They grow proud of their collective power, and passionately unfriendly and insincere towards all those whose opinions and judgments do not coincide with those of the body to which they belong. In this way individual power and the sober religious idea of self-improvement are not only weakened, but actually tend to generate in them rude feelings of arrogant presumption and harsh ideas of violence, such as belong to the callous worldling who has lost all idea of ever being better and stronger than he is. *Esprit de corps*, in the religious as well as in the civic sense, is not a spiritual product. It is a fleshly thing, which produces the same results as one-sided intellectual or physical education. Our theory of elementary education has thus an important bearing on the question of maintaining equilibrium in the education of man's powers.[1]

## Of Teaching Methods in General.

35. I will now proceed to consider what the theory of the Elementary Method has to say with respect to educational appliances. Conformity to Nature generally demands the greatest simplification of these appliances, and all my pedagogical work has been based upon this idea. At first, my purpose was confined to an effort to effect the greatest possible simplification of them, with the object of making the practice of the school more like that of the home. This idea naturally led me to try to organize sequences of educational exercises, which in all branches of human learning and activity should start with the very simplest, and proceed in continuous and unbroken gradation from easy to more difficult, keeping

[1] *Cf. How Gertrude Teaches her Children*, p. 137.

step with the growth of the pupil's powers, taking their
cue from him, always stimulating him, never causing him
weariness or exhaustion.   The possibility of a straightforward psychological achievement of this idea depends
on the recognition of the difference between the method
of unfolding man's fundamental capacities, which follow
certain unchangeable laws, and the methods adopted
in teaching special branches of knowledge and special
dexterities in which those powers are applied.

These last differ from each other as completely as the
objects which we strive to know and put to use, and as
completely as the position and circumstances of the
individuals concerned differ.   The Elementary Method
proposes to avoid confusion by giving the first place to
the methods of developing capacity.   These are constant.
We cannot, of course, put powers to practical use until
they are developed.   It does this admirably, inasmuch as
in the whole series of exercises for developing and applying
our powers it seeks to perfect each step before a forward
move is made.   In this way it produces in the pupil,
both by the exercises for developing his powers and those
for applying them, a conscious effort towards perfection,
which is not only calculated to bring into closest agreement the method of developing the capacities with that
of training in their application, but is also likely to make
high standards of work habitual.

## Is our Ideal a Chimera ?

36. For the moment I shall leave the various consequences of this point of view.   Before going further I will
consider the question, Is not this our theory of an Elementary Method a mere dream ?   Does it give the ground-
work of anything that is really practicable ?   I am often
cogently asked, Where can one really find an example
of its working ?   My answer is, Everywhere and nowhere !
There are solitary illustrations of its feasibility everywhere, but you will find it in perfection nowhere.   It
has never been tried with a completely organized equip-

ment. No elementary school or institution exists which corresponds to our ideal in all its details.

But man's knowledge and capacity grows in piecemeal fashion in all its branches; even what is highest and best in our culture has been arrived at in this way. Educational progress is similarly piecemeal. Man goes now forwards, now backwards. No condition occurs, or can occur, which entirely meets our demands. There are unconquerable obstacles in human nature itself which prevent its being carried out on a scale of completeness. Characteristically human weaknesses of intellect and of heart, the inner, Divine nature of which chafes beneath the mantle of our corruptible body, does not suffer us to attain absolute perfection at any point. Even the most able of men, in all his endeavours to perfect himself in this or that way, must say with Paul, " Not as though I had already attained, either were already perfect, but I follow after, if so be that I may attain."[1]  If this is true of individuals, it is infinitely more true of all collective strivings after culture.

No institution, even it receive both material and spiritual help and encouragement on a royal scale, can succeed in making the theory of the Elementary Me.hod a perfect practical method for the training and instruction of all types of children. I repeat that human nature is constitutionally opposed to the introduction of this lofty theory all at once in its universal and perfect form. All our knowledge and all our skill is partial, and will remain so until the end of time. Our progress in knowledge and skill, even the advance in our ideals (inasmuch as these are determined by the limited progress of individual men and individual communities), must be halting and incomplete, leading us at times to place obstacles in the way of those who are actually contributing to the improvement of the existing state of things.

37. We must say it without reservation : a method of education and instruction corresponding completely to our idea of an Elementary Method is not conceivable in practice.

[1] Phil. iii. 12.

Into whatever prominence you bring its principles, however much you simplify its measures, however clearly you show the theoretical consistency of its practice, external consistency is inconceivable; every individual man will carry out its measures differently in accordance with his own individuality. In one case a man's impulse to put the theory into practice will come from his heart; he throws himself into the task with all the ardour of his love. Another's power is intellectual; he seeks to achieve his object through the clearness and accuracy of his ideas concerning it. Again, another will seek to achieve it through the practical and professional capacities with which he is specially endowed. It is well that it is so. There is genius of heart, genius of head, and genius of hand. God has created them. Some men are endowed in particular directions disproportionately beyond their fellows. They are the "millionaires" of those inner sources of moral, intellectual, and physical capacity, but, in the depths of their triune nature, they are animated by individual egoism in no way different from that which moves the "millionaires" of finance and power who live in our midst. Like the millionaires, the variety of the demands which their special gifts occasion, produces a whole series of dependents who are actually interested in maintaining the predominance of a particular craft, or a particular point of view, and set themselves in opposition to others who have also special but different interests. It follows that the general equilibrium is not disturbed, but that the patchwork type of progress which is characteristically human is kept up. It is necessary to recognize this as the natural method of progress in knowledge and in power, and as bound up with the reality of human welfare.

38. So long as we do not realize this, we must regard the theory of the Elementary Method as a delusion, and consider it impossible to put it into practice in its entirety. But as soon as we recognize that its aims are those of human culture in general, and accept as natural the piecemeal advance of knowledge, with the consequent hindrances

to progress, then we are admittedly in line with the final
purpose of humanity, and we think no more of the dis-
credited idea that we are deluded folk who take pleasure
in dreaming idly of the impracticable.

39. No! It is my duty to work towards an all-em-
bracing human purpose, for that cannot be eternally
impracticable; it must not be thought of as such.    This is
exactly the position we claim for our theory of the Elementary Method    Although such an aim can never reach
inner perfection in the forms and figures of actual practice,
nevertheless men who are uncorrupted and undisfigured
by the culture of their day cannot help working towards
it, and their efforts have effected such degree of attainment in morals, intellect, and physique, as the civilized
world has achieved.    Similarly, every principle of natural
education, every sound method of instruction, is its work.
I repeat that our ideal is everywhere in evidence, and yet
nowhere.    In its perfection it is nowhere; as partially
expressed, as an object of effort, it is everywhere.    To
ignore it entirely is to ignore all that is Divine and eternal
in man—the very essence of human nature, the only
really human thing in us.    Making the methods of education conform to Nature's laws (that is to say, the theory of
the Elementary Method) is at bottom nothing but bringing
them into harmony with the indestructible characteristics
of that eternal spark of Divinity which is always in conflict
with our lower sensuous nature.

To seek the satisfaction of sensory nature is characteristic of animal, as opposed to distinctively human,
purpose.    It follows, therefore, that the doctrines of the
theory of elementary education, which springs from the
life of the soul itself, are in constant conflict with the
whole web of sensuous artifice and with the overpowering
claims of the flesh.    The general opinion of those who
are giving attention to the problem of educating the people
as a whole, rather than to the problem of the education
of the individual, is not friendly to the consideration of
its claims and of what its measures might accomplish.
This is inevitable.    The practical organization of national

education demands power, skill, and effort of a physical character, rather than moral and intellectual. But carnal desire of every sort must be in complete subjection to mind, and the spirit of the Elementary Method as we conceive it works towards the sincere recognition of the necessity of such subjection. When I consider how I have striven for the recognition of our ideals, I remember that there was very little sign of them in the elementary schools for the people. I worked with all my might for the simplification of the common forms of popular education as the most effective method of combating successfully current educational evils. But my lofty ideals were pre-eminently the product of a kind, well-meaning soul, inadequately endowed with the intellectual and practical capacity which might have helped considerably to further my heartfelt desire. It was the product of an extremely vivid imagination, which in the stress of my daily life proved unable to produce any important results. I was rather like a child who thinks himself in battle with powerful opponents, in support of his fanciful ideals. The more the child persists in his dreamy efforts, the more prolonged is his defeat. Under such conditions, I naturally could not produce anything more than suggestions, sometimes vivid and brilliant, but on the whole ineffective. As you would expect, however, a natural method of education, based on man's spiritual nature, generally does appeal to individuals, and that in proportion to their own spirituality.

40. Whilst the unnatural artificiality which springs from worldliness and self-seeking, the charms of sensuous pleasure, the force of imitation, and the powerful influence of the crowd, are poisonous in their influence on man's primitive nature, on the other hand a natural course of Elementary education, followed with sincerity of aim and with concentration of purpose, always exerts a powerful influence on man's spiritual nature. It makes him more susceptible to moral and intellectual stimuli by freeing him from self-consciousness. The methods of Elementary education, directed as they are to the im-

provement of the race, offer effective opposition to the attractions and to the consequences of artificiality in life. The wisdom of all the ages tells in unambiguous terms how great is the effect of conformity to nature when we are concerned to educate and quicken our powers. This is exactly what is claimed by the theory of the Elementary Method whenever it comes into contact with unspoiled human beings. But life should not be regarded from the visionary standpoint of complete perfection, but in full view rather of its fragmentary impulses and their exciting causes, each impulse being an effort towards an ever-approaching perfection.

41. I will now examine from the moral, intellectual, and physical points of view the results of our attempts to investigate the influence of Elementary educational methods on human culture, without losing sight of the fundamental principle, that *Life is the great educator.*

## " Elementary " Method and Moral Training.

42. (a) The theory of Elementary Method touches the moral life of the child in so far as it makes its whole procedure dependent on the instinctive feelings that attach to parenthood and family life.

It is indisputable that faith and love, which are the God-given foundations of all true morality and religion, begin and develop in the intercourse between parent and child. We cannot boast of having had experience in school with children from their cradles upwards, but our methods are nevertheless, in their moral aspect, applicable to early infancy ; indeed, they apply to the moral nature far earlier than it is possible for them to be used in their intellectual and practical aspects. The child loves and trusts before it thinks and acts, and the influence of home life stimulates it and raises it to the moral level, which is taken for granted in what we think and do ; and we can say—in spite of our lack of experience with infants— with the utmost conviction, that the simple procedure of Elementary Method which makes children of any age capable of sharing what they know with other children about them, has preserved the moral force of the school, and produced there the feeling of brotherhood and sisterhood. We have at various epochs in our common life seen this mutual feeling of love and confidence produce results striking enough to convince onlookers that our way of working was a successful extension of the moral influences of home life, thereby bringing us nearer to a practical solution of a problem of urgent importance in our time.

## " Elementary " Method and Intellectual Training.

43. (b) On the intellectual side, we accept the same fundamental principle, *Life educates.* Just as moral education begins in inner experiences—*i.e.,* in impressions which touch our feelings—so the education of the intellect results from the experience of objects which act as stimuli upon our senses. Nature brings the whole range of our sense-impressions to bear on life. All our knowledge of the outside world is the result of sensory experiences. Even our dreams come from that source. The common impulse towards development which our senses share with all our potential capacities, compels us to see, hear, smell, taste, feel, touch, walk, and so on ; but our hearing, smelling, tasting, feeling, touching, walking, is only educative in so far as the eye is directed towards right seeing, the ear towards right hearing, and so on. This education in the right use of our faculties depends upon the impressions being properly matured which the objects concerned have made upon our senses. Wherever impressions have not perfectly matured, then we do not apprehend the object in its full sensory significance. We only partially apprehend it. The perception is not educative. It does not affect the educative possibilities of our nature as it might. The result does not satisfy our nature, and, to that extent, the procedure adopted has not been natural. Just as the instinctive feeling of parenthood forms a Divine centre for the natural development of moral

education, so must intellectual education proceed from a centre which is capable of bringing to perfect maturity the immediate results of sensory experience. In this way only will it become educative and natural. Clearly such a centre can be found only in the round of domestic life which the child watches from morning to evening from the cradle upwards. It is indisputably the repeated experience amongst objects, their frequent and varied appearance, which brings his sense-impressions to maturity and perfection. Wherever there is home life this is true, and outside the home there is no place in which the objects appeal to the child's senses, from early infancy, so persistently, so uninterruptedly, so diversely, and in such a variously human way. No other impressions are so naturally educative as these.

### Life Educates.

It is here that one feels the need of distinguishing between human faculty and its development on the one hand, and the particular practical use to which capacity will be put on the other. Practical use will, of course, vary with family circumstances, but in every case it should be, as it were, automatically connected with the fundamental faculties which have been developed in the individual. These furnish the basis for the training of the practical faculties. And, since the methods of developing human faculty are in principle the same in all ranks and in all circumstances, whilst the methods of developing practical abilities are infinitely various, we must consider the principle, " Life educates," from two points of view. First, do the influences of life favour the natural development of faculty ? And, second, do the situations of life teach the child in a natural way to make practical use of his faculties when they are developed ? The answer is simple. Life develops human powers, even under the most diverse circumstances, in accordance with unchanging laws, which apply equally whether the child concerned crawls in the gutter or is heir to the throne.

As to the putting capacities to use, vital influences are always in perfect harmony with diversity of circumstance, rank, and condition, and equally in harmony with the peculiarities of the individual himself. This latter influence is therefore in its nature quite different from the former.

44. We may now see what lines our art will follow in stimulating the natural development of the sensory activities in infancy. Its business is to bring to the child's notice in a striking and commanding way the sensory objects of home life, and in this way to make them educative in the best sense of the word. The Elementary methods of training sensory experience are simply psychological devices for stimulating innate impulses to self-development. They represent an endeavour to make the sensory impressions of objects educative, by encouraging him to concentrate his attention upon them.

## Words and Things.

45. This method of training sense-experience also stimulates the development of the powers of speech, inasmuch as, when sensory impressions are really educative, they give rise to the need for expression.

46. The natural training of the faculty of speech is thus intrinsically and intimately related to the process of nature in the development of sensory activities, and the methods of the educator must be similarly related to each other.

The training of the faculty of speech is based upon life, as is the training of the senses. The principle, " Life teaches," is just as true and just as trenchant in the development of the one as in that of the other. Agreement of procedure can therefore only be really achieved by linking all our methods to the home life of the child and to the whole range of perceptual experience that belongs thereto.

Sensory impressions should, however, be distinctly apprehended before the child learns the arbitrary catchwords which express them.

47. Whenever we put empty words into a child's mind, and impress them upon his memory, as if they were real knowledge, or genuine means of acquiring it, even when neither his feelings nor his experience of things are in a position to furnish clues to their meaning, we are obviously deviating from the principle, " Life teaches." We are sowing the seeds of an artificial use of the Divine gift of speech. We are sowing the seeds of callous insincerity and shallowness to which is due so much of the blundering arrogance which is characteristic of our time.

The principle " Life teaches " in this connection lays it down that the faculty of speech is a means of putting to use the knowledge acquired through sensory experience. It begins of necessity with the naming of objects that come under notice, and advances to the changes which they undergo. The more extensive and definite our sensory acquaintance with objects and their qualities, the more extensive and definite are the natural foundations of the faculty of speech. Accordingly, the faculty of speech in every child depends upon the extent and accuracy of his sensory acquaintance with things, and if these are wanting, the teacher must first fill up the gaps.

48. The natural progress in learning his mother tongue, and the educational advantages thereof, are limited by his sensory acquaintance with the things about him. Just as the child requires many years to get clear ideas of the objects in his environment through varied contact with them, so it requires many years to bring him to the point of being able to express himself with accuracy about them. Moreover, natural progress in this direction depends on his being constantly and variously made to feel the need for greater accuracy. To extend and quicken his direct knowledge of things is the only true method of furthering, in a natural way, the acquisition of the mother tongue.

The outward manifestations of speech, the sounds themselves, unless intimately associated with the experiences which give them significance, are empty and idle. Only by the consciousness of this relation to experience do they become true human sounds. The initial preparation that comes from the words which the child hears spoken is for a long time merely mechanical, but this mechanical preparation for learning to read should not be neglected by those who are concerned in his reading lessons. The words which the infant hears only become gradually educative for him. For a long time, like the clanging of bells, the thud of the hammer, like the calls of the animals, and all other sounds in Nature, they only make a sensory impression upon him. But this impression is important for speech training. The impression as such gradually becomes perfected with his hearing. As his hearing becomes perfect, the power of vocal imitation is slowly developed. The child learns now to utter a number of word-sounds, the meaning of which he does not know ; but he is in that way prepared informally to grasp this meaning more easily, and to retain it more steadfastly, than he otherwise would be.

The Elementary Method, in cultivating the child's speech, limits itself to employing the impressions which Nature puts at random before the child's senses, but extends this natural process along definite lines adapted to his capacities and requirements.

This is inevitable. For just as it is essential for the training of the child's faculty of observation that the circle of observation objects in his surroundings should be comprehensive enough for the development of the knowledge that is necessary to him, but should not extend so far beyond his requirements as to distract and confuse him in essentials, so is it just as necessary that the linguistic range of the child, within the limits of which he is to learn to read, shall be comprehensive enough for the requirements of his position, but not so extensive as to confuse the relations which should exist between speech-power and the actualities of life. This point of view applies with equal force to all methods for developing and cultivating other human faculties.

Even the education of the poorest child, whose position and circumstances are the narrowest you can think of,

can never proceed too far on the lines of this natural
Elementary method, if we are concerned for the genuine
solidity of fundamentals. We cannot train him to be
too kind, too intellectual, too active and industrious ;
but in training him to put these powers to practical use,
we must, from the moment we take him in hand, keep
him within the limits corresponding to the demands of
his actual life. It is on these lines that the practice of
Elementary Method is able to preserve its principles in
training the child to use his senses for the acquisition of
knowledge, and in training him to talk.

Education, even in the first stages of the child's training, even in its efforts towards the development of the
faculties of speech and sense, must never stand in the way
of life's needs ; it must never aim to further knowledge
of things or of words unsuited to the child's position in
life, or likely to set up differences between home and
school—two institutions which should always be in
harmony. Education should never make the child discontented with, or unfitted for, his station ; it should
never create discord between the child and his life.

## DIFFERENCE BETWEEN DEVELOPMENT OF FACULTY AND TRAINING TO PUT FACULTY TO USE.

49. Such, then, is the importance of recognizing the
difference between the conformity to Nature in cultivating
human faculties and conformity to Nature in cultivating
their practical application. The difference between the
Elementary methods of developing our faculties and the
Elementary methods of training our powers of putting
them to use is closely related to the difference in the extent
to which the devices for cultivating the faculties of
language, observation, thought, and art must be applied
in the various ranks of life. The close connection of this
twofold difference shows how necessary it is that education in its initial steps should hold fast to the course of
Nature, both in the methods of developing our faculties
and in those for training our practical dexterities.

## Method of Teaching Foreign Languages.

The peace of the world and the true welfare of all ranks is dependent on the recognition of this truth. The most sacred bonds of social life will be weakened from misconception in this matter, so far as it concerns domestic and public education. I will go farther. The "natural" method of acquiring any other language than the mother tongue involves, as I said before, the use of essentially different methods. They consist in the simplification of the process of changing the sounds of the mother tongue, the meaning of which is already familiar, into the sounds of another language which are not familiar.

If this process of transformation, from the psychological point of view, follows Nature, although absolutely different from the artificial and routine processes commonly employed, it will be found extremely easy. Experience shows that it depends on the following dictum : " Learning to speak is, *per se* (at least in the initial stages), not a question of intellectual training, but of listening to others, and trying to speak one's self." The knowledge of grammatical rules is merely a test as to whether the natural means of learning to speak and of listening thereto has achieved its object satisfactorily. Grammar is the end of a psychologically well-arranged method of learning to speak, not the beginning. But for a long time teachers have neglected to bring the general theory of speech to bear upon the problem of learning a foreign language. The more intellectual side of the work (*i.e.*, the study of grammar) must be postponed until the mechanical facility in speaking has been considerably advanced. Grammar rules will then make explicit what is already known implicitly. With regard to living languages, this is sometimes admitted—it should *always* be so—but it is absolutely denied with reference to the dead languages, and as proof of the position we are told that instruction in the dead languages, in spite of the alleged deficiencies of the routine methods of teaching the rudiments, has achieved in our days astoundingly good results, and that in its more advanced stages it has followed lines that psychologists would approve. However that may be, it is still true that the more elementary stages of instruction in the ancient languages cannot be considered satisfactory, whether from the psychological or from the more mechanical point of view. The admirable work in the higher stages has no proper psychologically or mechanically graded foundation. I am so sure of this that I venture to urge that the present routine process in learning the rudiments of the ancient languages is contrary to Nature. I know quite well how these words will be resented, coming as they do from one who does not know the ancient languages, and has no experience of the advantages which the method of teaching them claims.

But while, on the one hand, I recognize my incapacity to judge the more advanced instruction, and willingly concede everything which follows from this, on the other hand I hold that this very ignorance of the routine processes of language teaching has helped me to simplify the methods, by bringing them into psychological harmony with the course of Nature, and making it at once effective and fruitful. My ignorance, I say, has helped me in one way to investigate more fully the simplicity of this process of Nature in the acquisition of dead languages, and the psychological and mechanical bases of the process, than would have been possible for me if I had learnt the ancient and modern languages perfectly in the best of their routine forms.

50. I saw very soon that the methods of intellectual education which are based on the simplified teaching of form and number are imperfect, and as a rule ineffective in their results on education, if they are not allied with an equally effective simplification of language teaching. And, since I personally am quite unable to reorganize and extend the method of teaching number and form, not having had the necessary experience in these branches, I have given all my attention to the step which lies between the elementary but systematic training of sensory experience and the training of the faculty of thought.

My only claim to influence on the reorganization of the theory of elementary education lies in the department of language teaching.

51. The natural method of teaching every language is essentially the natural method of developing and training the faculty of speech, and is consequently very closely related to the natural method of developing sensory experience. It constitutes in reality an intermediate stage between the latter and the methods of training thought-powers proper. Language teaching forms, therefore, the necessary intermediate link between the intellectually stimulated sensory activity and the faculty of thought.

The means for developing this intermediate link are therefore necessarily mechanical in their initial stages. This is inevitable, and the faculty of speech is the organ which adjusts the impressions of sense-activity to the necessity for developing the faculty of thought.

52. These three faculties (sense, speech, and thought) are to be considered as the sum-total of all the means for developing the intellect, the origin of which is to be found in the senses and the successive stages of natural development of speech and thought respectively. The similarity between the methods of developing the sensory faculties and the faculty of speech strongly confirm this view. The method for developing sensory experience begins with real objects ; the recognition of their different properties and their different activities constitutes an efficient training for this faculty. Corresponding thereto, the primary method of exercising the faculty of speech begins with substantives ; these are followed by adjectives and verbs, thus forming the link between the method of developing sensory efficiency and the method of training the faculty of thought.

### LANGUAGE TEACHING IN RELATION TO LIFE.

The great educational principle, " Life teaches," is applicable to the utmost extent of its claims in respect of the development of sensory experience, and it is equally true and important when applied to the development of speech. One might say it was doubly true and doubly important when we consider the faculty of speech in its capacity as an intermediary link between the method of developing sensory experience and the methods of developing the faculty of thought.

The Elementary training of speech, if it is given when the child is learning to talk, is dependent upon the laws which govern speech development on the one hand, and on the other upon the infinitely dissimilar circumstances of the children concerned. Learning to speak does not result from language teaching; language teaching results from being able to speak.

However, it is not the dissimilarity of the forms of speech and idiom which determines the great difference in the manner in which linguistic facility should be developed; it is the conditions, circumstances, and environment; together with individual capacity which are the determining factors. In one case these things naturally extend the province of learning to speak, and in another naturally limit it. This applies to whole classes as well as to individual men.

Just as the objects of sensory experience, as well as the methods of employing them for the cultivation of intellectual and practical power, are more limited in the case of the agricultural labourer than for the professional or commercial man, so, on the other hand, these same objects and methods are more limited in the case of the city professional or commercial man than in the case of those who are being educated for an intellectual career, or more particularly than for those whose circumstances raise them above the necessity of attending to the establishment or maintenance of the economic position of their house and connections, with all the attendant restrictions and self-sacrifice which that means.

53. The undeniable significance and reality of these different classes in human society makes it clear that the artificial aids to language teaching both at home and at school must be brought into harmony with the real

foundations of the actual life of men and of the different
social classes.

Only in this way can they be recognized as being in
conformity to Nature, and as being conducive to the
actual well-being of the human race.

The methods employed in training the faculty of speech
must, therefore, as a general rule, be very differently
organized in each of these classes and ranks. They must
in each case satisfy the requirements of the position, but
in no case must they degenerate into an obstacle to well-
being and to tranquillity.

They must always be associated with the objects which
are available for training in sensory experience, and with
the things which are essential for the cultivation of moral,
intellectual, and practical power. If language teaching is in
harmony with them, its influence cannot fail to be good.

54. The child of the soil and the whole class of landless
agricultural labourers must learn in their language lessons
to express themselves accurately about everything which
has to do with their calling, their duty, and their environment ; they must also be able to express themselves spontaneously concerning what is elevating or edifying in their
religion with simplicity, sincerity, and fervour. The
heartfelt language of prayer should be acquired in the
dialect of the lowliest huts. In the happy spirit which is
characteristic of their age, children's command of speech
must be equal to the needs of their emotional life, just as
it should enable them to take full advantage of their surroundings and circumstances. But laborious toil is their
lot in life, and their language lessons must not set up
interests which would undermine the bases of their happiness and well-being. For this reason it is important that
men should not be led by their lessons into the habit of
idle chatter. They should learn to speak only after
deliberation ; the association of speech with thought
should be absolute.

The tendency to chatter which an unpsychological
method of speech training may easily produce is extremely
injurious, and particularly so for those who must earn

their bread by the sweat of their brow. Education should enable men to follow their particular calling with godliness and honour. We of the present generation call ourselves cultured, but do we take pains to insure that time is not lost on useless accomplishments which should be given to the serious acquisition of what is immediately necessary?

55. Of course, the artisan and professional class, including the landed proprietor, who belongs to this class by reason of his estates and his industrial interests, needs a more extensive linguistic training ; but this, too, must be based upon the realities of actual life.

The fundamental bases of citizen honour and comfort, and of the modest rectitude of the artisan, commercial, and professional class, used to find admirable expression in the superior linguistic training they received in the ordinary way of their lives—the books they read, for example—as compared with the advantages which the rural population as a whole enjoy.

The Church hymnal, and, in part also, the songs that belonged to their trade guilds and corporate life, their workshop rhymes, etc., were a genuine testimony to the development of a language faculty which was in harmony with their lives, and stirred the deep places of their souls without disturbing their social content. So with them we must return to the natural principles of former times. At present we give them a large vocabulary relating to things which are either useless or which have no bearing upon their general welfare, whereas in respect of the real requirements for their moral, domestic, and civic welfare, we give in general a vocabulary that is already too limited, and is growing more so every day. Even since my childhood we have grown conspicuously less careful in this matter.

The burgher class require a burgher language, based upon the realities of their actual life and calculated to stimulate burgher interests. This we do not provide, because—at any rate, in many of our towns—there is no such thing as burgher life, and as long as this is so, there can be no burgher language.

56. The burgher class requires the language neither of the *bon ton* nor of the different kinds of the *mauvais genre du ton*. They have no connection with the realities of the genuine burgher life ; indeed, they are directly opposed to the public and private welfare of this class. I will not discuss the language training which is acquired by the burgher class through the general frequenting of the municipal promenades, the theatres, and the casino, nor what is gained by reading-circles and other such public facilities for language teaching.

57. The professional and higher classes gain just as little help from the modern spirit as the burgher and agricultural classes.

It seems as if we thought that the higher classes must learn to think and to live by being able to speak, and not that it is life which compels them to learn to speak and to think. Thus it comes about that the training of the power to deal with real situations, which is the natural basis of speaking, thinking, and living, is as good as lost. The essential motive for the practical training of the powers of sense, of speech, and of thought, has disappeared.

The consequent gaps in the training of individuals are great and of serious moment. Of what use is an excess of the power of application when the powers to be applied are themselves lacking ? Faculties untrained, badly trained, or unnaturally trained, from the point of view of their influence, are even worse than complete absence of faculty.

I must not put too much confidence in this idea of mine, but I would urge the point of view upon the upper classes for their serious deliberation. Their dignity, welfare, and independence, and the welfare of all the dependent classes, are bound up with the question.

58. The necessity for extending, strengthening, and quickening the capacity for culture among the upper classes is really just as urgent as that of making the knowledge and linguistic powers of the lower classes harmonize with their actual needs. To endow them extravagantly with knowledge which is not only superfluous and unproduc-

tive, but even injurious and disadvantageous, is surely mistaken, especially when it goes with very slight attention to the cultivation of practical ability, to say nothing of the increasingly superficial habit of thought and judgment which is engendered.

## How a Child Learns to Speak.

59. To return to the question of the natural method of developing the faculty of speech. *How does the child learn to speak, and how is it prepared beforehand therefor?* From its birth the child is just as observant of the tones which fall on its ear as of the objects which are brought to its consciousness by the sense of sight or by any other of its senses. The training of those organs by which the objects of his sensory environment are brought into consciousness is closely bound up with the training of the organs of speech.

The child at an early age feels within him the power of being able to reproduce the sounds which he hears, and this power becomes more active, like every other human faculty, by the spontaneous impulse to put it to use. By use the speech organs are actually, though imperceptibly, strengthened from day to day.

Crying, which the child does not need to learn, is in its varied articulations the first utterance of the innate faculty of speech. Next come sounds which have no connection with the articulations of human speech, but which possess a great similarity to the sounds of various animals. They proceed from the pressure of organs which are trying to develop in a purely instinctive fashion, and they have no connection with the human sounds uttered by those around them. It is only after several months that these sounds gradually begin to have a perceptible connection with the sounds of the vowels and consonants contained in our words, and to approximate to the sounds of some syllables and words which have been often spoken in their presence. The child now begins to imitate the easiest sounds which his mother says to him.

Learning to speak becomes daily easier and more pleasant to him, and is always associated in its progress with the cultivation of his sensory powers, exercised as they are in the circle of his home life and surroundings.

## RELATION OF WORDS TO THINGS.

Thus we see that, as regards the faculty of speech, it is life itself which really trains the human race and makes for progress. All the means which life affords for the development of culture must be utilized in order that advance may be uniform and harmonious. The training of the emotions, the training of the intellect, artistic and technical training, must develop in Nature's order if there is to be sound progress in language training. If each of these is regarded as a separate unit, it means a departure from the natural principle ; it means the substitution of the artificial devices for true and genuine means of developing our faculties. We make children read before they can speak ; we attempt to make them read by means of books ; we prevent them forcibly from becoming familiar with actual objects—the natural basis of speech —and in the most irrational way we make the lifeless alphabet the starting-point of their sensory experience instead of a spirited firsthand acquaintance with Nature herself. Man must be able to speak correctly and with assurance about many things before he is sufficiently mature to read any book with intelligence. But in these days the appearance of skill is more sought after than skill itself, and all genuine means for cultivating the faculties are rendered worthless by the ever-increasing belief in spurious methods of development. If I consider now the method of learning to speak as it actually takes place (and this is the essential basis of language training), I see that the infant child hears from those around him a large number of verbal sounds, the meaning of which is at first quite unintelligible to him. Many of these, by frequent repetition, affect his sense of hearing; they become familiar to him, and he can imitate them skilfully without in the least comprehending them or guessing at their meaning. This premature, mysterious knowledge which the ear acquires, and this skill of the speech organs in repetition, is an essential preparatory stage for the real cultivation of the faculty of speech.

By anticipating the idea of an object through familiarity with the word which denotes it, the idea becomes indelibly impressed upon the child's mind from the moment when the object itself is associated by observation with the name. Consequently, it is of great advantage in language teaching, if the child has always been accustomed to hear conversation on various topics, particularly on those which concern his immediate neighbourhood and his own home. Listening to conversation has an influence upon the development of speech in all its aspects. In this way the child not only becomes familiar with an extensive vocabulary almost without being conscious that he is learning anything, he also picks up declensions and conjugations. That is of itself no small matter. However, when I leave the question of the natural laws which govern the mechanical development of language, and ask, How does Nature develop the deeper spiritual aspect of language? I find that linguistic training stands in most intimate relations with the natural development of experience, and proceeds step by step in uniformity with it. At first every object is perceived as an individual unit, and the process of analyzing the various parts of objects and regarding them individually is very slow. The varying conditions of time and circumstances affect the child's senses casually and disconnectedly before they are brought into clear consciousness comprehensively and connectedly. If Nature is given a free hand in the development of language, these are the lines which she follows. Objects are named without reference to their constituent parts or to their various qualities. Gradually and with the slow lapse of time a stage is reached at which these constituent parts are considered in detail; they also are named, and finally the child is able to express himself with precision and accuracy about those qualities which vary with time and circumstances. The Elementary system of education and al methods based upon it, provide that language teaching shall be wholly in conformity with Nature's plan of developing the child's capacities. It ceases at once to be Elementary if it deviates in the slightest from these principles. A child brought up on this method must not chatter before it has knowledge, nor talk about a thing of which it has no first-hand experience. Progress (both intensive and extensive) in linguistic training, if it is to be genuine, must follow this course, and only on this basis can it form the necessary link between experience and thought.

60. The art of language teaching provides the intermediate link between experience and thought, both of which are in process of development. The art of cultivating the first precedes that of cultivating the second. The methods of developing the faculty of thought are deprived of their natural foundations if a rational and comprehensive cultivation of experience has not preceded them. . . .

62. It is manifest that the pupil whom we are bringing up on a natural method must be able as a result of his linguistic training to express himself concerning the sense-impressions made by his surroundings and circumstances with the same degree of precision as the impressions have made on him. Unless the student has reached this stage in learning a language, there is a gap between his experience and his thinking which can only be remedied by the development of his linguistic powers.

## FOREIGN LANGUAGES.

63. Such is the problem of language teaching as viewed by psychology. The solution of this problem enables us to deal with another—that of teaching foreign languages. Is there a universal method for such teaching? Everything depends upon the recognition of the principle that experience leads to thought through language—first ex-

perience, then language, and then thought. The natural course in the development of the mother-tongue must be kept in mind. . . .

65. The method by which the child learns his mother-tongue is the prototype for all language teaching  The natural course is to proceed from the mother-tongue to the living, and then to the dead languages, because the first-hand knowledge of things which a child must acquire by learning a living language is more closely related to his actual life than that which must be first of all made clear and comprehensible to him if he is to have a real understanding of the dead language.

In all cases, however, the principles underlying this universal method of understanding and speaking a foreign language must be aided by mechanical and psychological teaching devices. We must utilize to the full all that the experience of ages has taught us in respect of such devices, knitting this on to what we know of Nature's own procedure. What Nature left to herself hindered by the undeveloped senses and organs of the infant child, slowly, uncertainly, and imperfectly achieves, the teacher arranges in sequences of teaching devices which are based upon the natural way of acquiring a language. Mere systematization gives it a power to which Nature alone could not possibly attain. This is, of course, only true if the devices are psychologically sound.

The fuller recognition of the natural method of learning the mother-tongue is therefore the true source of all devices for making the acquisition of other languages easy.

## Grammar in Child Language.

66. We are thus driven back to the careful consideration of how the child learns to talk—that is to say, of the relations between mother and child at home. Here instinct reigns supreme, and when the claims of society do not draw the mother away from her natural position, the relations of mother and child exhibit the natural process

of learning to speak to perfection. But the age has corrupted primitive maternal power, to the consequent damage of all subsequent linguistic work. Child speech has no relation to experience. The great object of the theory of the Elementary Method is to find how these established errors can be avoided ; above all, it seeks to use to the full all the possibilities of home life, in the first place, by putting a proper instrument into the hands of mothers, and, in the second place, by training the children themselves to impart their newly-acquired skill to their brothers and sisters.

First, the child learns to recognize and name things ; then their qualities and their activities—from the objects, that is to say, he passes to the adjectives, and then to the verbs. He learns these words unsystematically with the flow of time, but, spasmodic though his progress is, the words are always learned in phrases. The context enables the child to grasp the meaning of the words and their relation one to another. Because they convey a meaning, phrases are learned more easily than detached words, though, of course, in the solitary phrase individual words can only be partially understood. At the same time the child is getting command of grammatical changes in such words as undergo them.

The syntactical influence of those parts of speech which are not changed in form—prepositions, conjunctions, etc. —can be impressed upon the child by carefully collected examples, thereby assisting the otherwise slow natural process. This is particularly aimed at in our plan of elementary education.

### GRAMMAR IN ACQUIRING NEW LANGUAGES.

Exercises on these and all other parts of speech are given without a word of grammar, though grammar is of course introduced when the children have acquired practical command of the language. Precisely the same principles apply to the learning of a foreign tongue, though current teaching practice has forgotten it. How curious it is that uncultivated people teach their language in the right way! A French servant to whom one entrusts a German child for the sake of his French teaches him effectively and quickly by continuous conversation. The child can very soon express himself with ease about the things around him—a result which years of school devices do not achieve, in spite of the logic of their procedure. The servant's method is the natural method—hence its superiority.

67. The position of the man who finds himself in a foreign country where nobody speaks his language also illustrates my point. Necessity compels him to learn the language as he learned his own. He is soaked in its sounds before he knows their meaning, but the meaning and the power come. My own experiments have given further confirmation to my idea, though for a long time we could not apply it to any other language than the mother-tongue.

68. Nevertheless, I believe that it does apply to them, and that it represents the normal type of procedure in acquiring a language. We have worked with German (*the mother-tongue*) and Latin.

### Language the Middle Term between Sensory Experience and Thought.

69. But to leave this subject and go back to the relation between sensory experience and thought. Unless his sense-experience is peculiarly confused, man of his own motion seeks to get clear impressions of the objects amidst which he lives. But clear perceptions do not satisfy him. Again, he endeavours to organize them into a higher order of ideas. By bringing his varied perceptual experiences into relation he seeks to arrive at definite ideas. He compares them with each other, exercises his logic upon them, utilizes them in his judgment. All this is spontaneous on his part, and educators have all along been trying to reduce this spontaneous process to simple rule, and to free it from error. But they have gone as far

astray in regard to it as they have strayed in the more
elementary work of organizing sensory experience. Instead of careful practice in analytic comparison, they have
taught the rules of logical thinking. This is, of course,
to put the cart before the horse. Systematic logic is only
useful to those who are already clear thinkers. Its real
significance is otherwise lost, no matter how long students
play with it. It is a vain show of power, mischievous and
deadening in its effects.

70. Exercises in the development of thought power
must be brought into line with the methods of life itself.
Just as men do not become moral through talking about
it, so will they not learn to think except by actual thinking. The Elementary system regards form and number
as the simple natural provision for the transition from
simple perception to actual thinking. It uses them to
that end, and regards them as the proper basis for unfolding and training men's power of abstraction.

It must, however, be clearly understood that our
method of teaching number and form is not a series of
mechanical exercises and artificial devices for simplifying
and abbreviating arithmetic and mensuration. We do
not begin to teach number by the multiplication table or
other such paradigm. The basis of the work is an appeal
to the power of grouping, separating, and comparing
sensory objects, and we have no desire to abandon our
square of numerical relations for other devices which are
purely artificial.[1] We rest everything upon man's native
disposition to think. Man must learn to think over the
objects presented to his senses, to group, to separate, and
to compare them himself. As he does this, the power of
counting and measuring comes into being, as it were, spontaneously. Our method lays the utmost stress upon this
early work, and refuses to have anything to do with
mechanical tricks and abbreviations so much used in
elementary and higher practical arithmetic. Before the
child can deal properly with the variety of objects that
are capable of measurement and counting, he must grasp

[1] These squares are reproduced in G., pp. 195 and 199.

the general principle of quantity and measurement through a series of exercises on abstract forms.

71. To be successful, the devices employed must be in accord with Nature. They must, that is to say, be " elementary "; they must be carefully graduated in series which show no gaps from the barest rudiments to independent reckoning, leading even to simple algebraic and geometric problems.

72. This does not mean that boys of all ranks are to learn algebra and geometry. Different ranks and even different individuals require different degrees of attainment, and very few require advanced mathematical knowledge. It would be a good thing indeed if higher work were only attempted by those who show exceptional power, independent of their rank. Cases of this kind are a special responsibility. Unusual capacity should be given every possible chance, and, above all, it should be rightly guided. But even here the principle that *Life educates* must be recognized. We must be careful not to be out of harmony with the boy's circumstances, either actual or potential. His happiness in life is the first consideration. The loving care which we ask for exceptional children is not out of harmony with this principle, but rather strengthens it, nor is the case of mathematical ability different from ability in any other direction.

73. Mathematical training must be kept in strict relation to the boy's general intellectual progress. Specialization must not be forced upon him ; methods must be adapted to his spontaneous activities.

74. Although the impulse to analytic and synthetic thinking lies in the child, it does not follow that we may leave its development to chance. We must guide and stimulate him by methods calculated to give him both knowledge and self-reliance, such as those we have outlined for organizing his sensory experience, and for number and form.

### PRACTICAL SKILL.

I pass now to the question of practical skill. Like all other human capacities, the germ lies within the child. It develops into maturity only with exercise. Although it depends on the practical use of sense-organs and limbs, progress is intimately related to mental growth, and all our work in that connection is helpful. The internal and external factors must ever be kept in close relation.

75. . . . Soul, life . . . both constitute the very essence of practical skill, as they do that of sensory experience. External devices demand organization. We require an elementary gymnastic of the senses and of the limbs. The exercises must be adapted to the special nature of the case—those for the senses upon their physical constitution, those for the limbs upon the laws which govern the acquisition of control.

76. Although, as always, the impulse to activity lies within, the teacher must stimulate and guide it into right channels. If he adopts the " elementary " principle, he will use a graded series of exercises that will quicken and strengthen the ear for hearing, the eye for seeing, and the mouth for correct speech and song. So, too, with the limbs.

### THE PSYCHOLOGICAL MOMENT.

77. The child's own impulses induce free activity, and instruction must not hurry to interfere. It must only make demands for which the child is already prepared. When he *feels*, " I can do that now," then we may ask him to do it. The child must be allowed to take chalk, pencil, charcoal, etc., in his hand, and draw straight and crooked lines all over without attempting to interfere and correct. Only when the child begins of its own accord to imitate easy words, pleasant sounds, and to take pleasure in the changes and more accurate representation of his random strokes ; only when he is stimulated to imitate a greater variety of words and sounds, and to make his strokes more correct and varied, does the thought awaken

in him : " My dear mother can help me to do this, which I very much want to do, but cannot do properly." *Then* is the time when instruction can be offered to the child in a natural way ; then and then only should it be offered to him. In all departments of practical education the mode of procedure is the same.

78. All " elementary " methods advance from the simplest fundamentals by means of continuous and un-interrupted steps to the higher branches of knowledge. Inner harmony is preserved alike in its intensive and in its extensive progression.

79. The methods of training in any practical art are based in part on the sensory needs of primitive life, and in part on the character of the art itself. The higher achievements of architecture began with the decoration of the primitive man's hut. Had man not needed protec-tion against wind and weather, he would have built no palaces. Had we not felt the desire to get as quickly as possible from one shore to another, there would have been no naval architecture. Except for such circumstances, the very word *architecture* would hardly have been in-vented.

80. When our primitive needs were satisfied, the power we had gained in the process was spontaneously applied to the advance of the art itself. This new movement will have a profound effect upon education if teaching devices continue in harmony with historical origins. If, on the other hand, the practical basis of art is forgotten, and attention is given to developing the showy semblance of artistic power, this side of education will lose its useful-ness. It will be a source of weakness rather than of strength.

Higher artistic training must be subordinate to training for the actual needs of life. Indeed, on this basis alone can higher training flourish. Artistic power in any case depends primarily on the thorough training of the five senses. That is, of course, essential to sound experience.

### INTELLECTUAL FOUNDATIONS OF PRACTICAL SKILL.

81. On the intellectual side artistic capacity also demands the training of the thought powers, a knowledge of form and number, and efficient linguistic capacity. He who has learned to measure, to count, to draw, on " elementary " lines has got within him the intellectual foundations for his practical skill. It only remains to train the external dexterities necessary to the particular art which he desires to master. This is true both of music and of drawing. . . . The course of training for all mechanical dexterities goes through four stages : the first concerns the correct apprehension of forms; the second, power to reproduce them ; the third, delicacy in their representation ; and the fourth, freedom and independence in applying them. Experience has shown us that this is true of writing, drawing, singing, and piano-playing. . . .

### PRACTICAL SKILL AND LIFE.

82. The child who has grasped the elements of form and of number also possesses the intellectual foundation that is necessary for the performance of his duties at home and in his profession. The principle, *Life educates* is, however, less applicable to the richer classes than to the poorer. The latter practise from their cradle those mechanical devices which are needed in life. The children of artisans are always in intimate contact with their father's work, and derive enormous stimulus from it. They take their part in it, and master much of its detail. But in the case of the wealthier classes no such opportunities offer. Their children say : " We are rich ; we do not need these things." The idea that they can help to relieve the burden of life for their parents, and all the happy consequences associated with such an idea, never occurs to them. The same is true, alas ! of the children of those who are content to live in dependent admiration of their richer neighbours. . . .

84-90. We need to supply this gap in the education of the children of the wealthy, and to save them from the social evils of the day, but the same principles apply to this problem as to that of the education of the poor.

91. We aim at the restoration of parental interest and parental power in all classes. In my childhood I used to hear that the boy who was brought up from early youth to pray, to think, and to work, was already half educated. Nothing can be truer, and this is precisely the object of the " elementary " education we have in mind. It is a psychological instrument for assisting Nature in the unfolding of our physical, intellectual, and moral powers. An intelligent visitor who had been watching a lesson in number remarked : " *C'est un pouvoir, ce n'est pas un savoir.*" His comment exactly and clearly expressed the position and the difference between the " elementary " method and all others.

92. The method applies to the whole range of our knowledge and of our dexterities. Each branch of knowledge and each dexterity has its special character, which differs from that of all the others. The teacher in any one of these dexterities must, of course, have the special knowledge and special power that this implies. He must not only have complete acquaintance with the " elementary " training of our capacities, but also with the special branch of knowledge or of art to which he proposes to introduce his pupils. This is not so difficult as it seems, because when the teacher realizes the absolute necessity of carefully grading his particular branch of science for teaching purposes, he will also recognize that in principle the Elementary Method is the same as this necessary preliminary to the teaching of his subject. So, too, must he recognize the principle that *Life educates*, in accordance with which the aim and extent of his scientific teaching must be determined. . . .

94, 95. It is only when due regard is paid to the needs and circumstances of the various classes of society that we may safely consider our educational schemes as contributing wisely to national culture. If care is taken in this regard, its influence on the higher classes especially, and on all those whose vocation calls for a higher scientific education, will be good, on the one hand giving them full and adequate training for their profession, and on the other putting them in a position to pursue and apply in their own way their special studies.

96. Its influence on the artisan and the labouring classes would be equally happy. If it were adopted as a national system, it would on the one hand cool the ambition of those who, whilst excellently fitted for their particular station, are quite unsuited for any higher position, and on the other it would make the way easy for the specially gifted to use their powers in their own circle, to their own and to the common advantage.

### Sensory Experience in Relation to Higher Work and Natural History.

97. Consider the elementary exercises in sense experience, and the transition to thought proper through exercises in language. The sensory foundations being adequate and sound, we lead our pupils by progressive steps to definite ideas. We introduce them to abstract thinking in our lessons on number and form, and gradually pave the way to the scientific point of view. Consider Natural History as a case in point. However restricted a child's experience, he is sure to be familiar with half a dozen mammals, as many birds, fishes, insects, amphibians and worms. If he has learned to know them from his cradle up in all their essentials, and if he has learned to express himself about them clearly as the " elementary " method would teach him, such a child has obtained a sound and natural introduction to the point of view of the zoologist, ornithologist, etc. If circumstances are favourable, he can take up such a study with considerable chance of success. So it is with any other science. . . . Indeed, if the elementary method does not mean this, it is useless. Its value depends partly on ourselves and partly upon the environment, which is never entirely uneducative. Any child who has learned to look carefully at water at rest and in motion, or in its various forms—dew, rain,

mist, steam, hail, snow, etc.—and then again has learned to observe its various effects on other bodies, and can express himself with clearness concerning them, has already got the foundations of the physicist's way of looking at things. Similarly, the boy who is familiar with such phenomena as the solution of salt and sugar, and its recovery by evaporation and crystallization, fermentation, the conversion of marble into chalk, and of flint into glass, is as well prepared for the scientific in vestigation of these things as the country lad who knows thoroughly a few cottages, and can describe them in detail, is ready as it were to learn how to build them. And if such a lad has ability, he needs only the " elementary " training in form and number to take up the study of building in a much wider way.

98. When a child is brought up in this way from the cradle, it is impossible to say how far the careful training of his sensory abilities may carry him, especially if he has adequate training in the abstract treatment of his experi ences. Where capacity is great, method is easy of application, and is very far-reaching.

## GEOGRAPHY AND HISTORY.

99. But this advanced work has nothing to do with the confused verbal teaching which passes current nowadays. We hold fast to the principle *Life educates*. Our appeal is always to the child's whole nature. Even when subjects are concerned which are not really suited to children, the method makes an appeal to good sense, and makes as much as possible out of the situation. To take Geography and History as examples, though I do not recognize either as proper subjects in an elementary curriculum. If a child has to learn geography, the method provides a simple course of exercises in the names of mountains, rivers, and towns, and by making use of the ordinary geographical apparatus, he is taught through " artificial experience " the relative position of these places.

100. Both types of exercise are suited to children. Memory and sensory activity are especially strong in childhood. I should make every use of the neighbourhood for teaching geographical position and relations ; I should, in the first reading lesson, practise my pupil in reading and pronouncing the names of places of a given neighbourhood—for example, a river basin ; I should divide this into middle, upper, and lower districts, and drill the children in the names and positions of the most important places. In a second course they would learn the positions of smaller places in relation to the first. . . . The children would learn that such and such a place is so many miles in such a direction from so and so.

101, 102. This course would form a suitable introduction to the scientific study of geography, the nomenclature of which it would provide. It is, however, nothing but the materials for a house which is to be built later.

103. As to history, we can do nothing more. If we would not for ever spoil a child's chances of understanding history, we must not attempt to teach it to him as such in his early years. It is absolute nonsense to wish to make people acquainted with the spirit of an age far removed from that in which they live, long before they have any real acquaintance with the actual world about them. We must not attempt more than to provide them with such names of persons and places as will be useful.

104. Thus I regard such work as is possible with Geography and History as little more than mechanical exercises in speech, though I have already said that I regard this kind of exercise as most important.

105, 106. One of the great advantages of learning a new language is the opportunity it gives for revising and renewing our knowledge. Much of that which we learnt in relation to the development of the mother-tongue has faded, and now is the chance of bringing it back to life.[1] All that is wanted is a textbook conforming to the normal

[1] Pestalozzi appears to have in his mind the type of exercise to be found in the language primers of Comenius—the *Orbis Pictus*, the *Janua Linguarum Reserata*, etc. He refers specifically to Latin.

type. But I must proceed to the consideration of the idea of elementary education as a whole, and bring together what I have said of isolated aspects.

## HUMAN NATURE AS A WHOLE MUST BE EDUCATED.

107. Although I have not said so, the various devices for developing our sensory powers, our powers of speech and thought, and our practical experience—all are calculated to further the satisfaction of the needs of human nature as a whole. But in their isolation the cultivation of these faculties is not enough. There is always the danger of over-emphasis in one direction or another, which brings about internal disharmony. We cannot, however, answer the question what it is that makes education and instruction wholly natural until we have settled what is the specific character of human nature. We are thus carried back to the problem discussed in our first paragraphs. There we found it to consist in those qualities which man has over and above those which he shares with other animals. The cow has a soul and a life of its own, but it is not human. . . . The dog has a better nose, the eagle has a better eye, than man ; not only so, but they make better use of these organs. We cannot expect to approach their wonderful skill, which, great as it is, is not human. It only implies the use of instinctive power. The difference between it and man's capacity for thought and action, however humble, is clear. It is, indeed, so striking that when I hear the words, " Thou hast made us a little lower than the angels," I remember what is equally true : " Thou hast exalted us infinitely above all flesh and blood that wanders upon the earth ; Thou hast made us infinitely higher than the beasts of the field." . . . Human thought is in no way related to our fleshly organization. It is the Divine instrument which makes the body the servant of the mind ; only then is it truly human, and in absolute opposition to the thought-powers of the lower animals. In order to grasp fully the significance of what we mean by " according to

Nature," we must keep in mind that all our work is designed to affect the whole nature of man in which the various powers find unity.  It depends upon the harmony of our powers—a harmony which, when established, will affect our whole active life. . . .

111. Everything depends upon the successful establishment of the dispositions to love and faith.[1] . . .


DIFFERENT EDUCATION NEEDED BY DIFFERENT CLASSES.

119. Whilst the " elementary idea " insists upon the importance of considering human nature as a whole, it does not forget the necessity of dealing with the question in its due relation to the differences of position which exist among men.  Harmony between education and home circumstances is one of its first principles.  The child is taught to love all that is lovable in its own surroundings.  He learns to think about the things which are provocative of thought ; he learns to do, to wish, hope, believe, and strive in relation to the actualities of his life.  His powers develop in harmony with his life's needs.  His father's home, his father's social position, etc., are dear to him, and he shares the burden of them willingly.  He does not feel the restrictions placed upon him ; they have become habits.  We do not make a dreamer of him—one who has lost all sense of reality, and is unfit for the duties of his station.  However humble these may be, the boy is made a happy instrument for good within them.

120, 121. We need above all things an educational system which will take these differences into account. It will necessitate different provision for different classes. The citizen of the towns does not of course need a solider foundation in the elements than a countryman, but it is essential that different methods of developing his powers should be used, and different forms of application should be encouraged.  If the countryman's education is to put

[1] Pestalozzi repeats in greater detail what he has already said in the earlier paragraphs.  Compare also the *Views and Experiences* for the Moral Ideal (Letter III.).

him into the position of not needing to call in a carpenter for every board that needs planing, or to summon a smith every time he wants to drive a nail into the wall, so must the townsman's special needs be provided for. He must acquire a sound knowledge of the materials which are used in local industries, and receive such a mathematical and æsthetic training as will bring out any capacity for invention.

122. The case of children of the higher classes is quite different. They need nothing of the kind, nor does their environment offer the opportunity for such training. They will never have to worry about their means of livelihood. Intellectual and emotional life in their case is not to be stimulated through manual work. It should rather be the other way about—intellect and heart should stimulate the hand.

123. This point of view brings out the differences which should mark the educational arrangements of the various classes if the order of Nature is to be followed in the development of their powers, their knowledge, and their dexterities. . . . The happiness of the wage-earning classes depends entirely upon their practical capacity. Extensive knowledge has little to offer them. The higher classes need more knowledge, but only such as is solidly grounded in actual experience. Their practical capacity itself depends upon the wider acquaintance with things and their treatment, although the actual handling of them will fall to other people. The scientific classes need a deeper and wider training in methods of investigation.

124. Except in the case of those who are to be educated for special scientific work, Nature herself provides the very environment necessary for the educational needs of each of these classes. . . .

PARENTS OR TUTORS AS EDUCATORS.

135. Whilst assuming and providing for this, I am fully aware that I shall be mocked at for imagining that when my theory of elementary education is realized those

parents who are not compelled to do so will seriously give themselves up to their children's education. I do believe that this will happen in most cases, and I know that it is the habit of most parents in this class—if, indeed, it is not a matter of principle with them—to confess quite frankly that they understood nothing about education. They say they are obliged to entrust their children to paid teachers, and that they grudge neither the time nor the money spent upon the search for suitable persons. They do this apparently with great generosity, and often with unexpected success. The discovery of a really good teacher is as great a piece of luck as the winning of the first prize in a lottery. Although, as the proverb says, " A blind cow may find a horseshoe," such a piece of luck does not happen often, and many people who wish to secure a first-rate teacher by paying a large salary may get just as incompetent a person as if they had chosen the cheapest from motives of meanness. Such a misfortune often does happen to people of high rank and great wealth. That it is a very grave misfortune is evident from the number of men who have paid a heavy price for our erroneous and detrimental system of education, and bewail the consequences of their mistake. There are, however, brighter days in store. The time may come when noble men of every station, and more particularly of the highest, after serious reflection upon the qualities which are essential in a teacher, will arrive at sounder conclusions upon the subject. Animated by a parental zeal for Elementary education, they may then do their part in helping to substitute a better mode of procedure than that which comes from our present ignorance.

[*The essay closes with a further detailed examination of the principle of unity and harmony, which are so easily lost sight of in the effort to train this or that special capacity.*]

# INDEX

323

# SIGNIFICANT CONTRIBUTIONS TO THE HISTORY OF PSYCHOLOGY, 1750-1920

Edited and with Prefaces by

## DANIEL N. ROBINSON
Georgetown University

### SERIES A: ORIENTATIONS

**Volume I**

Condillac, Étienne Bonnot de. THE LOGIC OF CONDILLAC. 1809.

Brown, Thomas. SKETCH OF A SYSTEM OF THE PHILOSOPHY OF THE HUMAN MIND. 1820.

**Volume II**

Fichte, Johann Gottlieb. CHARACTERISTICS OF THE PRESENT AGE. 1889.

Fichte, Johann Gottlieb. THE WAY TOWARDS THE BLESSED LIFE, OR, THE DOCTRINE OF RELIGION. 1889.

**Volume III**

Taine, Hippolyte Adolphe. ON INTELLIGENCE. 1875.

**Volume IV**

Bain, Alexander. THE SENSES AND THE INTELLECT. 1855.

**Volume V**

Bain, Alexander. THE EMOTIONS AND THE WILL. 1859.

**Volume VI**

Herbart, Johann Friedrich. TEXTBOOK OF PSYCHOLOGY. 1891.

Lewes, George Henry. THE STUDY OF PSYCHOLOGY. 1879.

Lotze, Hermann. OUTLINES OF PSYCHOLOGY. 1886.

**Volume VII**

Romanes, George John. ANIMAL INTELLIGENCE. 1883.

**Volume VIII**

Ward, James. "PSYCHOLOGY." 1886.

Ward, James. PSYCHOLOGICAL PRINCIPLES. 1920.

**Volume IX**

Stout, George Frederick. A MANUAL OF PSYCHOLOGY. 1899.

**Volume X**

Elliotson, John. NUMEROUS CASES OF SURGICAL OPERATIONS WITHOUT PAIN IN THE MESMERIC STATE. 1843.

Esdaile, James. MESMERISM IN INDIA. 1846.

Macnish, Robert. THE PHILOSOPHY OF SLEEP. 1834.

**Volume XI**

SEMINAL RESEARCH PAPERS:

Classical Studies by J. McK. Cattell & L. Farrand (1896); J. Dewey (1900); L.W. Kline (1899); C.E. Sharp (1899); W.S. Small (1900, 1901); D.A. Spalding (1873); C.E. Spearman (1904); E.L. Thorndike (1900); and M. Wertheimer (1912).

## SERIES B: PSYCHOMETRICS AND EDUCATIONAL PSYCHOLOGY

**Volume I**

Herbart, Johann Friedrich. THE SCIENCE OF EDUCATION. 1902.
Froebel, Friedrich. THE EDUCATION OF MAN. 1887.

**Volume II**

Pestalozzi, Johann Heinrich. PESTALOZZI'S EDUCATIONAL WRITINGS. 1912.
Pestalozzi, Johann Heinrich. HOW GERTRUDE TEACHES HER CHILDREN. 1894.

**Volume III**

Sully, James. STUDIES OF CHILDHOOD. 1896.

**Volume IV**

Binet, Alfred. "Mental Imagery" (1892); "The Mechanism of Thought" (1894); "The Intelligence of Imbeciles" (1909).

Binet, Alfred; and Simon, Théodore. "The Development of Intelligence in Children." (1911).

Galton, Francis. "Co-relations and Their Measurement, Chiefly from Anthropometric Data" (1889).

Stern, L. William. THE PSYCHOLOGICAL METHODS OF TESTING INTELLIGENCE. 1914.

## SERIES C: MEDICAL PSYCHOLOGY

**Volume I**

Ribot, Théodule Armand. DISEASES OF MEMORY. 1882.
Ribot, Théodule Armand. DISEASES OF PERSONALITY. 1891.
Ribot, Théodule Armand. DISEASES OF THE WILL. 1894.

**Volume II**

Janet, Pierre. THE MENTAL STATE OF HYSTERICALS. 1901.

**Volume III**

Pinel, Philippe. TREATISE ON INSANITY. 1806.
Maudsley, Henry. RESPONSIBILITY IN MENTAL DISEASE. 1876.

**Volume IV**

Maudsley, Henry. PHYSIOLOGY AND PATHOLOGY OF THE MIND. 1867.

**Volume V**

Binet, Alfred. ALTERATIONS OF PERSONALITY. 1896.
Binet, Alfred. ON DOUBLE-CONSCIOUSNESS. 1890.

## SERIES D: COMPARATIVE PSYCHOLOGY

**Volume I**

Wundt, Wilhelm Max. LECTURES ON HUMAN AND ANIMAL PSYCHOLOGY. 1894.

**Volume II**

Morgan, C. Lloyd. INTRODUCTION TO COMPARATIVE PSYCHOLOGY. 1894.

**Volume III**

Haeckel, Ernst. LAST WORDS ON EVOLUTION. 1906.

Jennings, Herbert S. CONTRIBUTIONS TO THE STUDY OF THE BEHAVIOR OF LOWER ORGANISMS. 1904.

**Volume IV**

DARWINISM:

Reviews of *Origin of Species* from the major journals of the day (e.g., *Edinburgh Review, Fortnightly Review*, etc.).

Angell, J.R. "The Influence of Darwin on Psychology" (1909).

Baldwin, J.M. "The Influence of Darwin on Theory of Knowledge and Philosophy" (1909).

Huxley, T.H. "Evolution and Ethics" (1893).

Galton, Francis. NATURAL INHERITANCE. 1889.

---

## SERIES E: PHYSIOLOGICAL PSYCHOLOGY

**Volume I**

Whytt, Robert. THE WORKS OF ROBERT WHYTT. 1768.

Hall, Marshall. MEMOIRS ON THE NERVOUS SYSTEM. 1837.

Cabanis, Pierre Jean. MEMOIRS. 1823.

DuBois-Reymond, Emil. "On Secondary Electromotive Phenomena in Muscles, Nerves, and Electrical Organs" (1887).

Hall, G.S., and Hodge, C.F. "A Sketch of the History of Reflex-Action" (1890).

**Volume II**

Bichat, Xavier. PHYSIOLOGICAL RESEARCHES ON LIFE AND DEATH. 1827.

Spurzheim, Johann Gaspar. OUTLINES OF PHRENOLOGY. 1832.

Flourens, Pierre. PHRENOLOGY EXAMINED. 1846.

**Volume III**

Ferrier, David. THE FUNCTIONS OF THE BRAIN. 1886.

**Volume IV**

Magendie, Francois. AN ELEMENTARY TREATISE ON HUMAN PHYSIOLOGY. 1844.

Binet, Alfred. THE MIND AND THE BRAIN. 1907.

Huxley, T.H. "On the Hypothesis that Animals Are Automata, and Its History" (1874).

# UNIVERSITY PUBLICATIONS OF AMERICA, INC.
## 5630 Connecticut Avenue • Washington, D. C. • U.S.A.